Ruskin's Scottish Heritage

University of Illinois Press, Urbana, 1956

RUSKIN'S SCOTTISH HERITAGE

A PRELUDE

HELEN GILL VILJOEN

To
Barbara Gnosspelius
and
to the memory of her father
W. G. Collingwood
with abiding gratitude
for help and kindness
out of which my work has grown.

Contents

Introduction

This book has been written in the belief that for many years grave confusions have distorted all attempts to interpret the life and work of Ruskin, and that these confusions can but become the more seriously confounded until new foundations for Ruskin biography have been laid. To establish these foundations through the use of a new method — new, at least today, in application to John Ruskin — is therefore the chief function of *Ruskin's Scottish Heritage*. The present volume thus becomes a "Prelude" to a biography which must be based on this preliminary work.

In fulfillment of its special purpose, *Ruskin's Scottish Heritage* proceeds upon two levels. The first is signified by the narrative wherein, frequently for the first time, one meets the ancestors of Ruskin and, against these family backgrounds, reads the story of his parents before their marriage. This tale is told from the point of view of a biographer who sees this book in its relation to the whole of Ruskin's life and who therefore handles this material as though it veritably represented the first volume of a long biography. Thus viewed, *Ruskin's Scottish Heritage* appropriately ends with Margaret and John James Ruskin finally married and established in their London home, with hope and prayer that they will have a child. As narrative, then, this book presents material which in a "Life" has been, and henceforth will doubtless always be, contained in no more than several opening chapters.

The second level, represented by the notes, explains the detailed treatment of this narrative and, in consequence, its present length, at this point unavoidable if by use of the "new" method, two new premises are to be established as a basis for biography. These premises are extremely simple, although it seems to me that for Ruskin scholarship they can be startling in their implications.

First, however, as to the method: it is merely that of basing statements and interpretations upon evidence obtained from primary sources which, since the days when Cook and Wedderburn were editing *The Works of Ruskin* in their thirty-nine volume Library Edition, have not been studied for their interrelated meaning as a whole; primary sources, furthermore, which never have been used with due regard for their particular relationships, in time, to the period of Ruskin's life on which they bear. Apart from work on Ruskin, this would seem to be a valid method, elementary to common sense, not to mention scholarship. Applied to Ruskin, as this "Heritage" will show, it can provide a body of information that entails correcting many long-established errors and changing treacherously misleading preconceptions. But beyond thus supplementing present knowledge, it provides a fresh approach to Ruskin through which, eventually, we can reach a more clear understanding of the emotional and intellectual development expressed in his achievement as a human being who was almost as complex in personality as he was greatly gifted.

Such study of Ruskin manuscripts, together with a search of public records to which no biographer heretofore has turned, has led to the two premises on which all my work is based. First, I am convinced that it is folly to assume that the accounts of his own life which Ruskin gave in later years, conspicuously in *Praeterita,* should be accepted at face value, as though he spoke, literally and unreservedly, truths on which to base biography. Thus baldly stated, this may seem to be a premise which is self-evident. Yet only Ruskin's first biographer, Collingwood, has attempted to approach Ruskin's life and work as though the *Praeterita* account of family backgrounds, of Ruskin's parents and their early years, and of Ruskin's youth and subsequent development, demanded critical evaluation and reinterpretation in light of the tale told, *contemporaneously,* by the successive Ruskin manuscripts.

These manuscripts, supplemented by the search of public records, have likewise led me to my second premise: no more than one should regard *Praeterita* as an essentially sound foundation for biography should one use the Library Edition of *The Works of Ruskin* as a trustworthy source of information. Already, thanks to several recent publications from Ruskin manuscripts, the reading public has begun to realize that, as editors, E. T. Cook (later Sir E. T. Cook) and Alexander Wedderburn were highly selective and far from reasonably dispassionate. But no one has as yet suspected that through their imposing array of thirty-nine volumes, they had prepared, in actuality, a gigantic trap which not one subsequent biographer of Ruskin has managed to escape.

To establish the validity of these two premises is an essential purpose of *Ruskin's Scottish Heritage* as a "Prelude" to the biography which can then proceed with scant regard for the vagaries of Cook and Wedderburn, and with quiet acceptance of the fact that *Praeterita* pervasively expresses Ruskin's later moods and fantasies, while often adumbrating what was true in his emotional experiences as a child. Initially, however, the need to enlarge the province of our knowledge by presenting much new information about Ruskin's parents and ancestral backgrounds has offered an ideal opportunity to demonstrate, albeit at the secondary level of the notes, that Ruskin-biography can come to grief if it is based upon *Praeterita,* and upon the work of Cook and Wedderburn. Confusion, overlappingly intensified during recent decades, has been a consequence of their performance.

Nor, in the long run, it may be, will one regret the present need to dwell upon the family backgrounds. In our day it is widely realized that the fate of the individual seems rooted in the relationship between his parents and in their characters as shaped by their own earlier experiences. When, therefore, *Ruskin's Scottish Heritage* can be seen in its relationship to the whole "Life" of Ruskin, it may be found to have been, perforce, biographically experimental in that it will have shown how Ruskin's personality, in its uniqueness, was intellectually and emotionally integrated with the lives of his forebears. Certainly, the story of the early life of Margaret and John James Ruskin is needed if we are to understand their personalities and therefore the development of Ruskin during youth, precisely as the story of his youth is needed for an understanding of the man. Indeed, a fresh approach is needed from start to finish, if prevailing confusions are so far as possible to be dispelled. In English literature, I believe, only Pope has suffered as has Ruskin because of his own desire to shape men's understanding of his life and because of early editorial treatment of his manuscripts — a dual heritage seized unsuspectingly by critics of an age alien and hostile to the one which fathered each protagonist.

At the same time, one must recognize that Ruskin did not deliberately deceive. Writing *Praeterita,* he professed that he would tell no more than he thought wise, and he was doubtless unaware of the degree to which emotions colored his memories. Meanwhile he kept at Brantwood a great wealth of his own manuscripts with which he never tampered except, occasionally, to add a dated comment to the original entries in his *Diaries* — from which here and there, at widely separated intervals, he himself presumably (but not characteristically) cut out a page. Successive pages deleted at one point had been written by his wife (to judge from passing comments in his letters), and at least one other group of pages were removed — but, typically, the pages written while he was insane in 1878 were *not* destroyed. Thus it was as though Ruskin had consciously, and conscientiously, preserved a full record of his past, he having been one of the very few English men of letters who approved Froude's having told what Ruskin, with good reason, was convinced had been the truth about Carlyle. For himself, it clearly was such truth that he desired.

Hence, ironically, in 1900, when he died, these manuscripts — including not only diaries but also hundreds of letters, and unpublished passages of books — passed into the keeping of his literary executors: Charles Eliot Norton, Alexander Wedderburn, and, as a guiding spirit, Mrs. Arthur Severn. Mrs. Severn was the "Joanna" of *Praeterita,* who had "cared" for Ruskin during his last years and who, as Ruskin's heir, living on in Brantwood with her family, was prepared continuously to exercise protective custody, now as the chief guardian of his manuscripts and memory. As Joanna, she is a character who will become intimately known through the story of the final period of Ruskin's life; and even in this "Prelude" we catch a glimpse of her by way of family backgrounds, since she was a distant cousin. In her long devotion to John Ruskin she was not entirely selfless, but she was extremely loyal and kind; in fact, no one who loves Ruskin could fail to love Joanna, sympathizing with her many trials. Yet even as Joanna, Mrs. Severn did not love Ruskin with much depth of understanding, for she was not particularly intelligent, or critically perceptive. Rather, it was enough for her to love, worshipfully, as she remained in essence the dear Joan who had come from simple folk of Galloway, most proud of "family," and otherwise uncomplicated and conventional in her judgments. Now left in charge of Ruskin manuscripts, and in the end controlling what was published, Mrs. Severn could serve as an important agent in determining the image of John Ruskin that would eventually emerge.

As coexecutors, Charles Eliot Norton and Alexander Wedderburn were apparently content to serve in an advisory capacity. From his Cambridge (Massachusetts) home, Norton had kept in touch with Mrs. Severn through all the years of Ruskin's illness, so that now, without troubling him about details, Mrs. Severn could consult him as a trusted friend. Long ago, his beliefs about the duties of a custodian of manuscripts had been made clear to all of them when he and Ruskin had differed sharply in their opinions about Froude, whose life of Carlyle had seemed to Norton an "artfully malignant" and grossly indelicate "betrayal of a most sacred trust." [1] No less, the Ruskin manuscripts, as Norton knew, contained material which was intimately personal, with the added complication that during later years Ruskin's diaries and letters not infrequently reflected the suffering and instability that sometimes led to loss of rational control. Publication from such manuscripts might well present to almost anyone a disquieting problem, as Norton personally must have realized when he undertook to edit his own Ruskin letters. But no such problem was involved when, as a guest at Brantwood, he helped Mrs. Severn make a bonfire of Ruskin's correspondence with Rose La Touche because these letters were "too sacred for publicity." By way of comfort we are told that Ruskin's letters to Rose were "perhaps the most beautiful things he ever wrote" [2] — and we are left to reconstruct, as best we can, from brief diary entries and from peripheral letters carefully preserved by Ruskin's other correspondents, the developments in and the true nature of a complex emotional relationship which was the most immediately important influence on Ruskin's life and work for more than twenty years. Publishing his Ruskin letters — some of which have survived with parts relevant to Rose literally cut out of the manuscripts — Norton himself nonetheless cast light upon these matters, so that Mrs. Severn would reproach him: "I am sorry . . . for the introduction of poor Rose — . . . I thought when we made the little sacrifice in my beloved Deepie's [Dear Papa's] little garden here, that we had agreed to burn *all* the letters bearing on that subject — I have done so — and destroyed many since to myself, — and to others." [3]

In Alexander Wedderburn one finds a man who was still more "conservative" (in context a strange word) than was Norton, whose relatively full edition of Ruskin's letters in 1904 disrupted a relationship which had been courteously friendly. Nor could Cook, a few years later, have been acting without the knowledge and the sanction of both Wedderburn and Mrs. Severn when he persuaded Kathleen Olander to destroy three of her Ruskin letters which were critical of Mrs. Severn (other such letters have survived), promising that he would *mention* Kathleen's *name* in his biography "if she was willing to destroy" *all* the letters which were finally published in *The Gulf of Years!* [4] That other manuscripts, probably including the letters of Ruskin's Croydon grandmother (who was not a "lady"), were more successfully wiped out becomes evident. In 1912, the Library Edition having been completed, one of Ruskin's most loyal friends wrote to a member of the Millais family: "He [Alexander Wedderburn] and the Arthur Severns are as anxious as you are that nothing should be left that could ever, by accident, fall into the wrong hands in after years. He is *almost* certain that no such letters now remain at Brantwood, but will ascertain for certain. . . ." [5]

Nevertheless, after the work of Cook and Wedderburn was finished, there remained at Brantwood a treasure-trove of documents. Through these, in his own hand (at first in penciled script of early childhood, sometimes almost indecipherable) Ruskin told the story of his life and interests from day to day through many years in diaries made resonant by the innumerable letters which are their essential counterpart, until he finally put aside his pen, patiently to wait with courage undismayed for the release of death.

It is this story, as it emerges from these and many other manuscripts, that I herein begin to tell, seeking to create a new and genuine likeness of John Ruskin and, inseparably, also of his parents, and to communicate the truth as I have learned to see it through contemporary records that chronologically unfold a deeply moving and, to me, a tragic tale, marked by an almost classic unity in its development through strict, and often ruthless, causal sequence. For here the end is indeed in the beginning, with all that follows dramatically implicit in these days of "Scottish Heritage."

The total story is one which I desire to tell because I also know and love John Ruskin, in my own way at least as well as those who first had charge of his manuscripts, screening the documents they did not burn and through their selectivity tailoring the man so that he would approximate his ideal image as it was conceived by Mrs. Arthur Severn, supported by those other guardians who thus blindly and conventionally sought to serve what they believed to be his welfare. Ruskin once had told his father that he would take no such chance with anything that he designed for publication:

I should be glad not to write — or publish — just now — but if I write, I publish — having utter horror of executors after what I have seen of Turner's, and know of Byron's and Pope's. Probably the finest things of Pope are lost to us and what little of real good is in me would be sure to be burned — if I left it. I have seen enough of my friends' "selections" lately — to know this. ((I promised Mrs. La Touche, when I was in Ireland, not to publish anything on religion, of a serious kind, for ten years —)) so if I write anything like that — and die, it must take its chance. But politics I will not make posthumous — if I can get them printed. [6]

Necessarily, however, his more strictly personal writing and, indirectly, his more personal reputation, were at the mercy of his personal friends.

The great body of Ruskin's collection of his own manuscripts was preserved in the library of his home until the summer of 1930, so that, against the immediate background of a doctoral dissertation, I once had the opportunity to read these documents as a whole, with freedom to transcribe. This privilege was granted under the auspices of Mr. Collingwood, and through the kind permission of Miss Violet Severn, who then lived at Brantwood.

The Ruskin manuscripts were the only property of any value, I was told, that remained in Brantwood, where they had lain un-examined for almost twenty years. Mrs. Severn had died in 1924, leaving her property to her husband. When I was shown through the house, there were buckets catching rain that dripped in through the roof. The contents of the library, however, had so far been preserved from mildew by an old retainer who, on his own initiative, had regularly kindled a fire in the fireplace in that room. A number of items had been already lost to the collection by being sold to visitors — so that today one will sometimes find most interesting (albeit relatively minor) Ruskin MSS. in unexpected places. Always, for those who knew enough to value rightly what remained, there was the fear that the house might some day be destroyed by fire. And, at best, how much longer would it be before the content of that library would be scattered — who knew how, or where? The answer came some months after I had done what I soon knew to be preliminary work on a biography of Ruskin, helped all through those weeks by those to whom I am finally privileged to dedicate this book.

By the summer of 1930 the auctions had begun, first at Brant-wood, next at Sotheby's. For three days (as described in letters of two people who were present) buyers sat in the rain, beneath um-brellas in the Brantwood garden, often bidding blindly for prize packages that might turn out to hold Pear's Soap advertisements or, more luckily, perhaps a Ruskin drawing. Many letters were knocked off in unlabeled envelopes, among them those which Ruskin wrote to Effie Gray during their engagement — letters I apparently had missed because (the story goes) they had been placed under the board beneath a bookcase which broke through the floor when it was moved. Naturally, therefore, at that sale various manuscripts which I had studied simply disappeared: they were never listed in any catalogue, and as an aftermath of the whole outrage, no one had any way of knowing who had bought unlisted items or precisely what had thus been scattered. One of my correspondents tells me that at a somewhat later date he saw a heap of mildewed manuscripts piled for burning — possibly among them the autobiography, in diary form, of Rose La Touche. It is one document which I am most thankful that I copied as a whole, because through the years since, wishing to check the accuracy of my transcription, I have vainly tried to locate it again.

Not only manuscripts were destroyed or scattered: all items which remained within the library, including marked copies of books invaluable to scholarship (such books had originally called me to Brantwood), were nonchalantly contributed to this havoc, presided over by local auctioneers. The owner, Mr. Severn, reportedly was under the impression that everything which was significant in monetary value had previously been sent away for sale at Sotheby's. Intermittently, items of more obvious and ready value, such as Ruskin's collection of Scott manuscripts, had been quietly sold in earlier days (some during Mrs. Severn's lifetime), when it was also Mr. Severn's practice to sell an original Turner drawing and hang in its place the copy he had made, so that Turner drawings auctioned off at Sotheby's were not always what they seemed.

Thus, Ruskin's work and treasures had become to Ruskin's heirs (all have died by now) a matter of complete indifference except as a source of income, and these were days when "Ruskin" as a source of income was far into ebb tide. During the next year, at Sotheby's, important groups of manuscripts were picked up for very modest prices, and, so far as I can judge, not everything dispersed at Sotheby's was listed in the Catalogues; but what happened at those sales to certain major items could be more easily traced.

Fortunately for my work and not unfortunately for others — English or American — who still honor Ruskin, a great many of the manuscripts sold at Sotheby's eventually found their way into our libraries in the United States where, with utmost generosity, they have been made available to me for further study, together with many Ruskin manuscripts which had never found a home in Brantwood. Meanwhile I have done my best to trace the whereabouts of other documents, only once being refused permission to re-examine those which I had located. Mine has thus been a patient, time-consuming work which now enables me to say, rather wryly, that I feel confident that I have already gained the distinction of having read more unpublished Ruskin manuscripts than has any other human being who has ever lived, with the sole exception of their author. And it seems right to make this statement inasmuch as I never yet have read words written by John Ruskin which, if seen in context and with due regard for circumstance, could have become to him a cause for shame, as doubtless he himself best knew when he preserved his diaries (containing his records of his dreams, beyond those entries made after he had become insane) and his letters, including those which he himself may — or may not — have placed beneath that floorboard.

Yet to be sure, he too — however greatly gifted, and regardless of his insight and integrity — was but a human being with his share of human frailty, so that he also had full measure, and more, of suffering as well as of regret. His parents, he once remarked, should not fret about his welfare, "for you believe that [God] brings all right for everything and everybody; and I, that He appoints noble laws, and blesses those who obey them, and *destroys* them who do not." [7] In his own mind he seems never to have faced more than gropingly the problem of *how* the sins of fathers are visited upon the children unto successive generations — a problem on which this "Scottish Heritage" has some bearing. In another vein, but with equal pertinence, he wrote his father: "I have your pleasant letter about 'invulnerability' — but don't hope for it — Pope was not invulnerable — and there never was a shrewder man of the world. The best of all the heathens, Socrates — was made a laughing stock all his life by Aristophanes and the populace — and then poisoned — Only people like Lord Palmerston are invulnerable — men who never utter (or see) anything beyond a commonplace, and who care for nothing, and have good ready sense and wit." [8] Not "invulnerable," certainly, and conspicuously a victim of his heritage — by no means to be explained as merely physiologically transmitted instability — Ruskin will nonetheless be done the justice, in my story of his life and work (so far as lies within my power, comprehension, and objectivity of judgment), of being permitted to speak genuinely for himself. It is a privilege he has never yet been granted throughout a biography.

One important explanation of this fact is to be found in the use which Ruskin's biographers and editors initially made of his manuscripts. In 1893, Collingwood's *The Life and Work of John Ruskin* appeared as an "official" biography which remains, in my opinion, by far the best account of Ruskin that has been produced. To this work Collingwood could bring rich personal knowledge gained through many years of companionship as Ruskin's friend and secretary. When he was asked to write the *Life* he could communicate insight that was informed and sensitive, as well as helpful through determining nuances in what he sometimes said, necessarily leaving much unsaid, not only out of his regard for people who were still alive (for instance, the Millaises and the La Touches) but also for what Ruskin might consider right. For as Collingwood remarked in a late edition of the *Life*: "This book . . . had the advantage — and the disadvantage — of being written under [Ruskin's] eye; that is to say, he saw as much of it as his health allowed; and it received his general approval." Undoubtedly it also received the general approval of Mrs. Severn, whose protective custody of Ruskin was well established by the time Collingwood (to Mrs. Severn and her children almost a member of the family) was granted access to the Ruskin manuscripts.

They next were used by E. T. Cook and Alexander Wedderburn, for biographical backgrounds and editorial comment in their Library Edition of Ruskin's *Works* (1903–12), Cook's *Life of Ruskin* (1911) having been developed, without meaningful revision, from "Introductions" to the thirty-nine volumes, of which all but two had been published by 1909. Despite its shortcomings, this edition of the *Works* is of course indispensable to Ruskin scholarship, and to cavil against the editors' performance might seem to be ungracious. By providing a reliable and collected text of Ruskin's work, made usable through the huge "Index" (Vol. XXXIX) and equipped with bibliographical apparatus not only as a whole but also for individual items in volume after volume, Cook and Wedderburn have left all who are in any way concerned with Ruskin immensely in their debt. In this respect the Library Edition embodies the knowledge which Alexander Wedderburn had gained by editing collections of Ruskin's public letters and of his minor essays and by occasionally contributing an index to some reprint from the Ruskin canon, in the handling of which George Allen, first as Ruskin's publisher and now as Wedderburn's, had had some thirty years of practical experience. Cook, in turn, brought indefatigable patience to the annotation of the text, as well as his ideals about the making of an index (he would publish on this subject): as early as 1909, according to his diary, he had "finished 'colour' for the index," and in six years he had collected 10,000 slips returned for books he had consulted in the British Museum. "The brain aches," J. S. Mills remarks, "even at the record of this relentless toil. In the end every allusion, save one, was duly tracked home, and the wonder of this can be appreciated only by those who know something about Ruskin's 'esoteric allusiveness.' " [9] Thus overwhelmingly impressive, the Library Edition has helped to shape, and in fact has essentially determined, all subsequent study of Ruskin's life and work. It is consequently most unfortunate that this edition should also have defects which have made it seriously hurtful to Ruskin, the assumption always having been that beyond bibliographical information and meticulously annotated text, statements made by Cook and Wedderburn should be accepted as reliable. Yet no assumption could be less warranted.

As editors they worked at a pace set by Alexander Wedderburn's preparedness for his part of the task, as Cook (to use the words of his biographer) "took the labouring oar": that is, with what can seem unpardonable haste in view of the superficiality of their critical and interpretative judgments, and of gross mistakes in their imposing biographical introductions. Such lapses will not seem surprising if one considers how the Library Edition came into being. The project was not definitely conceived until nine months after Ruskin's death in 1900, when his books commanded such an excellent sale that Alexander Wedderburn, encouraged by George Allen, led Mrs. Severn to believe that from a collected edition of the *Works* the three of them could realize £30,000. The profit, they agreed, would be equally divided — although Mrs. Severn would ostensibly receive her share for the upkeep of Brantwood, inasmuch as in his *Will* Ruskin had expressed the wish to have income from his books devoted to this purpose. It was an arrangement to which Mrs. Severn had subscribed without enthusiasm and which, in retrospect, could seem to her, if not unjust, at least unfortunate in that she, in expectation, was rather indirectly scheduled to receive a mere £10,000, in contrast to those anticipated £20,000 to be divided between George Allen and Alexander Wedderburn.[10]

In the beginning, making plans, she and Alexander Wedderburn had hoped that Collingwood would handle that part of the work which instead became the special province of E. T. Cook — nor should one fail to realize the editors' eventual indebtedness both to Collingwood's biography and to his detailed editorial work: Volume II of the *Works,* for instance, is little more than a reprint of Collingwood's edition of the *Poems,* inclusive of its difficult and careful dating of material in that group of boyhood manuscripts. Collingwood, however, declined the invitation to participate, partly (there is every reason to believe) because he felt that the whole project was associated much too closely with thoughts of once more "selling Ruskin," at a profit, to increase the Severns' income. Nor did the principals fail to make it clear to Norton that such a service to the Severns, in the name of Brantwood, would be helpful.

With Collingwood thus unavailable, they turned to Cook, for whom the "financial terms," believed to have been £1,500, "were certainly not very attractive";[11] and for the others, the Library Edition evidently far from realized initial expectations, although it made a little money at the start. Sold in sets only, each volume was priced one guinea — two thousand copies of the Edition having been prepared for sale. Of these there was a surplus after the last volume had been issued: in 1912 unbound copies were consequently sold to The Encyclopædia Britannica Company, which sought to stimulate the market by advertising that an autograph Ruskin letter, in a red morocco folder, would be presented to everyone who purchased the Edition as thus offered,[12] in a blue binding. George Allen had died in 1907; by August, 1914, when his business was reorganized as George Allen & Unwin Ltd., the new firm acquired the remaining copies of the original edition.

As graduates of Oxford who had shared an interest in Ruskin, Cook and Wedderburn were old acquaintances. Years before, Cook had prepared a guidebook for the National Gallery, for which Ruskin had written a preface in which he commended the author's "industry and good sense"; subsequently Cook had published, as *Studies in Ruskin* (1890), a collection of miscellaneous and inconsequential articles originally written for the *Pall Mall Gazette.* He then became a more and more important journalist, ending as "joint manager for the Press Bureau for the censoring of English newspapers" during World War I: he had been editor of the *Pall Mall Gazette* (1890–92), of the *Westminster Gazette* (1893–99), and then of the *Daily News* until, in 1901 — "like a bolt from the blue" — this editorship was terminated by new proprietors, and Cook was left in grave need of a source of income. Thus "excluded from influential and responsible work for which he was uniquely fitted," Cook was free to spend the next ten years regularly writing political articles for the *Daily Chronicle,* with frequent contributions also to the *Sunday Sun,* and to act as a coeditor of the Library Edition. Of Cook's "amazing industry" there can be no doubt. But by no stretch of the imagination could his backgrounds have effectually prepared him to assume the editorial responsibilities of a biographer — a labor to be crowned by the standard biography of Ruskin, which "was wholly Cook's work." [13] His diary indicates that he had begun his editorial work during 1902.

Hence, in 1903, there began that phenomenal feat of publication: thirty-nine huge volumes in nine years, during which time Cook had still had energy to spare for the publication of his two-volume *Life,* as well as for his supplementary bread-and-butter writing. In 1903 Cook and Wedderburn apparently had hoped that *all* the volumes would be out by 1906! "It is no small labour," Wedderburn wrote Norton, on April 20, 1903, "and will take all my leisure [*sic*] for the next three [*sic*] years. But I am most fortunate in having E. T. Cook with me." [14] Biographically, what could be expected in the Library Edition other than much slapdash work, supported by useful although undigested compilation?

As a pioneer, Collingwood had done his work with perception and with care, but in the *Life* he had accepted a good deal on faith, and had made various factual mistakes. When Cook and Wedderburn used Collingwood's achievement (both editorial and biographical) as a main foundation for their further work, they were especially unfortunate when they undertook to make corrections: almost all the errors made by Collingwood not only were perpetuated but were multiplied. Indeed, the errors made by Cook and Wedderburn within the province of biography are so widespread that it can seem symbolic that the editorial work in the Library Edition should have *begun* and, for the main body of Ruskin's writing, should have *ended* with a mistake. Cook's "Preface" to the whole edition concludes with the remark that one of the two watermarks "of the unbleached paper made for this edition . . . is Ruskin's monogram." Actually this watermark is not Ruskin's monogram but, rather, that of Ruskin's father: it can be read *JJR* (John James Ruskin) as well as *JR* and there are books of John James Ruskin "with the same design as a book plate." [15] Another error marked the end, in 1909, when with Vol. XXXVII ("Letters," Vol. II), the editorial work on the body of Ruskin's writing was concluded by the publication of a letter of October, 1893, from Ruskin to Miss Susan Beever. At this point we find the last editorial note: "[What is believed to be the last letter written by Ruskin is here added in *facsimile* . . .]," whereupon the facsimile appears, entitled "The Last Letter." It is now possible to offer in facsimile two later letters — one to Lady Simon, written on March 3, 1894, and not unknown to Cook; the other dated "12th Oct. 1895" and written to Sir John Simon — so far as we yet know, really the last letter Ruskin ever wrote.[16]

The number and the latitude of biographical mistakes in the Library Edition can be seen, perhaps most easily, through a comparative examination of the Cook and Wedderburn "Family Tree" (*Works,* Vol. XXXV, p. 603) and the one herein presented, both versions being much indebted to the "Family Tree" originally prepared by Collingwood. Granted, Cook and Wedderburn were producing under pressure, with no small interest in making money.[17] But they should at least have taken time to be consistent in their errors, if not to consult records. From records they could have learned, for example, that Ruskin's Aunt Jessie did not marry a Mr. "Peter" Richardson of Perth and that "Mr. Richardson, of Croydon" was Ruskin's Uncle *George.* So, too, they could have obtained actual dates of birth and death for many members of the family, thus obviating the need for blanks that were, however, less befuddling than was the editors' more usual guesswork. They were far too casual in accepting Ruskin's chance remarks and his own repetition of mere hearsay. They also seem sometimes to have been deliberate in their preservation of what were, on occasion, Ruskin's deliberate misstatements. Like Ruskin, for example, they must have known that his mother was *not* a daughter of "Captain Cox of Yarmouth" inasmuch as they specifically refer to a *Birth Certificate* on which Margaret Ruskin is designated "daughter of William Cock of Croydon." From this same document Cook apparently obtained the last name of Ruskin's nurse, Ann[e] *Strachan* — so named in his biography and on this *Birth Certificate,* but elsewhere, to my knowledge, merely called "Nurse Anne."

So one could continue, as many a page in my own work will demonstrate, though I shall not belabor such details, even in this "Prelude." And it will become evident that beyond names and dates, one should never feel secure in accepting, without verification, any biographical or interpretative statement made by Cook and Wedderburn. Even after verification, many of their statements need to be reconsidered in light of relevant information which, typically, may have been withheld.

In general, sharing responsibilities for the biographical paraphernalia, they also worked without imaginative insight or genuinely sympathetic comprehension. At Oxford, Wedderburn had been one of Ruskin's diggers on the road at Hincksey, and now the editorial approach could not have been much different if Cook and Wedderburn had still been undergraduates engaged in hero worship.

In their attitude of reverential piety, which has placed them foremost among those who have made *Ruskinian* a term often used derisively, they were at one with Mrs. Severn, so that it becomes impossible to gauge how much influence, through her ultimate control, she may have had upon their work. Charles Eliot Norton, having first expressed his disapproval of the plan to gather in the Library Edition all of Ruskin's published work, seems subsequently to have been content to trust their judgment in selecting from the manuscripts. He, too, would exercise discretion while editing his Ruskin letters. Nevertheless, he published with a fullness that angered Alexander Wedderburn, as a coexecutor, into stopping the English sale of those two volumes. More quietly, Mrs. Severn was disturbed by Norton's inclusion of material that illuminated more than Ruskin's feelings about Rose La Touche: "Then our Beloved was so varied in his Religious views," she protested, rather plaintively, " — and to my mind was not a sceptic — and in later days I don't think the Parents were blamed for their bringing up of him — " [18] In Cook and Wedderburn she had agents whom she could consider more wisely faithful to the best interests of their victim.

In making their selections from the manuscripts, the editors seem to have been guided by two principles. First, nothing should be made public which might reflect adversely, from their point of view, either upon Ruskin or upon any member of his family, although (as a corollary to this first principle) if there was any conflict between the interests of Ruskin and of some member of his family, Ruskin should be favored. It followed that Cook and Wedderburn made almost no use of the family letters which cast light upon the long engagement of Ruskin's parents (to have published these more fully would have cast doubt upon the adequacy of Ruskin's understanding of his mother and her early life) and on events within the home of Ruskin's Scottish grandfather, who seems to have been considered the skeleton in the family closet — obviously not to be displayed. Nor did the editors publish widely enough from Ruskin's letters to reveal the destructive intensity of his conflict with his father and the toll upon his health and work exacted by resentments that mounted through the years and finally left him burdened by a weight of guilt which was no less heavy than it was unwarranted. Inevitably, when such material is withheld (and at this point I give no more than the briefest indication), the whole picture — its shadows at once lightened here and darkened there — becomes so grotesquely distorted that the man whose strength enabled him to bear prolonged and intense suffering while yet functioning creatively can in our day be made to appear a weakling and a hypocrite.

As their second and related principle, all that Ruskin said auto-biographically, especially in *Praeterita,* about his life and that of his parents should be given unqualified editorial support, unless some assertion was so glaringly at variance with an established date or other obvious fact that perforce a footnote must be added to indicate that in this detail Ruskin's memory must have been at fault. Such footnotes naturally enhance the impression that with these exceptions, all statements in *Praeterita* should be accepted at face value.

Perhaps the spell cast by *Praeterita* — because the spell that it can cast is one token of its imaginative and creative power as well as of its inner truth as an expression, profoundly moving and suggestive, of mood and memories and fantasies during Ruskin's old age — perhaps that spell, together with adulation and preconceptions, blinded Cook and Wedderburn (though it did not blind Colling-wood) to the significance of what they must have read in manuscripts. To be sure, not even momentarily would I risk seeming to imply that *Praeterita* is not a most important source of knowledge about Ruskin's early years, and about his parents, too. Biographically, how-ever, it presents complex problems. As a culmination of Ruskin's life-work and experience, it is subtly and immensely resonant, and it is often marked by irony (used repeatedly against himself) and by hostilities as well as by much reticence in the course of its free flow and tenderness. Cook and Wedderburn, nonetheless, apparently assumed that in *Praeterita* is to be found the literal and unadulterated truth which should be used as a point of departure for editorial comment and, unhesitatingly, as the rock foundation upon which to build biography.

One result of this lamentable assumption was that, through their selections from the manuscripts, they documented, in effect, by their thirty-nine volumes, the absolute reliability of Ruskin's portrayal, in *Praeterita* and elsewhere, of his father and his mother and of his early years, and consequently of the whole course of his experience and development as a personality. And never once since they produced that long array of volumes has any biographer failed to found his work upon *Praeterita* as though in it one finds the Ruskin-gospel, to be read verbatim and uncritically accepted, as though one were an Evangelical turning to his Bible.

As one more element destined to increase eventual confusion, there was — incompatibly — the editorial policy of collecting all the work of Ruskin that had been already published, with the inclusion of his public and his private letters. This policy was faithfully pursued with only one exception of which I am aware — amusingly, a public letter of 1852. In Venice, some weeks before, the jewels of Ruskin's wife had been stolen. As a sequel to the incident, Ruskin had been challenged to a duel. Gossip brought this news to London, where there was some unpleasant talk, to the chagrin of Ruskin's father — who urged the wisdom of this letter. In view of Ruskin's habitual and sometimes unsuccessful struggle to voice his thought through public letters in spite of the paternal censorship, it seems delightfully incongruous that the one letter in this category which Ruskin's editors were willing to ignore should have been written at the insistence of John James Ruskin.[19] Less amusingly, the decision to include all published letters had caused trouble in 1904 when, as has been already said, Charles Eliot Norton aroused editorial consternation by issuing his Ruskin letters in two volumes:[20] eventually these letters must be incorporated in the Library Edition, even though Norton had been guilty of what could be considered serious editorial indiscretions. This event was typical of difficulties which evolved, in that the policy of including everything already published could sometimes conflict with the two principles which generally seem to have determined editorial selections from the unpublished manuscripts at Brantwood.

Before they finished, Cook and Wedderburn had collected and reissued numerous letters which significantly supplemented their selections, so widely scattered through their introductions to earlier volumes that at the end of six years, when they concentrated on the "Letters" in Volumes XXXVI and XXXVII, it is entirely possible, if not highly probable, that they themselves did not realize how much they had revealed, all told. Nevertheless, momentarily and intermittently, they *had* shed light on various problems — frequently, in biographical introductions and editorial notes, by having published fragmentary passages, sometimes wrenched misleadingly from the letter as a whole; occasionally by having published a letter without indicating that parts of it had been omitted; unavoidably, by having published all those other letters thrust upon them after passing through the hands of other editors, whose treatment of the original they seldom had a chance to check.[21] They did not, however, make it possible to see events in context and to interpret individual episodes in Ruskin's life, or Ruskin's isolated remarks, as part of a consistent and illuminating whole. What reason is there to suppose that they themselves ever had perceived the whole? If they had, they gave no inkling of it, either in the Library Edition or in the *Life* which Cook produced therefrom, without correcting factual errors he had made in editorial introductions and with undiminished faith in the literal truthfulness of *Praeterita,* as he assembled and developed what remains the "standard" life of Ruskin, called, of late, "a classic."

Meanwhile, interest in Ruskin had waned more and more so that the Library Edition became indeed a drug upon the market. (There was no red morocco folder when I bought my set in London, I believe in 1932, for about $30 — the volumes in original wrappers, with uncut pages — and there were other sets from which to choose.)

By the 1920's, a new generation of biographers took over, to make the Library Edition their happy hunting ground while using that invaluable Index too exclusively as a tool. Now Ruskin's story of his life was often read with not entirely friendly eyes — Ruskin having written *Praeterita,* between psychotic episodes, for the entertainment of a friendly reading public as he sought escape from extreme loneliness and suffering during his old age, trusting his readers to recognize and to discount his irony, with a responsive kindliness. In the changed climate, Cook and Wedderburn, through the collected *Works,* could be provocative to those who now would exercise on Ruskin new techniques of popular biography, not without regard for the new approach to individual behavior provided by twentieth-century psychologists. And now again, as in Pope's day —

> The flying rumours gathered as they rolled,
> Scarce any tale was sooner heard than told;
> And all who told it added something new,
> And all who heard it, made enlargements too,
> In every ear it spread, on every tongue it grew.[20]

Not unrelatedly, these new biographers would express the iconoclasm of a period when not the qualities reflected in significant achievement but, instead, the vulnerabilities (real or supposed) of erstwhile heroes could best satisfy the spirit of a time that also fostered challenge to age-old values in our civilization, particularly those concerned with love and with religion — many of these values, beyond that rationalistic Waste-land of the twenties, to be contemptuously stigmatized "Victorian."

And among Victorians, no one offered richer opportunities for caricature (not always hostile) than did John Ruskin — "moralistic" champion of the good, the beautiful, the true in art as reflective of the character of the artist, the life of man, and the attributes of God; dreamer who "ignorantly" attacked the mechanism and cocksureness of late nineteenth-century science, "sentimentally" proclaiming admiration, hope, and love to be the sources of power behind all that makes for life and human welfare; mystic — even from the first — in his own ultimate comprehension of a spirit at work within the universe, with intuitive apperceptions more and more spontaneously communicated through the "formlessness" of later books; foe of "liberty," and advocate of Empire and paternalistic capitalism — except for his cry against machines and laissez-faire, as likewise against faith in the "Almighty Dollar" ("blasphemy") and against the "getting-on" of a few at the expense of many — as he pleaded for a return to the ways of days-of-old, as Sir Walter Scott first had led him to envisage them; knight-errant, too, who chanted woman worship according to traditions linked to the school of Courtly Love. All this: while in his personal life he revealed neurotic maladjustments and as a climax, with seemingly convincing proof, could be charged of late with having been deliberately cruel to his own wife, as the son of hateful parents, he himself "incurably" impotent — than which no shame could seem more great to virile manhood in an age impotently ridden by its hatreds and its fears, with Ruskin's "Storm-Cloud of the Nineteenth Century" now shutting out the Sun, world-over.

In our day, too, speaking of Ruskin's mother's death, one writer could remark, "And so the old hag died"; and a reviewer would rejoice that for Ruskin personally, agony of spirit became so unendurable that he escaped through losing contact with reality. Close beneath the surface, great cruelty, ignorance, and barbarism are at work within our age, and as one very minor incident in their course, they have also hit John Ruskin. But he would have been far less vulnerable as a target had his more private manuscripts initially been entrusted to a Froude instead of to the friends who so effectively prepared the way for those who were, or have become, his forthright enemies.

One need not pause for more than general comment on the biographies produced during the second phase of Ruskin scholarship, dating from the 1920's. Until quite recently, it has been assumed that whatever needed to be known about Ruskin manuscripts had been representatively published by Cook and Wedderburn or, at best, that their selections needed merely to be supplemented by whatever group of manuscripts (his *Diaries,* for example) any single individual chanced to have at his command. No one, so far, has been in a position to subject the work of Cook and Wedderburn to critical appraisal, or has suspected that, as editors, they could be seriously misleading. Assuming, consequently, that Ruskin's portrayal of his parents must have been, if anything, too charitable, and accepting at face value his account of his experiences during childhood, some of these later biographers undertook to entertain the public by psychoanalytical interpretations, although, in general, they were equipped to do little more than apply what had become clichés of Freudian thought at its most mechanistic. And obviously even the most enlightened and conscientious study that embodies psychoanalytic insight invites travesty if interpretations (such as those offered by Wilenski) are based on information which through unobjective and uncomprehending selectivity has been distorted from the start. Moreover, problems created by the Library Edition could not be solved without considerable work. Yet Cook and Wedderburn were not alone in having hastily prepared to "sell": witness their factual mistakes unfailingly incorporated in later books, in the face of public records available to all, which would have made corrections possible.

In addition, years have passed since Cook and Wedderburn collected Ruskin's work, supplementing it by material drawn from memoirs of his day. Yet to my knowledge, no one except Derrick Leon has bothered to do any reading, worthy of being so designated, in the nineteenth-century memoirs from which Cook and Wedderburn made selections to suit their special purposes. Nor has anyone, except Joan Evans, more than scratched the surface of material scattered through memoirs published after 1910 (the last date included in the Cook and Wedderburn Bibliography) and therefore often difficult to locate. Through this interim, the sheer bulk of Ruskin's writing, all but overwhelming even in the Library Edition, has been substantially increased through further publication of his letters, sometimes handled with the care and objectivity which distinguished Leon's presentation of the La Touche Correspondence, and sometimes with the scant attention to detail and the high degree of partisanship which marked Admiral Sir William James' treatment of the Ruskin-Millais Correspondence (*The Bowerswell Papers*).

As yet, however, no one has attempted to discover how any editor handled the documents at his disposal, although to do this checking is a fundamental need, as has been exemplified by the result of Joan Evans' dispassionate eclecticism in combination with her failure to evaluate the sources which guided her interpretation of Ruskin's personality and thought, and doubtless therefore her selections from his *Diaries,* as she told the story of his life. Hence, after critical appraisal, all of this material remains to be assimilated. The work of Admiral James has already served to muddy still more darkly the onflow of biography; for the Whitehouse "Vindication" scarcely served its proclaimed purpose, although Ruskin's "Statement to his Proctor" (as therein presented) naturally has value as another fully published manuscript.

Against these backgrounds, I am undertaking to present Ruskin's life and work in a biography which, if its purpose is successfully achieved, may help to usher in a third phase of Ruskin scholarship. Therefore necessarily, beginning with this "Prelude," I challenge beliefs long established and universally supported by tradition and achievement in the Ruskinian world. In effect, I am returning to the point which Collingwood had reached when in 1893 he published the official *Life*. In so doing, I have resources which were not at his disposal: knowledge of many manuscripts unavailable at Brantwood, and of letters and memoirs published during the last sixty years; a viewpoint cognizant of developments in twentieth-century psychology; and, not least, the text of Ruskin's work as it was so invaluably assembled, annotated, and charted by Cook and Wedderburn. As to my over-all endeavor, I can but hope that as I in turn retravel The Old Road, guided by those documents which serve as signposts year by year, I may not go too far astray before finally reaching *Praeterita,* then to return with Ruskin "by a commodius vicus of recirculation back to Howth Castle and Environs. . . . A way a lone a last a loved a long the / / riverrun, past Eve and Adam's, from swerve of shore to bend of bay. . . ."

As a beginning, it seems essential to undertake to reconstruct, so far as possible, the early life of those two most unusual personalities, Margaret and John James Ruskin, whose extraordinary influence on their son's work and fate would outlast their mortal lives. To this end (not fully realizable), I have herein made use of five main sources: (1) the correspondence of Ruskin's Scottish grandmother (Catherine Tweddale Ruskin), now owned by Mr. F. J. Sharp, of Barrow-in-Furness, Lancashire, who has helped me with great generosity; (2) letters of John James Ruskin in which he describes his early career in London, now among *The Bowerswell Papers,* in The Pierpont Morgan Library; (3) unpublished passages scattered through manuscript and/or corrected proof of *Praeterita* and *Dilecta,* now in the Yale University Library, with certain sections missing; (4) letters of those who conducted in my behalf investigations of public records in Scotland and in England, as I shall specifically recount, with a depth of appreciation I could not well express; (5) published memoirs — virgin territory for Ruskinians — which unfold the social scene in the late eighteenth-century Edinburgh of which John James Ruskin was a product and which, therefore, deeply colored Margaret Ruskin's life-experience.

More incidentally but realistically, I must also mention my own knowledge of the personalties of Margaret and John James in their actual relationships with Ruskin as I have learned to know the trio in the course of many years of work with letters of all three, in large part unpublished; and with the scattered wealth of *Juvenilia* — boyhood letters, poems, sermons, stories, drawings, journals — in which, knowing Ruskin's parents at the start, one finds implicit the actual story of his childhood. This will be a story not unlike the one recounted in *Praeterita,* yet there will be significant — in my opinion, crucial — differences. Therefore to know John James and Margaret Ruskin through their early years is more genuinely to understand the family life which they created shortly after leaving Scotland and, as its far counterpart, the writing of *Praeterita* as thereby we return to earlier days — not alone of Ruskin as he spun his tale about his parents and their backgrounds. For, as I have already noted, it is in his treatment of their early life that one most readily can recognize *Praeterita* to be shot with fancy and with symbolism, and sometimes, I suspect, with fantasies which Ruskin personally had had during the childhood he relived imaginatively, with a resurgence of old emotions, while writing his autobiography. To prepare his present readers to discriminate between fact and symbol (as in the incident of his suddenly forswearing Evangelicism during a Sunday in Turin), and to see, as an inevitable result of the lives of Margaret and John James Ruskin before their marriage, those years of childhood which for Ruskin held the future, are also functions of this book. Thus (to elaborate an earlier remark) *Ruskin's Scottish Heritage* becomes one product of a period when men have learned to comprehend how forces — family and environmental — which determine the securities and insecurities of parents, likewise determine their subsequent behavior and thus affect their treatment of their children so that, as ancient wisdom knew, the "sins" of fathers, and of their fathers, can leave a mark from generation unto generation. It is not often that surviving documents provide such opportunity.

It is also an opportunity imperatively to be used as a means of substituting for caricature, particularly of Ruskin's mother, a semblance of reality — a reality which cannot be recaptured if one begins with the young Margaret who first was animated in *Praeterita.* This young woman of *Praeterita* was obviously someone Ruskin never knew, Margaret having been thirty-eight years old when he was born; and she also was a character created with considerable hostility, although he loved his mother very deeply. (Ruskin was notably ambivalent about both his parents.) Nor will reality be found, except for later years, by turning to the impressions left upon those who saw her briefly, as visitors at Denmark Hill, when she was anywhere from seventy to ninety, by then an almost blind old lady, set in her ways and not without her eccentricities. Even for the later years reality should not be sought in letters, editorially selected from among those written by a daughter-in-law who hated the whole family, not without some cause but not with objectivity. Least of all will reality be found in a tradition created by biographers who have stressed all that Ruskin satirized in his mother (his treatment of her Evangelicism having been sharpened by his experiences with Rose La Touche) — these biographers habitually selecting the details expressive of his disguised animosity and minimizing, or omitting, those details originally designed to soften the effect, while rounding out their picture of the younger mother through evidence that shows her, rather incompletely, during her old age. It will, however, help us to approximate reality if we begin by recognizing that the younger Margaret whom her son envisaged in *Praeterita* is predominantly a character whom he himself created.

To be sure, cutting cloth of the imagination as he told the story of his parents' early life, Ruskin did use a scattering of facts to guide the general pattern: John James' father *did* lose his mind and die a suicide, and his mother *was* the daughter of a Presbyterian minister, and she probably eloped; Margaret *did* attend Mrs. Rice's day school, and her father *did* die "of a broken leg . . ."; John James, in turn, actually attended the Edinburgh Royal High School and he married Margaret after working nine years to repay his father's debts. Thus one learns to look for some nucleus of truth from episode to episode within *Praeterita;* in fact, dealing with this early period, I have only once been seriously disappointed in my attempt to find it: records give no sign that Margaret's father, or his father, originally came from Yarmouth. And what Ruskin wrote had for him, as it has for us, imaginative truth so that, turning to the later years for an example, no one should feel disconcerted upon finding in a letter of his *wife* an account of a dinner table conversation held with Gladstone which in *Praeterita* is used to illustrate how Ruskin courted Charlotte Lockhart! That conversation was another bit of truth, used, in its own way, to communicate a further truth: what Ruskin felt about himself, in retrospect — masochistic in self-mockery. Moreover, in *Praeterita* he professedly would tell the reading public no more than it was good for them to know, insofar as he could charm them (more immediately, such understanding and delighted friends as his Isola — Lady Mount-Temple, and "Lacerta" — namely, Mrs. La Touche, with whom there had been a reconciliation) and could amuse and solace himself. Poetry, even prose-poetry about one's own life, is written, is it not, chiefly to instruct and to delight?

In the *Praeterita* portrayal of John James he was, however, relatively realistic, partly because he understood his father better than his mother, and also, I believe, because he was much more vividly aware of his real feelings toward John James, both in love and in hostility, first as child and then as man, although in his emotional relations with his father and his mother Ruskin did not outgrow the child: that also was a part of his Scottish heritage.

In the manuscript version of *Praeterita* it is curious to see how automatically he capitalizes *Father,* usually writing *mother* without a capital, even in such a combination as "my Father and my mother" — curious because Margaret was in fact, both as wife and mother, habitually in "lower case," even as she had been, one gathers, during girlhood in her home in Croydon, and as she would remain through all the years she spent in Scotland — waiting, serving, all her youth away, with far more than stern bare bones of help from her Bible and from God, Evangelically (or Presbyterianly) interpreted. Next, as mother, Margaret would channel, not undeliberately, her son's affections into worship of that Father, household god, who very early found his alter ego in the son whom he adored with a love as ultimately self-centered as it was all-consuming and self-doubting in its pride — hurtfully projecting his own lack of self-respect into his treatment of the son through whom, vicariously, he found compensatory satisfactions.

As early as Ruskin's years at Oxford, resentments against his father took their toll upon his health (he then thought, he says, that he was losing all his teeth), and they finally drove him, for self-preservation, into the intensely conscious anger (always swiftly smothered) which was expressed in several letters often quoted from the Library Edition. Thus more fully aware both of the excessive love which he had felt for Father as a child and of the excessive bitterness of his resentments during later years, Ruskin was consciously protective of John James when he wrote *Praeterita,* as becomes apparent through passages which he withheld from publication. This protectiveness, however, leads in its own way to a distorted picture and scarcely gives a hint of the extreme insecurities that motivated the behavior of his father as yet another facet of the Scottish heritage. Yet these insecurities must be clearly recognized and understood if John James in turn is not to be victimized through caricature. This development could easily occur — partly because of the letters he wrote George Gray, published (often incompletely and usually out of context) with merciless (probably because uncomprehending) editorial comment in *The Order of Release,* and publicly received with no great charity; but chiefly because John James Ruskin, in actuality, was the main agent of destruction in his son's life. And yet, "In tragic life, God wot, / No villain need be. . . ."

Finally, a more accurate portrayal of the early life of Ruskin's parents will make it possible to see their son, nineteenth-century-London–born though he was, as a child of Scotland through his direct heritage of the cultural and intellectual life that distinguished Edinburgh when John James Ruskin was in process of development as a young man, so that Margaret, too, when she reached the Scottish capital, learned to share her future husband's early interests, and admirations. Then for John James these cultural interests lay largely dormant during many years, as he worked with concentrated drive first as a clerk in the offices of two Colonial Brokers and next as the head of his own firm. But after he and Margaret had established their cloistered home, they were ready to pass on to Ruskin all that they themselves had learned either to admire or, with participation, to enjoy — be it the poetry of Erasmus Darwin, or the *Sermons* and the *Rhetoric* of Hugh Blair, or the poems and the novels of Sir Walter Scott; natural science (above all, geology) and architecture (particularly Gothic), or gardening, with keen delight in flowers; correct pronunciation, and English etymology, or romantic landscape painting, and sketches that recorded topographical detail; Tory faith in politics, strongly tinctured by the class consciousness of feudal days and intermixed with an intense distrust of Whig reform, and of "liberty" — or a religious faith which was at one with that of Scottish Presbyterians, and colored by the superstitions which were especially prevalent in the Scottish countryside. All of this, as we shall see, was in the very air that men of Edinburgh breathed in the late eighteenth and early nineteenth centuries, and all this reappears distinctly, either in the *Juvenilia* or in the early memories of John Ruskin.

The danger is, perhaps, that what I now maintain may sound too neat; nonetheless, no one could legitimately deny that the cultural heritage which came to Ruskin during his most formative years and which determined his life work reached him almost exclusively through his parents, and represented what they themselves had gained when they resided in that city which was the self-flaunted Athens of the North. Nor would the philosophy of Dugald Stewart (incidentally inclusive of political economy as a branch of moral philosophy) and of Professor Thomas Brown, and the aesthetic theory of other Scotsmen, be unhelpful when their son wrote *Modern Painters I,* although by then he had been exposed to influences other than those exercised by his parents. Nevertheless, surely John James Ruskin would have whetted his son's interest in the work of famous teachers at the university which he himself could not attend, although it was within walking distance of his home? But however that may be, John James and Margaret, between them, left John Ruskin unique among nineteenth-century men of letters in his combined pursuit of scientific knowledge, literature, and painting. Great breadth of interests was characteristic of the ideally Cultivated Gentleman in the Edinburgh of their youth: as G. T. Garratt said, speaking of Lord Brougham, "A clever young Scotsman was expected to take all knowledge for his province, like Francis Bacon or Teufelsdröckh."

It is now a pleasure to turn to my indebtedness to those who have helped me in my work. To many, my specific thanks must be reserved for later volumes, though everything I have received is implicit in this *Heritage* which realized itself, at first like an unwanted child in an already too-large family. To all who have made possible this book by making possible what will follow it, I now express my unforgetful gratitude.

Extending back through many years, this gratitude first leads to memory of days when Mr. Collingwood made accessible to me, through the kindness of Miss Violet Severn, the Brantwood manuscripts. I went to Coniston, introduced by the late Professor Arthur

Beatty of the University of Wisconsin, who had directed my doctoral
dissertation on John Ruskin and who then followed, with faithful
interest and unqualified encouragement, my work on this biography.
Material which Professor Beatty was the first to read, as part of
a short opening chapter, could not possibly now be published without
my expressing deepest gratitude to him. Likewise, I express my thanks
to Mr. Collingwood, in memory, for having opened to me the door
of opportunity; and to his daughter, Barbara Gnosspelius, as a most
meaningfully living presence, for the sympathetic help she gave me in
those days — such help having also been bestowed frequently and
open-handedly thereafter. There could have been no more perfect
introduction to the world of Ruskin than that which I received
through their great kindness, that spot of time-and-space — at one
with thought of them and of their home — having lived on, inex-
tricably, as part of my own present. It is therefore with pleasure
deeply felt that I have dedicated *Ruskin's Scottish Heritage* to Mrs.
Gnosspelius, and to the memory of her father.

I also express heartfelt thanks, personally and professionally, to
Professor George B. Parks of Queens College, and to Dr. Gotthard
C. Booth, psychiatrist in New York City. To them I am indebted
for much help which is intangible; they have never failed me during
years when work could sometimes seem to be both endless and
unrewarding, as well as unproductive except in my own hive of
slowly accumulating manuscript, which each of them was kind
enough to read in part and to discuss with me. To Dr. Booth I am
more specifically indebted for my general understanding of the com-
plexities involved in "heritage." To Professor Parks I am most immediately indebted for the interest he has generously and variously
manifested in this volume, which has profited from advice and criticism he gave after reading it, as a whole, in manuscript.

To those who have helped me through correspondence about the
Ruskin family backgrounds I am deeply indebted not only for specific
information, often vivified by photostats and photographs most generously contributed, but also for one of my most surprising and altogether happy experiences in Ruskinian adventure. I could not
possibly express with adequacy the depth of my appreciation to all
who gave their thought, their time, their knowledge and resourcefulness to research conducted in response to what sometimes must

have seemed to them to be my endlessness in query. The extensiveness and over-all importance of this part of my debt can be indicated only through the implications of my notes and appendices.

To Mr. E. A. Hogan, Registrar General for Scotland, I feel an all-encompassing gratitude for what he once called "an effort to restore some of the literary and artistic and, if it comes to that, the human past." His response to my first letter of inquiry led to all that followed in this realm; through search instituted because I had asked whether the dates of the death of Ruskin's Scottish grandparents might not be located even at this late hour, he discovered many details about the Edinburgh Ruskins, together with the maiden name of Ruskin's mother. Thus Mr. Hogan also led me to suspect that no one heretofore had made a serious effort to discover facts about the Ruskin family backgrounds. For a while it had seemed unlikely that the two dates initially desired could be obtained: Scottish records for those days are incomplete and the Scottish grandparents had been buried without there being any trustworthy clue as to *where* or *when*.

To Mr. Alexander J. Tait, City Librarian, and Miss Ethel Leslie Watson, Principal Assistant of the Sandeman Public Library, Perth, I am particularly indebted for having run down those two dates (in consultation with Mr. Hogan, who was the first to tell me), and for having provided much information about the Patrick Richardsons of Perth (the family of "Aunt Jessie"), gained in the course of their main search, as well as for having investigated in my behalf the history of Bowerswell. Miss Watson was likewise especially kind in checking and rechecking problematical names and dates and in offering various suggestions more generally related to my interests.

To Mr. W. D. Collier, Keeper, *Edinburgh Gazette,* I am indebted for knowledge that no Award of Sequestration (or bankruptcy) was published in the *Gazette* for John Thomas Ruskin, the grandfather, at the time of his financial failure; to Mr. Lloyd Mead of The Vintners' Company, London, for knowledge that the name of John Thomas Ruskin does not appear in the "Freedom Book" of the Vintners' Company; to Mr. Ernest Morris, F. R. Hist. S., campanologist, and author, for knowledge that evidence which has been cited to prove the presence of Ruskins in Leicester during the eighteenth century is without foundation in fact; to Miss Vera J. Ledger, Research Assistant, London, for having located the will of Ruskin's great-great-grandfather, John Ruskin of Cheshunt, Hertfordshire, and related items; to Lambert & Raggett, genealogists of Watford, Hertfordshire, for evidence which demonstrates that eighteenth-century London Ruskins came from Cheshunt, Hertfordshire, where Ruskin's great-grandfather was born, and for having located the will of this great-grandfather, and related items.

To Dr. D. S. M. Imrie, Rector of The Royal High School, Edinburgh, I am indebted for investigation of old High School records that contain one piece of information which has proved invaluably helpful; to Mr. C. S. Minto, City Librarian and Curator, Central Public Library, Edinburgh, for further information about John Thomas Ruskin entries in Edinburgh Directories from 1780–1810; to Mr. A. B. Paterson, City Librarian, and Mr. C. W. Black, Depute City Librarian, The Mitchell Library, Glasgow, for seeking to determine whether any copy of the Scottish National Covenant now in Glasgow could have come from the library of Ruskin's great-grandfather, the Rev. James Tweddale of Old Luce, Wigtownshire; to the Rev. Malcolm Pollock, present Minister of Ladyburn Church, Glenluce, and to the Rev. David Galloway, present Minister of Old Luce Church, Glenluce, for historical information about the Old Luce Church, Mr. Galloway having also most kindly examined the Kirk Session Minute Book kept during the ministry of Ruskin's great-grandfather.

To Mrs. Oscar Gnosspelius, as Curator of the Ruskin Museum, Coniston, I am indebted for information about Ruskin's *Birth Certificate,* and for the dates of birth and death of members of the Severn family.

To Mrs. Thomas J. Telford of Grasmere, from whom I obtained the Ruskin family miniatures, I am also indebted for my first knowledge of when Ruskin's great-grandfather, John Ruskin of London, died, and for information about family letters and other matters.

To the Rev. Dr. Newell E. Wallbank, Officiating Minister of the Priory Church of St. Bartholomew-the-Great, London, I am indebted for having initiated investigations of the London Ruskins as former residents of his Parish, and for knowledge that no Ruskin epitaphs have survived in the Great Churchyard.

To Mr. Raymond Smith, Librarian and Curator, Guildhall Library, London, I am indebted for information, obtained from records in his keeping, about the London Ruskins, inclusive of the marriage of Ruskin's maternal grandparents.

To Mr. T. E. Callander, Chief Librarian, the Central Library, Croydon, I am indebted for the results of a varied and most rewarding search: information about the Croydon backgrounds of Ruskin's mother (inclusive of Mrs. Rice's Academy for Ladies — a most difficult bit of business, although it can appear but passingly in this book), in course of which he located the family graves in Croydon's churchyard; knowledge that the maternal grandfather's family name does not appear in Yarmouth records but occurs in Croydon records of the eighteenth century; many facts about Margaret's parents which help to bring to life the environment in which she spent her girlhood as daughter of the keepers of the King's Head Tavern, as niece of an Aunt Mary, heretofore ignored (whose husband also kept a tavern in the neighborhood), and as sister of "Aunt Bridget," about whose life and family further information has been provided; and as though all this were not sufficiently God's plenty, Mr. Callander entrusted me with old photographs of now-demolished sites connected with the family history, and with related aids.

Not only the type of help I have received, as indicated by these paragraphs, but also the spirit in which that help has uniformly been bestowed, leaves me, as I have already said in letters, humble in my hope that in my work I may have been enabled to use to some degree commensurately the riches thus placed in my hands through human kindness in alliance with the selfless and international concerns of scholarship in its effort to restore, as Mr. Hogan said, our human past.

It is with such thoughts that I now seek adequately to acknowledge the great help I have received from Mr. F. J. Sharp of Barrow-in-Furness, Lancashire, whose ownership of *The Catherine Tweddale Ruskin Correspondence* I discovered, as though by yet another act of Fors, after years of searching vainly for these letters. Among the Brantwood manuscripts, they had chanced to be almost the first I studied, after which they disappeared at auction so that I could only regret, with self-reproach, the shortcomings in my transcriptions from letters which I feared might have been permanently lost. Then one day I sent Mr. Sharp a request for permission to use quotations from other manuscripts in his possession, of which I had found typed copies in The Pierpont Morgan Library, and soon

I knew that day to have been most fortunate for *Ruskin's Scottish Heritage*. Since then, by correspondence, Mr. Sharp has helped me through consultation about specific problems, upon which he has brought to bear the wide and detailed knowledge he has gained during his long study of Ruskin's work and manuscripts; through supplementing my initial harvest from the "Catherine Correspondence" while helping me with my original transcriptions; through giving me information drawn from other material in his carefully selected and altogether invaluable Ruskin Collection; through providing photographs of Ruskin's " 'Last' Letters," of "The Calvert Check," and of Aunt Jessie's home in Perth, together with transcriptions of the *Deed of Indenture* of John Thomas Ruskin and of other manuscripts, in part or whole, as acknowledged in my footnotes. More than this, he has fortified my faith in my own work by his good wishes and participative interest. Only through the spirit of this work could I hope to express, significantly, my thanks for such sustained and generous support, the more meaningful to me because of Mr. Sharp's desire to serve the interests of Ruskin. My gratitude to Mr. Sharp is not merely commensurate to the rich harvest gained, for the "Heritage," through our correspondence.

Returning to compatriots, I find myself widely and likewise deeply indebted, though now my thanks can be more readily expressed because although the help I have received has not been less generous or meaningful, it has been somewhat less unusual. First, however, I must pause, as at an international bridge, to thank the British Information Service of New York, for unfailingly wise guidance when I would telephone to ask how I should address yet another inquiry. At home there are the Queens College friends and colleagues to whom I am grateful for various assistance: Drs. Robert H. Ball, Israel Baroway, Phyllis Bartlett (Mrs. John Pollard), Dwight L. Durling, Dorothy Jones (Mrs. Ernest van B. Jones), James R. Kreuzer, Harold Lenz, Max Patrick, Irving Ribner (now of Tulane University), Esther K. Sheldon (Mrs. James F. Bechtold), James E. Tobin, Marianne Zerner.

In our libraries there are those to whom I am particularly grateful. From Drs. Joseph H. Brewer, Robert A. Colby, the late Sidney Mattis, and Mrs. Ruth B. Oakley, of the Queens College Library, I have repeatedly received invaluable aid. I am also individually indebted to Mr. Archibald R. DeWeese of the New York Public Library, where I have done almost all my background reading, seldom failing to find whatever publication might be needed, however esoteric it might seem, and ever helped by the resourcefulness and courtesy of members of the staff. To Miss Marjorie G. Wynne, Librarian, Rare Book Room, I express sincere appreciation for all that made my work pleasant as well as greatly rewarding in the Yale University Library, with its wealth of Ruskin manuscripts. In all which I have been seeking to achieve — from my first return to manuscripts that were originally at Brantwood — I am inexpressibly indebted to the Yale University Library.

And now once more by way of long ago, I thank Miss Elizabeth B. Norton for having most kindly granted me permission to read and to transcribe from the correspondence of her father, Charles Eliot Norton. I likewise thank those librarians in the Treasure Room of the Harvard College Library who were the first to produce for my research a trunk containing what were then uncatalogued manuscripts.

To Mr. F. B. Adams, Jr., Director of The Pierpont Morgan Library in New York, I am so greatly and variously indebted that I become, once more, keenly conscious of the inadequacy of words. To Mr. Adams I am most tangibly and immediately indebted for having made available for illustrative use in *Ruskin's Scottish Heritage,* through photographic reproduction, documents which Mr. Callander entrusted to my care, together with photographs of Ruskin family miniatures I personally have acquired, most reassuringly aware that I am supported by his judgment of their value; and for his having permitted me to use, before they were catalogued, Ruskin-Millais manuscripts contained in a wonderful trunk owned by The Pierpont Morgan Library: this trunk still holds *The Bowerswell Papers.* While working with these documents I frequently received most kind help from Dr. George K. Boyce, then Curator of Manuscripts, and day after day, when I grew puzzled while making my transcriptions, from Mr. Curt F. Bühler and other members of the staff who were in charge of the Reading Room. More recently I have also been most generously helped by Mr. Herbert Cahoon, present Curator of Manuscripts.

It was this work with *The Bowerswell Papers* that precipitated *Ruskin's Scottish Heritage,* while enabling me to evaluate the handling of these documents in *The Order of Release* and to understand more fully the whole episode of Ruskin's marriage. Therefore, both for this "Heritage" as a first fruit and for much that remains to be recounted I am immeasurably indebted to The Pierpont Morgan Library — with all that I have thus gained inseparable from the great kindness of Mr. Adams.

To conclude, I should like to express my gratitude to an editor, Dr. Donald D. Jackson, and to his assistant editor, Miss Rachel E. Anderson, who have significantly helped to make this book at least better than it would have been without their creative criticisms and suggestions. Their patience, too, has gained my special gratitude as — until even later than the *eleventh* hour — further information, casting further light upon some episode or problem, would arrive so that some passage in the manuscript would have to be once more revised. All told, I have good cause to remember "My First Editor" with most sincere appreciation.

Formally, but appreciatively, I now thank those who have granted me permission to use material under their control. For quotations from MSS. in their possession or in their custody, I am indebted to officials of The Houghton Library, Harvard University; of the Ruskin Museum, Coniston; of the Rutgers University Library; and of the Yale University Library; to Mr. F. J. Sharp, of Barrow-in-Furness, Lancashire; to the Trustees of The Pierpont Morgan Library. For illustrations, I am indebted to The Croydon Corporation, Croydon, Surrey; to George Allen and Unwin, Ltd.; to Mr. E. A. Hogan, Registrar General for Scotland; to The National Galleries of Scotland; to Mr. F. J. Sharp; to Mr. Raymond Smith, Librarian and Curator, Guildhall Library, London. For quotations from books of which they hold the copyright, I am indebted to Charles Scribner's Sons and to John Murray (for passages from Admiral Sir William James' *John Ruskin and Effie Gray,* variantly entitled *The Order of Release*); to the Columbia University Press and to Constable and Company, Ltd. (for passages from Sir Herbert J. C. Grierson's *Sir Walter Scott, Bart.*); to E. P. Dutton and Company (for passages from J. S. Mills' *Sir Edward Cook, K. B. E., A Biography*); to George Allen and Unwin, Ltd. (for passages from the Library Edition of Ruskin's *Works*); to the McGraw-Hill Publishing Company (for passages from *Boswell's London Journal,* as edited by F. A. Pottle).

1

The English Ancestors

The life of Ruskin was affected so profoundly by his parents' needs and values that the true beginning of his story lies hidden, for the most part, in the backgrounds and events which shaped the personalities of his father and his mother. They themselves, by middle age, were loath to speak of days which had left memories of financial failure, insanity, and suicide, and which — more serious by far — had undermined the self-respect of Ruskin's father. Something of his shame of his own family John James Ruskin apparently communicated to his son who, in the course of working on *Praeterita,* noted in a diary: "24th February Tuesday [1885] Y[esterday] a terrible day of chagrins and difficulties —

finding my Croydon Grandmothers lost letters to my mother, and my Ruskin grandfathers apprentice indenture to a vintner in London in 1776 — and the news from Africa of attack on our camp. All humiliating and grievous." [1]

Writing his autobiography, he explained that he had been "stupidly and heartlessly careless" of the history of his family: "not till after my mother's death did I begin to desire to know what I could never more be told." [2] More fundamentally, it would seem as though he had early learned not to question: as he explained, "I had however from childhood formed the habit of letting my mother speak just of what she chose — and of nothing more, knowing that there was much both in my fathers family and her own, which she did not like to speak of." [3] Similar reticence would screen his own portrayal of his family background — he, in turn, the one reluctant to relate even so much as he knew. [4]

It was not alone because of this reluctance that etymological speculation frequently enriched by sentiment has to this day served as a substitute for factual knowledge about the Ruskins' origin. During his old age, Ruskin himself is reported to have been "keenly interested" when he learned that he had probably descended from a Scottish family known in the eighteenth century by their occupational name — "na Rusgan" or "na Chlann Rusgain," that is, the clan of bark-peelers, since rusg means rind, peel, bark in Gaelic, with Rusgan signifying someone who strips bark. In the course of the investigation which led to this conclusion, a man who would have been a distant cousin wept upon perceiving, in a picture of John Ruskin as a youth, the face of a beloved brother John who long ago had died. Local folklore indicated that in 1715 the great-great-grandfather of John Ruskin had left the Land of Lorne to follow the Earl of Argyll as his chieftain, and had fallen wounded at the Battle of Sheriffmuir. Those were days when Scottish nobles were divided in their loyalties, some supporting the Hanoverians and others wishing to restore the Stuarts to the throne.

Read as a whole, this is an amazing tale, gleaned through the ingenious research of a Gaelic scholar, Dr. Alexander Carmichael. So well graced is it by fancied bits of circumstantial evidence that in 1946 the not incautious Dr. George F. Black included "Ruskin" in *The Surnames of Scotland,* citing the work of Dr. Carmichael. [5] For his part, Dr. Carmichael may have been inspired by Collingwood, who, in 1893, opening a discussion of "The Ruskin Family" in which no progress has been made,[6] introduced a ghost that can still be counted on to make its spectral reappearance. "The name," Collingwood observed, "seems to start up in the eighteenth century . . . with a solitary Ruskin in Edinburgh, as if he were some immigrant known by his place of origin, — one of the many who drifted into the towns of that period, seeking safety or a field of labor, with clan-name either concealed through prudence, or too common to identify him. We find a kirk of Roskeen . . . on the firth of Cromarty, — a Gaelic name. . . . About this dimly seen person we only know that his son [Ruskin's paternal grandfather] was famous for his handsome looks. . . ."[7] It is therefore not surprising that perhaps the most reliable of Ruskin's twentieth-century biographers asserts: "All that can be said with certainty is that a John Ruskin appeared in Edinburgh in the earlier half of the eighteenth century, whose son was John Ruskin's paternal grandfather. . . ."[8] Obviously it is not thus that Ruskin's story, rooted in the story of his parents and their forebears, should continue to be told.

Those who would prefer to read a more realistic tale, gained — not unimaginatively — through the employment of a more pedestrian method, must be content to start with little more than a glimpse of scattered facts, realizing that these facts will help to focus vision.[9] With the eighteenth century drawing to its close, the opening scene is Edinburgh. Here Ruskin's father, John *James,* spent his first sixteen years of life, and the social atmosphere which then impinged on his development was to be reflected ever after in his own character, as though in mirror image. Self-defensively, he would remark in later years that he did not have one happy memory from his youth to help him. Though doubtless he exaggerated when he made this statement, no one would have found it easy, in the Edinburgh of those days, to have been the son of a mother who was by birth genteel and of a father who had occupied, for almost twenty years, the socially contemptible position of a petty tradesman.

This father, John *Thomas* (Ruskin's paternal grandfather), had come from London after about twenty years of residence in the Parish of St. Bartholomew-the-Great. There he had been born, in 1761,[10] and there, in 1780, his father, John Ruskin, had been buried in the Great Churchyard at the age of forty-five. This John Ruskin, the great-grandfather, had originally come from the Parish of Cheshunt,

Hertfordshire. Baptized there on January 3, 1735,[11] he was the third child of a John Ruskin who, in 1731 (probably within a month of burying his first wife), had married Mary Adams. Their first child, Robert, had been born in 1732, and their first daughter, Mary, in 1733; late in 1734 they had their John. Sometime between 1738 and 1746 (a period for which there is a gap in Cheshunt registers) they evidently had three more children — Jane, Ann, and Thomas, or, according to his father's spelling, "Tomass." For on November 25, 1747, when Ruskin's great-great-grandfather made his *Will*, "being in ill state of health but in perfect mind and memory," he specified that each of his three daughters (Mary, Ann, Jane) and three "Suns" (Robert, John, Thomas) should receive "twenty pounds of good and lawful money of grate Britain being to be paid at the years of one and twenty and it is my Will and desire is [*sic*] that if any or either of these children should should [*sic*] dye before the age of one and twenty that the said sum of twenty pounds shall remain in my dear and loving wifes hands Mary Rusking witch I make my hole and sole Executrix . . . John Ruskin signed. . . ." [12] In 1742, his name — "John Ruskin . . . of Cheshunt" — had found its way into the County Records as a "yeoman" bound over to "answer for assaulting" a resident of Hatfield. Finally, on February 23, 1753, his *Will* was proved at London "by the Oath of Mary Ruskin widow," "John Ruskins" having been buried in Cheshunt five days before.

Beyond this great-great-grandfather it is impossible, as yet, to carry back the Ruskin line. It is clear, however, that from early in the eighteenth century Ruskins had lived in Cheshunt, as well as in near-by towns of Middlesex; records of their marriages, births, and deaths, sometimes supplemented by a *Will,* inconclusively suggest family relationships. Perhaps a *Robert* Ruskin buried in 1719 had been the father in whose memory Ruskin's great-great-grandfather named his first "Sun" Robert, this name to be bestowed upon a son of his "Sun" John. With first names in that family linking the known generations, *William* also hauntingly appears — first in 1660 when, in Paul's Wharf, London, a *William* Ruskin married *Mary* Pew; and in Little Berkhamstead, also in 1660, *Thomas* Ruskin married *Elizabeth* Smith. (*William, Robert, Mary, Elizabeth* were all siblings of *John Thomas* Ruskin.) *John* emerges in 1686, when, in the village of Writtle, Essex, a John "Rusken" gave his *Will* by word of mouth to "Goodman" Green, making his son John his heir. Then in 1709 we find *John* Ruskin marrying Sarah Benton in Enfield, Middlesex; in 1713, again in Paul's Wharf, London, *Robert* Ruskin, a widower of Berkhamstead, Hertfordshire, married the widow Mary Crane, of Edmonton, Middlesex — he to be indicted, ten days later, for "scandalizing" a Mr. Thomas Hatton. (One gathers, variously, that these Ruskins were a hotheaded crew.) Next, in 1735, in Cheshunt, on the very day when Ruskin's great-grandfather was baptized, there also was baptized *"William* a Base son of *Ann* Mead supposed to be begot by *William* Ruskin." And there were other Williams too. More respectably, in 1734 the Spinster, Frances Ruskin, of St. Mary Stoke Newington, Middlesex, had made her *Will,* not forgetting her brothers Jeremy and *Robert,* or her nephew *John* Ruskin, or, by curious chance, the children of a relative — *John James.*

It is with reluctance that, at this point, one feels obliged to pause in the pursuit of ancestors, granting the morbidity of such an appetite. Scattered evidence that there were English Ruskins as far back as the fourteenth century has been offered heretofore, without, however, helping to resolve the mystery of Ruskin's more immediate family background. Hence it is good at last to know that in the early eighteenth century *"na Chlann Rusgain"* were evidently simple although not unprosperous folk of Middlesex and Hertfordshire, where their descendants lived, as laborers and farmers, well into the nineteenth century.[13]

John Ruskin, the great-grandfather, next appears in Marylebone, Middlesex, within the Diocese of London (here, perhaps not unrelatedly, Ruskin himself was to put Octavia Hill in charge of one of his experiments in social welfare after he had inherited some slum property, in 1864, from his father). Great-grandfather Ruskin was by now (1754) nineteen years old, and before long presumably received those £20 designated in his father's *Will.* If so, it was a nest egg which he modestly increased, for, in 1780, although his widow swore that his estate did "not amount to the Sum of one hundred pounds," he had left to her the administration of "goods etc. in different Archdeaconries or jurisdiction within the Diocese of London," having stipulated that after her death "all [his] personal Estate of what kind or nature soever . . . [should be] equally divided between . . . [such children] as shall survive . . . Said Wife." [14] On June 26, 1754, when they were "both of Marylebone," he married Mary Carswell.[15] In July of either 1755 or 1756, Ruskin's maternal grandmother, Margaret, was born at "35 minutes past 3" on a Saturday morning. In December of the next year there came her sister Mary — in biography an unknown member of the family, although in later years Mary lived near Margaret in Croydon, where Margaret made her living as a tavern keeper, as did Mary's husband.

Ruskin's great-grandparents soon moved into the Parish of St. Bartholomew-the-Great, where John Ruskin had found employment as the Parish Clerk before he made his *Will.* He was evidently living there by 1759, when his first son was baptized *William,* doubtless in honor of some member of the family, according to the well-established habit of those Ruskins. It is therefore interesting — as well as puzzling — that in 1745 a *William* Ruskin should have been buried in the Great Churchyard of this Parish, as had been a Jane Ruskin in 1753. By 1761 John Thomas Ruskin had been born, shortly after which his brother William died. In 1767 came the twins, Robert and Elizabeth, who after three weeks died; then in 1772 brother James was buried, "aged 8 mos." Thus, of all their children only three survived — Margaret and Mary, and John Thomas.

Not long after they lost William, John and Mary Ruskin had a miniature of John Thomas painted — his little face, low-necked white shirt, blue waistband (or top of trousers), all shown in an oval water color no more than one inch high. This likeness was set within a frame of turquoise that is now the center of a bracelet.[16] It may have been the bracelet of his mother, because a mourning ring in memory of the father of John Thomas was subsequently made as a matching piece of jewelry; this ring also has an oval frame of turquoise which surrounds a bit of brown hair identified by the inscription engraved upon its mount: "JOHN RUSKIN / *Ob*[*it 1*]6*th*. *of May* / 1780 aged 48 [*sic*]." [17] The links which make this bracelet, attached to the miniature and wrought in bars embossed with leaves of gold, may have been designed in later years. If so, this piece of jewelry could appropriately have been made for Ruskin's mother, inasmuch as in the little picture of John Thomas as a child of about three years old, Margaret Ruskin could readily enough have seen her son (except for the straightness of his hair) as Northcote painted him when he in turn had reached the age of three — their resemblance, as toddlers separated by the passage of approximately sixty years, having been as striking as it remains evocative.

John Thomas next appears as of February 7, 1776, when, aged

fifteen, he was indentured to Robert Walker, "Citizen and Vintner of London, to learn his Art" and "to serve from the Day of the Date hereof, until the full End of Seven Years. . . ." In this apprentice-ship he spent at least four years because on the back of his *Deed of Indenture* there is the entry: "Vintners' Hall / to wit / the 3 day of April 1780 the within named apprentice by consent of both Parties is turn'd over to William Chatfield, Citizen & Vintner of the same trade for the rem^r. of his term / Willm. Bedell, Clk." [18] Such a change is said to have been possible only if a master died. Almost immediately (on May 16, 1780), John Thomas lost his father, after which there is reason to suspect that he did not work out the term of his indentured service. John Thomas Ruskin was a headstrong man, and he may well have been a headstrong youth. When his father, eight days before death, had willed the whole of his estate to his wife Mary, he had thought it wise to specify that it should "be by her possessed without the control or interference of my children or any other person. . . ." [19] More significantly, when John Thomas left for Scotland, his name was not enrolled in the "Freedom Book" of the Vintners' Company to show, as was the custom, that after satisfactorily completing his apprenticeship, he had "take[n] up his Freedom and in due course his Livery." [20] So far as can be de-termined, he did not practise the Art of Vintner during all his years in Scotland, although biographers — faithful to tradition stemming from the words of Collingwood — have habitually assumed that of course in Edinburgh he "set up in the wine trade. . . ." [21]

Perhaps John Thomas did not simply run away from home or from William Chatfield, because by February, 1783, he would have finished his apprenticeship; and it was rather more than nine months later that he became the father of Janet Ruskin — to be known better as "Aunt Jessie." By then John Thomas Ruskin had become an Edinburgh grocer, as is recorded in the entry of his daughter's birth: "December 5th 1783 / John Thos. Rusken [*sic*], Grocer and Catherine Tweedale [*sic*] his Spouse Old Kirk Parish, a Daughter Born 20th November last named Janet. Witnesses [*sic*] Alexander Manners Grocer Bapd. by the Rev^d. Dr. Henry." [22]

An English Ruskin having found his Scottish home and Scottish wife, henceforth there would be Ruskins traveling from Scotland into England, and then back to Scotland, until finally we find the child John Ruskin traveling thus, within his father's borrowed carriage, as *Praeterita* recounts. And even though his Ruskin ancestors were men of Hertfordshire and Middlesex, there nonetheless was that in Ruskin's personality which could appropriately have stemmed, as has been said, from Scottish ancestors who had dwelt for centuries " 'amid the silence of [these] storied glens — who read the auguries of Life and Death in the eagle's scream and the black-bird's song, and who in early, mystic times amid these scenes, worshipped the great nature-forces — the Sun and the Moon, and the Earth-gods, by the Cromlech and the Serpent-mound on the shores of Loch Nell.' " [23]

Before the time of the child John's traveling to and fro, Margaret Ruskin, the sister of John Thomas, would have a daughter Margaret, who in her turn would set forth for Edinburgh to join her uncle's family. There she would be influenced by her Scottish aunt and would fall in love with her cousin, John James Ruskin. He in his turn would set off for London, so that he and Margaret would thereafter travel back and forth for visits.

Eventually, in London — as though rounding out a cycle which, having been renewed, would be extended far into Ruskin's lifespan — John James and Margaret had the boy who was to find in them, as well, the auguries of Life and Death, together with his Sun and Moon, and Earth-gods, with the end of his own life so strangely yet so naturally swinging back to its beginnings.

2

Edinburgh — Old and New

In Scotland, centuries of internecine strife and of struggle against England had found final manifestation in the Rebellion of 1745, when Prince Charles Edward, last of the Stuarts, had arrived from France. Through *Waverley,* Ruskin would learn to love Prince Charles — by no means as "The Pretender" but rather as "Chevalier" of the St. George for whom he too would raise his banner, first spelling out in childish verse the romance of battles as recounted by Sir Walter Scott.[1] For when Sir Walter Scott was young, there still were people who had danced in Edinburgh Castle at the ball where Cavaliers had welcomed this descendant of their fabulous Queen Mary. With their defeat in

1746, years of civil war were ended, and there was no longer need for Edinburgh to remain a city fortified by the Castle and by walls which had been raised against rebellious nobles and marauding or invading English forces.

The Old Town stretched out, turtle-like, from east to west atop its ridge, with the Castle for a head and Holyrood Palace for a tail, and High Street lying like a backbone in between, while narrow alleys — "wynds" or "closes" — extended right and left, like ribs. In these "wynds," gabled houses rose story upon story, some of them twelve stories tall — an "amazing" height, Sir Walter notes in *Guy Mannering*.

Through Boswell's words, we can hear and smell that city to which John Thomas Ruskin came only five years after Samuel Johnson had been induced to visit Scotland:

Mr. Johnson and I walked arm-in-arm up the High Street to my house in Jame's Court; it was a dusky night; I could not prevent his being assailed by the evening effluvia of Edinburgh. I heard a late baronet of some distinction in the political world in the beginning of the present reign observe that "walking the streets of Edinburgh at night was pretty perilous and a good deal odoriferous." The peril is much abated by the care which the magistrates have taken to enforce the city laws against throwing foul water from the windows; but, from the structure of the houses in the old town, which consist of many storeys in each of which a different family lives, and there being no covered sewers, the odour still continues. A zealous Scotsman would have wished Mr. Johnson to be without one of his five senses upon this occasion. As we marched slowly along, he grumbled in my ear, "I smell you in the dark!" But he acknowledged that the breadth of the street and the loftiness of the buildings on each side made a noble appearance.[2]

The city being what it was, social status usually was designated not by a street address but rather by the floor on which one lived, inasmuch as rank by rank and floor by floor the social classes rose to better light and air. In earlier days, Brown Square had been occupied exclusively by families of the upper classes, after which Jame's Court (where the well-born Boswell had his home) and George Square (to which Scott's father moved his family after losing several children while a resident of College Wynd) became addresses which in themselves denoted one's "respectability." Shopkeepers, like the working class and other humble folk, were generally housed in cellars or on the street floor, darkly dismal in those unclean, narrow alleys, with two to three rooms for a fairly prosperous family and with the front room of the ground floor holding the tradesmen's ware. Above the lower classes lived professional men; then, in the upper half of gabled building, enduring steep dark stairs, came the gentry and the nobles. Yet, even among those who lived in the upper stories, the rate of infant death was fearful.[3]

With the coming of peace, increasing commerce brought prosperity, and men soon were longing to draw deeper breath than they found possible within the confines of historic Edinburgh. At first some few had made their homes outside the south wall, and to the west. But toward the north there lay a great plateau, beyond a once protective marshy gulf, and it was here the city ought to spread. Therefore, the Town Council enlarged domain and passed decrees, arranging finances until, by 1772, the North Bridge was in use. Then building mushroomed on that north plateau, with good citizens such as Alexander Nasmyth much interested in city planning as the environs of Princes Street took shape. Coaches multiplied astonishingly on those more commodious streets, as coachmaking became one of the new industries established during this period when older industries no less phenomenally expanded.[4]

This movement from the Old into the New Town steadily progressed. Of the nobility, all but the most conservative or impoverished had migrated before 1790,[5] seeking the less crowded quarters where more lavish entertainment characteristically replaced conviviality in taverns and sociability at teatime with no more than a few friends. With the city thus expanding, there was more than ever need for workers, grocers, merchants — newcomers who gravitated into the Old Town, which in time was to become the slums of Edinburgh. Into the nineteenth century, however, it was respectable to live there, although the degree of one's respectability continued to be indicated, almost as much as formerly, by one's floor: ". . . the quaint old social arrangement had hardly been impaired even up to the year of *Marmion*." [6]

In the Edinburgh of the 1780's, then — regardless of the difficulties an apprentice to a London vintner may have had — there was much to attract a young man reaching out adventurously toward a career.

3

John James Ruskin's Parentage

It was here in Edinburgh, in some dark lower room of Old Kirk Parish, that Catherine Tweddale had borne to "John Thos. Rusken, Grocer" their first child, in 1783, shortly after her own twentieth birthday.[1] The girl-mother had come from quite different surroundings; to say the least, she was the daughter of a minister, which was in itself enough to give her a modicum of social standing and, in general, a position in marked contrast to the one bespoken by her present habitat and by her husband's occupation.

Moreover, Catherine's mother was an Adair of Galloway. One of her brothers, Andrew, was the minister of Whithorn Parish; the other was the Dr. John Adair, Surgeon-General, who, in 1759 at Quebec, had attended General Wolfe when he was dying, and who, fortunately for John James Ruskin, would not forget Catherine when he made his will.[2] Catherine's mother had a sister, Mary, who had married the Rev. James Maitland; Mary became the mother of the Rev. John Garlies Maitland, and finally, through a second marriage of her grandson, the Rev. James Maitland, she became the great-grandmother of Ruskin's distant cousin, James Charles Maitland (*d.* 1915) of Kenmure Castle.[3]

Catherine's grandfather had been Captain Adair of Little Genoch, who had married Jean Ross, also of the landed gentry and, as Catherine would not fail to tell her son, a highly cultivated lady.[4] Such facts are not without their special meaning, for if Catherine had not had just cause for pride in her family, with its traditions of good education and good birth, the life of John James Ruskin might well have been eventually less rewarding, although more immediately less harassing because of his own inescapably two-class parentage in that Edinburgh of his youth.

In long view, these backgrounds had a bearing upon what John Ruskin came to feel about his family and, more indirectly, about society at large. There was something childlike in the humiliation he experienced on discovering those "grievous" letters of his Croydon grandmother, as well as in the pleasure with which, six months later, he heard about his "Galloway Ancestry," and planned to publish his discoveries.[5] For, thanks to Catherine, friends and relatives could trace his ancestry back and back until, through Mrs. Arthur Severn and another distant cousin, he realized that he, too, was graced by some "dim gleam of ancestral honour."[6] Well knowing what would please Ruskin, Collingwood related picturesquely, in the official *Life*, that Catherine's birthplace had been "the old abbey of St. Ninian,"[7] erstwhile church in Whithorn — the Candida Casa (White House). Located on a promontory extending into Wigtown Bay, the abbey had been built in the fourth century when, as Bede recounts, the monk Ninian went north to convert the heathen. In the thirteenth century a second Abbey of St. Ninian had been built upon the site of the Candida Casa. Here had been "deposited relics of the patron saint and hither flocked crowds of pilgrims, of whom were kings and queens of Scotland, 'For the dear grace of St. Ninian's bones.' "[8] Long before the birth of Catherine, however, only roofless walls remained to mark the ruins, reminding visitors of this historic tale.

Reflecting Brantwood atmosphere through analogous associations (doubtless also feeling kindliness toward Mrs. Severn, the "Joanna" of *Praeterita*), Collingwood would more factually recount, in a later edition of the *Life,* that Ruskin was descended from "two great families, the Agnews and the Adairs" (Mrs. Severn's maiden name was *Agnew*): this fact therefore made it possible to assemble a galaxy of distinguished men as Ruskin's kin, regardless of how indirect or remote the connection. We are told, for instance, that Ruskin's paternal grandmother's great-great-grandmother was "a near kinswoman of the celebrated Sir Andrew," commander of the Scots Fusiliers at Dettingen and " 'the bravest man in the British army' ''; that this lady's son married the great-aunt of Admiral Sir John Ross, the Arctic explorer, and of Field-Marshal Sir Hew Dalrymple Ross;[9] and naturally, that Catherine's great-great-grandmother had been Mary Agnew — one of the innumerable cousins of Sir Andrew Agnew, whose father is said to have had twenty-one children and whose family (one might add) had possessed "Lochnaw Castle" for almost four hundred years.

On Ruskin — "poor gipsy herald," [10] as he once called himself — such interests and attitudes had made, in his far, personal past, an inescapable impression. In *Praeterita* he had spoken much less freely than his readers would infer about his aunts who had married a Perth tanner and a Croydon baker, relatives who did not leave him, as he confessed, "entirely at ease." [11] Conversely, he had been delighted when he was told that Grandmother Catherine's father, his own great-grandfather, had had in his possession that major document of Presbyterian Scotland, the National Covenant, which in 1638 and 1639 had been distributed in multiple copy, with the text of the Covenant, inscribed on sheepskins, made available for signatures in every parish. Catherine's father — so the story runs — had received "the National Covenant of the Scottish Covenanters" from his uncle (another Rev. James Tweddale, 1685–1757, minister of Old Luce), who had received it from an aunt, who had received it "from Baillie of Jarviswood, who was suspected of having it in his possession, and was executed." [12] This document, Collingwood believed, was sold with the library of Catherine's father "at his death . . . and is now [1900] in the Glasgow Museum." [13] And Catherine's father *may* have owned a copy of the Covenant which is now in the Kelvingrove

Museum — a sheepskin "signed by many of the great covenanters (noblemen, barons and ministers), as well as by many other sub-scribers from various counties." [14] Nevertheless, in the Edinburgh of Sir Walter Scott and of Ruskin's father, one would have had far more prestige had one's own ancestor, like Waverley's, been honor-ably beheaded while serving in the Royalist cause.

Family connections such as Catherine's undeniably were significant, as her son, John James (made more poignantly aware of his own connection with a Grocer), would prepare *his* son to comprehend — even before he introduced the world of Waverley to Ruskin as a child. There is no trace of snob or sycophant in Ruskin, but the class consciousness and respect for rank which characterized his father colored feelings he himself developed during youth. These attitudes were reflected in his thinking and behavior to the end: in St. George's Guild, he would become the "Master" in what was essentially a feudal lord's relationship with followers, and his Utopia (witness *Time and Tide*) would have been an hierarchical society in which each man "knew his place." More crudely, it was thus in late eight-eenth-century Edinburgh; and so it was, more philosophically, in the concept of the Great Chain of Being to which Ruskin, as a "Tory-Radical," had been from earliest days receptively disposed.

How and when John Thomas found his Catherine remain among the facts unknown. According to the terms of his indenture he was not free to marry until his contract as an apprentice had been com-pleted.[15] Clearly, therefore, they were not married until some time after the spring of 1780, when he changed Masters. Then, as has been noted, after he met Catherine they may have waited until, legally, he gained his Freedom on that 7th day of February, 1783. Or, truly taking Scotch leave, had he gone to Edinburgh before he first saw Catherine, there to meet and take her as his wife when he was only twenty or twenty-one? It seems especially unfortunate that, so far, it has been impossible to discover where and when these two were wed.[16]

Catherine's father, who had died in 1777 at the age of forty-four, had been the minister of Old Luce Church, in the village of Glenluce (Parish of Old Luce), Wigtownshire, where he had officiated for nineteen years as successor to his uncle, the Reverend James Twed-dale. Built in 1636, theirs was a very simple church, as well as "one of the poorest in the country." [17] Like the surrounding region, the

Parish of Old Luce was a sparsely populated district which had been impoverished by prolonged political disturbances and by religious persecution, nowhere "more severely felt than in Galloway" [18] and nowhere symbolized more strikingly than by the Wigtown Martyrs — old Margaret M'Lachland and young Margaret Wilson who, in 1685, staunchly Presbyterian in their resistance to the Test Act, had been tied to stakes and drowned by an incoming tide.

The quality of faith which had survived the "Killing Time," as that period was called, had left its stamp upon the very faces of the people: an eighteenth-century traveler, whose misfortune it had been to start his Scottish travels by entering Galloway for his first week-end, observed:

There is nothing of the gaiety of the English, but a sedate gravity in every face, without the stiffness of the Spaniards; and I take this to be owing to their praying and frequent long graces, which gives their looks a religious cast. . . . Next day I expected, as in England, a piece of good beef or a pudding to dinner; but my Landlord told me, that they never dress dinner on a Sunday, so that I must either take up with bread and butter, a fresh egg, or fast till after the evening sermon, when they never fail of a hot supper. — Certainly no Nation on earth observes the Sabbath with that strictness of devotion and resignation to the will of God: they all pray in their families before they go to church, and between sermons they fast: after sermon every body retires to his own home, and reads some book of devotion till supper, (which is generally very good on Sundays;) after which they sing psalms till they go to bed.[19]

Doubtless it had been thus at least since the 1620's, when "anti-Romanists" walked almost two miles from their village and deliberately reduced to ruin the Abbey of Glenluce, built in 1190, where Robert Bruce had signed a Charter while making a pilgrimage to the Abbey of St. Ninian. And so it had remained through generations in which every child of Presbyterians would "commit to memory the shorter Catechism and the 'proofs,' " while being trained to accept, unforgettably, the doctrines of justification, sanctification, and redemption.[20] And if it was thus in the average home, what must have been the practice and the training in the home of Catherine's father as the village clergyman?

From a Kirk Session Book for the years 1724–75 one gains a glimpse of the Glenluce congregation. The number who attended a periodical communion service "seems to have ranged between 143 and 273" [21] from a population which by 1801 comprised only 1,221 inhabitants, no marked changes either in population or in way of life having taken place in Wigtownshire before the coaches, boats, and railroads of the nineteenth century induced a typical revolution. Under Mr. Tweddale's ministry they were, it seems, a godly group because although they struggled to maintain themselves through agricultural pursuits, they once contributed £39, 13s. "on behalf of a 'New Yoark' congregation," and again, in 1752, £4 sterling "on behalf of the 'suffering protestants' of North America," though toward the building of a bridge across the River Dee they gave, all told, precisely "six pence Scots." [22] And when, in 1745, there was once more a Jacobite rebellion, once more raising threat of "Romanism," they observed "a day of fasting, humiliation, and prayer . . . 'on account of insurrections and risings in the north headed by the Pretender's eldest son, and for the manifold sins and immoralities reigning in the land.' " [23] Then finally, on October 24, 1757, after only three days' illness, "the Reverend and worthy Mr. James Tweddell" was lost to them — "[33] years Minister in this place and justly regretted by all ranks in the parish." [24]

Ten months later, Catherine's father joined them (on August 10, 1758), an eligible young bachelor. Son of John T. Tweddale, "Bailie of Midcalder," he ended his first year of ministry by marrying (on September 26, 1759) Catherine's mother, thus becoming a son-in-law of two important county families, with their many consequential relatives. But of most immediate importance, Catherine's mother (eleven years older than her husband) was a daughter of the Captain Thomas Adair of Little Genoch who had married Jean Ross of Balkail.[25] Hence, as the first surviving grandchild through this marriage and as a pet who would not be forgotten by the Captain's son, her Surgeon-General Uncle John, Catherine must have had familiar contacts, during girlhood, with the gentry of that district, where prestige as well as life depended on the ownership and working of the land.

Here were rivers where the salmon swam, and valleys with low hillsides, softly rolling, with good grazing grounds for cattle, and for sheep whose wool was not surpassed by any that came from Galloway, then famous for this product. It was still a primitive countryside, with undrained marshes, unfenced fields where yokes of oxen ploughed the soil, inasmuch as horses, after all the years of raiding from the South and North, remained scarce and costly. Peasants lived in hovels made of stone and turf, while village homes were thatched, and only farmers and the upper classes knew the luxury of candles made at home from the boiled fat of sheep. Women always spun their thread from local wool, this thread made into cloth by local weavers and dyed brown by local herbs.

During these years, when young Catherine went to visit relatives, it must have been on horseback (no Wigtown horse would have been surprised at carrying two) across the hills and moorlands, following paths impassable to carriages. There were no roads in Galloway deserving of the name before 1780, when Parliament imposed assessment.[26] For gossip, there would have been the latest doings of the smugglers as they clashed with sheriffs — a persistent token of hard times in that country with its wild and jagged coastline; or of the cattle which had died from "elf-shot" — because it was well known that the old flint arrow heads of Galloway were worked by witches, fairies, and elves, and then shot to cause a bloat in animals that perchance had also fed on clover;[27] or of the latest ghost (for ghosts notoriously prevailed in Galloway), which a minister might be called upon to "lay" if it should prove especially troublesome. For home companionship, there would have been her younger sister Janet and their brother James. Not long after Catherine's marriage, Janet would also live in Edinburgh, likewise married to a "merchant," Alexander Brodie[28] — of whom one hears no more in family history; James would become Collector of Customs at Wigtown, and the grandfather of "Joanna," Mrs. Arthur Severn, known at Brantwood as "the cousin," familiarly called "the Coz."

When she was fourteen, Catherine lost her still-young father, her mother having died two years before.[29] Within a few weeks of her father's death, the Reverend William Learmont became the parish minister and of course would have occupied the vacated manse.[30] Relatives would then have taken in little Janet, brother James, and Catherine. In the home of Uncle Andrew, minister of Whithorn Abbey, there already were nine children, while at Sorbie their Aunt Mary, wife of the Reverend James Maitland, was mothering seven. So probably they joined their grandparents — Captain Thomas Adair and the former Jean Ross of Balkail, whose accomplishments, as revealed in her old age, Catherine would remember.

Four to six years after she became an orphan, Catherine met John Thomas Ruskin and fell headily in love. A miniature painted after they were married, when his rather curly hair was already touched with gray, shows a face that was alive, intelligent, and strongly masculine in contour and in features.[31] One cannot doubt that in John Thomas Ruskin, as Collingwood has said, Catherine gained a "handsome young husband" [32]: firm-chinned, and ruddy in complexion; dark-eyed, with sweeping brows; high-cheeked, with nose that is aggressive, as well as a model for his son's. As a type, the personality is suggestive of command, as though, had this man come from a different background, he would have made his way in law, or Parliament, or still more, perhaps, in military service. Desiring Catherine, he might well have overridden circumstance.

In a matching miniature,[33] Catherine is very feminine indeed with necklace, lace, and an elaborate coiffure. Wisps of curls are most carefully arranged to grace her forehead and to swirl until they overhang her eyebrows, falling down from beautiful brown hair piled high in a soft roll that serves as a crown, from which there sweeps a triangle of lacelike stuff that falls upon her shoulder. Catherine herself, as rival to this hair-do, is not too easy to find out. Yet the widely opened, eloquently large brown eyes are inescapable, and hers were lips that curved most naturally to smile. An altogether gentle, unconventionally pretty face, with skin almost as white as her lace and strands of pearls. Here, however, there is little hint, if any, of the reserves of earnestness and strength within her character. Rather, one can see the wife prepared, by temperament, to do what her husband wished; the girl, not uninterested in dress and fashion, who might have thought of life in Scotland's capital as more attractive than were the days and ways in well-born, homespun Wigtown — a girl in love who doubtless was persuaded to elope, as Ruskin said she did, should "Family" have objected, as members of her family doubtless did.[34] For beyond Catherine's time there was in Wigtown (where "Joanna," or "the Coz," also spent her girlhood) what one nineteenth-century native called a "terrible and deadly disease" — *gentility,* "very fatal all over Scotland, but in the West Highlands and in Galloway its ravages are most awful." [35]

And now, somewhere seeking the daughter of the manse, descended from the County Families, came a young man, unestablished, unconnected — not even qualified to practise the Art of Vintner; this young man whose charm and drive could not conceivably have made him, as a husband for our Catherine, other than appallingly "Inferior." Yet Catherine's joy in him, one gathers from this surprising miniature (she scarcely looks like the daughter of a minister), outlasted her first years of marriage; and apocryphally there would be handed down the winning, though unlikely, tale that shortly after Jessie's birth a friend surprised her "dancing a threesome reel, with two chairs for her partners; she having found at the moment no other way of adequately expressing the pleasure she took in this mortal life, and its gifts and promises." [36]

These next were realized, memorably, when she became the mother of John James, born May 10, 1785. "Robert Stewart Grocer and William White Iron Monger" were asked to witness the entry of this birth, on which "John Thomas Risken [sic]" called himself ambitiously, a "Merchant." [37]

It was to take John Thomas eleven more years of work, finally helped by Catherine's inheritance, to gain public recognition that he was a "Merchant" rather than a "Grocer," this distinction being chiefly connotative but not therefore less important. As the *Monthly Magazine* remarked in 1798, "In Scotland every little retail shop-keeper is dignified by the title Merchant," [38] and not long thereafter, in his *Dictionary* of the Scottish language, Jamieson defined *Merchant* as "A shopkeeper, a pedlar," to wit, " 'A peddling shop-keeper, that sells a pennyworth of thread, is a *Merchant.*' " "Wholesale and retail dealers alike passed under this name," Chambers recalled in 1859, "as is still, indeed, the case to a considerable extent in Scotland, where it has always been remarked that there was a peculiar liberality or courtesy in the distribution of names and titles." [39]

Long ago a "Merchant" had belonged "to a superior class of traders" who were "dealers in imported goods" and had occupied the luckenbooths on High Street, "in more retired situations," — in contrast to the tradesmen of the "Land-Market" who sold the "inland" wares in open booths or "laigh shops." [40] Then, as shops increased in number, with the highly miscellaneous stock of neighbor-hood grocery stores conveniently at hand,[41] the difference between a Merchant and a Grocer grew less and less clear cut. Nevertheless, late into the eighteenth century *Merchant* as a descriptive epithet appreciably signified superior dignity; when Peter Williamson prepared his first *Directory* for Edinburgh (1773–74) he preserved the old distinction through arranging citizens rank by rank, with due regard for the local Aristocracy of Law: "Lords of Session, Advocates, Writers of the Signet, Lords and Advocates Clerks, Physicians, Noblemen and Gentlemen, Merchants, Grocers. . . ." [42] Hence, when John Thomas Ruskin, flanked by his friends William White, the Iron Monger, and Robert Stewart, Grocer, styled himself a "Merchant" on that proud registry of his son's birth, one finds a straw which indicates the direction of the wind.

Yet, within the world in which John Thomas lived, it was accepted axiomatically that no more than a Grocer could a Merchant be a Gentleman, even should he rise to become a wholesale dealer. This simple fact is overwhelmingly important in the life of Ruskin, as it will take the story of his life to show. Motives are seldom unalloyed, and to generalize through almost any sweeping statement is to oversimplify. Nevertheless, it seems just to say that Ruskin was not undeliberately "made" a "Gentleman" (at first, most satisfyingly, a Gentleman Commoner of Christ Church College, Oxford) by a father who had spent his youth as the son of a Grocer, highly sensitized because his Mother *was* a "lady," and who thus had been convinced, emotionally, that he himself was not, and could never be, a Gentleman.[43] Therefore, tellingly, because in his own right John James could not be a Gentleman according to the standards of the world from which he came, he undertook to live, vicariously, that other life — his "Son's" (he always capitalized "my Son"). Thus seeking self-fulfillment, often to their mutual frustration, Ruskin's father would indulge in behavior that has caused him to be called "a prince of snobs." [44] And Prince of Snobs he will emerge, sometimes most offensively, though in this role, at his worst he can arouse compassion as he shows the wounds which he himself was dealt when young, while at the same time he helps to sow the seeds of tragedy in that well-loved other life which of course was not his own — though this was more than he himself could ever clearly comprehend.

Williamson's *Edinburgh Directory* shows the route that John James traveled as his father's son, and, no less, his mother's child. When John Thomas Ruskin registered his son's birth, he probably felt free to call himself a *merchant* because by 1785 he had acquired a shop: "John Ruskin, grocer, head of Kennedy's Close" appears in the *Directory* for 1786–88. "This Kennedy's Close," we learn, "was immediately to the west of the Tron Kirk, and was adjacent to the west side of the present Hunter Square. The shop was, in fact, on the ground floor of the tenement, behind or in which the famous George Buchanan died." [45] George Buchanan, it may be

Fig. 1. The Calvert Check, February 8, 1868.

Fig. 2. John Thomas Ruskin, *c.* 1764. A miniature attached to a bracelet.

Fig. 3. John Thomas Ruskin, *c.* 1795? A miniature.

Fig. 4. Catherine Tweddale Ruskin, *c.* 1795? A miniature.

Fig. 5. Dr. Alexander Adam, 1808. A portrait by Sir Henry Raeburn.

Fig. 6. "Aunt Jessie," Mrs. Patrick Richardson of Perth, *née* Janet Ruskin, *c*. 1804? A miniature.

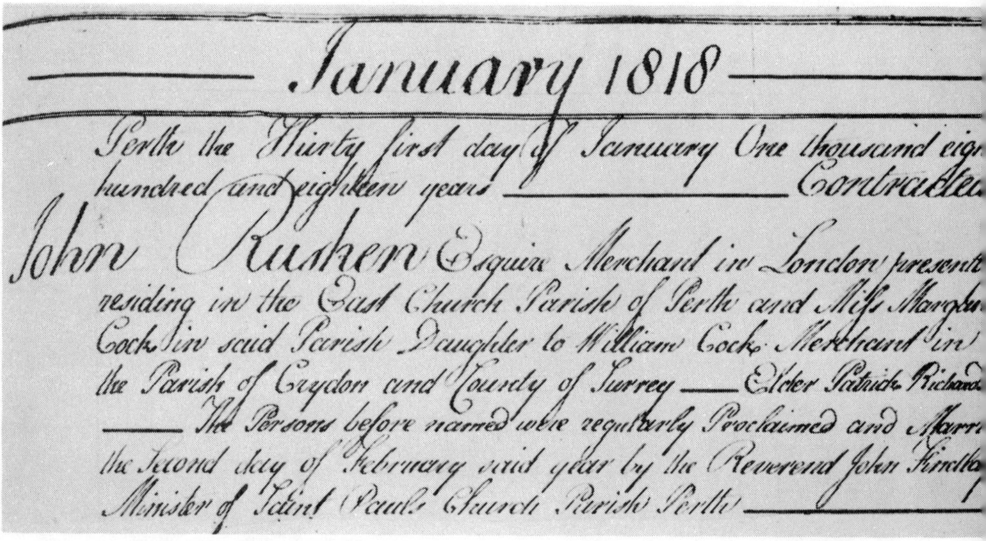

January 1818

Perth the Thirty first day of January One thousand eight hundred and eighteen years _____ Contracted

John Rusken Esquire Merchant in London present residing in the East Church Parish of Perth and Miss Margaret Cock in said Parish Daughter to William Cock Merchant in the Parish of Croydon and County of Surrey _____ Elder Patrick Richard _____ The Persons before named were regularly Proclaimed and Married the Second day of February said year by the Reverend John Findlay Minister of Saint Pauls Church Parish Perth _____

Fig. 7. Entry of the Marriage of Ruskin's parents, John Rusken (*sic*) and Margaret Cock. February 2, 1818.

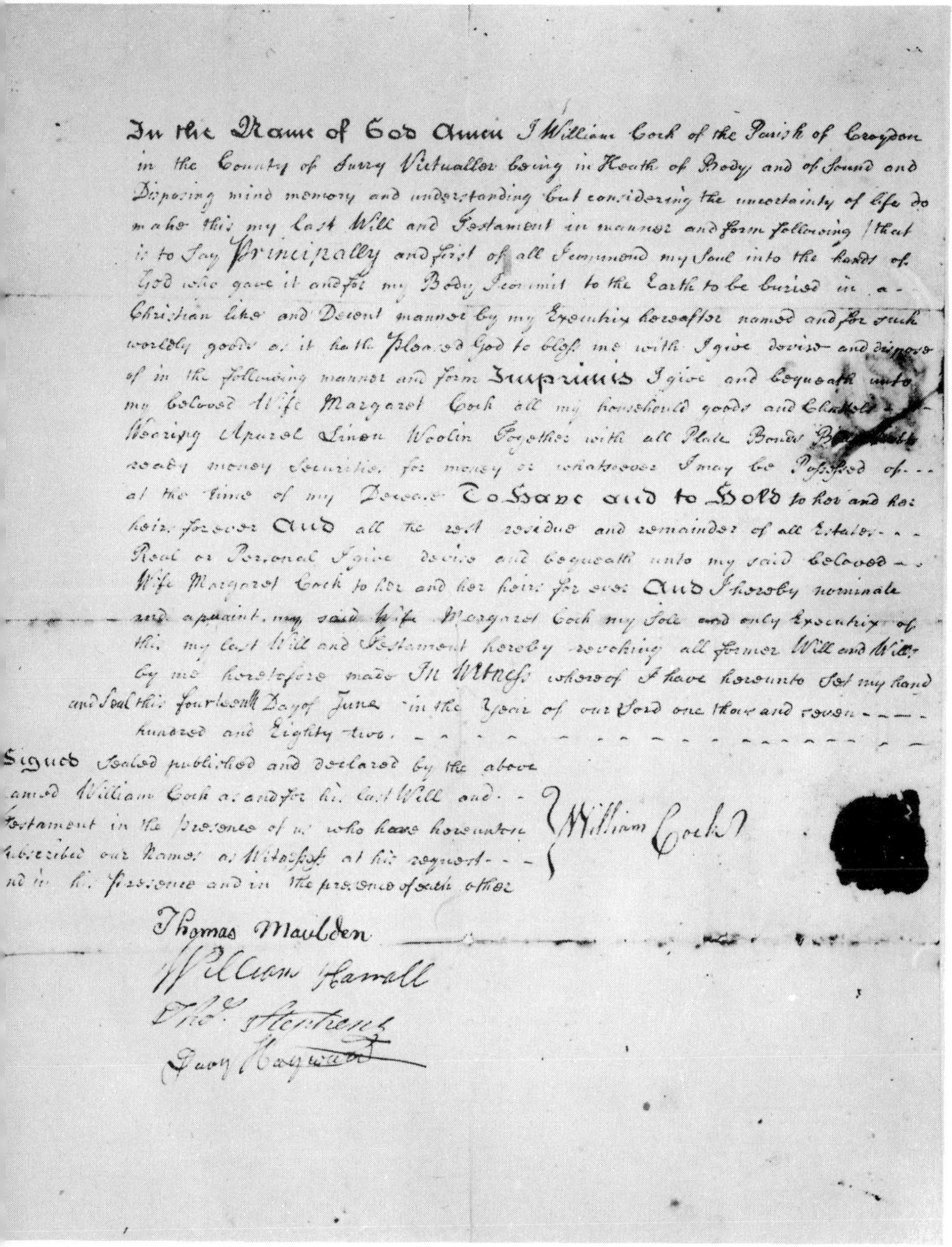

In the Name of God Amen I William Cock of the Parish of Croydon in the County of Surry Victualler being in Health of Body and of Sound and Disposing mind memory and understanding but considering the uncertainty of life do make this my Last Will and Testament in manner and form following that is to Say Principally and first of all I recommend my Soul into the hands of God who gave it and for my Body I commit to the Earth to be buried in a Christian like and Decent manner by my Executrix hereafter named and for such worldly goods as it hath pleased God to bless me with I give devise and dispose of in the following manner and form Imprimis I give and bequeath unto my beloved Wife Margaret Cock all my houshould goods and Chattels Wearing Apparel Linen Woolin Together with all Plate Bonds Bills securities ready money Securities for money or whatsoever I may be Possessed of at the time of my Decease To have and to Hold to her and her heirs forever And all the rest residue and remainder of all Estates Real or Personal I give devise and bequeath unto my said beloved Wife Margaret Cock to her and her heirs for ever And I hereby nominate and appoint my said Wife Margaret Cock my Sole and only Executrix of this my Last Will and Testament hereby revoking all former Will and Wills by me heretofore made In Witness whereof I have hereunto Set my hand and Seal this fourteenth Day of June in the Year of our Lord one thousand seven hundred and Eighty two.

Signed Sealed published and declared by the above named William Cock as and for his Last Will and Testament in the presence of us who have hereunto subscribed our Names as Witnesses at his request and in his presence and in the presence of each other

{ William Cock }

Thomas Maulden

William Hamall

Thos Mertens

Geory Haywood

Fig. 8. The Last Will and Testament of William Cock, "Victualler" of Croydon. June 14, 1782.

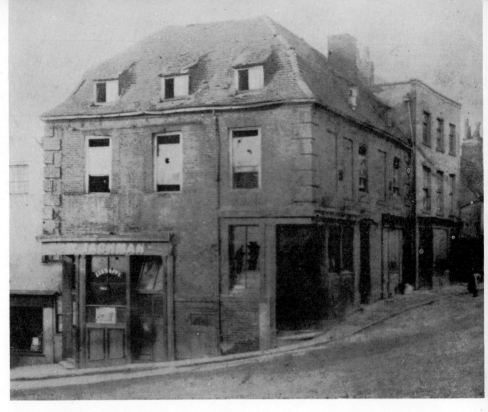

Fig. 9. The Old King's Head Public House, *c.* 1890. Photograph of a now demolished site.

No 167 } William Cock Batchelor of the Parish
and Margaret Ruskin Spinster both of
this Parish were
Married in this Church by Banns
this Nineteenth Day of June in the Year One Thousand Seven Hundred
and Eighty . By me Owen Perrott Edwardes Curate
This Marriage was solemnized between Us { Wm Cock
Margaret Ruskin
In the Presence of { John Scott
Mary Ruskin

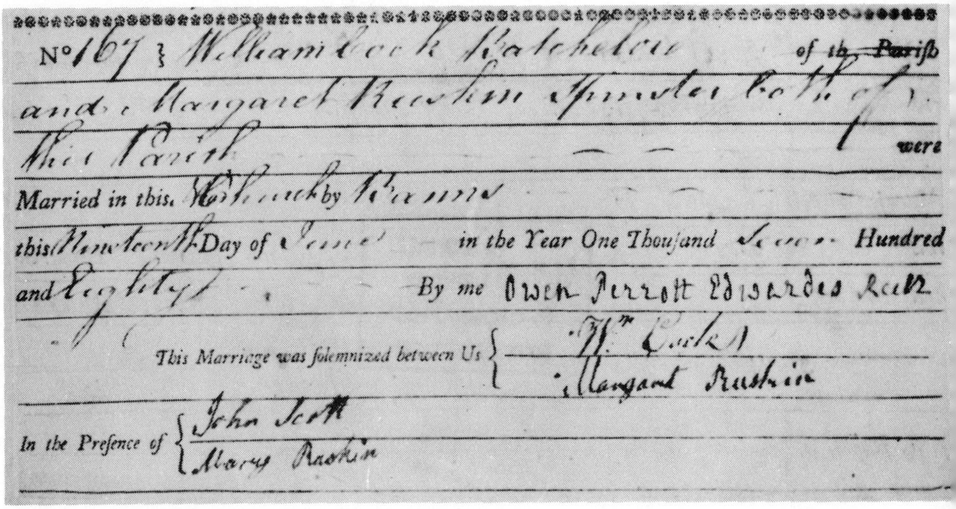

Fig. 10. Entry of the Marriage of Ruskin's grandparents, Margaret Ruskin and William Cock. June 19, 1780.

Fig. 11. "Aunt Bridget," Mrs. George Richardson of Croydon, *née* Bridget Cock, *c*. 1804? Steel engraving of a miniature.

Fig. 12. John James Ruskin, *c*. 1804. A portrait by Sir Henry Raeburn.

Fig. 13. Thomas Brown, M. D., 1806. Engraving of a portrait by George Watson.

Fig. 14. John Thomas Ruskin, *c.* 1815? A miniature.

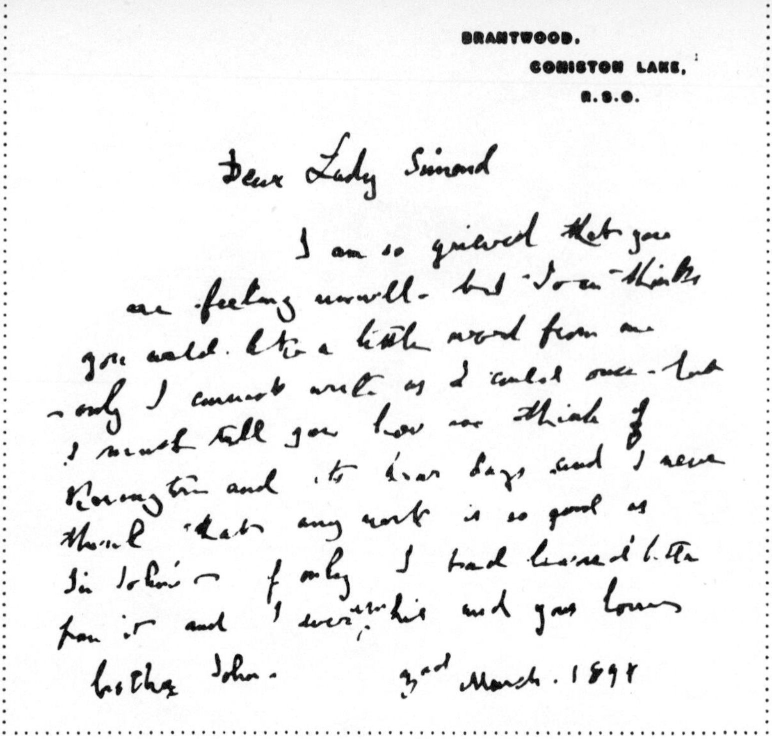

Fig. 15. A Letter of "3rd March, 1894" to Lady Simon.

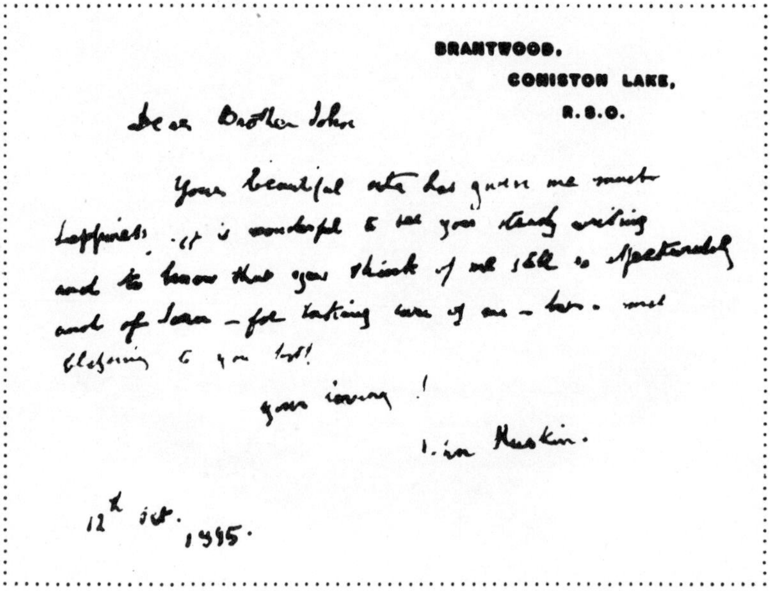

Fig. 16. A Letter of "12th Oct. 1895" to Sir John Simon. The "Last" Letter?

remembered, was the historian and poet who had been a tutor of
the sons of James V, and also of Queen Mary, and assuredly his
name serves as a graceful adjunct to the Ruskin domicile, suggesting long-persistent atmosphere. In 1790–92, the address changed
to " 'head of Morrison's Close,' which was in the High Street on
the north side, halfway between Leith Wynd and North Bridge
Street." Then, from 1793–96 they lived " 'opposite Blackfriars'
Wynd' — the same locality as Morrison's Close." [46]

For Catherine, these must have been the years which shaped the
woman — in all ways, a gentlewoman, who will emerge more clearly
as the mother of John James and of our most strictly Evangelical
"Aunt Jessie" and as a shaping influence on Ruskin's mother, Margaret, who would spend the better part of her young womanhood in
the household of Aunt Catherine. The life which Catherine came
to know as a grocer's wife would seem calculated to have burned
away frivolity while setting her more fundamental traits of character
— these traits associated not with the gaiety of passing visits to
estates of County Families but with the sobriety of a settled atmosphere in the home of a village clergyman, as well as with traditions
that had produced the Covenanters, and then the Martyrs of her
Wigtown. "There was a year of my life," Catherine would tell
her son, "that I maintained myself and two children on twenty pound,
the bread too was ½ the loave that year: we did not indeed live
very sumptuously nor shall I say our strength improved much but
I did not contract one farthing of debt and that to me supplyed the
want of luxuries." [47]

Then in 1794 her uncle died and left her £1,500.[48]

Two years later, John Thomas Ruskin could at last transport
his family into New Town, where he became "John Ruskin, merchant, 15 St. James Square." [49]

4

John James' Years at the Royal High School

In 1795, his mother having received her legacy, John James Ruskin (ten years old) entered the Royal High School. By this time he would have known how to read and write, and how to do arithmetic, perhaps taught by Catherine rather than at some school for which his parents would have had to pay a fee. Through the *Memoirs* of Adam Black (Edinburgh publisher and civic leader), who was one year younger than John James and whose parents made good money through having furnished the front room of their lower floor as a shop where they sold country produce, we hear about the early education of a boy whose later schooling was strictly parallel to that of John James Ruskin.

When he was about four or five years old, Adam Black had been sent off to school.

It was of the old-fashioned sort. "Our schoolbook," he says, "was the Bible, or any other book we chose to bring. No grammar was taught, no geography; no explanation was given of the meaning of words; no questions were put, except the questions of the Shorter Catechism." ¶This school Adam Black attended till he was seven years of age, when he could read, write, and do a little arithmetic. . . . His religious education certainly was not neglected. Family worship was as regular at home as breakfast and supper; and on Sunday the children, after being twice at church, had to learn the Shorter Catechism, "with proofs," under penalty of going without the luxury of tea and bread and butter, allowed to them only on that blessed day. . . . Those of a more advanced generation may look back with a sympathetic shudder on such Sundays as these, filled up with religious exercises from morning to night, "spending the whole time," as the Shorter Catechism prescribes, "in the public and private exercise of God's worship, except so much as is required for works of necessity and mercy." But it cannot be denied that our country and its people have owed much to the stern discipline of our fathers. . . .[1]

The custom was to have a child begin his five-year high school course when he was eight, the Scotch high school having been in reality a grammar school that specialized in Latin, though during their last year at the Royal High School, fifth-year students made an incidental bow to Greek. In Edinburgh, the boys were likely to repeat their fifth year because the Rector, Dr. Adam, was an unusually rewarding teacher. But by and large, students finished high school as they reached thirteen, and so the universities began by giving relatively elementary work which led into training for professional careers.

Under James IV of Scotland, in 1494, the Privy Council had decreed " 'that barons and freeholders should put their eldest sons to the grammar school, 'till they should be founded in Latin, and thereafter should study law, for three years, under penalty of twenty pounds. . . .' "[2] Although this edict was not enforced (the first Edinburgh High School was erected in 1578), in Scotland the study of law had become, traditionally, occupation for a gentleman. By the eighteenth century it had evolved that boys of every social class had opportunity for education, including study in a university; therefore, men whose families were distinctly middle-class were becoming lawyers, especially Writers to the Signet, with increasing frequency.[3] At the universities, tuition was kept low and the term was limited to six months so that during long vacations, sons of poorer families — the peasant's son, Carlyle, for instance — could help earn money needed while they carried on their studies, sometimes with relentless sacrifice if, like Carlyle, they had to live away from home.

It would mean much to Ruskin, in sentiment, that his father had been graduated, under the regime of Dr. Adam, from the High School of Sir Walter Scott;[4] and, he might have added, of Lord Cockburn, Lord Brougham, Lord Jeffrey, and of other distinguished men who had been students but some few years before John James sat in the schoolrooms they had frequented. From them we know the very costume John James wore as "a High School lad of Edinburgh,"[5] to use his son's fond and unsuspecting phrase. But what we do not know, except inferentially, is why, when he left the Royal High School, John James could not realize his heart's desire — to study law — by entering the great university within such easy reach of his own home.

What he experienced as a boy attending the Royal High School it is, however, possible to judge. Partly because so many of its graduates achieved distinction, this school, under the Rectorship of Dr. Adam (1768–1809), has been recurrently discussed, the supposition being that it gave the very best available in elementary education in a country notable for its progressiveness in providing citizens with opportunities for school. The new High School building, begun in 1777, had five classrooms on its second floor, with four Masters, each carrying forward the same group of boys through four years, and then passing on his class to Dr. Adam for the fifth year, which the more privileged students could continue through a sixth year, during which they shared Dr. Adam's schoolroom with the fifth-year students, "promiscuously mingled."[6]

At the Royal High School, traditionally, the sons of Edinburgh's upper classes began their schooldays together with the son of anybody who could pay tuition, even unto an Adam Black, whose father, having prospered as a grocer, next would make good money as a mason. Hence, the sons of "duke to cobbler" would sit side by side for six hours every day, learning Latin, except for six weeks of vacation from mid-August to October. Year by year the size of classes grew, rising from 120 in the group of 1781 (when Lord Jeffrey entered) to 167 in Dr. Adam's class of 1809. Seldom university graduates and never trained to teach, the Masters solved the problem of instruction by having their hundred-odd boys recite in unison — for example, while committing rules to memory through repeating them aloud in Latin, the theory being that the more rules learned, the better. For self-instruction, there was a library from which students could withdraw books if they paid a shilling fee — which John James Ruskin paid no more than once in his career.

In memoirs, graduates of the Royal High School were prone to dwell upon their year, or two (for approximately half), with Dr. Adam. There were, however, four preceding years characteristically dismissed with some perfunctory comment. Sir Walter Scott, for instance, notes that he learned little through this earlier period, although he expressed no resentment against that "worthy" man, Luke Fraser, who also gained a kindly word from later pupils. Nevertheless, according to Sir Robert Christison, "Fraser . . . retired from the school with the reputation of a merciless tyrant." [7] Luke Fraser may have been more merciful, however, than was Sir Robert's father, who had charge of John James Ruskin.[8] Severity remained the mode under Dr. Adam's rectorship, during which all masters flogged their boys as standard discipline. "Two of the masters, in particular, were so savage, that any master doing now, what they did every hour, would certainly be transported," [9] Lord Cockburn notes as he describes conditions which prevailed while he was there — for six years, through 1792. One of these two men is left unnamed; the other was the tavern friend of Robert Burns, "Willie" Nicol who "brew'd a peck o' maut" — "an excellent classical scholar" but "a savage fellow" — "worthless, drunken, and inhumanly cruel to the boys under his charge," according to Sir Walter Scott.[10]

Relatively speaking, John James was fortunate in having entered high school when Mr. Christison received the entering group. This must have been in 1795, since Mr. Christison was governed by the usual four-year cycle and had received new classes in 1787 (Lord Cockburn's class) and in 1791 (the class of Adam Black). Two years older than the average student in his group, John James doubtless had had to wait until his father could afford to pay tuition, although, if Catherine had received her legacy without delay (*i.e.,* in

1794), his parents may have waited still another year because they were unwilling to expose him to extreme brutality by starting him in William Nicol's class of 1794.[11]

It was bad enough to be a schoolboy under Mr. Christison, "to whose uncontrolled discipline" Lord Cockburn had been subjected. He was "a good man, an intense student," Lord Cockburn grants; in 1806 he was, in fact, appointed to teach Latin at the University, where, his son protests, he was much loved by his students. This, however, was a love which the young Carlyle did not share.[12] And at the High School, Lord Cockburn states, Mr. Christison was

as bad a schoolmaster as it is possible to fancy. Unacquainted with the nature of youth, ignorant even of the characters of his own boys, and with not a conception of the art or of the duty of alluring them, he had nothing for it but to drive them; and this he did by constant and indiscriminate harshness. ¶The effects of this were very hurtful to all his pupils. Out of the whole four years of my attendance, there were probably not ten days in which I was not flogged, at least once. Yet I never entered the class, nor left it, without feeling perfectly qualified, both in ability and preparation, for its whole business; which, being confined to Latin alone, and in necessarily short tasks, since every one of the boys had to rhyme over the very same words, in the very same way, was no great feat. But I was driven stupid. Oh! the bodily and mental wearisomeness of sitting six hours a-day, staring idly at a page, without motion and without thought, and trembling at the gradual approach of the merciless giant. I never got a single prize, and once sat *boobie* at the annual public examination. The beauty of no Roman word, or thought, or action, ever occurred to me; nor did I ever fancy that Latin was of any use except to torture boys.[13]

"My father . . ." Sir Robert Christison recounts, "was . . . a genuine Scandinavian in frame — tall, broad-chested, long-bodied, strong-limbed, very muscular in every way, with small features for his size, calm determination in his looks, and of intense though quiet energy." Said to have been "the strongest man in his parish," he once, on foot, overtook a run-away pony at full gallop.[14] And although his son challenges the charges of Lord Cockburn, Adam Black likewise recounts: " 'These four years [under Mr. Christison] . . . were years of cruel bondage. The great educator was the *tawse,* a long thick leathern thong, cut into stripes, which, brought down with great force on the hand, was very painful, often leaving marks of coagulated blood. Every day this teacher of the young . . . was administered more or less liberally; no boy altogether escaped,' " although, as Adam Black makes clear, Mr. Christison was a master who showed "a partiality for the sons of the great." [15]

The atmosphere outside the classroom was one of rowdiness and insubordination, starting with strife between the Masters and the Rector. In 1772 Dr. Adam had published a textbook Ruskin would begin to thumb, according to the good old Scottish custom, when *he* was eight years old — Dr. Adam's *Latin Grammar,* the "best," the "very best grammar ever written," he reiterated in *Praeterita.* With this grammar on the market, Dr. Adam wished to have it used in the Royal High School instead of the long standard text by Ruddiman, who gave rules in Latin whereas Dr. Adam presented them in English. But after 1778 not one member of his staff would use his book, which he himself continued to employ. This issue led to such a violent quarrel by 1785 that the four masters asked the Town Council to support their use of Ruddiman, pleading that it was absurd to have students introduced to a new book in their fifth year. Periodicals of the day carried "ridicule and abuse" of Dr. Adam's grammar,[16] a committee from the University was appointed to make recommendations, and in 1786 the Town Council ruled that only one Latin grammar should be used in the Royal High School — that grammar to be Ruddiman's.[17] Dr. Adam, nevertheless, quietly went on using his own grammar,[18] and was knocked down one night by William Nicol. Fortunately he was never prosecuted by the city, and so, in John James' home, Dr. Adam's *Grammar* engendered loyalty unto the second generation.[19]

The boys shared, with zest, the prevailing spirit, surely no more restrained than were their elders in expressing their hostilities. By ancient custom they conducted "bickers" in the alleys of the city, and serious accidents sometimes marked their feuding, analogous to the "gang-warfare" in some cities of our day. This pastime was by no means limited to students of the High School. Sir Walter called it "only a rough form of play," though he remarks (in the course of the Green-breeks anecdote) "it happened that the children of the higher classes were often pitted against those of the lower, each taking their side according to the residence of their friends." [20] As a resident of George Square, Scott notes that he fought under the "patrician standard," whereas Green-breeks was the "plebeian champion." Less fortunate in the location of his home, Adam Black also recalled these bickers: "The aristocratic boys of George Square, sons of peers, law lords, and other dignitaries, came out against the 'blackguards' of the Bristo Street quarter, as they called them, of whom Adam was one." [21] Within the precincts of the High School, according to Lord Cockburn, "The hereditary evils of the system and of the place were too great for correction even by [Dr.] Adam; and the general tone of the school was vulgar and harsh. Among the boys, coarseness of language and manners was the only fashion. . . . No lady could be seen within the walls. Nothing evidently civilized was safe." [22]

Predominantly, however, these boys came from the best homes of Edinburgh, center of the cultural and intellectual life of Scotland, and stronghold of the aristocracy, with the Judges and the Advocates holding proud position. In the second decade of the nineteenth century, when time had somewhat modified *ancien régime,* Lockhart's "Peter" wrote to *Kinsfolk:* "I have already told you, that the Bar is the great focus from which the rays of interest and animation are diffused throughout the whole mass of society, in this northern capital. . . . Into whatever company the stranger may enter, he is sure, ere he has been half an hour in the place, to meet with something to remind him of the predominance of this great jurisprudential aristocracy." [23]

As to the older generation, we can see them and their parents ranged in Raeburn's portraits — "descendants of those truculent nobles who did so much to make the romance of Scottish history; of a crowd of lairds, driven off the land by the stress and results of the '15 and the '45; mingled with an aristocracy of intellect and of official position in the Church or the Law." [24] These portraits show us, too, the new life that had flooded into Old Town as it overflowed its confines, with tradesmen making money until, no less, a John James Ruskin would also sit for Raeburn. Raeburn himself, however, could never mingle freely with the upper classes he portrayed, for he had spent some years of childhood in an orphanage and then had been a jeweler's clerk. The founder of that orphanage had been Heriot, one of the few merchants Sir Walter Scott portrayed with sympathy; but Heriot had died in 1624, and his "hospital" had become yet one more historic monument. Elsewhere, Scott repeatedly would indicate the sharp divisions which gained one the respect or the contempt of fellow creatures in that Edinburgh of his youth, "long the Mecca of social snobbishness, drawing its lines very sharp and clear. . . ." [25]

As a close-knit social organism, it was potent in effect upon others than John James, left longing to get his toe hold as a lawyer. One can, in fact, perceive its influence upon two men of an earlier generation. To James Boswell, as the first son of Lord Auchinleck — an *Advocate* — it had given an ineffable self-assurance. Surely no one ever could have known his own weaknesses better than did Boswell. Nevertheless, it simply never occurred to Boswell that in his own unspoken (wherefore speak the obvious?) right as a "Gentleman" he would not be welcome anywhere, to anybody, be it a Lord Eglinton or a Duchess of Northumberland, or a Queen's brother; nor did Boswell hesitate to rebuff Lord Eglinton when he grew careless in observing the amenities due to a Gentleman-by-Birth. Samuel Johnson, with his own reverence for hierarchy, was fondly and respectfully aware of Boswell's antecedents, in whom Boswell freely, yet naturally, confessed well-founded pride. During early days of friendship, "I gave [Johnson] an account of the family of Auchinleck, and of the Place. He said, 'I must be there, and we will live in the Old Castle; and if there is no room remaining, we will build one.' This was the most pleasing idea that I could possibly have: to think of seeing this great man at the venerable seat of my ancestors." [26] Had there been no "ancestors," the young Boswell of Edinburgh, and of its Royal High School, could scarcely have achieved his ultimate significance, so integrally related to his own vast aplomb.[27]

In contrast, Sir Walter — his father a mere Writer to the Signet, whose father had worked a rented farm, although Sir Walter's mother also had been born a "lady" — was left (in spite of family residence) eager to enhance the social standing of his forebears while at the same time behaving with deference to his "superiors" and emblazoning "the armorial bearings of his forefathers" (thus Lockhart) upon the roof of Abbotsford; eventually he began his *Autobiography* by explaining, at some length, precisely *why* his birth "was esteemed genteel." Nor did Lockhart (much too well aware that Keats was *not* "a gentleman") fail to comment on the "modesty" of Sir Walter's statement as he in turn marshaled evidence, most abundantly, which would substantiate Scott's claim to gentility — a claim which to Scott had thus become insistently important because in earlier years he had been made aware that though his birth was not what he called "sordid," it was in fact distinctly middle class. Therefore, despite his father's being Whig, and Presbyterian, during

High School days Scott became a Tory and, as he said, "hated
Presbyterians, and admired Montrose with his victorious High-
landers. . . . In all these tenets there was no real conviction on
my part, arising out of acquaintance with the view or principles of
either party. . . . I took up my politics at that period, as King
Charles II. did his religion, from an idea that the Cavalier creed
was the more gentlemanlike persuasion of the two." [28]
Although he seems to have been happy with his classmates, he saw
no more of High School friends belonging to the upper classes after
he left the University to join the apprentices who were studying, in
his father's office, to be Writers to the Signet. Then, as Lockhart
says, he entered a class in Civil Law which "brought him again
into daily contact with . . . his earlier acquaintance of the higher
ranks. . . ." [29] And so he discovered, Sir Herbert Grierson explains,
"that none beneath the level of an Advocate — leaving soldiers and
the aristocracy aside — could in Edinburgh be accounted a gentleman. In consequence, those ambitions were quickened which were
to determine the direction of his life, to assert for himself his
proper place in the social scale, whether law or literature should
prove the appropriate lever." [30] Nevertheless, Sir Herbert likewise
notes, Scott could "use his good sense to discount [romantic senti-
ments]. . . . When his son Walter demurs to the connection with
trade of the bride proposed to him . . . Scott reminds him that they
are themselves but cadets of cadets, and tells him that his sister
Anne, 'makes herself a little ridiculous with her airs' — her Edinburgh airs." [31] Fortunately, however, both for Lockhart and for
Scott, Sir Walter's ancestry was not discernibly contaminated by a
tradesman.

To have been born a tradesman's son in Edinburgh of that day
was to have been stamped with social stigma. Desire for literacy
in Bible-reading Scotland had served the cause of democratic education, and through the countryside there was a peasantry with sturdy
self-respect and with independence known of old to Presbyterian and
Whig. Nonetheless, Edinburgh of the 1790's, with "the line of
demarcation between classes . . . drawn with a clearness that is now
unknown," [32] was not a place remembered with affection by Robert
Burns, however (briefly) fêted; nor could Carlyle's emotional
security have been increased by his own (somewhat later) stay
within that atmosphere.[33]

By the time of Burns' first visit (1786), streets on Sunday were filled with people who were no longer gravely headed off to church, and within a few years no Whig dared to raise his voice. Hard drinking was the fashion, and was indeed one token of a gentleman; while every tradesman closed his shop at eight and went off to his club for a convivial hour or two before he so much as thought of returning to his family. "This was universal and unfailing." [34] Within the homes of the well-bred, all social drinking was genteel, each cup being prefaced by a "sentiment" (platitudinous to a degree) or by some personal toast.[35] When the toasts began, they were likely to continue, as at a gathering in 1782 to honor a deceased Lord Brougham: his coffin is reported to have subsequently fallen off the lurching hearse at the head of the funeral entourage and to have tumbled down the bank into the river as the mourners obliviously and hilariously drove on toward church, to be astounded when they sought to place the lost body into its ancestral crypt.[36] Cursing was another "mark" and "right" of Gentlemen — a privilege particularly exercised in cursing their "inferiors." [37] It greatly helped to be submissive if the inferior knew his place. Obsequiousness was essential to the survival of the fittest among tradesmen, many of whom were extremely prosperous in a social order which they evidently did not find disturbing.[38]

As to the sons, there is no reason to suppose that social prejudices were not carried into the schoolground, or that John James Ruskin could have been especially happy as he traveled daily from a grocer's home into the notoriously brutal atmosphere of the Royal High School, for his first personal experience with the aristocracy and gentry. Again, Scott is revealing as he recalls his own response to a fellow student at the University, "an excellent Greek scholar," who once protested against Scott's refusal to study Greek: "My stubborn pride received this advice with sulky civility; the birth of my Mentor (whose name was Archibald, the son of an innkeeper) did not, as I thought in my folly, authorize him to intrude upon me his advice." [39] As we shall see, John James Ruskin was never to overcome his shame that, still worse, *his* wife was the daughter of a *tavern*keeper. Yet, inevitably, he himself had learned to know his place, and he never would forget it. This, however, must have been a lesson integrated with his knowledge that *his* Father was *not* content to be a Grocer and that, except for mésalliance, his Mother was Genteel. Hence, in the course of his development, probably made vulnerable by attitudes, atmosphere, and values in his home, John James lost what he once called his "self-respect." [40] It is rather more than likely that as one unit inseparable from the totality which shaped his character, these school years significantly helped to do the damage.

What he gained, if he was like the rest, came primarily from Dr. Adam, of whom John James' son would always speak with reverent affection. Ruskin's remarks of course were colored by his thought of all the happy hours during boyhood he had spent in study directed by his mother. But for Dr. Adam and his much-debated grammar Ruskin had a special feeling which would naturally have been implanted if John James told his child what others wrote when they remembered Dr. Adam. He was by aptitude a teacher, and even though he had to lecture in a crowded classroom, he could hold attention as he gave immediacy to the thought and ways of men he brought to life — Caesar, Livy, Sallust; Terence, Horace, Virgil. By the time John James became his pupil, he had also gained wide and undisputed recognition as a scholar through his *Roman Antiquities, or an Account of the Manners and Customs of the Romans Designed to Illustrate the Latin Classics* (1791) — another textbook Ruskin used as a child and subsequently treasured.[41] In Scott's tribute to Dr. Adam there is a revealing touch of patronage, but there is likewise record of a typical experience: "It was from this respectable man that I first learned the value of the knowledge I had hitherto considered only as a burdensome task." [42] Even Dr. Adam could not eradicate the harm done by traditions that had spawned snobbery in local homes and practice. But at least within the sanctuary of his classroom, no student from a humble home was made to feel the onus of his birth.

Dr. Adam, too, had come from a humble home: on his father's rented farm, he would recount, he had sometimes been the neatherd and, while at the university, he had known poverty so acute that he kept warm by means of exercise and studied with his friends at night to share candles he himself could not afford to buy, suffering from hunger as he lived on penny loaves and oatmeal porridge. As a personality he could, however, feel without defiance that a man's a man for a' that, and this, in part, was what he tried to teach his boys, who marveled at discovering, when he paused to talk by way of illustration, that what Latin authors wrote could be challengingly — or even dangerously — pertinent to their own lives.

In Scotland, through this period, Henry, Lord Dundas was effectually a tyrant who by means of bureaucratic Tory patronage had silenced those who wished reform, and in the classroom Dr. Adam eloquently dwelt on Brutus and the Gracchi, nor did he "check his fervour when in Livy's page the vice of the Tarquins, the excesses of Appius Claudius, or the tyrannies of the Patricians were perused." [43] His pupils carried home their tales of what he said, until, in days when the French Revolution was raising tempers in alarm, old acquaintances no longer bowed to Dr. Adam on the street. For a while he grew less vivid and specific in exemplifying his "Republican" ideals, although he would not utterly capitulate. What was the word for "King"? — and *Rex* would come the answer. " '. . . another word?' " *Tyrannus*. " 'Right, sir,' said the Rector, with a peculiar emphasis." [44] Francis Horner (political economist who joined Francis, Lord Jeffrey, Lord Brougham, and other Whigs to launch the *Edinburgh Review*) would acknowledge gratitude "for the most valuable impressions in all subjects of political opinion," [45] and Lord Brougham would recall related themes: "Among his favorite topics was inculcating love of independence, the duty and comfort of making one's own fortune, and relying on one's self alone. Then he would chide a pupil's idleness or inattention; and if the lad was of the higher orders, 'But *you* will get a post or pension when the others are working their way up-hill.' " [46] To the political indoctrination, John James was not receptive; but precepts about more general conduct he would not forget.

Such lessons became personalized to suit each pupil's need, for Dr. Adam knew his groups so well as individuals that he remembered every boy he taught, through more than forty years — or so at least Sir Walter Scott believed.[47] In retrospect, they themselves might sometimes feel inclined to smile when they spoke of his conviction that their hours with him had been alone responsible for all they had achieved in their careers; but they agreed, without dissent and with impressive earnestness, that he had been important to what they valued in their lives. And to someone like John James, who henceforth would depend upon self-education and, still more, upon working his own way, Dr. Adam must have been immensely helpful. " 'The old man, from his own hard struggles with poverty in early life,' " Adam Black recalled, " 'was rather favourable to the sons of those in the humbler ranks . . .' ";[48] while Lord Cockburn records that "he delighted in the detection and encouragement of every appearance of youthful talent and goodness," [49] and inspired "especially the timid and the backward," encouraging "by praise, play, and kindness." [50] "Then the delights of learning in all its branches formed a constant theme," and his pupils often caught his ardor. "Stirred by his precepts and example," Lord Brougham recounts, "I spent the months during which I was kept from school by indisposition in reading and trying my hand at composition." [51]

Speaking always "with great natural eloquence" that was both forceful and concise, Dr. Adam enabled them to share his feeling for the significance and beauty in those books through which he was their guide. "He was always extolling the ancient writers. . . . But he ever dwelt on their works having been the result of the greatest care, and of each being a monument of industry. . . . The eloquence of the old orators he would descant on by the hour, and show that its success was due to diligent preparation." [52] "His great learning, his able and useful works, and his irreproachable character, as well as his untiring diligence and exemplary patience in the discharge of his duties, commanded the respect of all, and endeared him to those who had the inestimable benefit of his instruction." [53] Thus, long after John James left that schoolroom, the influence of Dr. Adam would help to shape events in yet another life.

A year before Dr. Adam died, fourteen pupils commissioned a Raeburn portrait; in it he sits with one hand holding a book and with the other raised admonishingly while a smile lurks in his eyes and on his "fine sagacious face, so curiously expressive of love and laughter." [54] Then one day in his classroom he was stricken by apoplexy, followed by a brief illness which brought delirium so that he was back again in school, still speaking blame or praise and saying as he died: " 'But it grows dark — the boys may dismiss.' " [55] This was in December, 1809, shortly after Carlyle had entered Edinburgh University. As an old man, Carlyle would tell John Ruskin how, on the day of Dr. Adam's funeral, he had joined a crowd that waited before the High School, where the body had been placed the night before. As the coffin passed, watchers "uttered a low 'Ah me! Ah dear!' or the like, half sigh or wail — 'and he is gone from us then!' ¶'The sound of the boys' wail is in my ears yet,' said Carlyle." [56]

5

John James Is Led to a
Decision

Leaving Dr. Adam, John James watched others than patricians start their work in the University, now undertaking mathematics (they would be through the first three books of Euclid by the end of their first year); seriously studying Greek, together with more Latin; and pleasurably profiting as Dugald Stewart — didactic, oratorical, and not abstruse in praise of virtue — caught the torch from their beloved Rector. As time passed, John James would never overcome regret that he had not shared these opportunities. Even when his own success as a merchant had yielded him a fortune, he nonetheless urged his friend George Gray not to try to start his son upon a mercantile career in London but to give him, rather, the opportunity to study law. "I used to envy," he recalled, "the family of the Tawses in Edinburgh, my School Companions — Sons of Steady Pious Father & good mother — They were all made Lawyers & all got on remaining always at home happy & industrious — I don't know now whether they are living. . . ." [1]

Financially there could have been no bar to John James' continuing his studies. When he was ready for the University, his parents had been living for at least four years on St. James Square, which was the oldest although no longer the most fashionable part of New Town.[2] Conceivably, by 1796 John Thomas had become more prosperous through his own management; or his mother may have died, possibly leaving property which had increased in value through the passing years, with her estate to be divided among the children, according to his father's *Will*.[3] But it seems far more likely that Catherine's heritage of £1,500 had enabled them to move into the New Town. Even so, Catherine's principal remained intact and provided enough income so that the education of her son, conforming with the traditions of her own family, could have been readily pursued, had there been no conflict in desire. In 1808, after her husband had failed in business, she would remind John James that she herself would have "£86 a year for life that your father cannot deprive me of. . . ." [4]

It seems amply clear that, as a husband and a father, John Thomas imperiously dominated his own household in ways not marked by wisdom. After almost fifteen years, having moved into quarters which meant comfort for his family, he had won public recognition, through Aitchison's *Directory,* that he was indeed a "Merchant." And although he had become a New Town Merchant who, within twelve years, would lose whatever substance he himself had gained, in 1800 he might well have wished his son to follow in his presently proud footsteps — and *his* wishes could not easily have been denied. It may be that John James was granted one more year (1800–1801) with Dr. Adam. Howbeit, he told George Gray that when he was sixteen (1801–1802) he was persuaded by his parents to leave for London to start his mercantile career.[5]

6

The Personality of Margaret Cox, as She Arrived from Croydon

Within three years, there occurred another change within that home, when John James' sister Jessie, on November 1, 1804, married Mr. Patrick Richardson of Perth. The minister of St. George's Chapel, Edinburgh, had performed the ceremony, although the contract had been signed in Perth, where the marriage, too, was registered.[1] The bridegroom, then thirty, was a tanner who liked to boast about his property.

Even so, John James Ruskin finally had to help support his sister's children, and was prone to talk, in later life, about the "speculative propensities" of Gentlemen of Perth.[2] The bride, as revealed by a miniature that shows her perhaps a year or two before her wedding (although she may be represented in her bridal dress), was indeed a lovely creature, than whom no girl ever could have been more tenderly and virginally young.[3] Fair-complexioned, with large, brown, pensive eyes and short brown locks that softly wave across her forehead, she sits posed against a distant landscape and blue sky suffused with pastel hues of sunset — her shoulders bare above a filmy, long-sleeved gown of white enwreathed with a cherry-colored ribband. There was something very feminine, natural, and delicate in the beauty of "Aunt Jessie" during her young womanhood before, as Ruskin phrased it, she was "brought down into Lowland life by her practical tanner." [4]

John Thomas is said to have arranged this marriage, to which Jessie, twenty-one, dutifully acquiesced. Good daughters were obedient in those days, and John Thomas apparently was wont to have his children heed his will. The Catherine he had swept away was a good wife — not uncritical, but loyal and submissive, well knowing that, if she would heed God's Word, no less than Jessie she must honor and obey. John Thomas consequently could determine Jessie's fate, at least according to impressions Ruskin gained from what he must have heard his parents say (he had been only five years old when this uncle died):

> My Father's sister had married, not to please herself but in a curious, patient apathy and unwise resignation of herself — according to my unwise Scottish Grandfather's reckless wish. Her husband was as opposite in nature to her as might well be conceived, made of extremely common material, with hereditary taint of unhealthy constitution and a corpulent habit alike of flesh and spirit, indolently unprosperous in his tanning business and ending in sudden apoplexy, leaving my aunt a moderate independence, and six children, with whom, leaving the large house and river-bank garden of Bridge End, she crossed the Tay to Rose Terrace.[5]

That John James loved his sister dearly seems no less clear than that she found scant happiness in either of her homes beside the River Tay. For Ruskin, Rose Terrace became a place charged with childhood memories, although when he last saw Aunt Jessie, he was only eight. Yet he always associated her with extreme gentleness, piety, and patience, and he was convinced that she had suffered deeply.

She had, all told, ten children, losing all but four of them before she died.[6] At Plymouth, when the news of *her* death reached her brother, he shocked his child into remembrance of his "deep distress of sobbing tears." [7]

Perhaps when Jessie married, or possibly before, Margaret Cox (to call her by her chosen name) had come up from Croydon, to remain with her Scottish relatives for many years as a daughter, sister, friend, and nurse. She herself had come, immediately, from backgrounds just as humble as were those which John Thomas had to some degree escaped and now would preferably ignore. Nor was she graced by any such connections as those John Thomas had effected through his marriage. On the contrary, Margaret's mother — the first-born in her family, and some years older than John Thomas — had married the William Cock whose very name would be deliberately blotted out. Nevertheless, in the parish register which contains the entry of her marriage, Ruskin's mother is designated "Miss Margaret Cock . . . Daughter to William Cock Merchant in the Parish of Crydon [*sic*] and County of Surrey. . . .";[8] and in his *Last Will and Testament,* made in 1782, William Cock called himself a "Victualler" of that Parish.[9] On Ruskin's *Birth Certificate,* a document known to Cook and Wedderburn, his mother is designated "Margaret . . . the daughter of William Cock" — a name likewise known to Ruskin, inasmuch as this *Certificate* was issued in 1837, when he was about to enter Oxford, and it was subsequently kept at Brantwood.[10] In 1837, his mother's name would not have come to him as a surprise if he had ever visited the grave of his Aunt Bridget: buried in the Croydon Churchyard, Bridget is designated "daughter" of "MARGARET COCK" on a gravestone which stands beside a tablet dedicated to the memory of "WILLIAM COCK." [11]

Ruskin's Croydon grandmother may have been the first to adopt the pluralism *Cox,* but it seems more likely that his mother chose this name, perhaps in consultation with her Edinburgh relatives, when she joined the household of her uncle. At best, the male of the domestic fowl did not provide a gracious name for any lady: in the time of *Gammer Gurton's Needle, cock* had signified a *servant;* next, more generally, it implied *"pertness: especially of lusty and swaggering youth";*[12] and in England, by the middle of the eighteenth century, it also had acquired anatomical connotations[13] which, in the United States, may have caused *rooster* to be adopted as a euphemistic substitute.[14] It is therefore possible that Margaret's mother, in her daily life, had become known by preference as "Mrs. Cox." (When Margaret returned to Croydon for a visit, the letters she received from Edinburgh were addressed to "Miss Margaret Cox.") Her mother nonetheless continued to be identified as "Margaret Cock" on legal documents and in an occasional record of her occupation as the keeper of a tavern. And although Margaret, in her uncle's home, could successfully have escaped her parents' name, from an Edinburgh point of view it would have remained a shameful fact, not to be denied, that her mother was indeed the keeper of this tavern which at first, apparently, had been managed by her father.

Center of a region famous for its hunting and its races — barely ten miles south of London on the main road to Brighton, Croydon was abundantly provided with inns and taverns patronized by sporting visitors, though during Margaret's youth it was still a country town. Antiquarians dwell upon its Palace (summer residence for the Archbishop of Canterbury) and its first Church of St. John the Baptist, mentioned in the Domesday Book and in 1867 destroyed by fire. And they almost always pause to talk about its formerly phenomenal number of ponds, filled by rivulets that ran from springs arising under the western side of High Street, to serve as tributary heads of the Wandel — Ruskin's " 'bright Wandel . . . of divine waters,' " [15] "loveliest stream in the English midlands," [16] singing "with constant lips of the hand which 'giveth rain from heaven' " :[17] Wandel fed by "streams to which my mother took me when a child, to play beside." [18] The first chapter of *Praeterita* would be called "The Springs of Wandel," one of which Ruskin would dedicate to his mother: "In obedience to the Giver of Life, of the brooks and fruits that feed it, of the peace that ends it, may this Well be kept sacred for the service of men, flocks, and flowers, and be by kindness called MARGARET'S WELL." [19] Beyond mere reason it infuriated him, in later years, that this spring, and the Wandel, should have been befouled, they having come to symbolize for him, emotionally, all that he most loved about his mother.

The Croydon Ruskin had known as a boy had already grown into "a large and handsome market town"; [20] but when Mother had been very young, Croydon had had fewer than eight hundred houses, laid out about its central mile of High Street, with the old Town

Hall (torn down in 1807) in use as a public market patronized by the
surrounding countryside. At the southwest corner of the Town Hall
there was still a whipping post, and at its rear (in 1812) a movable
public pillory had been deposited; on Surrey Street, in front of *The
Three Tuns,* the stocks remained. Every morning, in those days,
His Majesty's Mail Coach drove up High Street en route to London
and every evening it returned to Brighton, with its scarlet-coated
driver and the guard who blew his horn. Regularly, too, on every
weekday fifty coaches rattled through the town, making twenty-five
trips north and twenty-five trips south, with passengers stopping
at *The Crown,* although the mail coach patronized *The Green
Dragon,* where post boys were awaiting their turns for duty, clad
"in white cord breeches, . . . short blue jackets and white hats" as
they gossiped with their red-coated Reigate brethren.[21] Through the
night great vans drawn by six cattle, two abreast, rumbled down the
street, hauling in from countryside the market stuff; and when the
mackerel ran, fish vans with their freight for London always stopped
at Croydon.

In proper season came the fairs — in July the Cherry Fair, when
the market area "was full of stalls for the sale of cherries, gingerbread, toys and sweetstuffs, while swings and roundabouts afforded
amusements." [22] (When Margaret was growing old and rather
different from her earlier self, her husband wrote a friend: "I am
sorry to see Camberwell fair at an end . . . Mrs. R is very angry
at the View I take of Camberwell fair abolition, but I tell her
I am quite sure She has bought there ten times the Quantity of
Gingerbread Nuts aye & consumed the same, that ever I did — ") [23]

Of an evening there was music, a barracks for five troops of horse
having been erected in 1794: the "band of the Royal Waggon Train
was a very fine one, and used, by its splendid performances, to con-
tribute much to the happiness of Croydonians." [24] The audience,
thereafter, had a large choice of inns and taverns if they were in a
mood for further recreation. Up High Street they would find *The
Greyhound,* which dated from the sixteenth century, as did *The
Crown* and *The Swan.* Round about, of later vintage, there were
such hostels as *The Hare and Hounds, The Fox and Hounds, The
Horse and Crown, The Gun.* Then, too, there were *The George,
The Royal Oak, The King's Arms, The Rose and Crown* . . . The
list seems endless: the names of twenty-three Croydon inns and/or

taverns have been preserved on their old signs, and there were many with names unpreserved by any such memento.

Sometimes, with thought of Ruskin's antecedents, there is a reference to *The King's Head Public House* — or, as Ruskin preferred to call it, the "King's Head Inn and Tavern," demolished shortly after 1890.[25] *The King's Head* was, however, no more than a tavern — "a small tavern in a humble part of Croydon," with two bars and three bar parlors on its ground floor.[26] Above this place of business were two stories, one an attic which had gabled windows; on the floor beneath, three other windows of good size opened upon Market Street. All together, there was space enough to house in comfort a small family. Built on a corner, *The King's Head,* as Ruskin would recall, "present[ed] its side to Croydon market-place, its front and entrance door to the narrow alley which descends, steep for pedestrians, impassable to carriages, from the High Street to the lower town." [27]

Pursuing memories omitted from the published version of *Praeterita,* he recounted how his father finally revealed to him precisely where Margaret had once lived and worked, and (so Ruskin states) had been born — this birthplace being but two short blocks away from the home of his Aunt Bridget, where he had often been a guest, sometimes with his father, during childhood: "Very late in his life, my Father on occasion of a drive with me to Croydon, first showed me my mother's birthplace, with a gentle sadness, not unmixed with shame. Little, to the end, he knew my real character, either in its faults or strength, nor understood that he lost no honour with me for having married a tavern-keeper's daughter; but much for spending a whole morning in worship of the furniture and spoons of George the 4th." [28]

As to Margaret's father, he was probably a relative, possibly the son, of Benjamin Cock, a Croydon carpenter who died in 1778.[29] William, two years later, was described as a resident of the Parish of St. Bartholomew-the-Great, where John Ruskin (the great-grandfather) had died in 1780. So there had been a meeting between William Cock and Margaret Ruskin, followed by their marriage, on June 19, 1780, in the Priory Church of St. Bartholomew-the-Great, with a John Scott and either Margaret's mother or her sister, Mary Ruskin, serving as their witnesses.[30] They are next heard of as residents of Croydon, where Martha, widow of Benjamin, had died on December 17, 1780; and as parents of Margaret, Ruskin's mother, born on September 2, 1781, and duly baptized in Croydon's Church of St. John the Baptist.

A "Victualler" in 1782, William Cock was probably already tenant-landlord of *The King's Head* — doubtless, as Ruskin said, his mother's birthplace. At this time, having £30 to spare, he bought "twenty rods of land" along Pump Pail Street, where, before his death in 1787, he had built nine freehold cottages, in turn bequeathed by his wife to her daughters.[31] Their second child, Bridget, had been born on October 3, 1783. Then, when Bridget was four and Margaret six years old, William Cock "died of a broken leg at London. Aged 33," [32] leaving to his "beloved wife . . . all household [*sic*] goods and Chattels," [33] together with the tenancy of *The King's Head* as the chief means of supporting herself and their two children. Located across the street from the rear of the Town Hall and Market Place, it was conveniently at hand for those who brought in the vans of garden produce and for all who gathered there to shop. Mrs. William Cock could not have been unprosperous, because by 1799 she evidently no longer lived above her place of business but, rather, occupied "an unidentifiable house in the vicinity." [34]

Thus it happened that through courteous exaggeration William Cock could be designated a "Merchant" of Croydon when his daughter Margaret was married, even as he would more surprisingly be transformed by his grandson (with childlike fantasy animating this part of *Praeterita*) into "a sailor, who used to embark, like Robinson Crusoe, at Yarmouth, and come back at rare intervals, making himself very delightful at home. I have an idea he had something to do with the herring business, but am not clear on that point; my mother never being much communicative concerning it. He spoiled her, and her (younger) sister, with all his heart, when he was at home; unless there appeared any tendency to equivocation, or imaginative statements, on the part of the children, which were always unforgiveable." [35] In the next metamorphosis, effected by biographers (initially, by Collingwood), William Cock could readily emerge as the by now traditional "Captain Cox of Yarmouth," whose *vita* not unnaturally remained undiscoverable.

Finally, one night (to resume Ruskin's tale) the sailor-father, now "two and thirty," was "trying to ride, instead of walk, into Croydon;

he got his leg crushed by his horse against a wall; and died of the hurt's mortifying." [36] And there may be considerable truth in this account of the death of William Cock. Beyond the official record of a "broken leg" as the cause of his demise, there is the fact that Margaret retained all through her life an irrationally intense anxiety about horseback riding,[37] to the incongruously disproportionate, yet telling and recurrent, discomfiture of her son as an adult — this discomfiture expressed in its emotional totality through self-mockery in the *Praeterita* account of his "burning shame and misery" as a child who fell off horses, absent-mindedly, and who therefore no longer was permitted to take lessons at a riding school.[38] There is usually, thus, some dimly tangible foundation for fantasies elaborated in *Praeterita.*

Analogously, the factual basis of the tale that Grandfather William was a sailor becomes discernible — first in the handwriting of Ruskin's father when, in 1837, he was preparing his son's *Birth Certificate* for use at Oxford University and thereon improvised the information that his wife, Margaret, was the daughter of William Cock of Croydon, a *"Master Mariner"!* [39] It is not likely that John James Ruskin ever told his son that he had married Margaret as the daughter of that "Crydon Merchant" who had been, in fact, a "Victualler." More remotely, Margaret, too, may well have helped to build the legend out of the hearsay from her own past as, far back in his childhood, she entertained her boy. Then, discussing *Cock* as her maiden name, she might naturally enough have said that among her forebears there were sailors who had been connected with the herring fishery — because in the dialect which as a girl she would have known, *cocks* were "small boats, from two to six tons burden, used in the herring fishery." [40] More than once, in later life, Ruskin would manifest a special interest in the herring industry;[41] finally, in *Praeterita,* he recalled how tirelessly, when he was very young, he had demanded stories about a certain fisherman in a picture painted by his father.[42] Hence, it seems highly probable that the fantasy about his Croydon grandfather, as a sailor-herring-fisherman, stemmed not only from that statement of his father on his *Birth Certificate* but also from some story that his mother told him during his early years, harking back to the dialectical meaning of her own name. The trouble comes, of course, from founding Ruskin biography and, derivatively, much else in Ruskin scholarship, upon a literal acceptance of what Ruskin chanced to say in the imaginative re-creation represented by *Praeterita*.

What caused Margaret to leave her mother, Ruskin said specifically, in *Praeterita*, "*I do not know* . . ." [43] (my italics), though on another page he did not hesitate to state that as "a consummate housewife" ("rapidly growing into . . . a natural, essential, unassailable, yet inoffensive prude"), she "was sent for to Scotland to take care of my paternal grandfather's house . . ." [44] after which, so far as he knew (or this at least is what his careful phrasing leads one to infer), no "sentiment, accident, admiration, or affection [disturbed] the serene tenor of her . . . stewardship. . . ." [45] And yet apart from the so-called serenity of Margaret's stewardship (a grotesque assumption, in light of the story of these years), the statement does not satisfy common sense if one should say, more realistically, "to take care of her Aunt Catherine's house." Aunt Catherine, it seems clear, was — and remained — entirely capable of taking care of her own house, first in Edinburgh and, afterward, in Perth.

When Margaret left Croydon for Scotland is likewise a question that must first be shorn of confusions induced by *Praeterita*. In Ruskin's fantasy, his mother knew his father when John James was still attending high school, and Margaret *may* have gone to Edinburgh before 1800 — her uncle's family having moved into those doubtless more commodious quarters in the "tenement" on St. James Square. Or she may have joined them in early 1802, when John James left for his first period of work in London — an event which Ruskin believed to have occurred in 1809, so that his discussion both of his father's early mercantile career and of his parents' engagement became misleading. Or, as already noted, she may have joined them in 1804, to take the place of Jessie; or, for her own sake, at almost any time between 1800–1804, simply because she personally needed change: she once referred to a breakdown in her health as though it had occurred when she was in her early twenties. [46] Thus to state with stress precisely what remains unknown may also help to clear the air. All we really know is that through the discussion of his mother's early life, Ruskin transformed the actual experiences and personality of Margaret. Nevertheless, even if not quite as Ruskin says, when Margaret joined her uncle's family she received as well as gave. Catherine, her son said, "had a heart large enough to embrace the whole human race, but with universal love combined peculiar prudence." [47] These words no less are applicable to Margaret, upon whom, for many years, Aunt Catherine would bestow as much love as though she had acquired, in reality of flesh and blood, a second daughter.

Temperamentally, the two were kin, which may explain why Margaret was asked to live with this aunt and why she preferred to remain in Edinburgh, knowing that her mother was not without companionship as she earned her living at *The King's Head*. When Bridget left their home, it would be to settle in four rooms above her husband's bakery, within one hundred yards of her mother's place of business,[48] and there, before long, Mrs. Cock had grandchildren to visit. And only three doors from that bakeshop was *The Bear,* a tavern kept by a George Roberts who had married Mary Ruskin,[49] the sister of Margaret's mother. A year younger than Mrs. Cock, Aunt Mary may have come to Croydon from the Parish of St. Bartholomew-the-Great when the widowed Margaret needed comfort. There she would have met George Roberts as a neighbor known through business. Nine months after her brother-in-law William's fatal accident, Mary had become George Roberts' bride. Within three years, she had had three children, the youngest named in honor of his uncle, John Thomas of Edinburgh, after which no more is heard about Aunt Mary and her family. Both she and her husband had died some years before their niece Margaret married John James Ruskin, and the three cousins who had been Margaret's younger playmates may have left Croydon long before she first took her child to visit his Aunt Bridget — when he would have heard no more about *The Bear* as formerly the home of an Aunt Mary than he heard about *The King's Head* as the birthplace of his mother.

North of Croydon, within thirty miles, there were other relatives about whom Margaret must have heard, or whom she may have known, when she was young. For in Cheshunt, the Robert Ruskin (*b.* 1732) who was her mother's uncle, in all probability had married Hannah Adams in 1753,[50] to become, in 1755, the father of another Robert — presumably a first cousin of Margaret's mother. This (Cousin?) Robert Ruskin remained in Cheshunt as a farmer who would die in 1818, having become the father of a Robert Ruskin (identified as "labourer," "yeoman," "farmer") who was so obstreperous that his name, together with his father's, is more than once repeated in the records of the Hertford County Court. In

1810, for instance, he was indicted for assault; in 1815 he was sentenced to one month in jail for having attacked a "page" who was conducting to the Parish Pound of Cheshunt "a gelding belonging to him, which had been found trespassing. . . ." The year before, his father had received a "recognizance — to keep the peace towards Martha, wife of Robert Ruskin junior." Next, in 1815, Robert (junior?) was incarcerated "as an insolvent debtor," his "petition" having been dismissed because he had " 'omitted to state in his Schedule five Beasts, three Calves, two Ponies, and a Cart and Harness, which since his commitment to Gaol he hath authorized his Wife . . . to sell . . . for £50 and upwards without the consent or knowledge of his Creditors' "; and in 1817 he was once more indicted for assault. In earlier years, an *Ann* Ruskin of Cheshunt had been indicted (1779), then discharged, for stealing money; and shortly after Robert Senior died, *William* Ruskin, "labourer" of Cheshunt, having been indicted for "stealing two fowls," was sentenced to six months at "hard labour in the bridewell" — after which (in 1825) he was "committed for larceny." *James* Ruskin, in 1821, was ordered to appear for questioning about the child of Mary Cassell (both of Cheshunt); and in 1826 *John* Ruskin of Cheshunt received a recognizance "to keep the peace toward Ann Smith, widow." One does not know how closely John, James, William, Ann, were related to the Robert Ruskins, but it is clear that the two Roberts were in the public eye during the period of Margaret's residence in Scotland. One may therefore wonder whether Margaret's mother may not occasionally have referred to the doings of those Cheshunt Ruskins in the "lost letters" which Margaret's son would find "grievous" and "humiliating," and consequently whether it was quite accidental that the English origin of the Ruskin family should have remained a mystery which baffled Ruskin and his editors. Curiously enough, it was on the very birthday of John Ruskin — February 8, 1887 — that Alexander Wedderburn chanced to note that James Ruskin, a laborer of St. Albans (near Cheshunt) appeared before a jury of which Frederick Ruskin, a Cheshunt farmer, was a member.[51]

Or did those lost letters grievously evince no more than the relative illiteracy, if not the relative vulgarity, of Ruskin's English grandmother? The only specimen of her handwriting which is known to have survived is her signature upon the record of her marriage; although one must make allowances for nervousness at such a moment in a woman's life, the script in which she wrote her name does not suggest that she had been well educated.[52] Married (1780) when she was twenty-five years old, she at once had entered the environment of public houses near the market place of Croydon, where she herself, for twenty-eight years after her husband's death, supervised the two bars and three bar parlors of her tavern. Hence, apart from any news about the Cheshunt Ruskins, those letters, as a revelation of the level of her personal development and interests, could have been distressing — first of all, perhaps, to the daughter who received them.

What this daughter's life was like in her mother's home even Ruskin does not try to tell us, though he reanimates his mother's school days, having evidently had at least one fact at his disposal — the name of her headmistress. In a trade directory of 1791, one of the five schools of Croydon was advertised as "Mrs. S. Rice's 'Academy for Ladies.' " To be sure, the implications of this name ought not to be uncritically accepted, in that "the description 'Academy for Ladies' was in all probability supplied by Mrs. Rice herself; the practice still obtains in [England] of allowing those whose entries appear in a trade directory to supply their own description, and the opportunity for a puff has seldom been lost." [53] Yet his mother always spoke of "Mrs. Rice" with "respectful praise," Ruskin would recall, as he himself most readily supplied details to show how she, in contrast to her sister Bridget, had behaved in the "country school" which was, he did not fail to note, "quite fashionable (for Croydon). . . ." [54] Then, easily enough, everything which characterized his mother (and some things which did not) could be ascribed to the influence of Mrs. Rice, who thus, through Ruskin's fictional technique and skill, became established as the source of Margaret's Evangelicism, of her taste in reading, of her "purity" in speech, of her "consummate" competence as a housewife, and even of her feeling of inferiority because her "early education" had been, supposedly, "deficient."

Seeking now the actuality, one would seem to find, once more, the nucleus of truth within *Praeterita*. For it is possible, indeed likely, that Margaret, as Ruskin says, was "taught evangelical principles" by Mrs. Rice, inasmuch as the personal background of his Croydon grandmother might well have predisposed her to entrust the instruction of her daughters to an "Evangelical." Margaret Ruskin's mother had married William Cock "by Banns," which suggests that she personally may have been a Presbyterian Dissenter. Nor is it at all unlikely that through his English as well as through his Scottish ancestors Ruskin was the product of a long line of Evangelicals. From the time of the Restoration, Cheshunt had been "a stronghold of Non-conformity." [55] When the son of Cromwell could return to England, he had made his home in Cheshunt, which had been a place of rendezvous for Nonconforming ministers under Charles II. In 1715, the "Presbyterian congregation [of Cheshunt Parish] numbered three hundred hearers." [56] By the last half of the century Cheshunt College had been founded to train Dissenting ministers, and it was subsequently "certified as 'a place of worship for Protestant Calvinistic Methodists.' " [57] In 1753, Robert Ruskin of Cheshunt had been married "by Banns" — and interestingly enough, in 1683 Robert "Ruskyn," a husbandman of Little Berkhamstead, had been convicted for attending "an unlawful conventicle at the house of Israel Mayo," who would be remembered for having hazardously made his home in St. Albans a place for Nonconformist worship before the Toleration Act was passed. It would therefore seem as though Ruskin's mother, as a girl, might have been predisposed to heed any teaching of evangelical principles which she received from Mrs. Rice.

Nevertheless, for the final shaping of her faith, it would surely have been more important that she spent years of her young womanhood with her Presbyterian Aunt Catherine, the mother of Ruskin's memorably evangelical Aunt Jessie. According to the Croydon Parish Registers, both Margaret and Bridget had been baptized into the Church of England. But when Margaret left Aunt Catherine, to settle in London as a wife, she chose to attend not an Evangelical Chapel, but a Caledonian Church in Hatton Garden, whose congregation then "was in its infancy." [58] And Margaret would have her son baptized by a Presbyterian chaplain, the Rev. James Boyd, who not long after would return to Scotland to serve as "Minister of the Parish of Ochilbree — in the Presbytery & County of Ayr. . . ." [59]

As to *Praeterita,* it will doubtless be agreed that the distinctly oversimplified account which Ruskin gave of how his mother came to be an Evangelical can scarcely be considered a satisfactory basis for biography.

Similarly, the *Praeterita* account of what Margaret achieved under the tutelage of Mrs. Rice would seem to represent little more than

Ruskin's daydream, with the so-called "defects" in Margaret's "early education" providing him with a too-facile explanation of his mother's lack of ease in social contacts after she was married. While attending the Academy of Mrs. Rice, Margaret probably acquired the knowledge and the skills which most girls of that day received in elementary school: accuracy in spelling, legibility in penmanship ("in good round hand"), grounding in arithmetic, neatness in sewing, facility in housework, together with the religious instruction which was part of the curriculum in all schools of her time — doubtless, under Mrs. Rice, Evangelical.[60] Doubtless, too, as Ruskin thought, there was some improvement in her speech, and some development of taste in reading, though it seems clear that Margaret would have made the most significant advances in her speech and reading while she lived in Scotland.[61]

Mrs. Rice also must have given some attention to deportment, possibly with stress upon good posture; yet this acquirement, for which Margaret would be repeatedly remembered, likewise bears the stamp of Edinburgh. The well-bred Scottish woman of that day never lounged in her chair, as we learn from Lockhart's account of Sir Walter's mother, eldest daughter of John Rutherford, Professor of Medicine at Edinburgh University, and therefore a recipient of the best education available to young ladies of her city: ". . . even when she approached her eightieth year, [Mrs. Scott] took as much care to avoid touching her chair with her back as if she had still been under the stern eye of Mrs. Ogilvie." [62] Mrs. Ogilvie "was supposed to be the *best-bred* woman of her time in Scotland"; consequently when she *"finished off"* young ladies, she "taught [them] to sit quite upright. . . ." [63] It was a convention which would be reflected in Ruskin's own ideas about the proper training of young ladies — as he recalled his mother, at this point with approving tenderness: "The beginning, and very nearly the end, of bodily education for a girl, is to make sure that she can stand, and sit, upright; the ankle vertical, and firm as a marble shaft; the waist elastic as a reed, and as indefatigable. I have seen my own mother travel from sunrise to sunset, in a summer's day, without once leaning back in the carriage" — she too (as an essential part of the whole picture) with a waist "elastic as a reed." [64] When she was in her sixties, her husband, back from a business trip, would write their son: "I found your Mama looking on my return as if her countenance was become a reflector of all the Beds of Roses seen from her Window — not red but really fine pink & white but I found her the other morning not being able to complain of complexion, in some chagrin because time alters her figure she says for the worse." [65] And if, that evening, there was company, with Margaret sitting like a Lady but still showing some of her old shyness, let us not suppose that this difficulty was primarily a heritage from Mrs. Rice's day school.

It is more likely that, rooted in her far past, the trouble came from her relationship with Bridget. As personalities, she and Bridget were very different types although, as human beings, they loved each other with a loyalty that could withstand hard test.

One sees on Bridget's face, in an engraving from a miniature, the gaiety and kindness, and the potential mischief, on which Ruskin dwelt when he portrayed her character,[66] saying that at Mrs. Rice's school she had been the "plague and pet." Plague and pet she might well have been, both in her school and in her home — this younger sister who, after she had married, would contentedly remain in the near neighborhood of Mother.

Margaret's youth had left her feeling (doubtless even as a schoolgirl) a deep need to earn approval by becoming better than she was, perpetually recognizing, nonetheless, that except in the sight of God, she seemed to be inferior. For the younger sister had "more wit," and was much more confident of receiving love in her own right, and would laugh at Margaret (Ruskin would recount impressions of his childhood) with warm affection and with all the kindness of her generous heart.

It was typical, Ruskin added (now having made his father part of the whole picture), that Bridget should have taken a stray dog into her home, to make "affectionate" and "brave" the "snappish, starved vagrant." [67] No more, eventually, loving Margaret, could Bridget have shut her door to John James Ruskin, though he would close *his* door to her and hers. For she long since had found her share of happiness through marrying an "entirely honest . . . baker," whereas John James (commemorated as "an entirely honest merchant") had remained excessively defensive against his own unfortunate connections with petty tradesmen.

Even in her marriage Bridget might have seemed to be superior because George Richardson had wanted her before she had reached twenty; in fact, by 1803 she had become a mother. George Richardson, it seems, was not a native of her town, nor were her marriage rites performed in Croydon.[68] Inevitably one thinks of Patrick Richardson and wonders whether George and Bridget may have met somewhere in Scotland while she was visiting her sister and other relatives in Edinburgh, although no record of her marriage has been found in the most likely Scottish registers.[69]

Wherever her George may have come from, he settled down to run his bakery within that short walk from *The King's Head,* and through the naming of his children he would seem to have retraced the entire Ruskin family history, except for no commemoration of Aunt Catherine. First there was *John George* (Bridget's grandfather, John Ruskin, with perhaps a glance at Uncle John of Edinburgh; secondarily, her husband). Then came *Margaret Mary* (Bridget's mother and sister; her grandmother Ruskin, and Aunt Mary); next, *William Ruskin* (now her father, William Cock, with "William Ruskin" reappearing as a family name), after whom, in 1808, arrived *George James* (now *her* husband in the foreground, probably with an initial tribute to John James). Then, in 1810, shortly after Margaret had become engaged, there was that gala christening of a too-soon-lost *James Tweddel Adair.* Margaret had been visiting her sister not long before this child was born, and Aunt Catherine had written: "Bridget is getting a strong family indeed. May God give them grace and make them blessings to her. I hope she is beginning to see of what value her life and health is [sic] to her young family and not wearing out her strength by fatigue as she used to do. — Remember me affectionately to all friends and to your *Mother* in particular." [70] By 1811 there would be a *Charles Thomas* (probably, for once, in commemoration of some member of her husband's family, with a secondary gesture to John Thomas); finally, in 1814, a *Mary Bridget* would complete this conspicuously Ruskinian family of George Richardson — "an altogether gentle, loveable, innocent old man in gaiters — of [torn] a figure something between M Pickwick and M Lillyvick — and a baker of altogether excellent bread." [71] He would survive his Bridget for many many years, but would never more be heard of until, in *Fors Clavigera* as in *Praeterita,* he was remembered for his occupation and his honesty, and for having been the husband of his wife, his own name never having been so much as mentioned heretofore.

Bridget was perhaps as dominating as she was loyally affectionate;

on occasion, it could be, despite its warmth her laughter may have hurt. Yet Margaret also dearly loved her Bridget. Sometimes, if not regularly, through these and later years, she went back to Croydon, apparently staying with Bridget rather than with her mother; and there were frequent visits after she had married, when John James was traveling to gain orders for his sherry. ". . . I have now no sister nor friend with whom to divide the time of your absence," [72] she would remark after Bridget died (in 1830).[73]

Nevertheless, after his marriage Father kept "mother's relatives . . . out of the house," [74] Ruskin would observe, elsewhere explaining at greater length, in another passage of *Praeterita* left unpublished: "Also, we were in the habit of drawing perhaps too severe a line between the social standing of Merchant and Shopkeeper — so that my Father did not think himself losing cast — especially when it was in the way of business, by inviting to his table even the least of his country correspondents who supplied the cellars of the neighbouring squires; but would never extend the same encouragement to the thriving grocers, haberdashers, or tallowhandlers with whom he every day, nevertheless took his corner in goodfellowship in the morning coach from Herne Hill to the city. This rule was observed only the more strictly because we had to enforce it with Roman equity in the case of our own relatives at Croydon. We condescended indeed to stay with *them* sometimes, for their glorification in their Surrey sphere: but only received at Herne Hill their occasional forenoon visits[.] I never remember seeing my uncle, aunt, or any of my cousins but Charles, at Herne Hill dinner." [75] *Cousin* Bridget did, however, eventually cause some slight embarrassment by marrying "a Mr. Fox . . . of rank somewhat above a tradesman — just enough to be uncomfortable." But before long, luckily, "they went out to Sydney. . . ." [76]

All things considered, it could not have been especially easy for the young Margaret to have entered a household and the more general social environment which thus abidingly had fashioned John James Ruskin. Notwithstanding her lack of self-assurance and of ready wit, Margaret's was a much more complex and intrinsically a far more consequential personality than was Bridget's, however Ruskin may have weighted the scales when he discussed them — too well remembering how his mother, on one birthday, had denied him a "radiant Punch and Judy" brought to him by his Aunt Bridget.[77] In thought-

fulness, intensity, and self-restraint, Margaret would seem to have
been less like her sister than she was like Jessie, who became her
close friend during years when, in Perth, they lived near one another.[78] Nevertheless, to do her justice, although she was so different
from Aunt Bridget, Ruskin's mother was not without capacity for
mirth: "Far on the contrary," Ruskin himself would protest against
impressions he himself had overwhelmingly created, "there was a
hearty, frank, and sometimes even irrepressible, laugh in my mother!
Never sardonic, yet with a very definitely Smollettesque turn in it!
so that, between themselves, she and my father enjoyed their
Humphrey Clinker extremely, long before *I* was able to understand
either the jest or gist of it. Much more, she could exult in a harmless
bit of Smollettesque reality," as when Nurse Anne, facing a monas-
tery as she sat upon a railing, fell over backwards. "My father could
not help suggesting that she had done it expressly for the entertainment of the Holy Fathers; and neither he nor my mother could ever
speak of the 'performance' (as they called it) afterwards, without
laughing for a quarter of an hour. ¶If, however, there was the least
bitterness or irony in a jest, my mother did not like it. . . ." [79] Yet
even so, with Margaret laughter did not rule the hour. She remained,
rather, always eager to "improve" herself, presumably because long
before she had arrived in Edinburgh, she had been made to feel that
devastating need to *earn* approval . . . in contrast to her mirthful,
harum-scarum younger plague-and-pet (born when Margaret was
only two years old) who could so effortlessly win and hold affection,
and who was always so content to live within the orbit of her mother.

Unprepared to move with ease in the class-conscious circle of her
uncle, Margaret could find solace in her Aunt Catherine. For Aunt
Catherine not only loved but also justly valued this niece who, no
less than the more earthy Bridget, had her kindness and her loyalty,
together with her patience, submissiveness, integrity, and good mind
— this Margaret who was proud as well as shy, while ever seeking
to become more worthy. As a girl, she probably was not the "faultless" housekeeper Ruskin would envisage as the product of Mrs.
Rice's day school. Yet by the end of her long years in Scotland,
Margaret would have learned the ways of her Aunt Catherine, and
could bring into her husband's daily life the habits of his mother.

The eventual superiority of Margaret's household management
may well at times evoke a smile. One catches a glimpse of it at first

through Effie Gray while she was an unmarried guest at Denmark Hill and therefore not as yet entirely hostile. "Mrs. Ruskin," Effie observed drily, "is at present dusting her china which occupation she performs daily." [80] But it is Margaret's husband, writing from Chamouni, who gives a more panoramic view of her management, when she was over seventy: "I trust she will get home as well as she now is — Our absence has been long but it was not a mere Change of air that was wanted but a release from Household Cares — It may seem strange that with so small a family & so inhospitable a Board there should be any Household Cares; but as Charles Dickens' Raven used to perch on his window & drive imaginary horses with great skill all day, so Mrs R. seems at home to drive an immense imaginary establishment all day & the servants though of 10, 20 & 40 years standing are very considerate in not acting without authority & so contrive to worry their mistress all day for orders and Instructions about anything or nothing so that living at an Hotel is perhaps a very salutary Relief. . . ." [81] Thus Margaret gradually had fortified herself by a routine which, in her special sphere, made her, also, Consequential.

And yet beneath obvious absurdities, she had preserved distinctly compensating ways and values. Notably there was the family's relationship with servants, genuinely vestigial of Scotland's feudal past and a token to John Ruskin of what relationships between an employer and the employed ought to be. As James Nasmyth tells us, describing his own home in Edinburgh, "there was always a most cheerful and intimate intercourse kept up between the children and the servants. They were members of the same family, and were treated as such. The servants were for the most part country-bred — daughters of farm servants or small farmers. They were fairly educated at their parish schools; they could read and write, and had an abundant store of old recollections. . . . They became lastingly attached to their masters and mistresses, as well as to the children . . . and . . . they left us, for the most part to be married. . . ." [82] One thinks of all the servants who, through their devotion, became a part of Ruskin's life; of the old "Mause" of his Aunt Jessie; of Nurse Anne, who had not yet joined Catherine's household, though there would be no parting when it was time for Margaret to go, at last, to London as a wife. One thinks no less about the Margaret who never dismissed any servant, even under gravest provocation —

as when her son's lower lip was permanently marred;[83] and whom, except to marry, no servant ever left. On one occasion she would comment, writing to her husband: "Cook goes today[;] this morning when she came to take orders she thanked me for all my kindness [she] said the 9 years she has been in our house had been the happiest nine years of her life and that she wished she could show her gratitude in more than thanks[.] This is gratifying." [84] Once asked the function of an "ancient maid," Margaret, now eighty, would explain — still sitting upright: " 'She, my dear, puts out the dessert.' " [85]

But probably the deepest bond between Catherine and Margaret, as they grew into each other's lives, was the religious faith in which Catherine's niece was patterned after her own heart — the special quality of this faith by no means suggesting that Margaret had sprung a full-fledged Evangelical out of Mrs. Rice's nest. Going to her Aunt, Margaret was entering the home of a Catherine who had reached her forties not without receiving strength from God in time of trouble, so that the creed which she had once been taught in her Old Luce church and home had been confirmed in all it meant to heart and spirit, while being manifested through her own fulfillment of her duties as a mother. True, along those shadowed paths over which she had traveled, she may have sometimes heard and, with reservations, been persuaded by the voices of the "Moderate" clergy, because it scarcely could have been without her sanction that her son would once or twice perform in amateur theatricals.

Yet Catherine otherwise had shut her ears to all that made for skepticism, while changing old God-fearing ways. ". . . remember," she would warn John James, "no woman without the fear of God, can either make a good Wife or a good Mother — freethinking Men are shocking to nature, but from an Infidel Woman the Good Lord deliver us." [86] Or she would express concern about temptations to her son which might attend his life in London: "I hope, my dear John, amidst all your throng of business you take time to read your Bible and to reflect on what you do read. And beware, my love (as you value your own peace either here or hereafter), of forming friendships with those who make mock of Religion. Such friendships lead to destruction, for no one who lives without their God can be trusted as a friend. Those who are Rebels to their God can never be good to anyone." [87] And sometimes, as to herself, her thoughts of God flowed naturally from her pen, leading to a page of meditation and of prayer after she had learned that her son would probably recover from an alarming illness: "Friday. A day to be remembered while I have being O Lord let me praise thee. . . ." [88] Catherine had led her daughter Jessie to a font of piety which would never fail her need; beside the strictness of his Aunt Jessie's principles, Ruskin found his own mother's Evangelicism pale.

It was, however, more than creed that Margaret shared with Catherine, although the years of living with *this* Aunt must have more and more confirmed whatever hold evangelical beliefs may at first have gained on her in Croydon. Catherine would have taught John James no less earnestly than she taught Jessie the creed which to her signified Salvation. John James had been acceptant, never to be too seriously troubled by religious doubt, although, in the wake of David Hume, skepticism widely permeated Edinburgh thought. But whereas John James Ruskin reverently acquiesced to the articles of faith, Margaret participated in Catherine's doctrine with her *heart,* so that within her own personality a religious creed became emotionally, imaginatively, wedded to experience. Margaret's temperament was truly religious, as John James' was not. And it was this temperament which Ruskin would share with his mother — a temperament which largely shaped his own experience of life and never changed with creed. So, too, one meets the religious temperament of a Carlyle or Blake, in contrast to the dominantly rationalistic mode of understanding in a Leslie Stephen or a John Stuart Mill.

For the present, however, in her personality and ways Margaret resembled her Aunt Catherine, so that in this Croydon cousin John James could respect, from the first, what he revered in his own mother, and next in his sister, finally to trust implicitly in his wife. Through a faith beyond but yet together with their creed, both Catherine and Margaret had resources which could never help John James to achieve serenity; and in Margaret, faith would lead to a dogmatism which could be made maddening by her serene self-assurance. There was no room for argument because she had thought-and-*felt,* and therefore *knew.*

In such dogmatism one likewise finds, it may be thought, a definite resemblance in her son — as he, not incongruously, would find his mother's creed and quality of faith, and temperament, and most essential way of life, in Rose La Touche.

But Margaret now was young and subject to the influence of her

Aunt Catherine, with this Aunt's love, ideals, and power of personality. Predisposed to mutual understanding, they grew more close as years of trouble served to deepen sympathy. "My own dearest Margaret," Catherine would write, after they had lived together for some time, "you do not know how dear you are to me. I think when I want you I want the half of myself. I trust we shall never long be parted in this world." [89]

7

The Edinburgh Margaret
Knew

More impersonally, Margaret had entered an environment that helped to nourish all her married life and to determine its distinctive qualities, so that her son, in sympathies and vision, became far more a product of his parents' Edinburgh than of his native London. The Scottish capital she knew was still a small metropolis,[1] though the self-styled and acknowledged "Athens of the North." It had been the center of the Scottish Renaissance (two hundred years delayed) that marked the last half of the eighteenth century: looking back on Boswell, Smollett, David Hume,

and Robert Burns, together with Mackenzie, Macpherson, and a host
of other men with less abiding reputation, Sir Walter Scott voiced
national pride while saying that " 'in those days there were giants in
the north.' " [2] Now Scott himself was at the threshold, to make known
the people of his land as they had been of old, according to his vision,
and as he wished them to remain. And it was not in spite of Ruskin's
father and his mother that *Praeterita* begins with challenge: "I am,
and my father was before me, a violent Tory of the old school; —
Walter Scott's school, that is to say, and Homer's."

By way of paradox, likewise so typical of Ruskin's life, Scotland
also gave an Adam Smith to head the school of laissez faire, with
various beliefs to be embraced by prosperous merchants, in time to
the discomfiture of John James Ruskin's son. There were also men
of science, with Edinburgh University stressing scientific knowledge
to a degree as yet inconceivable in any English university. The
geology that led to intellectual revolution through the nineteenth
century, after Lyell began to publish, had been already sketched by
Hutton, whose theories now were being illustrated by Professor Play-
fair. The work of Joseph Black, who had discovered latent heat while
teaching chemistry at Glasgow, had been succeeded by the research
of Edinburgh's Sir John Leslie, who kept abreast of what was going
on in France and, with his fellows, swiftly made significant the
Edinburgh Royal Society (founded 1783). With the continent shut
off by war, English visitors turned more and more habitually to
Scotland and its capital; and now their sons sometimes attended
Edinburgh University, notable for its Department of Philosophy and
School of Law, and for what remained through years to come the
most outstanding School of Medicine in Britain. Pure science had a
way of going hand in hand with application: in 1788 a boat (with
Robert Burns as passenger) had been propelled by steam; and steam
would soon be used to till progressive farms — James Watt, of
Glasgow, having started yet another revolution through his work
in engineering. Thus, intellectually and technologically, Scotsmen
helped to forge the future even as they cherished the feudal past,
medievalism having dominated Scottish life and culture far into the
eighteenth century.

At a somewhat lower level, the arts were also flourishing. There
was much interest in the theatre: by writing *Douglas* (long believed
to be a major contribution to tragic drama), the Reverend John

Home notoriously had helped the Moderate clergy to dispel religious opposition to theatrical performances. Now Mrs. Siddons' brother prospered as owner of the Theatre Royal, where Mrs. Siddons, Mrs. Jordan, or John Kemble recurrently performed, while amateur theatricals provided interlude.

In the graphic arts, Raeburn was named automatically with Reynolds and Van Dyck, and Alexander Nasmyth fathered the Scottish school of landscape, while incidentally producing scenery for theatricals and cultivating landscape gardening upon great estates. In England, to be sure, landscape gardening had long since lost its novelty. But at this time, in Edinburgh, interest in flowers and in gardening spread until, in 1809, it was formally expressed in the founding of the Royal Horticultural Society. In 1780 the Society of Antiquarians had been founded and, shortly after, the Highland Society of Scotland. Gradually men began to look at trees and hills and sunsets, and to sketch "from nature," with Scott soon giving a tremendous impetus to their delight in an uncultivated but historic landscape. By 1826, Nasmyth's pupil, John Thomason, would be illustrating works of Scott, helped by Joseph Mallord William Turner. At the Trustees Academy, apprentices were trained in good design for textiles, carpets, and the like. This school was supported from estates that had been confiscated in 1715 and 1746, and was "the prototype of all the schools in the United Kingdom founded for the art-education of the people, in connection with national manufactures. . . ." [3]

Nasmyth's friend, Sir James Hall, President of the Royal Society, was writing *On the Origin of Gothic Architecture* — a work combined, in personal life, with his investigations of volcanic origins and with Huttonian-Wernerian debate. John Jamieson, a northern Samuel Johnson, had turned to his *Etymological Dictionary of the Scottish Language*. In 1802 the *Edinburgh Review* became *must-reading* for every "genteel" family, [4] with an influence to be counteracted (after 1809 — and appeals from Walter Scott) by the *London Quarterly* until, in 1817, Edinburgh produced *Blackwood's*. Scott's *Minstrelsy* was out by 1803, and then Scott shared, through his own poetry, what he had seen and heard and felt as the first great "romantic" traveler through Scotland.

Thanks to intellectual ferment and to hard work blessed by good return — including leisure — the middle class provided an ever enlarging reading public comprised of individuals who found it fashionable to cultivate knowledge, urbanity, and taste. The Reverend Hugh Blair had greatly helped until he died in 1800, after which his *Sermons* and his *Lectures on Rhetoric and Belles-Lettres* were popularly read, and otherwise diffused, in every English-speaking land for almost half a century. Minister at St. Giles Cathedral, Professor at the University, and "pillar in the edifice of civic pride," [5] Blair taught religious values that were approved, for style and sentiment, by followers more inclined to skepticism and gentility than to religiously dogmatic ardor; and with clear application, Blair readily explained the concepts which should guide the literary and artistic judgments of an eighteenth-century gentleman. (The young John Ruskin knew his Blair.) As Mathieson has said, ". . . the remark of Voltaire on reading Kames's *Elements of Criticism* was scarcely more ironical than true: 'It is an admirable result of the progress of the human spirit that at the present time it is from Scotland we receive rules of taste in all the arts — from the epic poem to gardening.' " [6] And it may be no less, though unironically, a comment on the workings of the human spirit that we should find in Ruskin, from his very early childhood, all but the whole gamut of the interests in this city of his parents' youth — interests which, in all their multiplicity, he would pursue as though his essential being had been shaped during some prenatal stage.

Socially and economically, it seems inevitable that Ruskin's father should have been a Tory. It was not merely that the Tories, under Dundas, had acquired a strangle hold on civic life, though the significance of this should not be minimized. Economically, it meant that even the banks were "overawed," and discriminated against suspected Whigs. Legally, it meant that anyone charged with "sedition" because of an unorthodox opinion could be, without appeal, transported to Australia for fourteen years by a jury hand-picked by a Tory judge. Practically and symptomatically it meant that Alexander Nasmyth turned from portraiture (*e.g.*, of Robert Burns) to landscape painting because he would not heed warnings and hence found patronage withdrawn. Such conditions could scarcely have developed except for popular hysteria, which here as elsewhere stemmed from 1789. With the French Revolution, the word and concept, *liberty,* became anathema, with connotations of "the people," soon associated with mob violence and with what are now called *purges.* "Tradesmen of 'Jacobinical' sympathies had their credit stopped at the bank. Housewives refused to buy unless from shopkeepers of approved loyalty." [7] "Every thing," Lord Cockburn said, "not this or that thing, but literally every thing, was soaked in this one event." [8]

John James had been only four years old in 1789, but while he was growing up, conservative opposition to revolutionary principles was being strengthened, first, by wide reaction against revolutionary methods and, next, by terror activated through Napoleonic conquest. From the start, Whigs became suspect as they urged electoral and other such reforms, but suspicions changed into the most extreme and personalized intolerance when war with France began in 1793 and as subsequent events upon the continent provoked dread of an invasion; and, even more, by 1796, of "the expected blow from the 'accursed dagger of domestic treachery.' . . . In the articles of the Edinburgh Volunteers, nothing was said of serving against a foreign foe; but the members formally reprobated the doctrine of universal suffrage and Jacobin political principles. . . ." [9]

By 1800 no able-bodied man could live unmolested if he had not at least enlisted as a Volunteer in the Home Guard (Scott was leading his Light Horse Troop by 1797), and at the University, professors drilled upon the grounds. Since Tory ideology was now the creed of patriots, any wish for change, any whisper of reform, or even any independent thought was eloquent of treason, as Lord Cockburn noted while describing the intensity of local feeling. At the University, Dugald Stewart became ostracized, and the Whiggish Dr. Thomas Brown, who also had defended Hume, was thought unfit for an appointment until 1810.

In historical perspective, Tory principles were a heritage of the aristocracy, as feudal lords and Cavaliers. But when Ruskin's father was a youth, Tory principles were also basic to a merchant's livelihood and to general social intercourse. "The frightful thing was the personal bitterness. The decent appearance of mutual tolerance, which often produces the virtue itself, was despised; and extermination seemed a duty." [10]

In view of home environment and of personal sensitivity to social pressures, it would have taken someone with a mind much more original, and more brave than that of John James Ruskin to have heeded the social criticism Dr. Adam must have masked by 1799, when John James was ready for his classroom. Indeed, the political ideals of Dr. Adam bore fruit through those who could afford to harbor independent thought because family backgrounds made them socially and economically secure — but even after they had launched the *Edinburgh Review* (as malcontents inspired by Sydney Smith), Francis Jeffrey found it wise to wait some years before he made their mouthpiece a forthright organ of the Whigs.[11] "Indeed," Lord Cockburn notes, "the suppression of independent talent or ambition was the tendency of the times. Every Tory principle being absorbed in the horror of innovation, and that party casting all its cares on Henry Dundas, no one could, without renouncing all his hopes, commit the treason of dreaming an independent thought."[12] John James was left with ingrained fear of independent thought: as a father, he never lost his terror as his son ventured a new book, and he never failed to suffer disproportionately under an unfavorable review.

As to Ruskin's "violent" Tory principles, they both were and were not what his father's were before him. Originally, Tory terrorism, wedded to hysterical suspiciousness of Liberty and Revolution, could browbeat any merchant family into conformity[13] unless, perchance, they gladly shared the day. But then, when *Waverley* appeared (1814) John James became a convert to the novels of Sir Walter Scott, who despite his breadth of human sympathy assuredly was not without his weaknesses as sycophant and snob: "the people of the town," John James would read, "chiefly engaged in mercantile pursuits, were not such as Waverley chose to associate with." Scott, too, had lived through that reign of terror with his insecurities, and deferential admiration of the upper class, together with a desire to be successful. In convictions, he had reverted, as an adolescent, to those of "Beardie" Scott — the grandfather who had fought at Preston and then had vowed, perhaps apocryphally, that he would never shave until a Stuart sat upon the throne. During his days in the Royal High School, such convictions could not have hurt Scott's popularity (Scott's father, as already noted, was a Whig); and as time passed, his political beliefs became, in overtones of feeling, scarcely less fanatical than had been those of "Beardie." When Scott began his work as novelist, he projected these beliefs into the medieval past, and consequently, in Scott's novels, John James could find what he himself believed, herein far removed from what to him had been so painful in personal reality. It was a pleasant form in which to pass on to his son his Tory creed. That son, throughout his life, on principle, would never cast a vote.

8

Family Life and Interests

Politically acceptable, John Thomas Ruskin participated in the social life of his community, although one should not assume, on the basis of a letter which John James received from Dr. Brown (published in *Praeterita*) that the Ruskins characteristically associated with families of the intellectually élite. Yet only in this circle, had they brought a proper passport, might their peers have been inclined to disregard the fact that John Thomas had been a grocer and was known, at present, as a "Merchant" — "that is to say," as Lockhart specifies, "a dealer in everything from fine broadcloth to children's tops." [1] "There was no class in the community so little thought of as the mercantile," Lord Cockburn notes, describing life in Edinburgh around 1800. ". . . They had no direct political power; no votes; and were far too subservient to be feared. The lairds were not merely more deferred to, but were in the height of their influence. . . . our Scotch commerce was only dawning; and no merchants, great by mere force of their wealth, had made either themselves or their calling formidable." [2]

Scarcely unaware of social hierarchy, John Thomas still did not rest content with the advances he had made. By 1802 he was acting as the "agent in Scotland" for a Mr. Moore, in whose home John James lived when he first went to work in London. By 1805, in Stark's *Directory,* John Thomas Ruskin had risen to the rank of "Agent." [3] Nor were his interests as an "Agent" confined to Edinburgh: "he is very busy just now preparing for his North Journey," Catherine wrote her son in 1807.[4] Meanwhile, in Edinburgh, no doubt he was still conducting his more strictly personal business as a "Merchant," for it was during 1808 that John Thomas Ruskin suffered his financial failure, after which it seems as though he went on serving Mr. Moore. Venturesomely (as was his way), Cook asserts that Mr. Moore was an "army contractor." [5] There is no shred of evidence to support this supposition, whereas the family letters of this period variously suggest that even as an "Agent," John Thomas Ruskin was "a trader in small wear." [6]

However that may have been, a New Town Merchant-Agent was more socially acceptable than was an Old Town Grocer, and could engage in the pleasures of the middle class. For residents of New Town there was, in addition to their club life, a good deal of private hospitality. We hear of Sunday supper parties when Adam Smith (*c.* 1790) was "at home" to guests not formally invited; of even more informal entertainments in the home of Thomas Brown (after 1800); somewhat later (*c.* 1810), of Alexander Nasmyth's welcoming guests who dropped in to pass the evening, bringing

the last new thing in science, in discovery, in history, or campaigning, for the war was then raging throughout Europe. . . . ¶The supper usually followed, for my father would not allow his visitors to go away empty-mouthed. The supper did not amount to much. Rizard or Finnan haddies, or a dish of oysters, with a glass of Edinburgh ale and a rummer of toddy, concluded these friendly evenings. The cry of "Galler sou!" was constantly heard in the streets below of an evening. . . . The freshest of oysters, of the most glorious quality, were to be had at 2s. 6d. the hundred! And what could be more refreshing food for my father's guests? These unostentatious and inexpensive gatherings of friends were a most delightful social institution among the best middle-class people of Edinburgh. . . [7]

Such quiet and unpretentious interchange of hospitality might well have characterized the "pleasant" home John James remembered leaving with regret, probably in early 1802. But looking back upon the entertainment which his father offered subsequently (doubtless while he was again in Edinburgh, c. 1804), John James wrote Miss Mary Russell Mitford: "I also had a father more magnificent in his expenditures than mindful of his family; so indiscriminate and boundless in his hospitalities that, when the invited guests arrived, he would sometimes have to inquire their names." [8] As once his father's trade in Old Town had shamed John James, so now his father's flowering as a resident of New Town would have caused distress, if only because the family must have feared that they were running into debt. Especially, Catherine would have longed to entertain their friends through hospitality which was within their means; and she would indicate that her husband's temper had not made life easy for their son as he approached the age of twenty. Eventually, expressing his impression of his whole experience in Edinburgh, John James told his son: "I have not one pleasing association of my childhood or youth to help me." [9]

The years which Catherine had spent among the lairds of Galloway now would have enabled her to play her part as a poised and gracious hostess, while those which Margaret had spent in her tavern home of Croydon would have become a most grave handicap, with circumstances favoring the return of every ghost of earlier inferiorities. With none of the spontaneous self-confidence of Bridget, she was entirely unprepared to move with ease in a community and home permeated by awareness of social class and the importance of "good birth." From hour to hour the very bearing of Aunt Catherine, regardless of her piety and love, could have been enough to signalize those differences that were not to be overcome by Margaret's learning to sit upright in her chair, while John James Ruskin's driving shame of taverns and of grocers is sufficiently suggestive of some force which must have been destructively at work within that household, perhaps not unrelated to the Lairds of Galloway. At social gatherings, Margaret could not dance, or play at the pianoforte, whereas dance and music were the mode, in imitation of aristocratic habits. She was unacquainted with classic authors on the tongue of every Edinburgh schoolboy, and she lacked the general knowledge which led to easy talk of Adam Smith and of Lavoisier. She had no command of any foreign language (German had arrived), or even of a foreign literature at second hand. And she could scarcely have done much more than wonder when she first heard references to Cervantes, Dante, Cuyp, Poussin and Claude, or to almost any one of those (Macpherson, Robertson, Mackenzie, David Hume, Hugh Blair, *et al.*) who so brightly ornamented Scottish culture during its "Augustan" — also called its "Periclean" — Age.

At the same time, this was a stimulating atmosphere which could challenge someone predisposed to make herself, ostensibly, more deserving of respect from those she loved — not that it follows, as her son fancied, that Margaret sought to show affection for John James "chiefly in steady endeavour to cultivate her powers of mind, and form her manners, so as to fit herself to be the undespised companion of a man she considered much her superior. . . ." [10] If, as Ruskin seems to have believed, Margaret was in Edinburgh by 1800, she would have seen a boy of fifteen graduating from the Royal High School; she did not become engaged to her Cousin John until she had almost reached the point of leaving Edinburgh, in 1809. Although by then she had been in love with her Superior Cousin for several years, the superiority and inferiority which *they* felt had little enough to do with "manners" or with powers of mind.

Nevertheless, having entered a society of relatively cultivated men and women, Margaret undertook, not unsuccessfully, to overcome remediable defects. This effort need not have been too strenuous because, as Erskine notes, "Whoever had read Pope, Addison, and Swift, with some ill-wrote history, was thought a lairnd lady, which character was by no means agreeable. The men thought justly on this point, that what knowledge the women had out of their own sphere, should be given by themselves, and not picked up at their own hand in ill-chosen books of amusement. . . ." [11] Yet even though her own deficiencies were widely shared, Margaret turned to books. For her, however, much which was intangible could not be remedied, and must have been endured from day to day, so that one result was a defensiveness which Ruskin would observe, misleadingly attempting to explain its cause: ". . . my mother always felt, in cultivated society, — and was too proud to feel with patience, — the defects of her own early education; and therefore (which was the true and fatal sign of such defect) never familiarly visited with any one whom she did not feel to be, in some sort, her inferior." [12] Surely, how-

ever, this problem of his mother's feeling insecure, socially, should
not be reduced to the limitations of her schooling under Mrs. Rice.
For when Margaret left Edinburgh, however otherwise inferior she
had been made to feel, she was by no means, according to either
English or Scottish standards of that day, a defectively educated or
an uncultivated woman.

How to carry on one's education through one's own efforts was a
subject which commanded interest in that home, John James Ruskin
also having had to find an answer after he left high school. Although
he may have spent a second year (Oct., 1800 — Aug., 1801) in Dr.
Adam's classroom, it is perhaps more likely that he went at once to
work, since he was older than the average graduate. He next spent
fifteen months in London, after which he was again in Edinburgh
for about a year. There he would have found his mother eager to
encourage his ambition to learn more than he had gained through
his long drill in Latin, with four years all but utter waste. The defects in such an education might not have greatly mattered to the
father who had set his sights upon becoming a successful Merchant,
and whose father's father had been illiterate (writing *Sun* for *Son,*
grate for *Great, hole* for *whole*). But in Catherine's family, the
men were usually university graduates, and the women did not take
pride in being ignorant. Her own grandmother, Jean Ross (Catherine
would recount), had been "a very remarkable woman. As a proof
of her learning, she was a good Latin scholar, & at the age of seventy
she could repeat from memory every syllable of Young's 'Night
Thoughts,' besides many other productions she had read." [13] Relatedly, when Margaret arrived, her Aunt Catherine would have
fully sympathized with her desire to overcome deficiencies — an
interest which was at one with John James' need.

So Catherine and her son turned, apparently, to Thomas Brown,
who would make his name as Professor of Moral Philosophy at
Edinburgh University, where he was now an undergraduate. From
her girlhood, Catherine must have known his mother — the widow of
a minister of Galloway, where, not far from Catherine's home,
Thomas had been born.[14] Then, when he was only two years old (in
1780) he had lost his father, whereupon his mother had moved to
Edinburgh. Soon Catherine was also living there, and they might
naturally enough have kept in touch with one another. Now Catherine's son was growing up, and needed some advice. "Even when

you were a mere boy," Thomas Brown would write a few years hence, "I was much delighted with your early zeal and attainments; and for your own sake, as well as for your excellent mother's, I have always looked to you with great regard, and with the belief that you would distinguish yourself in whatever profession you might adopt." [15]

John James, one gathers, had begun to find himself before he went away to London, with Thomas Brown helping him to formulate his plans for further study. When Thomas Brown next gave advice, he expressed his hope that John James (then twenty-two years old) would not let his Latin slip away, and added that, during a mercantile career, it should be relatively easy for John James to retain his knowledge of modern languages. Nor should John James regret the time which he had given to *belles-lettres* in preference to science, although henceforth he should acquaint himself with natural sciences. Most important, he must inform himself about political economy through mastering Adam Smith's *The Wealth of Nations*.[16] — Thus, all in all, it seems as though the shaping hand of Dr. Adam may again, most skillfully, have helped to mold the clay.

At this point one can achieve no more than a composite view of John James' cultural development during the year or two which he now would spend, intermittently, in his father's home. Perhaps before his first period of work in London, he had had the pleasure of performing in Home's *Douglas* and in "Monk" Lewis's *Castle Spectre;* and of studying under Alexander Nasmyth, who was professionally concerned with scenery for the theatre. Catherine could not have frowned too sternly on theatrical performances — and indeed, Margaret Ruskin, when her own son was young, was not averse to adding to the pleasures of a theatre party.[17] She had been at hand to see her Cousin John perform in Edinburgh, for "she was never weary of telling me, in later years," Ruskin would relate, "how beautiful my father looked in his Highland dress, with the high black feathers." [18] Her never-failing admiration of her cousin, with his high black feathers (they were echoed in his eyebrows), was perhaps no less important, in the long run, than all that Alexander Nasmyth taught him. Yet he learned much from Alexander Nasmyth, who had a commodious studio at the top of his house in York Place (No. 47), just opposite the home of Raeburn.

Here Nasmyth had been teaching landscape art since 1793, giving twelve lessons for two guineas and being generous with time and interest when he found a student genuinely responsive. Sometimes he would keep the class for a whole morning, taking up a brush to show a pupil how to get effects and regularly increasing interest by talk about "high principles of art." [19] Professionals would come to him for study, and his son Patrick became the "English Hobbema." But by and large, his groups were amateurs (mothers were often there with daughters) who simply found it fun to paint and sketch while learning how to look at pictures and at nature, as well as how to handle oil and water color. He also put much stress upon "the felicity and happiness" of pencil drawing as a means, first, of training hand to record what the eye observed exactly, and, next, of gathering memoranda which, long after, would vividly recall what had been seen — "the old streets, the pointed gables, the entrances to the old churches, even the bits of tracery. . . ." [20] There were sketching parties, during which the object was to discern the aspect of actual clouds and trees upon the actual landscape, for Nasmyth wished his pupils to perceive the beauty of the individual scene or sunset rather than to find effects habitually admired as worthy of "a Claude."

Despite this aim, Nasmyth's own pictures had the cast of something Claude, helped by some Dutch landscape artist, might have done; and when he painted home of nobleman or gentry, the country seat turned out to be more grandiose than a delighted owner might heretofore have thought. Nor could he ever find out how to give, through his own brush, the special atmosphere and colors that suffused the Scottish landscape. Nevertheless, he was the first to try to give, as though in portraiture, a likeness of the Scottish scene, for its own sake.[21] His pupils meanwhile learned to see architecture in surrounding homes and castles (he had also tried his hand at architecture), and beauty in their ruins . . . long valued as stone quarries; and something beyond a Claude, or timber, in a grove of trees.

For John James, regardless of how long, or intermittently, he may have studied under Nasmyth, such orientation (reinforced by developments in the *Zeitgeist*) was obviously more significant than any lack of talent in his use of oil or water color — though Ruskin called his father "no mean draughtsman." [22] Representing *Conway Castle* beyond its Firth, with cottage and a fisherman in the foreground, he produced a picture that would help him entertain his child, who eventually hung it with the Turners in his Brantwood bedroom.[23] He also did a *Lake Scene,* "with a castellated building on an island," [24] — a water color also to be treasured through the years, as was an *Edinburgh Castle* (17½ by 23½ inches) signed by Alexander Nasmyth: "the first picture," it seems clear, that Ruskin "ever saw with conscious eyes. . . ." [25]

What mattered most, however, were the lasting interests and the increased comprehension he acquired. Ruskin would recall his father sketching sights of Croydon Market Place, in India ink, while they were visiting Aunt Bridget. John James, within his limitations, became a good judge of pictures — always, regardless of his limitations, self-assured. He would take tireless pleasure in cathedrals, castles, and the scenery as, with his family, he retraced routes that also served, most practically, his interests as a merchant — this merchant eagerly awaiting a turn in the road that gave them some particularly fine "view," or fresh delight in grove of birches, "ancient" oak, or "mournful" yew; in stream and waterfall, or in some river quietly flowing beneath a bridge — preferably with arches.[26] When his sister "Jessie" died and he adopted Mary Richardson, who came to them with some ability to draw sights recognizably, he could realize that his boy ought to have a drawing master. Nor would he be inclined to grow impatient when, in course of travel, the young Ruskin wished to pause to make detailed and accurate memoranda, or to sketch some sight which they would otherwise inevitably forget.

It must have been after he returned to Edinburgh in 1803 that John James crossed York Place to sit for Raeburn,[27] a good friend of Alexander Nasmyth. This portrait is doubtless one more token of the extravagance of John Thomas, together with his pride . . . it might be thought not solely in his son, inasmuch as people who commissioned Raeburn portraits really had "arrived." Alexander Nasmyth, knowing John James personally, might well have acted as an intermediary. By 1804, Raeburn usually charged 20 guineas for a head,[28] and the Raeburn *John James Ruskin* shows a seated figure painted not quite half length, on a 29½ by 23-inch canvas, with no evasion of details in the composition as a whole.[29]

When Raeburn did this work, he had entered his last period, by then at ease with his technique and fully trained to grasp the individual character. By the end of the first sitting (there were usually

four or five, each lasting for an hour and a half), he was likely to
have decided on the traits that seemed to be at the core of his subject's
personality.[30] Public taste would popularize his *Boy with Rabbit,* but,
in general, he turned a keen mind and realistic vision on the Scottish
matrons, notables, and worthies who passed continuously through his
working day.

He thought it right to pose John James at pause in reading, with a
finger placed between the pages he had reached before he was dis-
tracted (a detail and a moment Raeburn also used when painting Dr.
Adam). The book is held upright in the foreground, resting on a
narrow table as a clear though unobtrusive symbol. The young man
sits relaxed, with his arms crossed, lost in daydream. His is a thoughtful and a not untroubled countenance as eyes look out from a world
within. Intelligence, imagination, sensitivity, are made the dominant
impression through total handling of the figure, with its narrow
sloping shoulders, that serves almost as a pillar for the fine head with
somewhat tousled hair; through the contours of the face and the
expression of the features; and not least through Raeburn's treatment
of the hands.

As distracting spots of light, hands for Raeburn presented a composition problem most easily solved by avoidance: he would manage
so that they often fell below the level of the picture or behind some
object; or he would cover them with a scarf, or sleeves or drapery.
There were critics who believed that Raeburn could not paint
hands,[31] although at times — as now — he portrayed them eloquently.
The fingers of John James are made to speak, and the hands are made
to seem all fingers — thumbs and the back of the right hand being
hidden by position, and the coatsleeve being drawn almost to the
knuckles of the left. One finger disappears in the book, but the
others are accentuated in their strong but tenuously slender length.
They may indeed have been a physical characteristic of John James
Ruskin, inherited by his son.[32] But in this portrait, Raeburn uses
them as a more striking symbol than is the book itself: as accents of
light, they catch the eye, and there is no mistaking what such hands
— made to work creatively with brush or pen, or book — have to
say about the young man's aptitudes and interests.

The dark horizontal of the left arm becomes a base for unsymbolic
superstructure as horizontal lines find echo in the mobile mouth, with
hint of sullenness in discontent, and in the brows that sweep above

the darkly brilliant, brooding eyes. It is a finely chiseled face and figure, with luminosity through the treatment of white neckcloth, face and eyes, and seven fingers. A Northcote portrait of his father reminded Ruskin of Reynold's *Banished Lord*,[33] and Reynold's title would not seem inept if it were used for Raeburn's portrait. Seeking out the "essence," Raeburn possibly, or even probably, idealized the facts. Nonetheless he shows the facts that he perceived, and if he was right in judging them the most essential, this youth could not have gone too far astray had he been permitted to follow out his "hankering after Law." [34]

9

John James' Life in London

Instead of pursuing a career in law, John James was pressed to go to London, although at first he was apparently enjoying life in St. James Square: "I too well remember when I was leaving my own pleasant Edinburgh home for London — the charming but false light with which my Prospects of Life in London were gilded by my Father & Mother — I was told of high connections & people whose Houses would be open to me — & of Pleasures of being noticed by many a friend, whose notice was honour, but whose Houses or whose faces, eventually I never saw. . . ."[1] Thus once more one seems to hear an echo of his father's voice, worldly in unrealistic fantasy, able to sway Catherine into acquiescence, faithful to pursuit of that mirage — the social prestige to be gained by a successful merchant, except that now, more glamorously, a son will be received by the élite of England's capital, where social barriers could also prove more easy to surmount.[2]

John James was then "16 years of age," [3] he says, which means that he set forth sometime before May 10, 1802; other information indicates that he was not too far from seventeen. Margaret had been twenty-one since September 2, 1801. In all likelihood, if she was as yet within that home she would have shared the pleasant expectations without too keen an experience of personal loss. If so, her phrasing of old memories proved misleading when as a woman in her eighties she described her reaction to what was doubtless John James' next departure — he then almost twenty, she approaching twenty-five: "She talked to me once also about her youth," Lady Burne-Jones relates; "how she had gone as an orphan [sic] to live with her aunt, who was her husband's mother, and how her love for him had grown. The vain effort at self-reproach that she made, when she told me of a night of passionate grief and tears spent upon the floor of her bedroom after he had first [sic] left home and gone away to business in London, was a clue to her nature that I never let go." [4]

Henceforth, events become far more kaleidoscopic in effect as these two found their way, with hurt, along the paths that finally converged in marriage. For the most part, they were separated, although John James returned to Scotland twice for more than passing stay, and Margaret saw him now and then when she returned to Croydon to visit Bridget and her mother. Twice she helped to nurse him through an illness; when she was not briefly with him, she was living quietly, like an older sister, with his mother, at the very least for fourteen years.

His parents' fantasies about the life that was awaiting his adventure had a twofold basis. Catherine's brother, James Tweddale, was now the Collector of Customs at Wigtown and, thanks to £8,000 which he had received after the death of his uncle, Surgeon-General Adair, he had become a landowner in Galloway.[5] He had also married Margaret McTaggart,[6] whose brother John was "one of the first Colonial Brokers in London." [7] By policy, the firm of John McTaggart did not employ "Connections" of the family, but James Tweddale had armed his nephew with a letter in response to which Mr. McTaggart "promised to look out" for the "Situation" that no

one doubted his influence could easily obtain. In Galloway, he was
not without prestige, having purchased, in 1798 (for £33,000), a
Kirkcudbrightshire estate. In London, apart from his own firm, he
had a nephew who was a partner in Arbuthnot and Company, of
Madras, and a son who was in the London house of Richard Kymer
Company.[8] At the same time, John Thomas had arranged to have
John James work for Fyfe Druggist[9] without compensation and to
board, meanwhile, with the Mr. Moore for whom he was an agent
in Scotland.[10] Thus John James started his experience of what it
meant to try to get established as a London Merchant. "Had I fore-
seen the true state of things — I should have paused — " [11]

The first reality turned out to be life with people who evidently
did not fully realize his financial stress as he did unsalaried work with
hope deferred by promises. Mr. Moore, he states, "received me into
his House for Bed & Breakfast & Tea except Sundays as he was
Roman Catholic — " Perhaps therefore on some Sundays he had no
food at all: "In the Roman Catholics [home]," he noted, marginally,
"I kept fast days too often — for 15 months." Meanwhile, at Fyfe
Druggist, his experiences began to build up backgrounds which caused
him to remark, speaking of another youth: "His pride will meet with
more mortifications as a London Clerk than at Perth under the
worst mishaps." [12] For seven years, "I plagued Mr. McTaggart who
with all his Influence could not help me. . . ." But for the present,
as a start, "I lost 15 months waiting & went back to Edinburgh."

There he stayed for what he vaguely called "some months," which
may have extended into 1805. This might well have been the time
when he observed, with long-remembered indignation, extravagances
in the entertainment offered by John Thomas, and when, incidentally,
he sat for Raeburn. Now his father, evidently prosperous, imperiously
wished him to remain in Edinburgh, while making him aware that to
remain could only aggravate their personal difficulties, without re-
solving his own need to get established. It was doubtless, too, a
period of ripening friendship with Margaret as he turned to her for
"encouragement in all his plans of life." And one might even wonder
whether he now also turned to her for what his son would call
"sympathy . . . in all his flashingly transient amours" [13] — thus suggesting that there may have been some disappointment to which John
James and Margaret would refer in later years.

Garbling and confusing evidence which (as so often) he had only half-digested, Cook asserts that, in Edinburgh, John James "had first been a clerk in the house of Mr. Moore, an army contractor [*sic*], with whose daughter he fell in love. She was a Roman Catholic, and her parents forbade the idea of marriage. He then [first] came to London, in 1810 . . . [!]" [14] Yet clearly, apart from Cook, the Moores were Roman Catholics, and obviously John James had lived with them in London, and certainly they had a daughter — to whom Catherine casually referred in her letters, though nowhere is there any reference to John James' having been in love with Miss Moore, or any hint of an objection to Miss Moore's religion. Conceivably, when Cook had access to early family documents he may have found some letter in which the Moores, for religious reasons, objected to the idea of John James' marrying their daughter. If so, when John James went back to Edinburgh, perhaps he turned to Margaret for sympathy, as *Praeterita* suggests.

Meanwhile, family pressure upon Mr. McTaggart may have become urgent, because, during 1804 or early 1805, John James "was called to London to go into Amyand Cornwall Co a German & Russian House, Amyand a Bank Director." [15] ". . . had your Father been pleased with your settling in London," his mother would write, "it certainly would have been a great blessing or had it pleased God his temper had been such that you could have settled at home even then in his line you might have been respected and happy[;] at any rate your present situation is certainly a most respectable one and if your health is not impaired by fatigue one which must ultimately be of infinite service to you whether you continue in it or not — there certainly is a chance if you keep your health in London from the respectability of your house that you are placed in a situation which will enable you soon to make your fortune — " [16]

By now (1805), as John James would say in retrospect, the once great concern of Amyand Cornwall Co. "was in a dwindling wav but out of compliment to Mʳ. McTaggart perhaps — they paid mᵉ £100 a year. . . ." For three years or more, he paid £60 for board "in a miserable Lodging House";[17] then, his father's business having failed, he informed his mother: "I have got a Boarding by going a small distance out of Town — abt £7 a year cheaper — this is a consideration." [18] Three nights a week, he notes, he worked till eight o'clock, and twice a week until eleven, and until four o'clock

on Saturday. "It was a miserable Life to me." What he did as an
employee he does not state, but he emerged knowing how importers
managed a large business. For with Amyand Cornwall Co. he spent
four years at work without one holiday, after which, ". . . at the
end of my Seventh year in London I found myself with this £100
a year. . . ."

He was still "plaguing" Mr. McTaggart, who at last — probably
in 1808 — heard about an opening in the "great House of Gordon
Murphy Co," which chiefly dealt with South America and Spain;

. . . happily for me, an Irish Clerk, . . . embezzled the petty Cash & I was
asked if I would undertake the whole Custom House Business, including the
clearing out the Ships for they employed no Brokers[.] I agreed at once but
found some difficulty for every Vessel that came to us from South America,
brought packages or articles contrary to Law & there was perpetual detention
& memorializing the Treasury but I kept my troubles quiet & fought on[.]
I thought I could hardly get into a worse Scrape than my Predecessor who
had, by a Blunder, got a Cargo worth £270,000 — seized and the House had
£500 to pay to get her released — I was to have £150 Salary but they
were satisfied & gave me £200 — I was now 23 [1808–1809] & my Father
was by good living getting behind — I saw my only dependence was here &
I seized every opportunity to make myself useful —

And indeed he put to excellent use this first real opportunity,
gaining, in addition to the Custom House, the management of Cash
and, next, a lion's share of the Correspondence. Three "Princely
Partners" owned the firm — Sir William Duff Gordon, Colonel
Murphy, and James Farrell.

The Cash Keeper was a young man of some Property & he came to
business on Horseback at 11 & 12 oClock — I was out getting Bills discounted
by Gurneys long before this — I thought I could manage Cash & Custom
House too — I displaced [Sir] Williams Cash Keeper — our payments were
£½ million a year on an average — Every morning at 9 for a long time I
met the wily Duncan Hunter to exchange accommodation Bills — I recollect
a warm Saturday in July 1810 on which I had £28000 to pay & at 10 oClock
I had only £10,000 at the Bankers — I raised the rest among the Jews &
Quakers — Sir Wm D. Gordon managed the English Correspondence with
Jamaica & Cadiz but he was member [M. P.] from Worcester & much
engaged — I heard him one night say he would write on an important
Subject next day to Cadiz — I knew his Sentiments — I wrote a Letter at
night & placed it before him next day — He read & signed & from that day
I had Cadiz & Jamaica Correspondence to myself except when Farrell wrote
a Letter — They raised my salary to £300 & gave me Rooms in the House
with the Junior Partner where I also dined every day he was at home —
Having Cash, Correspondence & Custom House I was safe enough if the
House had been so —

Unfortunately, the "Princely Partners" were extravagant, and by now he knew enough to understand that the business could not much longer bear the strain. On one occasion they sent abroad "in the Reid Irving fashion £150,000 in Goods for which no Return came — Murphys Brother having gambled all away . . ." There was "pressure & a course of Discounts commenced — " Sir William's outside interest also proved expensive: ". . . no Business could stand £25000 for Contested Elections £20,000 for House & furniture in Portland Place, £10,000 for Jewels to Lady Duff Gordon on her Marriage. I saw the House was going down — "

At this point ("about 1813"), Juan Pedro (known as *Peter*) Domecq approached him. M. Domecq was one of Gordon Murphy's clerks. He was also "nephew to Haurie whose Wines Gordon Co Sold — but Hauries & Gordon Co quarrelled," so that Haurie wanted a new London agent.

Domecq associated only with the Foreign Clerks — of whom there were Six or Seven. He had not exchanged ten words with me in as many months when he called me aside one day & asked if I would join him & be agent to his Uncle if he could get the appointment for us, — I said only on Condition of Gordon Murphy Co giving me leave — When I named it Sir W D. Gordon said he had plans of his own for me — but I was determined to avoid connection with such extravagance[.]

John James by now had spent the nine-years-without-a-holiday which his son would make proverbial. And so "I asked a few weeks for my Health after being 5 years there and 4 in Amyands without a Holiday, & at Gordon's We were often till 12 & 1, oClock — owing to Sir W^m. coming from House of Commons to City — I left by Coach for Edin^g in 1813 after being on Counting House till midnight — totally exhausted & was Seized with Typhus fever at Ferrybridge — " He consequently stayed at home for care and rest: "I was at Perth till 1814 — [then] I joined Domecq as agent for Sale of Hauries-Wine — " [19]

10

Margaret's Life in Edinburgh, and Engagement

Through John James' nine years without a holiday, Catherine and Margaret had had their own anxieties. By 1805, they, too, must have known the dangers and the temper that had impelled John James' return to London. Catherine, with her fear of debt, could have felt little joy as she perforce participated in extravagance: no member of the family (one gathers) had the power to guide — or thwart — John Thomas as he thus managed his own life and theirs most recklessly. Margaret, almost a daughter from the first, must by now have watched and played her rôle with feelings touched by more than filial, or sisterly, concern: her Cousin John, at twenty, back from fifteen months in London, would have become rather more than an appealing high school graduate, and when Margaret, during her old age, revealed the quality of the grief which she had felt after John James "first" went away to "business," it seems likely that she had in mind a night she spent (in tears upon her bedroom floor) after he had left his home for work at Amyand Cornwall's.[1]

Good had come to her, of course, as she received Aunt Catherine's love while sharing household work. But soon, with her uncle "getting behind" through "good living," her aunt would tell John James how contented she would be if she could have but "a neat little House and Garden in the country" [2] — where Margaret's great love of flowers (which eventually would mean so much to Ruskin) could have helped her also to gain peace. Meanwhile she would have had her needlework and books (her son would blame the failure of her eyesight during later years upon the fine needlework she did during her young womanhood). Before she married, she would have spent all too many years in Scotland, with needlework and books perhaps providing insufficient compensation during the last nine.

Yet when Margaret left her aunt, to manage her own home, she had learned enough to take over her son's education, through which, as one part of his Scottish heritage, she beneficently channeled on to him what she had gained. For one thing, she had "obtained her perfect skill in English reading," as well as mastery of cultivated English speech. These were endowments which became inestimably important to Ruskin's work, he himself accrediting them to her "hard effort . . . through the years of waiting . . . ; effort which was aided and directed unerringly by her natural — for its intensity I might justly call it supernatural — purity of heart and conduct, leading her always to take most delight in the right and clear language which only can relate lovely things." [3]

Apart from metaphysical considerations, it might at first seem strange that Margaret had gained purity of English accent during years when dominantly she was hearing Scottish speech. Educated Scotsmen, however, did not wish to seem provincial, and Scottish linguists had led the whole movement which fixed "correctness" in English pronunciation: therefore, especially in Edinburgh, Margaret would have become aware of the importance of niceties in speech. The first dictionary devoted to the pronunciation of English (published 1757) had been written by a Scotsman, James Buchanan; and others had followed until, in 1791, John Walker's *Pronouncing Dictionary* "won immediate popularity, and exerted strong influence not only in the last decade of the eighteenth century but well into the nineteenth century. Edition after edition appeared." [4] James Boswell, as a well-born youth, had taken lessons from an English actor to improve his speech, after which, in 1761, he had attended "lectures on English elocution" delivered in Edinburgh by Thomas Sheridan. "Many Scots in public life were becoming ashamed of their native Doric, and Sheridan, a fanatical believer in the powers of elocution, promised to teach a correct English pronunciation." [5] At the turn of the century, when Edinburgh University provided as good an education as could be obtained in the British Isles (some would say *the best*), young Scottish gentlemen were likely to be sent to English universities if for no other reason than to learn to speak like well-bred Englishmen.[6] "Correctness in language, which in the days of De Foe and Addison and Swift was often regarded in fashionable circles as a mark of pedantry, by the beginning of the nineteenth century had become established as a test of cultivation. 'Vulgar expressions,' Lord Chesterfield had said, 'imply either a very low turn of mind, or low education, and low company.' 'A false accent, or a mistaken syllable,' says Ruskin in the new century, 'is enough, in the parliament of any civilized nation, to assign to a man a certain degree of inferior standing forever.' " [7]

Clearly, in her uncle's home Margaret was far more likely to have become speech-conscious than she would have, had she remained in Croydon; nor would she have been averse to making a "hard effort" to overcome native impurities of accent which before long, in England, would signify "low birth." And there in England, according to Ruskin's memories, she would be tireless in her effort when, together, they did their morning reading of the Bible, he pronouncing one verse, she the next. This daily reading always has been thought of, exclusively, as a religious exercise, as indeed it was, primarily. Yet it should also be remembered that excepting through his mother, the young Ruskin seldom heard cultivated English speech.[8] Consequently, apart from religion, it may not be surprising that when, regularly, Margaret did the stint of Bible reading with her son, she struggled to get accents "correctly" placed, until ultimately only the slight burr of his father's Scottish "r" remained telltale. For as her son stressed: ". . . my mother was both able to teach me, and resolved that I should learn, absolute accuracy of diction and precision of accent in prose. . . ." [9] And so in turn it chanced that Ruskin, largely home-taught by a tavern-keeper's daughter, would find it possible to mix with Gentlemen Commoners of Christ Church College unhandicapped in this respect — as in much else, although what matters most to English prose is that from his very infancy his mother would attune his ear to the beauties of a language "rightly" read and spoken.

She also gained a wide knowledge of English literature — far beyond the scope of the King James version of the Bible, as one of its chief treasures, although for her the Bible was naturally the Book of Books through which, her son believed, she chiefly made him what he was. Of literature more generally, he once wrote: ". . . the effort [she] . . . had made to efface the faults of her own early education, had really concluded in her being a most graceful and accomplished English scholar. . . ." [10] It may be that in making this assertion he exaggerated her attainment. Nevertheless, his mother had read widely and with a sensitivity that helped her to inculcate abiding interests in a way which from the first would stimulate and shape her child's creative power. If, in the beginning, special pressures, feelings of inadequacy, motivated her desire for self-improvement, one may feel confident, in view of the end result, that before long she enjoyed for its own sake the study which might also help to make her less unworthy (as she and others viewed the matter) of the cousin with whom she had fallen very much in love.

On guard against referring to her youth, she yet would sometimes speak of Dr. Thomas Brown, who may have helped her find her way from book to book. Only three years older than Miss Margaret, Dr. Brown, a bachelor, lived quietly with his sisters and his mother, although he had been known in Edinburgh literary circles since 1798. In that year he was studying medicine at Edinburgh University, although, in the manner of the place and day, he had literary as well as scientific interests. Erasmus Darwin's *Zoonomia* was then creating quite a stir, and Thomas Brown had consequently gained attention by publishing a critique of Darwin's theory. (Margaret would acquaint her child with poems by Erasmus Darwin.)

Then, in 1801, at the age of twenty-three, Thomas Brown had published his own poems, in two volumes. Two years later he was granted his M.D. and started practice as a doctor of obviously more than usual promise since, in 1806, he was taken into partnership by the well-known Dr. James Gregory.[11]

In every human contact, it is said, Thomas Brown revealed the "tenderness and quickness of his sympathy," [12] which went hand in hand with special interest in problems of psychology. After he became Professor Brown, this interest gave his *Lectures on the Philosophy of the Human Mind* their individual stamp. "There was something in his voice, his look, and manner altogether, when he spoke to the old or the unhappy, that is seldom seen," one of his close friends observed, writing a *Memoir*. "His art consisted in the kindness of his own heart, which found its way to the heart. And many acknowledged, that while they felt the highest respect for his character, they could speak with more freedom to him than to their own relations." [13]

The friendship of young Dr. Brown apparently meant much to Margaret, as well as to her son, whose *Praeterita* account of their relationship has led to curious conclusions about the position which the John Thomas Ruskins occupied in Edinburgh circles, and about John James' eventual attainment in self-education. Thomas Brown seems to have had more than passing social (or professional) contacts with the Ruskins, as one might expect, since his mother and Margaret's aunt were probably old friends.[14] Naturally, therefore, writing to John James Ruskin in 1807, Dr. Brown sent "regard" from members of his family and recalled John James as the "mere boy" who had turned to him as a "literary advisor." Nevertheless, until John James came back from London in 1803, Thomas Brown himself had been a student, and therefore could not conceivably have been what Ruskin would envisage when he wrote *Praeterita:* "one of the chiefs of the purely intellectual circles of Edinburgh" [15] — a statement which encouraged readers to infer that John Thomas and his family circulated socially within this flight.[16] Nor had Dr. Brown achieved such intellectual leadership by 1807, when, regretting his delay, he once more undertook to guide John James. His letter therefore cannot be considered what Ruskin fondly thought — "a testimony to the position [my father] already held among the youths of Edinburgh. . . ." [17] In actuality, of course, by 1807 John James was matched against the other clerks of London. And by 1810, when Thomas Brown finally attained his university Professorship, the John Thomas Ruskins, together with Margaret, had already left the city.

Meanwhile, however, the young Dr. Brown could not have failed to please Miss Margaret Cox by manifesting interest in her cousin, whom he now (in 1807) advised, specifically, to concentrate on Adam Smith and to attend lectures upon chemistry, with supplementary study of Thompson's or Murray's text and of Dr. George Gregory's *Economy of Nature*. This advice would not be fruitless, in the long run: both of Ruskin's parents, but especially his father, cultivated in their child scientific interests from his early boyhood, and surely Dr. Brown had helped to stress that science should not be neglected in a well-rounded education. More immediately, however, one may wonder whether John James Ruskin could have found much leisure for the study Dr. Brown so kindly recommended.[18]

About Margaret, we know only that she was in her twenties when she was seeing the young doctor and that her son recorded his own observations as a child, Ruskin having been no less sensitive than is the average child in this realm of impressions: ". . . I noticed that she never spoke without some slight shyness before my father, nor without some pleasure, to other people, of Dr. Thomas Brown." [19] We do not even know what Margaret looked like during her young womanhood. Catherine, John Thomas, John James, Jessie, Bridget have all survived in some likeness of their youth; but Margaret has come to us only as her son conceived her youthful personality — creating legendary character — and as Northcote painted her when she was forty-five.

Looking at that portrait while remembering John James' still later praise of her complexion, and her own vanity about her figure, one can readily believe that she was now what her aunt called "hansome," and that if, as she told Ruskin, Dr. Brown came frequently to tea, he came not solely for the sake of contemplating her Aunt Catherine. In fact, dispelling her shyness, he might actually have found attractive, as a human being, the quiet and serious girl so much beloved by the lady he called John James' "excellent" mother. Ruskin, though (as is the way of sons), would envisage Mother as a fair maiden never young, while Dr. Brown became the perpetual Professor, with his beard forever gray. By thus projecting a son's vision into the pages of *Praeterita,* Ruskin found it possible to reason, with grave absurdity: "That the Professor of Moral Philosophy [*sic*] was a frequent guest at my grandmother's tea-table, and fond of benignantly [*sic*] arguing with Miss Margaret, is evidence enough [*sic*] of the position she held in Edinburgh circles . . . [!]"; hence, building on *non sequiturs* and still further fashioning legend, he concluded that Miss Margaret "was, thus, at twenty [*sic*], in a Desdemona-like prime of womanhood, intent on highest moral philosophy, — 'though still the house affairs would draw her thence'. . . ." [20] Once, as Margaret would recall — with more regard for fact — she lost her patience when the cook ran into her with a black saucepan and dirtied her white frock. The cook, she must have added with amusement, sorrowfully replied to her expostulation: " 'Ah, Miss Margaret, ye are just like Martha, carefu' and troubled about mony things.' " [21]

There was sufficient cause for care as Margaret shared the life within that home. In February, 1808, Catherine had had to tell her son that his father had failed in business, whereupon John James responded: " — you could not think you was [*sic*] telling me what I had no reason to fear was the case — so far from that I believe now that your affection has led you still to conceal the real state of your affairs — I should be comparatively happy did I think a Thousand Pounds the Amt of your Debt — " [22] But whatever the amount, Catherine was assured that her son would meet the obligation: "I have received all your letters," she replied,

and with feelings which words cannot express. I have shed tears of joy over them I have prayed God to bless to prosper to shower down eternal blessings on the head of my child, and you will be happy my dr John for pleasant is your conduct in the eye of your Maker[;] it is a commandment given with promise, and the prayers of your grateful parents will be heard, and he will bless you with life peace and prosperity I know well your heart — to a good Father you would sacrifice everything — but to a father so unstable as yours (pardon the doubt) if I thought it hardly possible you could perform your duty at a price so dear. Who then shall say that any trial is sent in vain — from this trifling change in our circumstances do I not know the value of my son even surpassing my fondest hopes — and what mother would not yield all they had on earth to be so blessed as I am — [23]

John James had told her, too, that he would never marry but, instead, would make her life his care. Catherine, in response, could also offer comfort:

I entreat my Dr John that you will not give yourself one moment's uneasiness about me — I will at all events have £86 a year for life that your Father cannot deprive me of, and tho I could not live very splendidly in a Town on this, yet with a neat little House and Garden in the country, it would afford all the means of life in fullness to Meggy myself and one servant. You forget, my D^r how much a woman can do without in domestick affairs to save Money — a Woman that has any management at all can live with more comfort on £50 a year than a Man could do on two hundred. . . . Now my Dr John let me never hear a fear expressed on my account; there is no fear of me; make yourself happy and all will be well, and for God sake my beloved Boy take care of your health, take a good drink of porter to dinner and supper and a little Wine now and then, and tell me particularly about y^r new Lodgings. . . .[24]

Evidently Margaret had also volunteered to sacrifice herself, and thoughts of her are interwoven with Catherine's protests that she would not have her son become "an old Batchelor" in preference to marrying her ideal of a wife;

— believe me my beloved Child I feel the full force and value of that affection that could prompt to such a plan — dear as your society is to me it would then become the misery of my existence — could I see my Child so formed for domestick happiness deprived of every blessing on my account. No my Dr John I do not know a more unhappy being than an old Batchelor ((The friends of his youth must pass away, and instead of the affectionate wife and dutiful child to cheer his declining years he stands alone in the world surrounded by mercenary strangers, without a being to love or be regarded by)) may God preserve my Child from realizing the dreary picture — as soon as you can keep a Wife you must Marry with all possible speed — that is as soon as you can find a very Amiable woman. She must be a good daughter and fond of Domestick life — and pious, without ostentation, for remember no Woman without fear of God, can either make a good Wife or a good Mother — . . . I have thought more of [your wife?] than you have done — for I have two or three presents carefully [hoarded?] for her, and I have also been so foresightly as to purchase two Dutch toys for your Children in case you might marry before we had free intercourse with that country. ((Indeed my Dr John the greatest happiness I can look forward to in Life is to see you with an Amiable young Wife and sweet young Child I know that your mother will always have a proper share of your love. Then instead of being tempted to wish myself out of the world for destroying your happiness my days would pass in peace and tranquillity in witnessing your Domestick enjoyments.)) Who can say what I can say "here is my Son — a hansome accomplished young man of three and twenty — he will not Marry that he may take care of his Mother — here is my Dr Margaret, hansome, Amiable and good and she would not leave her *Ant* (I mean Aunt) for any Man on Earth." Ah My Dear and valuable children, dear is your affection to my heart, but I will never make so base a use of it.[25]

By the next year (1809) when, through his work for Gordon Murphy Company, John James first earned enough to "keep a Wife," he and Margaret became engaged. Margaret, propitiously, had gone to visit Bridget in Croydon, in July of 1809, and so (greatly to the comfort of her Aunt Catherine) had been at hand to nurse John James through a spell of illness.[26] He was ready, she was there: what more natural than that their engagement should have occurred at this very time? Howbeit, to mark the day John James gave her the gold chain which she wore when Northcote painted her. (Now in the Coniston Museum, it bears no date.) Then Bridget's next child, born in January, 1810, was christened with a flourish *James Tweddale Adair*. And if anything that Ruskin said about his parents' early life warrants credence, it would seem to be that their engagement lasted for *nine* years.[27]

From the first, her uncle's debts overshadowed Margaret's engagement. Probably because a son of good repute had promised to assume his father's obligations, John Thomas Ruskin did not go through bankruptcy.[28] In the beginning there had been some talk of a return to London — a move which Catherine did not wish to make, even though her son had offered them a welcome. "I doubt my love we must remain in Scotland for the first three years," she replied; "I fear your father could not look right to his business [as an agent] were he to live in England, but of this I will be able to speak in my next when I hear what he says if Mr. Moore continues your Father in his business I think he will wish to have it more carried into England and less in Scotland in that case the[re will?] be no obstacle to [our being?] in England." [29] But she would not have her son imposed upon:

As your Father seldom knows his own mind two hours together, you may still expect some hints from him about coming down, but do not trouble yourself in the least — argue the matter with good humour and talk with cheerfulness of your future prospects to him, and that will put it out of his head. I was obliged to send your letters to your Father —— I sent them with reluctance as I was afraid he might when with your uncle take some undue advantage of your offer to come down — if I find he has done so I shall write your uncle directly and tell him the true situation, and how your feelings have been wrought upon to make such an offer — the goodness of my child shall not be concealed[;] I care not what anybody thinks, so that your character be established.[30]

Among the creditors, Mr. Moore himself may have been the one chiefly concerned. For although at this point one can do no more than conjecture, the hypothesis that John Thomas had been spending money which he should have been remitting as an agent is supported by such facts as are available. These facts do not by any means suggest that he was an "embezzler" or even that he had been deliberately dishonest. And apparently he did not lose his work as an agent.

Nevertheless, he had manifestly been unbusinesslike, as well as most unwise, in conducting his affairs. Catherine obviously feared that Mr. Moore would not continue to employ him. At the same time, Mr. Moore had known John James Ruskin for more than five years, and by 1808 he would have also known the dependability and promise which John James was showing in his work. Clearly too, having learned about his father's failure, John James turned at once to Mr. Moore in consultation, and he knew what Mr. Moore was writing to his father at this time. "I have seen the letter of Mr. Moore that you allude to indeed my dr I do not conceal anything from you," [31] his mother gave assurance, in the letter thanking him for having said that he would pay his father's debts. And as late as 1817 — two years after John Thomas had become an invalid who could not attend to *any* business, John James wrote his mother, "I am sorry you should have deferred what you have to say on Mr Moores business because your letters come always to hand if I tell you where to direct and the more so because on the letter that comes after you do not remember the subject you defer, I beg to hear directly regarding Mr Moore & everything you have to say [address] to post office Leeds — " [32] It was during 1817, nine years after he had made his promise, that John James made his final payment on whatever sum his father owed — among others, it seems not unlikely, to an employer whose interests had been hurt by the headstrong ways and general mismanagement of John Thomas Ruskin. John James himself in later years would state, according to his son's version of his words, that he had paid those debts because he would never have it said that Ruskin's grandfather had "injured" any man.

Remaining in Edinburgh for almost two years after he had failed, John Thomas evidently carried on his work as an agent. ". . . you know my D^r we must be near a Post Office," Catherine wrote John James during the autumn of 1808, "else I could find delightful little houses entirely in the Country but that would not answer your Father's business. . . ." [33] In July, 1809, he still was carrying on that business — which then had taken him to Morpeth (Northumberland). From Morpeth, John Thomas forwarded to Margaret, who then was visiting Bridget in Croydon, one of his wife's letters, having added a brief note: "Miss Margreat Cock [*sic*] must bring this carefully down with her to Scotland, after perusing it Only Herself, this contains a good Hit or two for your poor Uncle, God mend him I say." [34] Catherine finally decided that they ought to move to Dysart, Fife, where, in October, 1809, Margaret was with John Thomas while her Aunt was supervising the removal of the household goods in their Edinburgh home: ". . . tho we have had two of Dod's men all day we have got little or nothing packed [the 'Dysart Sloop' — name illegible] is to sail on Friday morning so all must be on board tomorrow and please God my Dr Margt we will I hope be with you on Saturday or Monday. . . ." [35] Thus, definitively, the Edinburgh work and hope of almost thirty years had ended for John Thomas.

As to the engagement which had become involved in these events, it would please Ruskin to fancy that before it had occurred, there had been, for John James, "all his flashingly transient amours" to call forth Margaret's sympathy, and that she in turn had been delighted when her cousin chose her "much with the same kind of serenity and decision with which afterwards he chose his clerks." [36] Certainly it would seem, rather, as though John James had chosen her as meeting an ideal his mother had held up, perhaps with thought of Margaret; he surely found in her his mother and his sister, together with his wife. It was not thus, precisely, that he chose his clerks, although in Ruskin's comment there is (as we shall see) the sting of an unspoken yet essential truth.[37] Catherine's feelings about her son's engagement are reflected in a letter which she wrote in 1812: "When you left me, my Dr Margaret, I felt so unhappy that I thought I would not be fit for anything . . . I beg of you to assure your Dr Mother that I am very deeply sensible of her kindness and I hope in God that she will never have cause to repent of it. She may be satisfied that in this she is parting with you to friends who are truly sensible of your own worth and who will ever prize you as dearly as if you were indeed their own Child and that I have now the right to look upon you as my daughter is one of the greatest comforts I have at this moment upon Earth." [38]

For Margaret, with her heart won before she fully gave herself emotionally as John James' fiancée, there would have been deep happiness which, too quickly, suffering replaced. From the start she must have known that hers would be a long engagement, and she would have therefore been prepared to wait. Patterns of behavior do not often radically change, and in all her later life (as her son was well aware) Margaret steadfastly subordinated her own desires to what her husband wished [39] — she, in her important province, fully honored by his trust. Now, loving and religiously obedient both as foster-daughter and as a prospective wife, she would have shared, much more than "amiably," ideals which said that John James had no right to his own home so long as Catherine's home and his name were shadowed by the father's debts. Catherine's feelings and John James' character being what they were, immediate marriage had become but one more luxury with which they must dispense, making now a sacrifice which Catherine would accept. For Catherine once had sacrificed the very food her children needed, so intense was her aversion as she contemplated debt — and she seems always to have been most optimistic about the fortune which her son would swiftly make. John James desired to make the sacrifice for reasons more complex.[40] And Margaret — with her uncle serving as a foil — would never deliberately wish to have her cousin other than as he was: exemplary in prudence, caution, honor. Meanwhile she would be content to let him pay off debts in any way which he thought best, even though this meant that years would pass before he met the monetary obligation.[41] But what she was *not* prepared for were the changes in her uncle.

Leaving Edinburgh, she had lived with John James' parents in Dysart, Fife (Cook adds, "in a small house by the sea"),[42] after which they went to Perth — John James' destination when, seeking rest at the end of his five years with Gordon Murphy, he was stopped, somewhat beyond halfway, at Ferry Bridge (Yorkshire) by typhus fever. "My d^r Margaret starts by this night's coach," his mother responded to the news;

if she can get forward she will be with you on Tuesday Morning. I would have accompanied her but I am quite uncertain about your Father he has been waiting at Newcastle to meet you. He may be on his way home I might pass him on the road and were he to arrive and find me absent without any previous knowledge of your illness the shock would be too much for him. I have written to your Father by this post in case if letter finds him at Newcastle he will be with you on Tuesday too, but this is quite uncertain and the only relief I can find is in the prospect of Margt being with you, since I am deprived of that comfort myself it is the only plan that can give me peace. . . .[43]

Six days later she learned that John James would recover: "A day to be remembered while I have being O Lord let me praise thee. . . ." [44] But still she shared thoughts of her son with consideration for the husband who was waiting at Newcastle to hear from Margaret: ". . . he is much distressed[;] you must soothe him and take good care of him when he comes — " [45]

With Margaret and his father, John James reached his mother, to convalesce either in the home of Jessie, with whom her parents may have been living, or in some house which they had rented in that neighborhood. Two years later (by April, 1815) they are known to have been living at Bowerswell,[46] where John Thomas died. This house in 1827 was owned by a Perth lawyer, George Gray, who had by then become John James' and Jessie's friend. In 1828 he would become the father of Euphemia, who would become John Ruskin's wife. There is, in fact, a story that Euphemia was born in the very room in which John Thomas Ruskin finally died by his own hand.[47] Margaret, visiting "Aunt Jessie" in 1827, called on Mrs. Gray; but she would not cross the threshold of that home, Bowerswell having become for her a house of horror and of superstitious dread.[48]

It was, one gathers, after John James had returned to London to act as Haurie's agent and therefore after Margaret had been engaged for about five years, that her uncle started to oppose the plans for an eventual marriage. John Thomas had been so effective as he raised objections that once more he seems to have swayed his Catherine into acquiescence. These facts become apparent through a letter John James wrote his mother during April, 1815, just after Margaret and his father had been with him in London. Then, as they returned to Perth, he had gone to Stirling, beside himself with fear lest Margaret had gone into a decline of which the outcome, soon, might be her death. Why his father had begun to make objections, John James does not explain. Whatever may have been the reasons and however they may have been expressed, these were of the many days so deeply sealed in Margaret's heart that in the end her son could say: "I never heard a single word of any sentiment, accident, admiration, or affection disturbing the serene tenor of her Scottish stewardship." [49] This astounding statement also tells its tale about the mythical Margaret of *Praeterita*.

To return to the present — it was April 13, 1815, and John

James was in Stirling. "My dear Mother," he opened his appeal,

> I am most wretched about Margaret. It is now too late to disguise my feelings but I cannot survive the sight of Margaret in very bad Health my feelings are unfortunately too strong for all I have to struggle with — I conjure you as you value your Sons Life not to see Margaret fall into irrecoverable Illness — My Sister is well protected
>
> Can you not come to a comfortable House in the Suburbs of London for a time rather than that Margaret should be sacrificed — my Father told me this morning She was in a very bad way besides her affection for me — I cannot exist under my present anxiety — Indeed it is cruel to let Margaret sink in this way — We must do something to save her or you must lose me — When my Father spoke kindly to her this morning — I saw by her bursting into Tears that she contrasted his words to her with his words to me in her absence which I acquainted her with as I keep nothing from her — poor thing she thinks that these attempts may operate on me & deprive her of all hope — oh my dear Mother as you have always loved me will you & my Dear Father assure Margt that you have both become reconciled to our union & be happy — or will you see her & me both fall sacrifices to this anxiety — Neither her constitution nor mine are fit for a long struggle — I have already said that if it leads to eternal Ruin I will fulfill my engagement with Margt — I hope my Dr Father will therefore no longer cause us any uneasiness — I have much to do — & unless Margt be well I can do nothing I shall not soon recover the shock I received on Monday
>
> Oh if you expect me to make some efforts to keep the family united — do not let her on whom my Life depends sink under my Father [*sic*] & your own displeasure — The state of our [wo]rldly matters requires that we should not oppose each other in other things to add to the distress — I beseech you to write me how Margt is — She got well in England & my Father says she is now in a bad way — She is dying & no one cares — Write me in Glasgow & remember my Dr Mother that Margts fate and mine are one — I feel this to day but too strongly — My dut[iful] & affect love to my Dr Father Your most dut & affec Son J.J.R.

Having folded his letter, John James added: "My Dr Father If you open this will you do me the kindness to say to Margt that you will never say any more against our union — you surely cannot wish to see her sink into her grave & if she sees you oppose our wishes she will / Your Dut & afft Son / J.J.R." [50]

It does not seem, however, as though John Thomas blessed this engagement after he became insane, with Margaret as a nurse.

11

The Founding of Ruskin,
Telford, and Domecq

Returning to London in 1814, John James had taken the last steps toward what can seem, in retrospect, an astonishing achievement for someone who began as an unsalaried clerk and thenceforth made his way through self-dependent effort. First he severed his connection with Gordon Murphy; the parting was with good will despite his joining M. Domecq to sell the Haurie wines which Gordon Murphy had been handling. Some time later, when Sir William acquired interests in Spanish wines, as a competitor of Haurie, he asked John James to be his agent — "So I was selling for two antagonistic Houses but I gave up Sir W^m. as I could not well keep both." [1] Meanwhile, getting under way, he realized that as Haurie's agent he was once more connected with a firm on the decline: ". . . Hauries shipments had sunk to 20 Butts — there was no established business in this — " [2] Nevertheless, at least for some time he continued to sell Haurie wine with vigor: "I went to every Town in England most in Scotland & some in Ireland, till I raised their exports of 20 Butts to 3000 . . ." [3]

In 1815 he had established, in the City, the offices of Ruskin, Telford, and Domecq, with 11 Billiter Street becoming their address because this property was owned by Mr. Henry Telford. Again John James had turned to the McTaggarts, this time to discuss the problem of how to raise capital, "for Domecq & I had only £1500 between us — " [4] If he himself had saved a little money, it could well have been with hope of some investment which might make it possible to clear away, in bulk, those debts . . . and would that one could know how large a sum he needed to gain such freedom! Mr. John McTaggart, Sr., had died in 1810 and had been succeeded by his son, in whose judgment John James had become a good financial risk. Henry Telford was a nephew of the deceased Mr. McTaggart, and had not only property but also money to invest. Scarcely less important, Mr. Telford had traits of character which could make him seem, from John James Ruskin's point of view, a sound venture as prospective partner.

After Mr. Telford's death in 1859, John James would write:

... we had been Partners for 44 years without a word of dispute or even a difference of Opinion. He was the Kindest hearted & most gentlemanly man I almost ever knew & is greatly regretted by many friends — As a Yorkshireman he was very fond of Horses & a first rate Judge — He enjoyed the Turf but this never gave me one moments thought or uneasiness for his Character was such that I felt it like an Impossibility for Mr Telford ever to Commit the Slightest Imprudence. He was never married & his Brother Mr. C. Telford of the Stock Exchange will chiefly benefit by his Death.[5]

"He was a perfect type of an English country gentleman of moderate fortune," Ruskin comments;

unmarried, living with three unmarried sisters, — who, in the refinement of their highly educated, unpretending, benevolent, and felicitous lives, remain in my memory more like figures in a beautiful story than realities. Neither in story, nor in reality, have I ever again heard of, or seen, anything like Mr. Henry Telford; — so gentle, so humble, so affectionate, so clear in common sense, so fond of horses, — and so entirely incapable of doing, thinking, or saying, anything that had the slightest taint in it of the racecourse or the stable. ¶ . . . Between him and my father there was absolute confidence, and the utmost friendship that could exist without community of pursuit. My father was greatly proud of Mr. Telford's standing among the country gentlemen; and Mr. Telford was affectionately respectful to my father's steady industry and infallible commercial instinct.[6]

As a partner, Ruskin adds, Mr. Telford's chief function was to conduct routine business when the Ruskins went off in his carriage on their long holidays.

As to M. Domecq, he returned to Spain to supervise the family vineyards in or near Jerez (originally, "Xeres") — a town not far from Cadiz, great shipping port for Spanish wines. Behind him was the reputation of his father's firm, established in Jerez in 1730 — "the oldest in the Sherry Trade." [7] His home, Macharnudo Castle, was in a countryside "where the vineyard has gained such great celebrity that there prevails a common belief in the inferiority of every other site of wine cultivation." [8] As *Xeres,* Jerez had given name to white wines once called *sherries,* later *sherry.* According to *Praeterita* (and here, cannot one catch some echo of the father's voice?), M. Domecq's vineyard was on "the most precious hillside, for growth of white wine, in the Spanish peninsula. The quality of the Macharnudo vintage essentially fixed the standard of Xeres 'sack,' or 'dry' — secco — sherris, or sherry, from the days of Henry the Fifth to our own; — the unalterable and unrivalled chalk-marl of it putting a strength into the grape which age can only enrich and darken, — never impair." [9]

Through the early years of John James' firm, it must have helped that Peter Domecq was Haurie's nephew, though before long "the quarrels of Haurie & my late partner Domecq gave us constant trouble — " [10] Independently, M. Domecq engaged in competition which by the time of Ruskin's youth, and love for M. Domecq's daughter, had gained him greater wealth by far than any known to John James Ruskin, who, lending a pamphlet to his friend George Gray, observed: "It may be a Spanish Exaggeration to say as on the pamphlet that he made a fortune in 2 years but with this I had nothing to do — Domecq had share of my London House but I had no Share of Xeres profits. I kept clear of Foreign risk . . ." [11] To greatly win or greatly lose, with a fine Spanish flair, was scarcely suited to the temperament of John James. "My father," Ruskin comments, "saw that he could fully trust Mr. Domecq's honour, and feeling; — but not so fully either his sense, or his industry; and insisted, though taking only his agent's commission, on being both nominally, and practically, the head-partner of the firm." [12]

To John James' whole endeavor and achievement what mattered in the long run was the quality of the wine which M. Domecq made from grapes of Macharnudo vineyards and dispatched, with pride, for British distribution. In later years, when John James consulted him about a rumor that overselling had caused deterioration in the product, M. Domecq replied: "You desired me to say something about our shipping. I wrote the following at the time on this sheet of paper:

'Every time we have exceeded our usual shipments, the idea of overship-ment has been insinuated into the minds of the trade; but it is well known that Mr. Domecq's stock of old sherries has been from the beginning by far more than adequate for the exportation he has ever had hitherto, and that his powers have increased in every respect instead of diminishing, by the constant exertions of his house, and by the addition for a long period of years of the produce of his immense vineyards, situated in the first-rate grounds of the country, the real advantages of which no one will dare to question. It would be besides a very short-sighted policy for any Sherry House to strain its shipment beyond its means, while you cannot expect to be moderately remunerated for your great exertion and capital, but by a long continuance of the business, the profits of which have ever been greatly exaggerated, etc. etc.' [13]

Either just before or shortly after the partnership was formed, John James went to Spain to observe with his own eyes those vineyards which his son would call the "main capital" of his father's firm.[14] The estate of Macharnudo would almost certainly have been more or less neglected during the long years (1808–1814) when Spain had served as the main battleground in the Napoleonic War; Peter Domecq's first work might reasonably have been one of restoration, as John James' son suggests in a poem written when he was sixteen and wished to celebrate his father's birthday. It may be that this poem, *M*^r *Domecq* / *Conducted to Machernudo* [sic] *by the Genius of Wine,* tells the tale of what John James himself had seen and then described to Ruskin as a boy, and assuredly it echoes John James' admiration of his partner's gift for making

sherry — with eventual reward of wealth and of considerable
prestige, in France, for M. Domecq's family.[15]

In "a dream" which yet was "no dream," the boy wrote, he had
found himself in Spain, where these vineyards lay before him:

6

Alas, and it filled me with grief
To see there no promise of fruit
For the insect was eating the leaf
And the worm was at work on the root.
Neglected for many a year,
Unpruned and untended they hung
The leafage was withered and sere,
And the vineyards looked sad in the sun.

7

When lo, oer the vine covered plain
Came one before whom the earth smiled,
The clusters blushed red as he came
Uprose, and empurpled the wild
He laughed, and he laughed loud and clear,
His temples were crowned with the vine
I rejoiced when I saw him appear,
I knew twas the genius of wine.

8

He walked on the hills, and the wreck,
Of the vineyards at once was renewed, oh,
For he brought with him Mr Domecq,
And pointed to wide Machernudo
He spoke and the hills laughed to hear,
And this one he said, shall upraise,
The fume of white wine far and near
Till all nations shall speak in its praise

9

He cometh, to be the erecter,
Of vaults upon vaults by a wink.
He comes, to make wine into nectar
He comes, that the nations may drink
Then England rejoiced on that day
Full loud was the noise and the rout.
There was raised such a thundering huzza,
That I woke in the rush of the shout.[16]

12

The England John James
Ruskin Did Not Know

In England, the scene was almost ripe to yield an enterprising Sherry Merchant excellent harvest. The year 1805, when John James began his salaried career, had been marked by Nelson's final triumph, at Trafalgar, over French and Spanish sea power; his realization of the desire to be himself a Merchant fell within the year of Waterloo, followed by a treaty that gave forty years of peace. From his position in two great commercial houses (eventually handling correspondence with Cadiz) he had watched Wellington's six-year struggle with Napoleon for the mastery of Spain. By 1807 — when Napoleon invaded

Spain — European markets had been lost because of the need to institute a blockade; not surprisingly, in view of international events, the exports of one Spanish house had declined to 20 butts of wine a year. With the Napoleonic Wars (outlasting twenty years) supported by the mercantile community, the anti-Jacobinism which had been the breath of John James' youth pervaded the world of businessmen still loyal to Tory leadership and bitterly intolerant of Whigs — who, as in the Edinburgh John James knew, could be made to seem seditious rabble-rousers so long as war beclouded the atmosphere.

Merchants, together with their employees, had sharply felt the pinch and the uncertainties of war. (One thinks of John James with his static £100 a year.) ". . . would the strain [Trevelyan asks] prove too much for the English middle and lower orders, whose business, employment and real wages were subject during these terrible years to vagaries of war prices and war markets? . . . Many merchants, like poor old Mr. Sedley in *Vanity Fair,* were broken by the sudden opening and shutting of markets, or the rise and fall of war prices." [1] The great export-import houses sought, and often found, new markets in the colonial empire, or they might lean more heavily on South American and other such connections. It was better, through those years, to have been learning than managing a business — as, with his imprudence, John Thomas Ruskin may have had sufficient cause to know.

There is no hint, however, that John James Ruskin recognized the more impersonal implications as he unfolded his personal narrative:

Now only observe — the first House Amyand Bank Director failed — the second House that was the greatest Spanish House of the day — failed & to amuse you — I send on loan & for careful return — a pamphlet setting forth the Situation of the third House [Haurie], I engaged with — you see that but by a kind of Luck I escaped from £100 a year in a decaying House & again by an unlooked for offer of Domecq from a falling House & after all when my House began we had to struggle against the Embarassment of the third House — . . . I run the risk of tiring you sadly with this History but you can only see by such details that what people call a nice pleasant Business has not been arrived at with little trouble & that in fact I am more like one navigating on a plank saved from the wreck of several larger Vessels — and patched up at length into a little craft for myself — [2]

He would have fair sailing as he navigated with superior skill, concentrating on the day-to-day routine of his endeavor while typically remaining unaware of the wider or the deeper meanings of events within the province under his command, though this became a province he himself believed he fully comprehended. Speaking of the "firm of which he was head partner," Ruskin remarked, with more than literal exactness, that its business was conducted "in a small counting-house on the first floor of narrow premises, in as narrow a thoroughfare. . . ." [3] These extremely narrow premises remained, until he died, the center of John James Ruskin's business life, in all its energy and thought.

By now he may have read his Adam Smith; yet he did not desire free trade, and his belief in laissez faire would not increase his sympathy for Whigs, not even after many other merchants gave support to the Reform Bill which enfranchised the mercantile community. His chief concern — to master practicalities of business method — had left him unprepared to understand or even to envisage as an encompassing reality, the transformations which were making England the world's "great workshop," where wealth would soon be overflowing the coffers of the middle class. For his countrymen were now achieving two of their far-reaching revolutions in their own characteristically undramatic way — under "settled government," as changes slowly broadened down "from precedent to precedent." By thousands, nameless individuals saw and sensed (although they did not intellectually grasp) what had been happening as the French Revolution and Rights of Man stirred the "friends of order" to dominantly counteroratory (most statesman-like in Edmund Burke), and as a nation united gave its conscious thought, and energies deliberately organized, to international events and all that made for victory at Waterloo, fit climax to the last dramatic Hundred Days.

Quietly, the while, in their own countryside, Enclosure Acts had multiplied through the last half of the eighteenth century as larger landlords gathered up small farms, and wastes once freely used for pasture, and fields once tilled by village folk in common cultivation. This development had scarcely begun to wane while John James was working in his counting-house: between 1793 and 1813, there had been 1,883 Enclosure Acts.[4] (Analogously, a century hence, farmers would be dispossessed on the great plains of the United States . . . to gather Grapes of Wrath, with individual bewilderment unalloyed by personal relationship with local landlord as, *en masse,* they too would seek the manufacturing centers, or seasonal employment at slow-starvation wage.) Thus, bit by bit, the Agrarian Revolution overthrew *ancien régime* of England. This Revolution had bounteously produced a crop of Displaced Persons as the English yeomen found themselves, in part, a sacrifice to more efficient cultivation; for landlords could now afford to introduce the new machinery and could even help prepare the way for Darwin by experimentally improving flocks and herds. (Rustics no less found their "iron servants," as Ruskin came to see it. "They had their goblin to pipe for them. They walked in procession after their steam-plough, and their steam-plough whistled to them occasionally in the most melodious manner it could.")[5] During twenty years of war, this change in the economy had filled the need to provide a rapidly increasing population with an increased store of meat and grains until the trading ships once more could freely visit worldwide ports, to return (especially, at that time, from Russia) with the life-sustaining gold of wheat. As this threat to the landed gentry materialized with peace, there were some months of highly publicized debate before the Tory Parliament (still overwhelmingly elected by the landed gentry) enacted the Corn Laws to protect the price of home-grown wheat regardless of the price of insufficient bread.

Meanwhile, in the cities, here and there, men first heard the hum of wheels and click of shuttles, steam-driven, in small and scattered factories. There was magic in these rhythms as they grew more intense in always concentrated although ever widening areas. By 1808, Blake had seen the mountaintops of Lancashire clouded by smoke from the mills. Thus Ruskin's "Storm-Cloud of the Nineteenth Century" gathered, darkly overshadowing the lives of those who sought the typhus-ridden slums. Sewage seeped into cellars packed as sleeping-quarters; opium stilled the cries of hungry infants who, too soon, would have to earn a wage. "Children under ten years of age, often only six or even only four or five years old, had to work twelve, sixteen, seventeen, even eighteen hours a day."[6] Crouching in mine tunnels, they helped the women dig and haul the coal; in the factories they did piecework, breathing air that bred disease, or served the new and dangerous machines.

Here there was no crash of guillotine to arouse conscience as the Industrial Revolution gathered sinew; nor was the public startled by awareness that what were truly frightful "slave camps" had developed, as — before Karl Marx — Charles Kingsley, among others, tried to show;[7] nor would such camps be dramatized by diverse devices deliberately implemented for mass-murder. It takes time to learn to see; it takes time for any civilization to grow hardened in and to brutality that can more and more elude the individual imagination as it crosses international boundaries through the ever-changing clasp of blood-stained hands. To his nation, John Ruskin seemed hysterical in 1863 (as perhaps, to some degree, he was) when he could not escape his own somewhat belated vision of an England drenched with blood.[8]

Yet it had all been there in first unmitigated flush of working order by the time that he was born — the year of Peterloo; the year when Shelley asked, in "Song to Men of England,"

> . . . wherefore plough
> For the Lords who lay ye low?
> . . . .
> The seed ye sow, another reaps;
> The wealth ye find, another keeps;
> The robes ye weave, another wears;
> The arms ye forge, another bears.

Blake, in a different mood, had already voiced what would become, with startling exactness in the replica, Ruskin's apperception and response as, like Blake, he pledged the power invested in his spirit to service of the Christ and of the England he envisaged, more than half a century later:

> And did those feet in ancient time
>   Walk upon England's mountains green?
> And was the holy Lamb of God
>   On England's pleasant pastures seen?
>
> And did the Countenance Divine
>   Shine forth upon our clouded hills?
> And was Jerusalem builded here
>   Among these dark Satanic mills?
>
> Bring me my bow of burning gold!
>   Bring me my arrows of desire!
> Bring me my sphere! O clouds, unfold!
>   Bring me my chariot of fire!
>
> I will not cease from mental fight,
>   Nor shall my sword sleep in my hand,
> Till we have built Jerusalem
>   In England's green and pleasant land.

There had been nothing in Ruskin's early experience to help him, from the first, to see England's green and pleasant heritage in relation to the political and economic scene in its reality. Yet this was the reality at the core of which John James Ruskin had been working from before his twentieth year, with endless opportunities for thoughtful observation after he began to tour great towns to sell his Haurie wine. Of course he did not wholly fail to recognize the wonder of the new machines and of mass production: now and then in later years he would take his child to see some "manufactory" (carefully selected), and in one of Ruskin's boyhood Red Books, when they were planning out a Tour of England and making notes on sights to see, John James entered under "Derby": "Famous silk mill on River built on Model from Italy[.] 100,000 movements by a single wheel. It turns 3 times in a minute & makes 73,728 yds silk each time." [9]

By then, Carlyle, in light of his own Scottish heritage, was brooding over what he saw as "Signs of the Times"; while Mill had been trained to understand the new political economy and, without undue reverence for rank or dread of Mobs and Liberty, the contemporary struggle for enfranchisement. Soon the streets of London would resound to the tramp of Chartists' feet.

Nevertheless, when Ruskin stood upon the doorstep of his life's work, he saw England as well as Scotland (region he first loved) as though his nation had remained not the actual England which pre-dated the Industrial Revolution but, rather, a land which was suffused by the atmosphere and attributes of feudalism and of Romantic poetry and landscape art — a land not far removed from that world which John James Ruskin had experienced during youth and then had re-experienced as actualities appeared, transmuted and transposed, in the novels of Sir Walter Scott.

In his later work, after Ruskin at last recognized, with shock, characteristics of the civilization which had been around him from the start, he would view Political Economy — curiously enough, but not inappropriately — as an adjunct of Moral Philosophy, even as it had been taught, distinctively, in those great days of Dugald Stewart and of Professor Brown, at Edinburgh University.

13

The Adult Personality of John James Ruskin

In his achievement and in personal relationships (notably with his wife and son) John James would show himself to be a product of those Edinburgh days so marked by loss as well as gain. Within his personality, the chief loss had been caused by inroads on his self-respect: aptly, he himself would call "want of self-respect" his "malady"[1] — a malady often manifested in adult behavior reminiscent of his earlier experience. His son once wrote: "You have of late often referred to 'your pride' — as if it were only an amiable weakness, to be indulged in almost meritoriously. ¶It has been the torment of your life, and a bitter and continual injury to mine." [2] For John James had emerged a highly egocentric individual, with an adamantine will. And it was not in spite of his own background that from the very start of his career this strong-willed, egocentric man had been dominated by a veritable passion to excel — this passion ever driving him to prove himself "superior" because, in inmost heart, so far as one can judge, he could never quite convince himself that somehow he was not, in actuality, "inferior."

This inherent conflict may help to explain his first remarkable success. In 1805 there must have been many a faithful, reasonably intelligent, ambitious London clerk who, ten years later — when war gave way to peace — had not become the head of his own House. When, in highly egocentric retrospect, John James told George Gray the story of his early years in business, he could casually refer to his success as due to "a Kind of Luck." [3] There was, in fact, more "Luck" than he himself apparently would recognize, in his having started out as the head of his firm just when he did. Of course it took good judgment and persistently hard work to raise the sale of Haurie wine from 20 to 3000 butts a year. But it also demanded a lot of customers who could afford to stock depleted cellars with good wines, including M. Domecq's sherry. As it chanced, such customers were less and less confined to the landed gentry, although this gentry remained prosperous, thanks to the Corn Laws.[4] Scarcely less, it required a high protective tariff against French goods: this tariff for many years had made French wines so much more expensive than those from favored Portugal and Spain that it was commonly believed "that French wines were naturally our aversion, and port and sherry our taste." [5] It is therefore not surprising that John James should have disliked the notion of free trade and, by 1848, should have observed: ". . . but the day for that [20 to 3000 butts] is past — I have now twice the trouble for a fourth of my former business." [6] During the next year, still more specifically, he remarked that wine agents "swarm like Locusts in Scotland & have filled that Country with rubbish — but we find the Wine Trade reduced 50% since Whigs & Free Trade — & other evils have fallen on the Country." [7] Nevertheless, when he died he left a fortune closely equivalent to one million dollars (in itself, in some sort, a token of superiority) — whereupon it was Ruskin's pleasure,

and not undeliberate comment upon John James' values as a merchant-father to disperse, within fifteen years, this part of his heritage.

That this fortune was not due primarily to luck, John James was
the first to know. Without John James, the firm of Ruskin, Telford,
and Domecq would not have lived. With John James, other partners
could have replaced Messrs. Telford and Domecq in a combination
which would perhaps have proved less happy while being nonetheless
successful. John James had trusted to no luck when he gave himself,
on joining Amyand Cornwall, to realizing what Dr. Adam had held
up, for "the lower orders," as "the duty and the comfort of making
one's own fortune, and relying on oneself alone." Nor had he trusted
solely to the virtues Dr. Adam praised, though Dr. Adam's eloquence and kindness had found in young John James a personality
prepared for lifetime practice of the "greatest care," "untiring diligence," "exemplary patience in the discharge of his duties." [8] Nevertheless, referring to the faithful Henry Watson, who became head
clerk of the new firm, John James himself would write: "I have a
Clerk most amiable, most honourable — who writes a good Letter —
he has been Clerk 31 years & never in my Life will be more & yet
I could not have hindered him from being Partner long ago —
had he so *determined*." [9]

Making this remark as part of a whole argument, John James
was momentarily content to overrate the actual ability of Henry
Watson. What matters is that John James had brought to his own
work not only adequate ability but such absoluteness of intent to
make his mark that no demands upon himself could prove too great.
Thus, through prolonged hours of dedicated service, unto nine years
without a holiday, he would first demonstrate that he was much
superior to other clerks. ". . . there may be a whole Staff of fine
youths in a large Colo[nial] Brokers," he observed. "It is not merely
the pleasing an Employer[.] There must be brought an unconquer-
abel *Will* & Power to Seize upon that which a hundred Competitors
are Striving to Keep from you —" [10] This passion to outdo competitors (and what was this if not the drive to show himself, each
time, superior?) became an invaluable contribution to his firm, to
which, as Ruskin said with multiple, and wonderfully laconic, under-
statement, his father brought "only his good, and extremely strong
will." [11]

In partners he could not well have been more blessed. Was not the one "a perfect type of English country gentleman" — "so gentle, so humble, so affectionate," and, one might add, so reassuring in accepting him with genuine respect? When John James went away on business, Mr. Telford occasionally would pay his wife the courtesy of a morning call;[12] when he had a son, Mr. Telford would bring a birthday present; when he went off to enjoy a holiday, Mr. Telford, "kindest of hearts & most gentlemanly man I ever knew," would provide them with his gentlemanly carriage. It must have greatly solaced John James Ruskin to have had, as "my Partner," Mr. Henry Telford — driving in to business from his country home; absolutely safe, but an English Squire in his love of horses.

M. Domecq was no more, in any sense, a rival than was Mr. Telford. Rather, far away in Spain, he lived in Macharnudo Castle, a feudal lord of vineyards. In later years, when he lived in Paris, he had what John James Ruskin accurately designated many "high Connections," including his son-in-law, the Prince de Bethune, who, with the Princess, sometimes stayed at Denmark Hill, these guests always welcomed by the senior Ruskins. His partnership with two such men, each one soundly practical in business, could not but have helped John James Ruskin serve their mutual interests with a minimum of stress.

The story of his relationship to his daily associates is, however, rather different, although complementary, inasmuch as in his routine work as head of the firm he managed his affairs so that he guaranteed himself incessant demonstration of his personal superiority. As an otherwise efficient man of business, he had one striking idiosyncrasy: in selecting clerks, he consistently chose men whose limitations were conspicuous: helpers who, because of their natural endowment, could not hope to win their way into any partnership, either with him or with another. Ruskin tells the story without asking *why* — and with good humor, in *Praeterita,* though he could be infuriated by his father with his clerks:

The chief fault in my father's mind . . . was his dislike of being excelled. He knew his own power — felt that he had not nerve to use or display it, in full measure; but all the more, could not bear, in his own sphere, any approach to equality. He chose his clerks first for trustworthiness, second for — *in*capacity. I am not sure that he would have sent away a clever one, if he had chanced on such a person; but he assuredly did not look for mercantile genius in them, but rather for subordinates who would be subordinate forever. . . . my father's clerks were, in many ways, utterly unfit for [their business]. Of which unfitness my father greatly complaining, nevertheless by no means bestirred himself to find fitter ones. He used to send Henry Watson on business tours, and assure him afterwards that he had done more harm than good: he would now and then leave Henry Ritchie to write a business letter; and, I think, find some satisfaction that it was needful afterwards to write two, himself, in correction of it. There was scarcely a day when he did not come home in some irritation at something that one or other of them had done, or not done. But they stayed with him till his death.[13]

Meanwhile, carrying home to Margaret his tale about each lapse, he had found a way of demonstrating no less regularly to his wife than to himself his own superior ability. And so what wonder that from day to day throughout the years he kept these clerks and went on counting off this rosary? There must have been some great need to fortify a major province of his life against old undertows of suffering and insecurity.

It was not enough, however, for John James to go on seeking and receiving, in his home and office, such reassurance that he was superior — even he, in his little craft, patched up from once-great ships that came to grief. Looking back, he could see the wreckage of another Merchant Craft, put together after years of effort and then conducted recklessly. His own humiliations had gone hand in hand with his father's ways of making and of spending money. Personally escaping the work of a tradesman (except perhaps as a child in his father's grocery), he nonetheless had shared the stigma, and had then accepted the fate of Merchant — whereas, had his parents heeded his desire, he might by now have been a Lawyer and, therefore, in his own right (according to the standards of his youth), a Gentleman. When he was in his sixties, he still remembered what professional careers had signified to his own boyhood, and he still harbored the old feelings: "I confess I should rejoice to see George [Gray, Jr.] get a Living *Professionally* — At the end of a not unsuccessful mercantile Life, I feel now that I would rather have been a very moderately endowed Edinburgh or Perth Lawyer than a very considerable London merchant." [14]

Since he had had to be a merchant, he at least had been a better Merchant than was his father. The epithets *extravagant, untrustworthy, reckless, hot-tempered, unsteady, impious, unstable, unmindful of his family* express, with overlapping shade, a composite judgment of John Thomas provided by Catherine and John James in spite of all their love. As a climax, from *their* point of view and in their inmost heart as they participated in the disgrace of overwhelming debt, the father's conduct would inescapably have led to an unspoken epithet most darkly overshadowing: *dishonest*. John James' repudiation of his father's ways, with all that led to mounting shame, need scarcely be spelled out in antonyms which would characterize this component in his drive to be Superior. At home and business, all his life would demonstrate the personal antithesis; and then, in famous epitaph, his son would place the spotlight: "He was an entirely honest merchant. . . ." [15]

He had been rather more than merely honest when he decided not to marry until he cleared away the load of debt. His son thought that he had spent nine years without a holiday, postponing marriage, to meet this obligation. It was not quite thus. He would not marry Margaret until the debts *were* paid, but he had spent four years without a holiday before he faced the need to pay those debts. That need, moreover, had been self-imposed, in further token of the intangible realities which drove him to excel. When Ruskin analyzed the problem, he could not conceive that there might have been a time — years before his birth — when he had not been at the center of his father's thought, or that his father might have had a mother whose "pride" meant more to him than Margaret's. Nevertheless, Ruskin knew his father well, and more than once protected him by not publishing passages which had been written for *Praeterita:*

Very certainly, had there been what is rightly called "love" on both sides it [the nine years' engagement] would have been impossible, and as things were, it was by my present judgment, unwise, and even wrong. That a son should pay his father's debts, if able to do so without injury to the force and happiness of his own life is alike reverend, and dignified in him, yet even so, not a part of his duty, but a grace beyond it: neither was it as a duty that my father did it, but for his own, nor perhaps less for my [*viz., his?*] mother's pride — most of all for mine [*sic* — eleven years before his birth!] "John shall never hear it said that his Grandfather had injured any man." As before noticed, his friends, as a body, — one or two perhaps with motives of their own — dissuaded him from the chivalry of such sacrifice to honour: without admitting them to be right, I very clearly see, at this distance of time, that the state of feeling in which my Grandfathers debts were paid had much in common with that in which my mother's relatives were kept out of the house. [16]

It is but another way of saying that, beyond the normal line of duty, John James was driven into demonstrating his superiority, this time as a Man of Honor.

As a personality, he had begun to pay the price when he first gave himself, without reserve, to gaining his chance for a career as Merchant. In fact, the John James who had sat to Raeburn might almost have smiled could he have seen his son, in turn, repudiate the ways of his father, together with the riches that had been accumulated at a cost to humane values. The first nine years best express the remorselessness of his demands upon himself as he channeled his libido into work, but from the age of twenty until he married at the age of thirty-three, he had spent himself in a concentrated drive to beat immediate competitors in relatively narrow work. True, the John James who must make his own way into partnership had begun by seeking further guidance from Dr. Thomas Brown. But how much strength of body or of thought or spirit could he have had to give to study of political economy, or to science, philosophy, poetry and art? Granted, John James remembered how "in the winter of 1811–1812 in a big ugly room, in a court off Fleet Street," he had heard Coleridge lecture,[17] and occasionally he found time to read Sir Walter Scott, and doubtless also Byron. But how much stimulation could he have found in his companions, or in the caliber of thought and of endeavor which overspread his world of lodgings in or out of counting-house? Who *could* have lived the life to which John James gave himself, without stultifying personal development? Subordinately, with stifled protest, the young man Raeburn saw was somewhere there, to be reanimated by a father's love and to seek self-realization in the person of a gifted child who would respond, with unforgettable intensity, to a devotion which was no less absolute than it was, in essence, egocentric. But the man who fathered Ruskin's childhood was in point of view and interests little different, as a human being, from the John James who had left his Edinburgh home. And although the need to demonstrate his own superiority against an ever-nagging doubt would scarcely have been different if he had studied law at Edinburgh University, the end result, in John James' stature as a human being, might well have been more satisfying to all of them than were the earnings from which he gave so generously — while still accumulating a fortune — as the merchant-father. There was a modicum of irony in Ruskin's last pronouncement on his father's life — "here lies an entirely honest merchant," as Raeburn's John James Ruskin would have known. And there was, too, a certain basis of reality for the absurdly childlike feeling John James kept on experiencing — that he might, himself, have been a Gentleman.

By the time he turned to his own business, his family believed that he had permanently hurt his health because of those nine years without a holiday.[18] When he at last returned to them for rest, they had nursed him through his convalescence from what Catherine called "that terrible [typhus] fever." [19] Forever after, he was ailing. And yet until his last two years of life he was never seriously ill,[20] except once (according to his son) through a few days of danger from an attack of erysipelas.[21] One also hears about a rupture,[22] about his sometimes stringent observation of a diet,[23] and off and on about the usual colds. Nonetheless, apparently with nothing much specifically wrong, he is referred to in *Praeterita* as a man "much broken in health," [24] while through the years his son expressed, in letters, sympathy evoked by illness, without ever having cause for serious anxiety or even an occasional alarm. Furthermore, John James' span of life was long; he died when he was seventy-nine, at work until the end, and ending work with a dramatic fitness. He had spent the evening upon two more of those most admirable business letters which once had added Correspondence to his management of Cash, and he was "very proud" of them. As his son adds — "Well he might be! they were monumental works of a master hand in its craft, splendid in writing, faultless in expression." [25] Therefore, still manifesting old compulsions, he had sat up till one o'clock, waiting to read these letters to his son, who never quite forgave himself for having found them such a mighty bore that, being tired when he got home, he praised the excellence of only one before he failed his father's need by letting his attention lapse. John James merely discontinued reading and said good-night. By morning he was ill; after several days of fever and delirium, his death took both his wife and son "wholly by surprise." [26]

Margaret, meanwhile, from the first days of marriage, had lavishly expended watchfulness and worry and attention on her husband's state of health,[27] which also always deepened Ruskin's sense of guilt when he went away, alone, for work and change. It may be that this was veritably part of the price they paid for broken health resulting from those early years without a holiday. But it seems likely that the explanation of such nagging illnesses, not interruptive of unflagging work, may have been more complex than they believed, and not unallied to needs which likewise shaped John James' more general conduct of his life.

He assuredly had served such needs when he became engaged to Margaret. As Ruskin said, had there been on both sides "what is rightly called 'love'" their long engagement would have been impossible. For her part, Margaret was enough in love to make him fear that she was dying when her faith that he would marry her was shaken. The trouble was that he must, and could, subordinate to more imperiously personal demands her love for him, together with his own great and not unloving need of her.

This dependence was twofold, with both of its sources apparent in his past. In Margaret he had found someone who was in many ways a counterpart of his own mother while yet she differed from his mother in that she was but a tavernkeeper's daughter and hence "inferior" to him as the Son of Catherine, born a Lady. But Margaret's birth from lower class was not without advantage. Branded by her backgrounds, according to the values into which her husband had been trained, she was graced by due respect for what his circle had to offer; by her desire to make good use of all her opportunities for self-improvement; and by her self-abnegating admiration for his brilliance and achievements. To some who, as Ruskin said, "could not bear, in his own sphere, any approach to equality," these traits would have been most telling in appeal. Home, no less than office, was also John James' sphere, this sphere in time becoming so peculiarly meaningful to him that he would never leave it to be the house guest of a friend.[28] Within his own four walls he felt secure perhaps not least because, as *Praeterita* attests, it was clear to all of them that to his wife and to her family he was superior. Upon one level, this could be a source of shame, as when at last he brought himself to show his son the place of Margaret's birth.[29] But it was more important that by having honored Margaret as his choice, he had provided (of course not too deliberately) what could be daily balm within his home for his own pride where it had been most deeply hurt. To this extent, John James had chosen his wife, as Ruskin said, much as he would choose his clerks — looking "for subordinates who would be subordinate forever." And Margaret — not only as his fiancée but also as his wife — could in some ways carry her subordination, at times entailing that of others, to a remarkable extreme.

At the same time, John James needed Margaret much as he had needed his own mother — trusting her, in her devotion both before and after marriage, as completely as he trusted his mother; knowing, *feeling,* her to be like his mother, from her daily habits to her inner life.[30] It would have been indeed appalling had he lost his Margaret — more concerned about his needs than about her own; faithful, patient, so long as he must be away to do his work; ever waiting sympathetically to welcome and, if need be, to soothe him on return. It was behavior such as any child is likely to expect from an indulgent mother and which many egocentric men, in our day as in his, expect of a wife to whom they have transferred the pattern of a mother-son relationship. And even though one cannot bear equality in one's own sphere, one nonetheless looks up to mother, often heeding governance while feeling her to be more wise and pure, in all ways more unblemished, more spiritual, than oneself. Therefore it is not incongruous that Margaret, while being made to feel inferior, should likewise have been given love marked by profound respect and reverent trust. As to the "in love," it might have been much better both for her and for her son had it been possible for John James to have given that also. But individuals are what they are, as they carry onward their own past. John James, with his ego and his insecurities, was one who could bestow devotion, even to excess, while remaining, ultimately, a human being who could give himself without reserve only to that central individual — himself.

14

Margaret's Years in Perth

While John James worked with twofold drive
— an excessive need to demonstrate superior
ability, now as head of his own firm, and the knowledge that his
own consent to marry was contingent on his making money —
Margaret was passing days weighted by a special burden of anxiety.
For in 1815, not long after accompanying her to London, John
Thomas Ruskin had become insane.

Here again, however, we have key information scantly supplemented by details. Nonetheless, there is a letter which John James
evidently sent his mother after she had written that his father was
no longer of sound mind. Answering with shocked distress, John

James told her that his father must not be committed to a public institution. Money, he explained, was scarce but would be provided so that John Thomas could be cared for in a private asylum should he prove unmanageable or dangerous. But John James stressed his hope that his father *could* be cared for in their home.[1] Two years later comes the only other direct glimpse of what evolved. Catherine then wrote a friend: "In answer to your kind inquiry, Mr. Ruskin, I am sorry to say, has not been in a good state of health these two years. He is better just now thank God, but quite unable to do any business and still subject to fits of low spirits. . . . My son has not been so stout since he had that terrible fever. He is doing remarkably well in business and was so fortunate as to form a connection with one of the most respected houses in Spain . . . this dear Son has given me 200 a year since the first of his fathers illness." [2]

Six years before, leaving Edinburgh after his career had foundered, John Thomas Ruskin had been only forty-eight years old. Thereafter, John James may have had to help his family through contributing from his salary, although until John Thomas became incapacitated, he evidently supplemented Catherine's little income through his earnings as an agent: as late as 1813 he was in Newcastle, presumably on business. Yet there is no reason to believe that he had found his way into a satisfying life as he tried to follow up connections doubtless made while he was still an "Agent" who could cherish the illusion of prosperity. True, his son had spared him the humiliation of becoming legally a bankrupt; but both before and after the retreat from Edinburgh — as his own Vanity Fair — John Thomas would almost inevitably have known the type of pain best understood through "poor old Mr. Sedley."

Another miniature, painted after he reached middle age, shows a face from which the old decisiveness has disappeared, as bewilderment and self-reproach ("God mend him I say") helped time to slacken lines which once had spoken drive and self-assurance.[3] And yet the bitter herbs which it had been his portion to consume had not destroyed his earlier attractiveness, though he had been transformed. For now beneath his whitened hair, the young man's dash and arrogance of spirit seem to have been chastened into an indeterminate gentleness which could stir compassion. Here, too, one finds a blue cravat prophetic of the one which Ruskin chose to wear, in later life, as a distinctive article of dress, as though he would make manifest identities and sympathies which may not have been entirely clear even to himself. There had been preserved, however, for his contemplation this likeness of his mad bad grandfather, whose blue eyes, accentuated by his blue neckcloth, John James and Margaret, it may be, could subsequently bear to speak of when they briefly dissipated their reserve. But it could not have helped a father's pride or self-respect that when John James established Ruskin, Telford, and Domecq, "It was an article stipulated that neither [he nor Mr. Telford] should have relations in the House." [4]

Speculatively, one seeks to put together the main events as John Thomas would have experienced them. From the first, if no more than a straw should rightly indicate direction of the wind, he had not been happily receptive to the thought of Margaret's becoming his son's wife: in 1809, when forwarding the letter which his wife had sent to Morpeth, he would have been more natural as well as kind, had he addressed his niece as *Margaret,* in preference to "Miss Margreat [*sic*] *Cock"* — the only indisputable appearance in the "Catherine" *Correspondence* of a name which could be used with a hidden sting.[5] And then it was not long before Aunt Catherine became protective as a wife: in 1813, her anxiety about her son, stopped at Ferry Bridge by typhus fever, had gone hand in hand with her concern about how John Thomas would react to this alarm. As she then wrote John James, she would have gone with Margaret to nurse him except that, if her husband returned home and found her absent, "without any previous knowledge of your illness the shock would be too much for him." Margaret, too, must "soothe" and "take good care of him" if he should travel to John James[6] — that only son who was so dear, and so important to them all.

Nevertheless, some months before his breakdown John Thomas was evidently once more acting like his imperious self as he undertook to save this son from a deplorable engagement, only to discover that in John James he now had met more than his match in strength of will. Hurt by his own failure, he must have found it comforting that in the chief commercial center of the world *his* Son had reached the goal which he himself, as a "Merchant," had briefly gained in Scotland's capital. Still harboring the values fostered by his Edinburgh life, did he think that John James ought to make a better marriage than the one which would come to them through Margaret

Cock, all but penniless in her own right and socially discreditable, as a tavernkeeper's daughter?

Judged by the impressions made on Ruskin and communicated through *Praeterita*, Margaret left her uncle's home convinced that she was socially inferior; and there are other indications that during her last years in Perth she had been made to suffer. It scarcely could have helped her cause that Ruskins who were highly undesirable as relatives still misbehaved themselves in Cheshunt; that Bridget had become the wife of the so-called "chief baker" of their town; and that her mother went on managing *The King's Head*, within ten miles of London, until the very spring when John James Ruskin founded Ruskin, Telford, and Domecq.[7] Then too, as his instability increased, John Thomas Ruskin may have lost his power to approve, objectively, a union between his son and a daughter of his sister.

He finally succumbed to an illness marked by spells of deep depression after a trip to London taken, it would seem, while his son's firm was being founded with the stipulation that no relatives would be employed. And it would be very easy to translate into the personal experience of John Thomas the generally accepted psychiatric theory that depression is a condition in which people punish themselves for a failure to have lived up to some ideal image of what they should have accomplished. The aggressiveness originally devoted to the acquisition of some objective in the outer world is turned against their own ego. The failure may obviously entail some frustration by the outside world, but the depressed person feels that it has been his fault that he did not overcome whatever obstacles have been in the way of self-fulfillment.

Thenceforth, adding hurt to hurt, John Thomas could have made his disapproval of Margaret's engagement keenly manifest, especially if, without command of reason, he disapproved for reasons surcharged with his own frustrations or with feelings about incest, even though ostensibly such feelings were not part of Protestant tradition. By April, 1815, the engagement clearly met his bitter opposition; before the end of June he had lost his sanity; in October, 1817, to cap "the serene tenor of [Margaret's] Scottish stewardship," he killed himself under circumstances which apparently left Margaret feeling that to marry her beloved cousin she must disregard the wishes of the dead.[8]

By then (1817) she had been living for at least two years in

Bowerswell,[9] a house which John James Ruskin is said to have sold to his friend George Gray, although a search of title-deeds reveals that this property was never owned by any Ruskin. There have been, all told, on the same plot of ground, three houses known as Bowerswell, of which the first, a modest home, was built at the beginning of the nineteenth century. In 1815, when Catherine, Margaret, and John Thomas are known to have been living there, the original owner sold the house to a James Henderson, who during the next year sold it to the Ruskins' second (possibly their third) landlord, a Mr. Patrick Taylor, who in turn disposed of it. Finally, seven years later, in 1827, it became the permanent abode of the family of George Gray.[10] It was a "pretty villa," one of the Grays recalled, and made a comfortable home until, with children frequently arriving and investments making money, George Gray had it torn down and replaced by a more commodious Bowerswell, which was reconstructed after being almost wiped out by fire in 1892.[11]

The first Bowerswell, however, was amply large for three adults, while for Catherine and Margaret it had a garden of not unhappy memory, together with a wide command over all the beauty of the countryside surrounding Perth, each Bowerswell having been built upon the Hill of Kinnoull.[12] In later years, Euphemia Gray would write Rawdon Brown that through the smoke of his cigar her father "very often" said, out "on the Terrace looking at the Grampians the Tay and our four Inches of Perth, that we look down upon, 'Do you know Phemy I think Mr Brown would enjoy a day or two here Eh!' "[13] In outward circumstance, therefore, the days and months, into the years, which Margaret spent at Bowerswell could not have been too desolate.

This was the period which left her intimate with Jessie, who lived near-by, "at Bridge-end, . . . [which] had a garden full of gooseberry-bushes, sloping down to the Tay. . . ."[14] And it was in Jessie's home that Margaret, seeing the joy that children bring, also sharply realized how ephemeral such joy can be, as she would not forget when she had, herself, an only child too anxiously to cherish. Ever deeply fond of children, she would tell her boy about the cousins who had not lived long enough for him to know, speaking of them so that into his old age Ruskin would remember little Patrick (in *Praeterita* called Peter), whom Jessie lost when he was eight years old, having made him "especially the corner-stone of her love's build-

ing. . . ." [15] This child "died of a decline on 9th. January, 1818" [16]
— only a few weeks before Margaret was married; and Margaret
vividly remembered the details of that pathetic illness.[17]

During the preceding year, Jessie had lost a Catherine, who died
when she was four: Margaret spoke "eagerly always about Catherine, who had been her favourite." [18] At the time of Catherine's
death, Jessie had also lost another daughter, Ruskin thought, for he
remembered how his mother told him that one night, when Jessie
could not sleep, "she saw the door of the room open, and two spades
come into it, and stand at the foot of her bed. Both children were
dead within brief time afterwards. I was about to write 'within a
fortnight' — but I cannot be sure of remembering my mother's words
accurately." [19] The second of this pair was probably the little girl
who had been given Margaret's name. Although there is no official
record of her death, Sievwright found it mentioned on the tombstone
of her parents: "Margaret died 9th. January 1817, aged 6 mo." [20]
On January 14, 1817, Catherine is officially recorded to have "died
of measles." [21] There was also a Helen, who died three weeks after
she was born. Before long there would be a Janet, likewise known
as Jessie, whom Margaret's child would have as his special playmate
while visiting in Perth — until she died when only eight. Thus
through the grief of Jessie and the love they shared, Margaret (already in her middle thirties) had cause enough to know that whereas
children do not always easily come, they can all too easily go.

At Bowerswell, there was "Old Anne" — as yet the young Anne
Strachan, to help them care for the invalid. Next to his father and
mother, Anne ("my father's nurse, and mine") became the human
being in whom Ruskin's life would be most deeply rooted in realm
of the emotions. Like many Scottish servants of that day, she had
joined the family as a "bare-foot child," [22] doubtless coming from
some farm. Ruskin says that she was then fifteen, which means that
she must have entered Catherine's home in time to help them nurse
John James after he returned to Perth with typhus fever.[23]

As Ruskin tells her story (not seeing, one would gather, how it
might cast light upon his mother's), Anne "had a natural gift and
speciality for doing disagreeable things; above all, the service of a
sick room. . . ." [24] Including four years in Perth, for fifty-seven
years she worked for Margaret, who seems, however, never to have
overcome the handicap of having started as the younger mistress, if

one may think of Margaret as a "mistress" in her Aunt Catherine's home. The young Anne apparently did not. Still, after Margaret was married, Anne followed her to London, where Margaret could not have hoped to find an attendant more devoted to her husband and her child, and to their household ways.

Nonetheless, Anne likewise had a

speciality for *saying* disagreeable things. . . . And she had a very creditable and republican aversion to doing immediately, or in set terms, as she was bid [*i.e.,* by Margaret?]; so that when my mother and she got old together, and my mother became very imperative and particular about having her teacup set on one side of her little round table, Anne would observantly and punctiliously put it always on the other; which caused my mother to state to me, every morning after breakfast, gravely, that if ever a woman in this world was possessed by the Devil, Anne was that woman.[25]

Beyond the humor, does it not, in its own way, help to tell the tale of early, and persistent, attitudes toward Margaret? Anne "was passionately devoted to her master and his son," Lady Burne-Jones recalled; but ". . . I once heard Mrs. Ruskin address the aged dame in a tone such as one might use to a tiresome child, whilst Anne retorted with a want of deference that was certainly not the growth of a moment." [26] In contrast (though Ruskin does not specify in deference to his father), "poor Anne remained verily servile in soul all her days. . . ." [27]

To complete the sketch, we need only add what Ruskin called his mother's "epitaph" on Old Anne's death, Margaret having reached the age of ninety: " 'She always persecuted *me*. . . . I think, of all the evil spirits I ever saw, she has acted worst to me. I blame myself entirely.' (Pause . . .) 'I ought to have sent her away three months after she came.' " [28] By then had Margaret grown so old that she could momentarily forget what had been her own position in her uncle's household? Or was she thinking of Anne's arrival in their first home in London?

From the first, however, she and Anne had had a community of interests which could help to hold them close to one another. Now, exposed to the peculiar strain which goes with watching, caring for, an insane member of one's family, she could not but have seen with gratitude Anne's will to serve and her talents as a nurse — "so that she was never quite in her glory unless some of us were ill." [29] When Anne went back to Scotland, perched outside on the rear seat of Mr. Telford's carriage, it would be with song that she first saw the "blue hills" of her land — "my Father's land," as her charge felt, with patriotic pride.

But there would be ambivalence in Margaret's heart when she returned to Perth, to seclude herself with Jessie and seem "curiously unimportant" [30] while their children played beside the Tay. Even in her own home Margaret could not quite escape her memories of that illness of John Thomas. Soon her son would prattle, writing to his father: "Mama is continually ((talking to me as if she had made the farthing bargain)) saying that I shall weary out my brain ((or brains))[.]" [31] It was always she who tried to hold him back through a quiet routine which would not overstimulate. "But papa," the boy would characteristically lament, with characteristic cheer, "alas I have just been up to mamma and she says not to write such a long letter to you so goodbye my own dear papa / Your affection[ate] & happy son. . . ." [32] Awareness of some need to guard his "brain or brains" would find expression in more than one of Ruskin's letters years before he deliberately directed rational power, together with resources of great courage and endurance, into a conscious struggle to prevent the recurrence of psychotic episodes.[33]

This awareness may have been instilled in early years merely because he had shown such precocity that any mother might well have tried to hold back such a child — which with John Ruskin was not easy, since he fully realized with what intense delight his father would receive every composition placed on the paternal altar. It would have been strange, however, had Margaret never given thought to hazards which might be intensified through a marriage of first cousins. And even if she was not troubled by such worry when she saw in her boy the physical resemblance to John Thomas Ruskin as a child, she nonetheless left Bowerswell with poignant knowledge of the fact that "brains" — and more particularly, Ruskin "brains" — could go awry. "((We restrain his poetic Efforts,))" John James would supplement, taking credit where none was due. ". . . If the Almighty preserves the Boy to me I am richly blessed but I always feel as if I *ought* to lose him & all I have — " [34]

Waiting to be married, living in an atmosphere which must have made her feel that even at long last, whatever service she might give, she would not be wholeheartedly approved as John James' bride, Margaret would have been something short of human had she not experienced resentments, though these resentments she would not have readily released. It seems peculiarly appropriate that she should have turned with special love to the 119th Psalm — the series of acrostic songs which read like a composite cry that God teach His servant who has been betrayed, despised, "ashamed" (sometimes translated "put to shame"), to remember His commandments and heed that Law which is His Word. It was a Psalm which she made her son commit to memory, despite the inordinateness of its reiterative length, so that it became "to my child's mind, chiefly repulsive — " even as in later years it was to him "of all the most precious. . . ." [35] He by then, as Margaret now, knew such trial as long ago had led to an afflicted people's chant of theme from song to song: "O that my ways were directed to keep thy statutes! / Then shall I not be ashamed, when I have respect unto all thy commandments." — "Remove from me reproach and contempt; for I have kept thy testimonies." / . . . / "The proud have had me greatly in derision: yet have I not declined from thy law." / . . . / "Trouble and anguish have taken hold on me: yet thy commandments are my delights." — "Consider mine affliction, and deliver me: for I do not forget thy law. . . ." And so what Ruskin called "one Agonizing Prayer" [36] goes on and on. "The 119th Psalm," Margaret once wrote her son, "is not, I think much read by you[.] I am sorry for it[;] to me it supplies daily prayers, confession, comfort, instruction so much more than I can give words to — You will I feel sure come to be thankful for it and to love it as I do — " [37]

No less suggestive is another glimpse we catch of the effect on Margaret's health of the atmosphere in which she lived — one would infer, from John James' letter to his mother (with the postscript to his father), not long before John Thomas lost his last hold on self-command.[38] Now it is her son who briefly draws aside the curtain, writing to a wife who had been enduring the strain of an unconsummated marriage — likewise devastating to her pride and engendering a fury of resentment as yet all but unexpressed (there would be time and ways enough for that) and scarcely recognized in its intensity (unforgiving) even by herself. Those still were days when women, trained into "obedience" as a biblical command supported by the social mores, might mysteriously go into "a decline," as they sought to stifle protests (if one may generalize, perhaps too sweepingly) by disciplining into godliness their rebellious adult selves. Sometimes, as with Elizabeth Barrett, relief from strain could seem to bring about miraculous recovery, or, as with Harriet Martineau, mesmerism worked strange cure;[39] sometimes, with strain alleviated (as it soon would be for Margaret), less serious symptoms might persist in other form. Meanwhile, those who helped to cause a thus destructive conflict would watch and worry, turning here and there, futilely enough, for medical advice. So it was that Ruskin, beginning the second year of his marriage, sought to understand an increasing weakness in his wife after she had spent some months in Bowerswell, a change which they had hoped would be beneficent — he meanwhile hard at work upon the continent, accompanied by his parents. Answering one of his wife's letters, he commented: "You say my mother is strong — but if you were to pass one of my mothers nights, you would remember it for some time — often she has to sit up in bed for hours together with pain all over the body: when she was your age she was weaker than you — literally, once, unable to lift a cup to her lips: she was made strong by being made to rub furniture." [40] — From whatever angle his remark is considered, is it not hair-raising? Yet who, one hundred years and more ago, was helped by understanding that such illnesses are, all but indubitably, psychosomatic?

Through the time of suffering which thus could drain her strength, as also through the days of her recovery, Margaret would have had for genuine support the quality of her religious faith — doubtless reinforced, as she revived, less by her rubbing of the furniture than by evidence that she could trust the steadfastness of her fiancé. Like him, she was limited in her development, despite what she had gained; and these limitations would help her to preserve, unmodified, the creed her son, in time, bitterly (and often unforgivingly) assailed. This creed, however, did far more than shape her reasoned and dogmatic understanding of the ways of God — else she could scarcely have communicated to Ruskin a living faith based upon a narrow creed with which, despite his analytic mind and scientific knowledge, he could not break for almost forty years.[41] It is "a great truth respecting human mind and nature," he would say, ". . . that, whatever the truth or error of the tenets represented by any superstitious creed that has had power in this world, the persons now familiarly accused of imposture did with their entire souls and hearts believe in them." [42] Thus Margaret indeed believed that her Bible was not only a record of miraculous events and of the early history of mankind but also a means of personal communication with her God. For her, articles of creed could serve as signposts to experience that transmuted formalized beliefs into personal awareness of spiritual realities and of truth "transcending all thought, and ordaining all conduct." [43] As soon as he "could conceive or think," Ruskin says, his mother's "unquestioning evangelical faith in the literal truth of the Bible placed [him] . . . in the presence of an unseen world. . . ." [44]

"Seek and ye shall find. . . ." One need not doubt the earnestness and constancy of Margaret's search. But one well may wonder what it was that shaped her personality and interests so that, shortly after she was married, she selected from the Bible the list of chapters Ruskin memorized as a child — chapters through which, he said, "she established my soul in life": [45]

Exodus	chapters	15th and 20th.
2 Samuel	"	1st, from 17th verse to the end.
1 Kings	"	8th.
Psalms	"	23rd, 32nd, 90th, 91st,
		103rd, 112th, 119th, 139th.
Proverbs	"	2nd, 3rd, 8th, 12th.
Isaiah	"	58th.
Matthew	"	5th, 6th, 7th.
Acts	"	26th.
1 Corinthians	"	13th, 15th.
James	"	4th.
Revelation	"	5th, 6th.[46]

Copying this list as it was written in his mother's hand, he evidently omitted Deuteronomy 32,[47] wherein Moses, offering his last prayer as leader of the Israelites (*they* about to enter promised land, to him denied), dwells upon Jehovah as God-of-Wrath at His most vengeful. Thus it was a chapter as appropriate for Margaret, in her Evangelicism, to have included as it was for Ruskin to have ignored when he published her selections as his most important heritage. That of the twenty-seven chapters she selected, he omitted only one as, to him, not permanently valuable, may be sufficient token of her knowledge of the Bible, and of her taste and acumen in judgment.

Of the published list, the first twelve chapters are the most provocatively interesting, except for Exodus 15 (the delivery of the Ten Commandments). Like Exodus 15, the last fourteen are such as might have been selected by almost any devout Christian of that day.[48] In contrast, the first part of the list would seem to represent a far more personal selection. Here, too, there is no chapter which in its own right is not conspicuous for meaning and for beauty — perhaps sufficient explanation of its presence. Yet, by no means everyone who had full knowledge of the Bible would have selected this group of chapters, out of all of the remaining riches, as those which he himself most deeply treasured. Why, then, these for Margaret?

In answer to a legitimate question, is it perhaps too fanciful to suggest that if one reads these chapters with thought of what would appear to have been happening to this woman during her years of residence in Scotland, they can most unexpectedly become an allegorical expression of her personal experience? For if Margaret — allegorically in the role of an Israelite — had long been made to feel inferior while "wandering" in a "foreign land" and had often been humiliated, if she had been promised a home with the man she loved and then with suffering had waited long for this her land of promise, if she had felt that she herself was sinful and that these trials were but chastisement imposed as a lesson by a God of righteousness to whom she trusted still for the fulfillment of her hope deferred, and finally if she felt that the "proud" had met most fearful punishment (He is also God of Wrath) whereas her prayers had been attended so that deliverance was effected and promise *was* fulfilled until with joy her cup was overflowing — if all this, then how easily, searching Scriptures for a personal message (as was the ingrained habit of her son as well as the habit of her sect), she might in truth have found preëminently significant the chapters she selected. One would by no means press this point. Nevertheless, it looms almost too discernibly to ignore, inasmuch as there is not one chapter in the first half of her list which, in light of what was apparently her own experience, would not have shared with Psalm 119 a beauty, helpfulness, and wonder that had become for her intensely personalized.[49]

To her, analogously, the unseen world could manifest itself in other ways. Thus it happens that in later years "superstitions," "feelings," "prejudices" might color her reactions to events, conspicuously those associated with her Scottish backgrounds. When her son's engagement was in prospect, her husband "ascertained," he said, that "to Scotland & most especially to Perth Mrs. Ruskin had an insuperable dislike — she has had so much misery herself in Perth that she has quite a superstitious dread of her son connecting himself in the most remote degree with the place — "[50] As to attending

her son's marriage in dread Bowerswell, her husband would explain
to Mr. Gray: "You expect that Mrs Ruskin & I should come
to Perth & nothing can be more reasonable — I at once acknowledge,
we ought to come; but with Mrs. Ruskins feelings & prejudices I
scarcely dare contend. . . ."[51] All about her, through these years,
were the superstitions of the Scottish countryside, though these were
doubtless much less real to her than to Nurse Anne, who would more
tangibly transport to London "her little library of Puritan the-
ology."[52]

Yet it was not eighteenth-century rationalism or skepticism, in
Edinburgh garb, that Margaret took to London for the child to
whom every Scottish glen would soon be "more or less enchanted . . .
with a general presence of White Lady everywhere,"[53] and who
throughout his life would have regard for "omens" and repeatedly
would search for evidence to support belief in ghostly presences —
he so curiously and intensely, both through training and in temperament a combination of the rationalist and mystic reflected not only
in his "age" but also in his parents, despite their being relatively
commonplace humanity. When Margaret entertained her boy by
reading Scott aloud, one can feel very sure that she was not un-
sympathetic to what Ruskin praised in later life as the stories in
which Sir Walter "freely accepts, and affectionately realizes, the
supernatural imagery consecrated by Scottish tradition,"[54] even as
he would condemn as "the deadliest sign of [Scott's] approaching
death . . . the form of incredulity which dictated to his weary hand
the *Letters on Demonology and Witchcraft.*"[55] Then too, indubitably, at Bowerswell there was Aunt Catherine, whose own parish in
Galloway had been so notable for wraiths and ghosts[56] and who
personally had "inherited" (as the older Ruskin gravely states) the
"gift of second-sight" which to his day remained in "that branch of
my family";[57] and in Scott's day (he elsewhere notes) the "faculty
of second sight" had been "well-attested."[58] Therefore, was it in the
least surprising that Jessie should have seen the apparition warning
her that two more graves must soon be dug?

As the years passed, there were refined in Margaret traits of
character which led to what Ruskin called a "purity of heart and
conduct" supernatural in its intensity.[59] Nor should this statement
be dismissed with sweeping skepticism as merely the tribute of a

fond son. For one thing, Ruskin was not uncritical of his mother, as the biographical tradition founded on his words attests. And for another, some such quality as he described might be expected to have emerged as one result of an essential conquest over self — this conquest gained through years of prayer and sublimating discipline. In actuality, Margaret had waited all her youth away without demand, faltering only when it seemed as though she might not still be privileged to offer to John James her love and admiration, with hope to be fulfilled only in due time — when he and God thought wise. Yet even then she doubtless sometimes knew, and sometimes doubtless showed through letters sent to London, the type of weakness she confessed in later years to a long-absent son: ". . . indeed I am filled with thankfulness through you, and would not have you in England [in contrast to his father's ever pressing him to due-date] while you think and feel as you do at present if I could bring you at this minute by a wish — but I cannot feel as I do when you are near me — I have not latterly been able to rest so much on the nothingness of time and the infinitude of eternity — I do miss you more than I have ever done because you have been more to me of late but still I have not the slightest wish that you should shorten your absence even by an hour — " [60]

Yet the self-conquest which she reached could not have been easy for a woman with her strength and forcefulness of personality — so self-assured and so dogmatic in beliefs, so matriarchal (although in some ways most important, undemanding) in maternity, while self-effacing as a wife; nor would that conquest ever be complete. For there would be those sleepless nights, spent sometimes sitting up in bed wracked by that all-over-body pain. And before the end of thirty years of marriage, on occasion (little wonder) she might plainly speak her mind. "She often provokes me," John James wrote to Effie's father, "by making Speeches to me that I am not flattered by but esteem remains on both sides — " [61] Sometimes, too, she would perhaps too much protest her gratitude for trials it still pleased God to place upon her, as when she broke her thighbone and evoked her husband's comment: "Mrs Ruskin's Constitution is good & her patience great . . . I had been ill from Octr last year & was getting nearly as well as I could ever expect to be — when the Alarm caused by the accident brought back my Complaints . . . ¶Mrs Ruskin's

Improvement under God is affected no doubt by her happy state of mind. — She is as full of Thankfulness, suffering from this fractured Limb, as some people would be at escaping from one." [62]

Nevertheless, at seventy-nine she *did* recover from that "fractured Limb," at least enough to get about, once impressing company by using a chair for her support in preference to John James' arm — as would befit her lifelong effort not to be in any way a hindrance to her husband.[63] For however many sleepless nights she may have spent, she made adjustments which did not sap vitality (she was ninety when she died), or gain for her a center of attention as the invalid. Yet she always had to be content with the "esteem" her husband offered her while finding his fulfillment in their son. Even so she spent her married life in serving him, "in every thought," her son said, "dependent on my father's wishes, and withdrawn from all other social pleasure as long as she could be *his* companion." [64] — "Mama is my Guardian Angel upon Earth," [65] John James once remarked. So when he died, he left her feeling that this time she need wait only for her own death — "not to be near him, not to be so high in heaven, but content if she might only *see* him, she said. . . ." [66] Surely Ruskin need not have altered his first phrasing of one statement in *Praeterita:* ". . . my mother was much the more deeply in love. . . ." [67]

In January, 1818, when John James was back in Perth and ready for their marriage, he was thirty-three and she was thirty-seven. She, however (Collingwood relates), "was for further delay; but with the minister's help he persuaded her one evening into a prompt marriage. . . ." [68] It was apparently a marriage as quiet as it was "prompt" — "the servants of the house having no suspicion of the event until John and Margaret drove away together next morning to Edinburgh. ¶In looking back to my past thoughts and ways, nothing astonishes me more," Ruskin concludes, "than my want of curiosity about all these matters; and that, often and often as my mother used to tell with complacency the story of this carefully secret marriage, I never asked, 'But, mother, why so secret, when it was just what all the friends of both of you so long expected, and what all your best friends so heartily wished?' " [69] And doubtless it *was* what their best friends desired. But had it been desired by the invalid of Bowerswell?

To conclude Margaret's life within those walls, there had been, within a month, three deaths of members of her family, each more shocking than the one before. The series began with the loss of her own mother, on September 29, 1817,[70] so that in all likelihood she would have been in Croydon when she received the news that on October 13 her Aunt Catherine had succumbed to "appoplexy [*sic*]." [71] Next, according to a story told by Derrick Leon after he had interviewed descendants of the George Grays:[72] "Through grief over his wife, who had fallen dead during the christening of a child of her daughter Jessie [possibly the Helen who lived only three weeks], John Ruskin had one day soon afterwards, at Bowerswell in Perth, ended his own life by cutting his throat. . . ." [73] There is evidence, obtained from a *Burial Register,* to support the gist of that tale which the Grays preserved: the body of Catherine remained unburied for a week, and it was only ten days after her funeral that John Thomas, dying "suddenly," effected his escape. — By way of epitaph, it is noted in the *Burial Register* that John Thomas Ruskin was a "Merchant." [74]

Surely, three months later, Margaret's hesitation about marrying John James was not unrelated to these events? During the insanity which had culminated in despairing violence, her uncle was not likely to have blessed a marriage he had set himself against not long before he had become insane; nor, under the circumstances, could Catherine have been wholly sympathetic. At the end, with John James returning to Perth for her funeral, the knowledge that his son was still intent on marrying Margaret — and was now, in fact, prepared to marry her — could scarcely have helped to assuage the father's grief. One also gathers that Perth friends and neighbors were well aware that John Thomas Ruskin would not countenance this marriage, inasmuch as ten years hence gossip would report that he killed himself *because* John James *had* married Margaret.

The story which thus indicates what townsfolk would have thought and said about the engagement after Mr. Ruskin put an end to his own life stems from Mrs. George Gray (Effie's mother), who told a niece how, in 1827, she had gone to Perth as a bride, driving "from Cuspar Fife straight to Bowerswell on the day of their marriage . . . and how she was received by her sister-in-law who showed her the bedroom and in doing so mentioned that this was the room in which old Mr Ruskin[,] J[ohn] R[uskin]'s grandfather committed suicide — . . . In less than a year after, Effie was born in that very room — The reason old Mr. John Ruskin took his life was, Aunt G[ray] said, because his only son John [James] R[uskin,] J[ohn] R[uskin]'s father — had married his first cousin, who had lived with them." [75] As to Margaret, one knows very well that she could not have easily disregarded one of God's Commandments even though the father (and possibly the mother) whose wishes should be honored had been put to rest in a nameless grave.[76] Why, except for thought of him (or them), could she conceivably have hesitated at this point until persuaded by her minister?

Be that as it may, by the end of January Margaret was ready to have Jessie's husband, as an elder of her church, enter notice in the parish register that her marriage, as "Margaret Cock . . . Daughter to William Cock Merchant in the Parish of Crydon [sic]" was "Contracted" to "John Rusken [sic] Esquire Merchant in London presently residing in the East Church Parish of Perth. . . ." [77] During the interim, she and John James doubtless had been living at Bridge End rather than at haunted Bowerswell.[78] By now John James would have settled all affairs attendant upon death, so that, wishing to get back to London, he might at last have been in haste to marry Margaret. However the event evolved, on February first their banns were "regularly Proclaimed" in church, one would assume for the third time because on Monday, February 2, they were married by the Reverend John Findlay.

That they kept this marriage secret, even from the servants at Bridge End — servants who, if typical, were almost members of the family, there seems no cause to doubt, in view of Margaret's reiteration of the story. One wonders what may have been the feelings of those servants, one of whom — Aunt Jessie's "very old 'Mause'" of "solemn, fearless, and patient faith," had known so well the man who had opposed this union. She had been, Ruskin notes, "my *grandfather's* [my italics] servant in Edinburgh" [79] and, when Jessie married, had gone with her to Perth; together with Nurse Anne, "Old Mause" was someone whom "my Saxon mother" did "not altogether [comprehend]," [80] which doubtless means that Margaret also had her troubles with this servant. Ruskin would recall her "wrinkled and worn face, moveless in resolution and patience, incapable of smile . . . I never can be thankful enough for having seen, in our own 'Old Mause,' the Scottish Puritan spirit in its perfect faith and force. . . ." [81]

It sounds as though, perhaps more strictly than did Margaret's minister, Old Mause may have believed that her former master's wishes ought to be respected — so that Ruskin, having known her as the servant of Aunt Jessie, recalled her likewise as the former servant of John Thomas, feeling puzzled that his mother should repeatedly have said that "the servants in the house" had had no suspicion of the actual event until she drove away next morning.

More generally, while Margaret lived in Perth, how much small-town gossip about her uncle, or about her long engagement and its right or wrong, had she had to face? At least with banns proclaimed in church, her pending marriage (about which she always talked complacently) had become a public secret. Might they have kept the actual ceremony secret merely because John James preferred, as he would say in later years (in connection with the marriage of his son), "to get quietly married & steal away & leave the good folks to talk it over the next day — but my notions may follow my nature which has always been rather retiring"? [82] Or was there perhaps a rather widespread poison in the air so that the bride and groom did not wish to open *any* channels to felicitations or to frowns?

15

John James and Margaret
Take to London Ruskin's
Scottish Heritage

On the morning after they were married,
setting out for the Promised Land with
Edinburgh as their first stop, John James and Margaret carried
with them Ruskin's Scottish heritage. As their son would say (once
more speaking of Sir Walter Scott): "Youth is properly the forming time — that in which a man makes himself, or is made. . . ." [1]
So it had been in Ruskin's own life, and so it had been with his

mother and his father. So, of course, it is with all of us to varying degree. But for Ruskin, because his parents had been fashioned into what they were, the degree would be phenomenal.

Thus it happens that their son, nineteenth-century-England–born and London-bred, was overwhelmingly a product of the Edinburgh of his father's youth, tinctured by the Scotland Margaret knew in somewhat later years. It was this which Collingwood characteristically perceived when he began his *Life of Ruskin:* "If origin, if early training and habits of life, if tastes, and character, and associations, fix a man's nationality, then John Ruskin is a Scotsman. . . . The writers who directed him into the main lines of his thought and work, not so much because he chose them as leaders, as because he was naturally brought under the spell of their inspiration, were Scotsmen. . . . The religious instinct so conspicuous in him is a heritage from Scotland; so is his conscience and code of morality. . . ." [2] All this and more was implicit in the man and woman who had begun their wedding trip, although the heritage of which they were the agents still cannot explain away life's mystery. For when all is said, the bride and groom (alas for Ruskin) were little more, if gauged objectively, than two rather ordinary geese who nonetheless, within the course of nature, would produce a swan.

As an initial good from pressures rooted in his ever-present long ago, John James was taking Margaret to the entirely modest home where they would pass four years before they moved to Ruskin's Earthly Paradise, Herne Hill. Yet 54 Hunter Street, Brunswick Square, could have seemed sufficient paradise to Margaret as the bride. John James unquestionably had once more acted as a man of honor while achieving one more triumph of strong will. At the same time, he had gained the wife he wanted — a wife who felt her own importance to the husband who might readily enough by now have won a younger woman of better birth and with more money than was provided by some cottages once built by William Cock. To leaven honor and esteem there were emotional satisfactions from which could be created the great peace and happiness that Ruskin knew through childhood — what child ever having known an earthly paradise unless his parents have found considerable peace of heart through one another?

Nevertheless, there must have been some serious insufficiency in their relationship — some need or needs that drove them into their lifelong clinging to their son as indispensable to their own happiness. Ruskin reciprocally was left with an imperative need to cling to them even when, at last, he sought to free himself from this destructive bondage: by then he was concerned about retaining his own health of mind as well as of body, together with his ability to work.[3] He himself would hold John James responsible for what he suffered, John James having been "a father [Ruskin said when John James died] who would have sacrificed his life for his son, and yet forced his son to sacrifice his life to him, and sacrifice it in vain." [4] Though oversimplified, the charge is just. For the cousin who had wanted Margaret, not too precipitously, and always treasured her as a wife who was to him emotionally reminiscent of his mother, found in their boy his *alter ego* — a son who could be made (it sounds absurd?) a "gentleman," and who could otherwise most lavishly fulfill the longings of that Edinburgh youth who had been robbed of self-respect but not of need to prove himself superior.

Nor could Margaret, having set up her husband as the Father upon Earth, on whom attention centered, adequately serve to check John James' extreme possessiveness, though after John James died, "I . . . was at first amazed," Ruskin said, "to find my own life suddenly becoming to her another ideal. . . ." [5] In his youth, training him to honor and obey, she may have sometimes been disquieted on perceiving that the child she also passionately cherished, commanded an intensity of admiration, hope, and love which she, as wife, must be content to give and not receive. In *Praeterita* Ruskin would make it clear that as a child he had felt insufficiently his mother's love, and he would also vividly recall what he had evidently felt as her hostility (as when she let him place his finger upon a hot tea urn, to teach him to obey) ; not unrelatedly, he would carry over into later life a curious conviction — repeatedly expressed, often with self-mockery — that he could never either love or be beloved. Always, as a mother, Margaret was overanxious, as was John James, in later years, whenever Ruskin went away; and during early years, why should John James have "always" felt "as if I *ought* to lose him & all I have — "? [6] Whatever may be answered, one cannot but conclude that for John Ruskin it might have been far better had both his parents been "in love." For the present, with thought of Ruskin's ultimate insanity, it must be enough to say that, as the grandson of John Thomas, he received from personalities that had been tormented during their own youth, a heritage scarcely less important or complex than the one which was transmitted physically through perhaps predisposing genes.

As the chief source of strength and peace within her home there was a Margaret prepared to trust her husband's wisdom, second only to the teachings of her God; content to honor and obey, knowing her unworthiness by values of his world yet confident of her own dignity as a child and servant of the Father who had heard her prayers, had punished the unrighteous, and had effected her deliverance as a great reward. It was a strange creature who would be created in her stead when Ruskin in old age relived his youth, finding solace through remembrance of things past and indulging his own fantasies about the youth and the young womanhood of his mother.

It is doubtful whether the real Margaret ever will acquire the vitality of the woman who thus usurped her name within the pages of *Praeterita,* although full publication of her letters to her husband and her son, supplemented (it may be) through those "humiliating" letters written by her mother, may greatly help to give her substance.[7] It seems already clear, however, that no more than she was the daughter of a Yarmouth sailor was she that Margaret who at twenty had been intent upon highest moral philosophy, as Professor Brown forsook his leadership of the highest intellectual circle to argue with her, benignly, while they drank their tea; or the Margaret whose serene Scottish stewardship was unruffled by any untoward happening or human sentiment; or the Margaret of rigidity and frigidity of body, mind, and spirit — that glacial prude who showed affection "chiefly in steady endeavours to cultivate her power of mind . . ."; in short, Margaret our "exemplary Croydon cousin," "perhaps the more in love. . . ." Still less was she the Margaret created by biographers who have made an initial caricature the more grotesque, first by ignoring all that Ruskin, in his ambivalence, said to soften the harshness of his portrayal; then by using without critical evaluation the memories of visitors who saw her, often casually, during her old age, sometimes to interpret their own memories to fit the woman they had subsequently met through Ruskin's words.[8] Ruskin himself, startlingly enough, would bury her (in fantasy if not in fact) in a coffin painted blue, symbolic color for purity, love, fidelity;[9] and in tenderness of truth, believing that in epitaphs men should speak the truth, he would have inscribed above her grave: "Here / Beside my father's body / I have laid / My mother's; / Nor was dearer earth / Ever returned to earth, / Nor purer life / Recorded in heaven." [10] In later years he sent to Dr. John Brown of Edinburgh another version of that epitaph: "In her place, / At her husband's side / Faithfully held in life, deserved in death, / I have laid / Margaret my mother / For whom, if any grieve, who honour me / Let them give to her their praise, / To me, their tears." [11]

It was the younger Margaret, just entering her prime, who now reached London at her husband's side. And it was here — in her own home — that she would reread the prayer of Solomon when he dedicated the temple:

I have surely built thee an house to dwell in, a settled place for thee to abide in for ever. / ... / And I have set there a place for the ark, wherein is the covenant of the LORD, which he made with our fathers, when he brought them out of the land of Egypt. / And Solomon stood before the altar of the LORD ... and spread forth his hands toward heaven: / And he said, LORD God of Israel, there is no God like thee, in heaven above, or on earth beneath, who keepest covenant and mercy with thy servants that walk before thee with all their heart: / Who hast kept with thy servant David my father that thou promisedst him: thou spakest also with thy mouth, and hast fulfilled it with thine hand, as it is this day. / Therefore, now, LORD God of Israel, keep with thy servant David my father that thou promisedst him, saying, There shall not fail thee a man in my sight to sit on the throne of Israel; so that thy children take heed to their way, that they walk before me as thou hast walked before me. / And now, O God of Israel, let thy word, I pray thee, be verified, which thou spakest unto thy servant David my father.[12]

Appendix A

RUSKINS OF LONDON, MIDDLESEX, AND HERTFORDSHIRE

The information assembled in this Appendix has been compiled primarily from contributions made by those to whom, in the "Introduction," I have expressed my most sincere appreciation. Now, however, I should like to add a word of special thanks to Miss Vera J. Ledger for having discovered the *Wills* of John Ruskin of Cheshunt and of Frances Ruskin, which set me on the trail of Middlesex and, more particularly, of Cheshunt, Hertfordshire records. These *Wills* precipitated the letter in which I asked Lambert & Raggett, Genealogists and Record Searchers, to investigate Cheshunt records for a key date — the baptism of a John Ruskin in either *1732* or *1735*, as well as for his marriage *c.* 1754. (See below, entries for *Jan. 3, 1734/5; June 26, 1754.*) Thus I introduced a problem which they pursued with skill until, regretfully, I found it needful to call quits to what by then could easily have become an effort to trace back and back the Ruskin family line. For much of what has so far been achieved, as herein presented, I have trusted to information sent me in letters from my various correspondents, whose words — and abbreviations — I faithfully present. The parenthetical number given after every item indicates the number of the source from which each detail has been obtained, as follows:

1. *Add. M.S. 39278. M. Is. at Cheshunt. Fo. 472;* in the British Museum Library. (Through the kind help of Lambert & Raggett.)

2. *Boyd MSS.,* "London Burials"; in the British Museum Library. (Through the kind help of Lambert & Raggett.)

3. *Boyd MSS.,* "Middlesex Marriages"; in the British Museum Library. (Through the kind help of Lambert & Raggett.)

4. Garrow, D. W., *The History and Antiquities of Croydon:* see pp. 382 and 393 for *Epitaphs* of Margaret (Ruskin) Cock, said to have died *aged 62* in 1817 (*b.* 1755?) and of Mary (Ruskin) Roberts, said to have died *aged 53* in 1809 (*b.* 1756?). For conflicting evidence, see below, Item 21. (The original register of St. Mary's, Marylebone, searched 1754–57 inclusive, does not contain a record of the baptisms of Margaret and Mary Ruskin, Lambert & Raggett have informed me.)

5. Hallen, A. W. Cornelius, ed., *London. St. Botolph Parish, Bishopgate Registers.*

6. *Hertford County Records, Notes and Extracts from the Sessions Rolls 1581 to 1833.*

7. *M. S. Index to Herts. Marriages;* in the British Museum Library. (Through the kind help of Lambert & Raggett.)

8. *Modern Transcript of the Register Transcripts of the St. Albans Archdeaconry,* Vol. IV; in the British Museum Library. (Through the kind help of Lambert & Raggett.)

9. *Original Registers of Cheshunt Co., Herts.;* in the Hertfordshire County Record Office, Hertford. (Through the kind help of Lambert & Raggett.)

10. Phillimore, W. P. W., ed., *Hertfordshire Parish Registers,* "Marriages": for *Datchworth,* see Vol. II; for *Little Berkhamstead,* see Vol. III.

11. Phillimore, W. P. W. and G. E. Cokayne, eds., *London Parish Registers:* for 1687, *Marriages at St. James, Duke's Place,* see Vol. II (no index).

12. Phillimore, W. P. W., *et al.,* eds., *Middlesex Parish Registers,* "Marriages": for *Enfield,* see Vol. V; for *Edmonton,* see Vol. VI. (Initially, through the kind help of Lambert & Raggett; only Vol. IX is indexed.)

13. *Publications of the Harleian Society. The Register Book of Marriages belonging to the Parish of St. George, Hanover Square, . . . Middlesex.*

14. *Publications of the Harleian Society. The Registers of Baptisms and Marriages at St. George's Chapel, Mayfair.*

15. *Publications of the Harleian Society. The Registers of Christ Church, Newgate.*

16. *Publications of the Harleian Society. The Registers of Marriages of St. Mary le Bone, Middlesex:* for *1754,* see Vol. 48; for *1781,* see Vol. 51; for *1797,* see Vol. 54.

17. *Publications of the Harleian Society. The Registers of St. Bene't and St. Peter's, Paul's Wharf, London,* "Marriages": for *1660,* see Vol. 40 (*Registers of St. Peter's*) ; for *1713,* see Vol. 39 (*Registers of St. Bene't*).

18. *Register of Baptisms 1716–1772,* GLMR. Ms. 6778/2; in the Guildhall Library, London. (Through the kindness of Mr. Raymond Smith.)

19. *Register of Burials 1716–1781,* GLMR. Ms. 6781/1; in the Guildhall Library. London. (Through the kindness of Mr. Raymond Smith.)

20. *Register of Marriages 1773–1786,* GLMR 6779/3; in the Guildhall Library, London. (Through the kindness of Mr. Raymond Smith.)

21. Transcription of birthdates entered in a "Family Bible," made by Collingwood for his "Family Tree." (Through the kindness of Mr. F. J. Sharp: see Note 11, p. 199.)

22. *Wills:* see Appendix C. (Through the kind help of Miss Vera J. Ledger, and of Lambert & Raggett.)

1660   Jan. 5   Ruskin, Thomas and Elizabeth Smith, married; Little Berkhamstead. (10)

1660   June 27   Ruskin, William and Mary Pew, married; St. Peter's, Paul's Wharf, London. (17)

1664   April 28   Ruskin, Robert and Mary Herrick, married; Little Berkhamstead. (10)

1683   March 11   Ruskyn, Robert, of Little Berkhamstead, husbandman; convicted for being present at an unlawful conventicle in the parish of Bayford. (6)

1686   Dec.?   Rusken, John, a Sawyer, died, leaving his "Goods" to his son John; Writtle, Essex. (22)

1687   Sept. 12   Riskin, Robert and Mary Pedle, married; St. James, Duke's Place. (11)

1701	July 6	Ruskyn, Jeremiah, bapt.; Northaw. (8)
1706	July 7	Ruskin, Philip, witnessed that Leonard Hancock, of St. Martins, had received the Sacrament as required by the Test Act of 1673. (6)
1707	Jan. 3	Ruskins, Aviss and John Ragg, married; Enfield Co. (3)
1708	April 11	Hester, daughter of Phillip Ruskins, bapt.; Cheshunt. (9)
1709	June 30	Ruskin, John and Sarah Benton, married; Enfield Co. (12)
1710	Aug. 21	Ruskyn, Jeremiah, buried; Northaw. (8)
1711	Nov. 25	Phillip, son of Phillip Ruskin and Hester, bapt.; Cheshunt. (9)
1713	June 2	Ruskin, Robert, of Barkhamstead (*sic*), Herts. (widower) and Mary Crane of Edmonton, Middlesex (widow), married; St. Bene't, Paul's Wharf, London. (3 & 17)
1713	June 12	Ruskin, Robert, of Little Berkhansted (*sic*), indicted for "scandalizing" Thomas Hatton. (6)
1716	Dec. 25	Ruskin, Ann, of Barkhamstead (*sic*), and George Phillips, of Esingdon, married. (10)
1717	Mar. 24	Elizabeth, daughter of Philip Ruskin, bapt.; Cheshunt. (9)
1718/19	Jan. 10	Ruskin, Robert, buried; Cheshunt. (9)
1719	Aug. 27	Wife of Phil. Ruskin buried; Cheshunt. (9)
1720		Ruskin, Eliz., and Thos. Hughes, married; St Gregory. (3)
1720	May 12	Ruskins, Phillip and Eliz. Bradwin, married; Edmonton. (3 and 12)
1720	Sept. 25	Ruskin, John and Helena Green, married; Little Berkhamstead. (10)
1729	Nov. 15	Phillip Ruskin's wife buried; Cheshunt. (9)
1729	Nov. 21	Joseph Ruskin's wife buried; Cheshunt. (9)
1731	Sept. 23	Mary, wife of John Ruskin, buried; Cheshunt. (9)
1731	Oct. 29	Ruskin, Elizabeth, of Northaw, and William Smith of Cheshunt, married; Datchworth. (10)
1731	Nov. 17	Ruskin, John and Mary Adams, married; Cheshunt. (9)
1731	Nov. 21	Ruskin, Avis and Willm. Grimwood, married; Cheshunt. (9)
1732	Aug. 30	Robert, son of John and Mary Ruskin, bapt.; Cheshunt. (9)
1732	Oct. 8	Ruskin, Phillip, buried; Cheshunt. (9)
1733	Dec. 5	Mary, daughter of John and Mary Ruskin, bapt.; Cheshunt. (9)
1734		Ruskin, James (aged) 42, buried; Bishopsgate, St. Botolph. (2 and 5)
1734/5	Jan. 3	John, son of John and Mary Ruskin, bapt.; Cheshunt. (9)
1734/5	Jan. 3	William, a Base son of Ann Mead, supposed to be Begot by William Ruskin, bapt.; Cheshunt. (9)
1735	Dec. 27	Ruskin, Benjamin, buried; Christ Church, Newgate. (2 and 15)
1741		Ruskin, Robert, farmer of Edmonton Co., died, leaving personal estate to his niece Elizabeth, wife of Thomas Prigg, Victualler of Stansted Abbott, Hertford; *Will* proved at London, Feb. 2, 1741. (22)

1742   Jan. 10   Ruskin, John, yeoman, bound over with Edward May-
nard, yeoman, both of Cheshunt, as sureties, to answer for assaulting Daniel Adams of Hatfield. (Note that John Ruskin married
Mary *Adams,* and appointed William Adams as "Trustee" in his
Will.) (6)

1742   Ruskin, Frances, spinster of Saint Mary Stoke Newington Parish,
Middlesex, died, having made her *Will* in 1734 and left bequests
to her brother Jeremy Ruskin, to the five children of her brother
Robert Ruskin, to her nephew John Ruskin and his children, to
her nieces Mary Fryar and Ruth James, to the two children of
John James, *et al.*; *Will* proved at London, Feb. 18, 1742. (22)

1744   Ruskin, Ann and Jn. Shepard, married; Mimms. (3)

1745   Nov. 17   Ruskin, William, buried in the Great Churchyard;
Parish of St. Bartholomew-the-Great. (19)

1747/8   Mar. 8   Ruskin, Jane, Infant, buried; Cheshunt. (9)

1752   Ruskin, Robert and Mary Pavitt, married; Mayfair, St. George.
(3 and 14)

1753   Feb. 20   Ruskins, John, buried; Cheshunt. (9)

1753   Feb. 23   Rusking, John, of Cheshunt; *Will* proved at London. (22)

1753   Oct. 24   Ruskin, Robert and Hannah Adams, married by banns;
Cheshunt. (9)

1753   Sept. 5   Ruskin, Jane, buried in the Great Churchyard; Parish of
St. Bartholomew-the-Great. (19)

1754   June 26   Ruskin, John and Mary Carswell, both of Marylebone,
married; St. Mary le Bone; Witns. — John Paine, Jane Sandress.
(3 and 16)

1754   Nov. 3   John, son of Robert and Hannah Ruskin, bapt.; Cheshunt. (9)

1755   Ruskin, Philadelphia and Wm. Meane, married; Enfield Co. (3)

1755   Nov. 14   Robert, son of Robert and Hannah Ruskin, bapt.;
Cheshunt. (9)

1756?   July 3   Margaret, daughter of John and Mary Ruskin, born
"35 minutes past 3, Saturday morning." (21; *N. B.,* however, 4.)

1757   May 1   Mary, daughter of Robert and Hannah Ruskin, bapt.;
Cheshunt. (9)

1757   July 16   Ruskin, Ann, of Cheshunt, and Alexander Smith, of
Beckingham, Kent, married; Little Berkhamstead. (10)

1757?   Dec. 6   Mary, daughter of John and Mary Ruskin, born. (21;
N. B., however, 4.)

1758   Oct. 10   Ruskin, Edmund and Mary Bigg, married; Bayford. (7)

1758   Dec. 27   Anne, daughter of Robert and Hannah Ruskin, bapt.;
Cheshunt. (9)

1759   Dec. 10   William, son of John and Mary Ruskin, born; bapt.
Dec. 25; Parish of St. Bartholomew-the-Great. (18; for birthdate,
see also 21.)

1760   May 26   Ruskin, Ellinor, Infant, buried; Cheshunt. (9)

1761   Oct. 22   John Thomas, son of John and Mary Ruskin, born;
bapt. Nov. 8; Parish of St. Bartholomew-the-Great. (18; for birthdate, see also 21.)

1762   Dec. 8   Ruskin, William, buried in the Great Churchyard; Parish
of St. Bartholomew-the-Great. (19)

1764   Nov. 14   Cock, Margaret, buried in the Great Churchyard; Parish of St. Bartholomew-the-Great. (19)

1765   Ruskin, Edmund: order allowing the appeal of Little Berkhamstead against a warrant removing Edmund Ruskin, Mary, his wife, and Jane, their daughter, from Bayford. (6)

1767   Mar. 2   Elizabeth, daughter of John and Mary Ruskin, born; bapt. Mar. 22; Parish of St. Bartholomew-the-Great. (18; for birthdate, see also 21.)

1767   Mar. 3   Robert, son of John and Mary Ruskin, born; Parish of St. Bartholomew-the-Great. (21; apparently Baby Robert never was baptised: see below, March 27, 1767.)

1767   Mar. 27   Ruskin, Robert and Elizabeth, buried in the Great Churchyard, aged 3 weeks; Parish of St. Bartholomew-the-Great. (19)

1769   Ruskin, John: orders adjourning the appeals of Nicholas Westcombe, Esq., against the poor rate at Flamstead and the appeals of Mary Smith and Henry Nutting against their assessments at Layston, quashing the poor rate at Cheshunt on the appeals of John Ruskin, *et al.* (6)

1772   Sept. 25   James, son of John and Mary Ruskin, born; bapt. Oct. 11; Parish of St. Bartholomew-the-Great. (18; for birthdate, see also 21.)

1773   June 14   Ruskin, James, buried in the Great Churchyard, aged 8 mos.; Parish of St. Bartholomew-the-Great. (19)

1779   Ruskin, Ann, of Cheshunt; indicted for stealing money from Robert Waters and discharged, no true bill having been found against her. (6)

1780   May 19   Ruskin, John, buried in the Great Churchyard, aged 45 years (having died May 16); Parish of St. Bartholomew-the-Great. (19)

1780   June 19   Ruskin, Margaret and William Cock, married; Parish of St. Bartholomew-the-Great. (20; see also Fig. 10 after p. 56, and Appendix B.)

1780   July 1   Ruskin, John: *Will* proved at London. (22)

1781   Aug. 17   Ruskin, Robert and Mary Fisher, married; St. Mary le Bone. (16)

1786   Nov. 20   Ruskin, John, buried; Cheshunt. (9)

1797   Jan. 31   Ruskin, Sarah and Johnson Sandon, married; St. Mary le Bone. (16)

1810   Ruskin, Robert, labourer of Cheshunt: indicted and acquitted for assaulting John Kemp. (6)

1814   Ruskin, Robert, farmer of Cheshunt: recognizance — to keep the peace towards Martha, wife of Robert Ruskin junior. (6)

1815   Ruskin, Robert Jr.: sentenced to one month in gaol and fined 5 *s.* for rescuing a gelding belonging to him, which had been found trespassing in a field belonging to Bryant Preston of Cheshunt and was being led to the parish pound by a servant of Mr. Preston. (6)

1815   Ruskin, Richard: released as an insolvent debtor. (6)

1815   Ruskin, Robert: his petition as an insolvent debtor dismissed because he had "omitted to state in his Schedule five Beasts, three Calves, two Ponies, and a Cart and Harness, which since his commitment to the Gaol he hath authorized his Wife . . . to sell . . . for £50 and upwards without the consent or knowledge of his Creditors." (6)

1816   Nov. 19   Ruskin, Robert the elder, of Chestnut: recognizance — to answer for the appearance of Robert Ruskin the younger, farmer, for assaulting Samuel Bennett. (6)

1817   Ruskin, Robert junior: indicted for rescuing some of his cattle which had been found trespassing and were being driven to the pound by Samuel Bennett. (6)

1818   July 2   Ruskin, Robert, died, aged 63; Cheshunt. (1)

1818   Dec. 14   Ruskin, William of Cheshunt, labourer: fined 10 s. for stealing wood. (6)

1819   Ruskin, Richard: account of W. P. Willson for conveying Richard Ruskin, among others, 73 miles at 1 s. each per mile, 36 l. 10 s. (6)

1820   Ruskin, William of Cheshunt, labourer: indicted for stealing two fowls, value 2 s.; six months hard labour in the bridewell. (6)

1821   Ruskin, James of Cheshunt: to appear, with William Seabrook, in respect of the children of Mary Ann Cassell of Cheshunt and Frances Miller of Puttenham, respectively. (6)

1825   Ruskin, William: committed for larceny; dismissed for want of prosecutors. (6)

1826   Ruskin, John of Cheshunt, labourer: recognizance — for Richard Adams of Cheshunt, labourer, to keep the peace towards Ann Smith, widow. (6)

1827   Ruskin, Joseph of Cheshunt, labourer: recognizance — to keep the peace towards John Schooledge of Cheshunt, labourer. (6)

1831   Nov. 2   Ruskin, Mary and William Hallam, married, St. George, Hanover Square, Middlesex. (13)

(The *Hertford County Court Records* contain no "Ruskin" entries after 1827, possibly because detailed "notes and extracts" from the Sessions Rolls do not extend beyond 1833. At the Winter Assizes of 1887, however, Alexander Wedderburn noted that Frederick Ruskin, a farmer of Cheshunt, was on the jury which tried James Ruskin, a laborer, for theft at St. Albans: see *Works,* XXXV, p. lxi, *n.*)

Appendix B

THE EDINBURGH RUSKINS AND THEIR DESCENDANTS AND RELATIVES OF CROYDON

The material herein assembled has been obtained through the generosity of those to whom I desire once more to acknowledge my indebtedness and to express my thanks, as will be specifically indicated when I list the sources.

This Appendix does not include data relevant to the family connections of the Scottish grandmother, Catherine Tweddale Ruskin: such information was gathered from Sir Andrew Agnew's *The Hereditary Sheriffs of Galloway*, Peter H. M'Kerlie's *History of the Lands and their Owners in Galloway*, and Hew Scott's *Fasti Ecclesiæ Scoticanæ*, and has been documented through references in footnotes. The source from which each item in this Appendix was obtained is indicated by the number given in parentheses, these numbers referring to the numbers in the list which follows:

1. *Burial Register of the Town of Perth 1794–1823;* in the Parks and Cemeteries Department, Perth. (Through the kindness of Mr. Alexander J. Tait and Miss Ethel L. Watson of the Sandeman Public Library, Perth.)

2. *Certification of the Birth of John Ruskin;* in the Ruskin Museum, Coniston. (Through the kindness of Mrs. Oscar Gnosspelius, Curator.)

3. Garrow, David W., "Epitaphs in Croydon Churchyard," *The History and Antiquities of Croydon . . .* , 1818.

4. *Inscriptions on Gravestones;* photographed (1953) in the Croydon Churchyard of St. John the Baptist. (Through the kindness of Mr. T. E. Callander of the Central Library, Croydon.)

5. *Parish Registers of St. John, Croydon;* in the Record Office, Town Hall, Croydon. (Through the kindness of Mr. T. E. Callander.)

6. *Register of Births and Baptisms for the Parish of Edinburgh;* in the General Registry Office, New Register House, Edinburgh. (Through the kindness of Mr. E. A. Hogan, Registrar General for Scotland.)

7. *Register of Births and Baptisms for the Parish of Old Luce, Wigtown;* in the General Registry Office, Edinburgh. (Through the kindness of Mr. E. A. Hogan.)

8. *Register of Deaths and Burials for the Parish of Old Luce, Wigtown;* in the General Registry Office, Edinburgh. (Through the kindness of Mr. E. A. Hogan.)

9. *Register of Proclamations and Marriages for the Parish of Perth, in the County of Perth;* in the General Registry Office, Edinburgh. (Through the kindness of Mr. E. A. Hogan.)

10. Ruskin, John: passing references to relatives, both published and unpublished. (For unpublished references, through the kindness of the Yale and Pierpont Morgan Libraries.)

11. Sievwright, S., *Supplement to Greyfriar's Burying-ground: Its Epitaphs and Inscriptions.* (Through the kindness of Miss Ethel L. Watson, who transcribed therefrom the "Richardson-Ruskin" tombstone inscription.)

1754		*Birth* of William Cock, victualler of Croydon, known as "Captain Cox of Yarmouth": see below, March 31, *1787.*
1756?	July 3	*Birth* of Margaret Ruskin: see Appendix A.
1757?	Dec. 6	*Birth* of Mary Ruskin: see Appendix A.
1761	Oct. 22	*Birth* of John Thomas Ruskin: see Appendix A.
1763	Aug. 15	*Baptism* of Catherine Tweddale Ruskin (said to have been born August 14: see Hew Scott, *op. cit.,* Vol. II, p. 349). "Catharine Tweddell Daur. to Mr. Jas. Tweddell Minr. here & Jannet Adair his spouse, was baptized the fifteenth Augt. j^m vij^c & sixty three by Mr. John Dickson Minr. of New Luce before these witnesses Thomas & John McCairlies in Balmesh." (From certified copy.) (7)
1764	Nov. 14	*Burial* of Margaret Cock: see Appendix A.
1774		*Birth* of Patrick (known as "Peter") Richardson, tanner of Perth. From tombstone inscription: *"Richardson-Ruskin* / Sacred to the memory of Mr. Patrick Richardson, who died 20th. July, 1824, aged 50. Also Janet Richardson, wife of the above, died 18th. May, 1828 aged 43 [*sic*]. Also their children, Margaret died 9th. January 1817, aged 6 mo. Catherine aged 4 [*sic*] years. Patrick aged 8 years. Helen aged 3 weeks. James, died 8th. May 1826, aged 18 years. Janet aged 8 years." (11)
1775	May 23	*Death* of "Mrs. Janet Adair Spouse to the revd. Mr. Jas. Tweedale Minr. of the Gospel in Glenluce . . . aged 53." (From certified copy.) (8)
1777	May 6	*Death* of "The Revd. Mr. Tweedale Minister of Glenluce . . . aged 44." (From certified copy.) (8)
1778	Apr. 26	*Death* of Benjamin Cock, carpenter of Croydon, aged 66 years. (5)
1780	May 16	*Death* of John Ruskin, of London: see Appendix A.
1780	June 19	*Marriage:* "William Cock Batchelor and Margaret Ruskin Spinster both of this Parish [St. Bartholomew-the-Great, London] were Married in this Church by Banns this Nineteenth Day of June in the Year One Thousand Seven Hundred and Eighty By me [signed] Owen Perrott Edwardes Rectr / This Marriage was solemnized between Us [signed] W^m. Cock / Margaret Ruskin / In the Presence of [signed] John Scott / Mary Ruskin." (See Fig. 10 after p. 56; for source, see June 19, *1780,* Appendix A.)
1780	Dec. 17	*Death* of Martha, widow of Benjamin Cock, of Croydon, aged 68 years. (5)
1781	Sept. 2	*Birth* of Margaret Cock, daughter of William and Margaret. (5)
1782		*Birth* of George Richardson, baker of Croydon. (4)

1783   Oct. 3   *Birth* of Bridget Cock, daughter of William and Margaret. (5)

1783   Nov. 20   *Birth* of Janet Ruskin (known as "Jessie"). (From certified copy headed "December 5th 1783" and otherwise fully quoted in text: see p. 42. (6)

1785   May 10   *Birth* of John James Ruskin: "May 27th 1785 John Thomas Risken Merchant and Katharine Tweedale his Spouse Old Kirk Parish a Son Born 10th Current named John, James, Witnesses Robert Stewart Grocer and William White Iron Monger, Edinburgh." (From faithful copy provided by Mr. E. A. Hogan, who mentions the "redundant comma between the John and the James.") (6)

1787   Mar. 31   *Death* of William Cock. (4) "4 Apr. 1787. Interred: William Cock died of a broken leg at London. Aged 33." (5)

1787   Dec. 11   *Marriage* of Mary Ruskin and George Roberts, victualler of Croydon. (5)

1790   Jan. 17   *Birth* of George Roberts, son of George and Mary. (5)

1791   June 3   *Birth* of Mary Roberts, daughter of George and Mary. (5)

1792   Oct. 23   *Birth* of John Thomas Roberts, son of George and Mary. (5)

1801   Oct. 4   *Death* of George Roberts, aged 44. (3)

1803   July 20   *Birth* of John George Richardson, son of George and Bridget; baptised 14 August, 1803. (5)

1804   Nov. 1   *Marriage* of Janet Ruskin and Patrick Richardson. "October 1804 / Mr. Patrick Richardson, Merchant in Perth and Miss Janet Ruskin in Edinburgh Daughter to Mr. John Ruskin, Merchant, Saint James Square Newtown, Edinburgh — Elder David MacLaren — The Persons before named were regularly Proclaimed and married the First day of November said year by the Reverend Mr. Charles Vincent, Minister of Saint Georges Chapel Edinburgh — Perth the Twenty seventh day of October One thousand eight hundred and four years — Contracted." (From certified copy.) (9)

1804   Dec. 22   *Birth* of Margaret Mary Richardson, daughter of George and Bridget; baptised 13 January, 1805. (5)

1806   June 30   *Birth* of William Ruskin Richardson, son of George and Bridget; baptised 27 July, 1806. (5)

1808   Sept. 16   *Birth* of George James Richardson, son of George and Bridget; baptised 30 October, 1808. (5)

1808   *Birth* of James Richardson, son of Patrick and Janet: see above, *1774*. (11)

1809   Dec. 30   *Death* of Mary, widow of George Roberts, *née* Ruskin; aged 53 (*sic*). (3 and 5)

1810   Jan. 20   *Birth* of James Tweddel Adair Richardson, son of George and Bridget; baptised 18 February, 1810. (5)

1810   *Birth* of Patrick Richardson (known as "little Peter"), son of Patrick and Janet: see below, Jan. 9, *1818*. (1)

1810   *Birth* of Catherine Richardson, daughter of Patrick and Janet: see below, Jan. 14, *1817*. (1)

1811   May 6   *Birth* of Charles Thomas Richardson, son of George and Bridget; baptised 25 May, 1811. (5)

1812   May 18   *Death* of James Tweddel Adair Richardson, aged 2 years. (5)

1814   Apr. 8   *Birth* of Mary Bridget Richardson (known as "Cousin Bridget"), daughter of George and Bridget; baptised 4 May, 1814. (5)

1815   *Birth* of Mary Richardson, daughter of Patrick and Janet: from W. G. Collingwood's "Family Tree."

1816   (Aug.?)   *Birth* of Margaret Richardson, daughter of Patrick and Janet: see above, *1774.* (11)

1817   Jan. 9   *Death* of Margaret Richardson, daughter of Patrick and Janet, aged 6 months. (11)

1817   Jan. 14   *Death* of Catherine Richardson, daughter of Patrick and Janet: "(aged 7) died of measles." (1)

1817   Sept. 29   *Death* of Margaret, widow of William Cock, *née* Ruskin. (4) Buried Oct. 5, aged 62 (*sic*). (3 and 5)

1817   Oct. 13   *Death* of "Catharine [*née* Tweddale] sp. of John [Thomas] Ruskin. *Age.* 52 [*sic*] *Disease.* Appoplexy." Buried "20th. Oct." (1)

1817   Oct. 30   *Death* of "John [Thomas] Ruskin, Merchant. *Age.* [none.] *Disease.* Suddenly." Buried "3rd. Nov." (1)

1817?   Oct.?   *Death* of "Helen aged 3 weeks": see above, *1774;* see also p. 167 and Note 73, p. 252. (11)

1818   Jan. 9   *Death* of Patrick Richardson, son of Patrick and Janet; "(aged 8) died of a decline." (1)

1818   Feb. 2   *Marriage* of John James Ruskin and Margaret Cock. See Fig. 7 after p. 56. "January 1818 / Perth the Thirty first day of January One thousand eight hundred and eighteen years — Contracted John Rusken Esquire Merchant in London presently residing in the East Church Parish of Perth and Miss Margaret Cock in said Parish Daughter to William Cock Merchant in the Parish of Crydon and County of Surrey — Elder Patrick Richardson — The Persons before named were regularly Proclaimed and Married the Second day of February said year by the Reverend John Findlay Minister of Saint Paul's Church Parish Perth." (From photostat in my possession.) (9)

1819   Feb. 8   *Birth* of John Ruskin. "No *439* / Dated the *30th* day of *November* 1837. / This is to certify and declare, that *John* the *Son* of *John James Ruskin* of *Billiter Street* in the *City* of *London Wine Merchant* and *Margaret* his wife (who was the daughter of *William Cock* of *Croyden* [*sic*] in the *County* of *Surrey Master Mariner and Margaret his Wife both deceased*) was born at the house of *the said John James Ruskin n°. 54* in *Hunter Street Brunswick Square* in the *County* of *Middlesex* on the *Eighth* day of *February 1819.* [signed] *John James Ruskin / Margaret Ruskin* The Parents abovenamed.

I certify and declare that *I was* present at the Birth of the Child abovementioned; and that such Birth took place at the time and place aforesaid. [signed] *Ann Strachan* of *Herne Hill in the County of Surrey Spinster formerly residing at N°. 54 Hunter Street aforesaid then the Nurse of the Said John Ruskin and then and now a Servant of the Said John James Ruskin.*

[Marginally printed and signed] Entered, Filed, and Registered, according to the custom in use amongst Protestant Dissenters, at the Registry of Births kept at Dr. Williams's Library, Red-Cross

Street, Cripplegate, London, this *6th* day of *December* 18*37*. By me [signed] *Richard Cogan* / Registrar." (Except for personal signatures other than his own, all the italicized material appears in the handwriting of John James Ruskin. Directions, printed on the form, called for information about "the business and profession, of the mother's father.") (2)

1819   *Birth* of Janet Richardson (known as "Cousin Jessie"), daughter of Patrick and Janet: see below, *1827.*

1824   July 20   *Death* of Patrick Richardson, husband of Janet: see above, *1774.* (11)

1826   May 8   *Death* of James Richardson: see above, *1774.* (11)

1827   *Death* of Janet Richardson, daughter of Patrick and Janet, aged 8 years: see Works, II, p. 285, *n.;* see also above, *1774.* (11)

1828   May 18   *Death* of Janet, widow of Patrick Richardson, *née* Ruskin, aged 45: see above, *1774.* (11) (Although Sievwright published "aged 43" rather than "aged 45," *May 18, 1828,* as the date of death is confirmed by other evidence, including an unpublished letter of 24 May, 1828, from John James Ruskin to George Gray; original in *The Bowerswell Papers.*)

1830   Dec. 12   *Death* of Bridget, wife of George Richardson, *née* Cock, "Aged 48 Years." (Bridget was, in actuality, 52.) (4)

1845?   *Death* of John Richardson, presumably of Glasgow, son of Patrick and Janet: in an unpublished letter of February 8, 1852, to his father, Ruskin refers to having had "John Richardson's death — announced to me at Vevay," when he was returning from Italy in 1845. (Original in the Yale University Library.) Various facts suggest that he was referring to John Richardson of Glasgow rather than to John George, the Croydon cousin who is said to have died in Australia.

1848   May   *Birth* of John Bolding, son of Parker and Mary, *née* Richardson: in an unpublished letter of May 24, 1848, to her mother, Effie (then Mrs. John Ruskin) refers to this event. (Original in *The Bowerswell Papers.*)

1849   June   *Death* of Mary, wife of Parker Bolding, *née* Richardson (of Perth): in an unpublished letter of 28 June 1849, to his wife, Ruskin refers to having received news, in Geneva, of this death. (Original in *The Bowerswell Papers.*)

1851?   *Death* of Mary Bridget Richardson, of Croydon: in an unpublished letter of February 24, 1852, to his father, Ruskin remarks: "But it is melancholy to think of my poor cousin Bridget dying there [in Australia] — almost of hunger. . . ." (Original in the Yale University Library.)

1861   July 1   *Death* of George Richardson, of Croydon, "Aged 79 Years." (4)

1864   Mar. 3   *Death* of John James Ruskin, aged 79 years.

1871   Dec. 5   *Death* of Margaret Ruskin, aged 90 years.

1875   *Death* of William Ruskin, physician of Tunbridge Wells and London, formerly of Perth: see *Works,* XXVIII, p. 604.

1900   Jan. 20   *Death* of John Ruskin, aged 81 years.

Appendix C

WILLS

The following *Wills* in the name of "Ruskin" have been found through a search (limited to the late seventeenth and the eighteenth centuries) which included, in Somerset House, the Diocese of Buckinghamshire, Cambridgeshire, Hertfordshire, Huntingdonshire, London, Middlesex, Peterborough, and Surrey. A search for the *Will* of John Thomas Ruskin in Scottish archives has been unsuccessful. No analogous search for "Cock" *Wills,* in an effort to establish the family history of William Cock, has been conducted, the number of "Cock-Cox" *Wills,* as revealed through a preliminary survey limited to the most relevant dates, having been, to me, necessarily discouraging. The *Will* of Ruskin's grandfather, William Cock, has, however, been located and is herein included: see Fig. 7 after p. 56. For the *Will* of Ruskin's Croydon grandmother, Margaret Cock, see Note 31, p. 219.

I. The earliest known "Ruskin" *Will* was given to "Goodman" Green by word of mouth on November 5, 1686 and was proved at London "(Dec.?) 13, 1686." (In Somerset House: Original; *Peculiar of Writtle, Essex / Calendar / 1618–1851.*)

John Rusken ye Elder lately deceaced in the Parish of writtle [near Chelmsford] in the County of Essex Sawyer did say unto Goodman Green of hiwood and unto Hezekiah Godsaf these words as follow one [*sic*] the fifth of nouember 1686

Giue unto my Son John Rusken all my Goods that I haue without dors. In Jeneral wheare of out of them he is to pay my debts and to bureime [bury me] and to pay my wife forty Shillings and I Doe Giue him all the Goods that are within dors that Ware his Gran-mothers,

How Green / Hezekiah Godsaf

Proven (Dec.?) 13 1686 / Heugh Green / Hekiah Godsaf / both sworn to / ye truth of this / will

II. *Will* of Robert Ruskin, January 18, 1741; signed by his "marke"; proved February 2, 1741. (In Somerset House. *Ref: Arch. of Middlesex (Essex & Herts.) / Pae flie / 1732–50 / folio 196.*)

. . . I Robert Ruskin late of Edmonton in the County of Middlesex ffarmer but now of Stansted Abbott in the County of Hertford . . . bequeath unto my Neice Elizabeth Prigg (Wife of Thomas Prigg of Stansted Abbott . . . Victualler) All . . . my household Goods plate Linen Rings and ready Money . . . IN WITNESS whereof I . . . set my Hand . . . this eighteenth day of January . . . One Thousand seven hundred and forty one, *Robert Ruskin* R *his marke.* . . .

III. *Will* of Frances Ruskin, May 29, 1734, with references to her Brothers Jeremy Ruskin and Robert Ruskin, to her Nephew John Ruskin, and to other members of her family; proved at London February 16, 1742. (In Somerset House. *Ref.: Tremley / 1742: Ruskin, ffrances — Middlesex — February — folio 65.*)

. . . I Frances Ruskin of the parish of Saint Mary Stoke Newington in the County of Middlesex Spinster . . . do make . . . this my last Will . . . Item I give and bequeath to my Brother Jeremy Ruskin Twenty pounds and in case of his Death to his Daughter Item . . . to my Neice his daughter ten pounds and in case of her Death to her Children Item . . . to my Nephew John Ruskin fforty pounds and in case of his Death to his Children Item . . . to my Neice the Daughter of Robert Ruskin ten pounds and in case of her Death to her Children. Item . . . to my Neice Mary ffryar Twenty pounds and in case of her Death to her Children Item . . . to her two Children ten pounds each and in case of their death to their Mother Item . . . to William James the Son of my Neice Ruth James ten pounds and in case of his Death to Mary ffryar Item . . . to the five Children of my Bro. Robert Ruskin's Daughter five pounds each and in case of the Death of any to the Survivors Item . . . to the two children of my Nephew Robert Warburton five pounds each, and in case of Death to the Survivor Item . . . to the two children of John James five pounds each and in case of Death to the Survivor all these several and respective Sums so given and bequeathed to the twelve Children above mentioned I will and desire may remain in the Hands of my Executors for to put them out Apprentices or else to be payable to them at the days of their respective Ages of Twenty one years or days of Marriages which shall first happen. . . . [Bequests to outsiders.] Item . . . to Sarah Smith my two best Suits of Wearing apparell and as to the Rest of my apparell I give and bequeath to my three Neices to be disposed of amongst them . . . desiring my Neice Mary ffryar may have the largest proportion . . .

IV. Original *Will* of John Ruskin, November 25, 1747; proved at London, by the Oath of Mary Ruskin, February 23, 1753. (In Somerset House. *Ref.: Searle / 1753: Ruskin, John, Hertford — February — folio 60.*)

CHESTHUNT in HERTFORDSHIRE November the 25: 1747 I John Rusking of the same do make this as my last Will and Testament as being in ill state of health but in perfect mind and memory I bequeath to my Sun Robert twenty pounds Item to my Sun John twenty pounds Item to my Sun Tomass twenty pounds Item to my daughter Ann the sum of twenty pounds Item to my daughter Mary twenty pounds Item to my daughter Jane twenty pounds of good and lawful money of grate Britain being to be paid at the years of one and twenty and it is my Will and desire is [*sic*] that if any or either of these children should should [*sic*] dye before the age of one and twenty that the said sum of twenty pounds shall remain in my dear and loving wifes hands Mary Rusking witch I make my hole and sole Executrix and I do appoint William Adams . . . in the parish of Chesthunt . . . as Trustee for my children — *John Ruskin* — signed and sealed in the presence of us Witnesses *Tho' Mills* — *Laios Nightingale* — *Mary Nightingale.*

V. Original *Will* of John Ruskin, May 8, 1780; proved at London, July 1, 1780. (In Consistory Court of London, *Register 1777–1781, f. 304.*)

I John Ruskin of the Parish of St. Bartholomew the Great London Parish Clerk do make this my last Will and Testament First I do hereby give and bequeath unto my dear Wife Mary Ruskin all my personal Estate of what kind or nature soever to be by her freely possessed and enjoyed without the control or interference of either of my Person or of any other Person whatever for and during the term of her natural life and after her decease I do hereby give and bequeath the Same or So much thereof as shall then remain unto my three Children Margaret Ruskin Mary Ruskin and John Thomas Ruskin to be equally divided between them or such of them as shall survive my Said Wife to share and share alike and of this my Said Will do nominate constitute and appoint my said Wife Mary Ruskin Sole Executrix and hereby revoking all others by me made do declare this to be my last In Witness whereof I have here unto set my hand the eighth day of May in the year of our Lord one thousand Seven hundred and eighty. /

[signed] John Ruskin

Witness / John Wyatt / Jn. Herring

1st July 1780

Mary Ruskin Widow the Relict of the Testator and Sole Executrix within named was duly sworn and that the Goods Chattels and Credits of the Testator do not amount to the Sum of one hundred pounds.

before me / And. Coltee Ducarel / Surrogate

Testator was late of the Parish of Saint Bartholomew the Great London and died May last.

This Will was proved on the first Day of July in the year of our Lord, one thousand seven hundred and eighty . . . by the Oath of Mary Ruskin Widow the Relict and Sole Executrix to whom Administration was granted being sworn duly to administer the deceased having at the time of his death goods etc. in different Archdeaconries or jurisdiction within the Diocese of London.

VI. Original *Will* of William Cock, 14 June 1782. (In keeping of the Central Library, Croydon, Surrey.)

In the Name of God Amen I William Cock of the Parish of Croydon in the County of Surry Victualler being in Health of Body and of Sound and Disposing mind memory and understanding but considering the uncertainty of life do make this my last Will and Testament in manner and form following 1 that is to Say Principally and first of all I commend my Soul into the hands of God who gave it and for my Body I commit to the Earth to be buried in a Christian like and Decent manner by my Executrix hereafter named and for such worldly goods as it hath pleased God to bless me with I give devise and dispose of in the following manner and form IMPRIMIS I give and bequeath unto my beloved Wife Margaret Cock all my househould goods and Chattels Wearing Aparel Linen Woolin Together with all Plate Bonds Bills Debts ready money Securities for money or whatsoever I may be Possessed of at the time of my Decease TO HAVE AND TO HOLD to her and her heirs forever AND all the rest residue and remainder of all Estates Real or Personal I give devise and bequeath unto my said beloved Wife Margaret Cock to her and her heirs for ever AND I hereby nominate and appoint my said Wife Margaret Cock my Sole and only Executrix of this my last Will and Testament hereby revoking all former Will and Wills by me heretofore made IN Witness whereof I have hereunto Set my hand and Seal this fourteenth Day of June in the Year of our Lord one thousand seven hundred and Eighty two.

Signed Sealed published and declared by the above
named William Cock as and for his last Will and
Testament in the presence of us who have hereunto
Subscribed our Names as Witnesses at his request   William Cock
and in his presence and in the presence of each other
      Thomas Maulden
      William Hawall
      Tho⁸ Stephen
      Davy Haywood

Notes

INTRODUCTION

[1] *Letters of Charles Eliot Norton,* Vol. II, pp. 135–36; from letter of July 5, 1882, to Mrs. A. Carlyle. In later years Ruskin sent to Norton what Mrs. Severn called "that dreadful letter," unrestrained in its satirical attack on Norton's persistent (and, in Ruskin's opinion, always unperceptive, often niggling) disapproval of Froude's work upon Carlyle. This letter, sent in three installments, I should not hesitate to publish at this point, if backgrounds had been appropriately developed — although when Ruskin dictated it to Mrs. Severn, he was not entirely sane. For years Ruskin had been aware that Norton had reacted to him as though he were a bad and foolish child who, incongruously, was also wise and gifted. Knowing himself to be in ultimately important ways superior in his own humanity, Ruskin had controlled his impatience against Norton as yet another loving-disapproving father-figure. But in 1889 there came the day when, *à propos* of Norton's edition of Carlyle's *Early Letters,* Ruskin spoke his mind with extraordinary incisiveness and acumen in "that dreadful letter" made hilariously brilliant through the very failure in restraint which was caused by mental illness.

This letter does not appear among the Norton manuscripts now in The Houghton Library of Harvard University, and naturally it was not included in the Library Edition, though it was known to Cook and Wedderburn.

[2] *The Works of John Ruskin,* edited by E. T. Cook and Alexander Wedderburn, Vol. XXXV, p. lvii (hereafter referred to as *Works*). In the following notes, "XXXV" signifies that a quotation from *Praeterita* has been used unless it is designated "from *Dilecta*" or unless a page reference in Roman numerals shows that it comes from the editorial introduction.

[3] From unpublished letter of December 20, 1904; original in *The Charles Eliot Norton Correspondence,* in The Houghton Library, Harvard University. *Deepie* (sometimes spelled *Dipa*) was an epithet Mrs. Severn used in her correspondence with and references to Ruskin.

[4] Unwin, Raynor, ed., p. 6.

[5] From unpublished letter of September 20, 1912, from Sara Anderson (one of Ruskin's secretaries during his later years) to Lady Charles Stuart Wortley, *née* Caroline ("Carrie") Millais; original in *The Bowerswell Papers,* in The Pierpont Morgan Library. Daughter of Lady (John Everett) Millais, *née* "Effie" Gray, Lady Charles Stuart Wortley began the collection of Ruskin-Gray-Millais letters from which Admiral Sir William James published *John Ruskin and Effie Gray,* distributed in England as *The Order of Release.*

[6] From letter of February 21, 1863, unpublished except for the sentence in double parentheses: see *Works*, XXXIV, p. 662, *n.*; original in the Yale University Library.

[7] *Works*, XVII, p. lxix; *destroys* is italicized in the manuscript, but not in the published version; original in the Yale University Library.

[8] From unpublished letter of August 26, 1862; original in the Yale University Library.

[9] *Sir Edward Cook, K. B. E., A Biography*, pp. 225–27, *passim*.

[10] These statements are based on letters which Mrs. Severn and Alexander Wedderburn sent Charles Eliot Norton between 1900 and 1905; their letters are the source of related information scattered through the paragraphs which follow. The original letters are in *The Charles Eliot Norton Correspondence* in The Houghton Library, Harvard University. Wedderburn's general plan for the Library Edition, drawn up in consultation with George Allen, was tentatively announced to Norton in a letter of September 21, 1900. In a letter of October 12, 1900, Norton objected to "a complete collection of all the Ruskin miscellanea. . . . Ruskin himself published, and allowed to be published far too much. . . . He has loaded his bark so heavily that there must be jettison of the great part of the cargo on the way down the rough river of Time." Norton ended by outlining a twenty-one volume edition which would "comprise all that can really be considered *opera*," and advised Wedderburn to "leave to the collectors trifles and momentary flashes of his wayward genius, and much of his later adventures in science." Refusing to be dissuaded from what in truth gives the Library Edition its permanent value, Wedderburn replied, on November 14, 1900, that it was for editors "to collect, not to jettison," which would be "the work of Time," after editors had shown everything from which selections could be made; George Allen and Collingwood, he added, agreed with him in this opinion. These letters do not reveal when Cook joined Wedderburn as coeditor. It was possibly as late as December, 1902, as J. W. Scott Robertson asserts (*Life and Death of a Newspaper*, p. 294), though Cook's biographer, J. S. Mills, remarks that in Cook's diary the first reference to the Library Edition occurs "early in 1902." (*Op. cit.*, p. 204.)

Mrs. Severn's letters show that through these years she was pressed for money and that, in her opinion, although Wedderburn always acted honorably, he never failed to take care of his own interests, and dealt with her far from generously. This impression about Wedderburn is elsewhere created: see Notes 14 and 17.

[11] Mills, J. S., *op. cit.*, p. 225. "Many a person," Mills continues, "obtains for a second-rate novel as much as Cook did for these thirty-nine volumes and the immense labour they represent." More specifically, Scott Robertson remarks: "Cook had a slender reward, £1,500 I think. . . ." (*Op. cit.*, p. 307.)

[12] One of the folders thus distributed is in The Pierpont Morgan Library. On the folder itself is printed: "ORIGINAL AUTOGRAPH LETTER BY JOHN RUSKIN PRESENTED WITH THE LIBRARY EDITION OF RUSKIN'S WORKS 1912." This folder contains a letter of December 11, 1913 from The Encyclopædia Britannica Company to Henry Champ, Esq., as follows: "Dear Sir, We have the pleasure to enclose you, in accordance with our advertised offer, the Ruskin autograph letter in the morocco case.

Yours truly, The Encyclopædia Britannica Company, Ltd." The autograph letter presented on this occasion is dated "2 April [1882]" and is addressed to George Allen. It deals with the handling of proof.

With appreciation, I am indebted to Mr. Stanley Unwin, Chairman of George Allen & Unwin Ltd., for my account of how The Encyclopædia Britannica Company happened to be distributing the Library Edition in 1912. William Allen (George Allen's son), Mr. Unwin notes, supplied a sufficient number of Ruskin letters so that one letter could be presented with each set.

[13] Mills, J. S., *op. cit.*, p. 227.

[14] From unpublished letter in *The Charles Eliot Norton Correspondence.* Editorial work on the first two volumes (1903) had been relatively simple because, as Wedderburn wrote Collingwood on December 9, 1902, "in the case of the Poetry of Architecture [*Works,* I, pp. 1–188] & Poems [the bulk of *Works,* II] you were paid a lump sum for your work." As to other Ruskin books that Collingwood had edited, Wedderburn remarked, in a letter of December 11, 1902: "There is no question of buying up your rights — but it is necessary to include Studies in Both Arts, Lectures on Landscape, & the Economist. . . . Do you object to this? or think any payment should be made to you. The legal question may be complicated — but I do not want any such to be raised. . . ." In his reply of December 12, 1902, Collingwood rather drily thanked Wedderburn for "explaining your intentions with regard to the Ruskin books in which I have an interest." (From letters in my possession.)

J. S. Mills relates: "The normal method of procedure was for the editors to meet twice a week, on which occasions Cook would submit for Mr. Wedderburn's approval the use he proposed to make of the latter's material, proofs also being subsequently sent. . . . It is possible that Cook scarcely realized when he undertook this colossal task the amount of work it would involve." When Cook was dismissed from the *Daily News,* in 1901, he "ran a risk . . . of being actually stranded," Mills notes (*op. cit.,* pp. 219–25, *passim*); and in 1911, when Cook lost his work for the *Daily Chronicle* and heard a friend congratulate him on having been freed from drudgery, he answered: " 'A rich man's view.' " (J. W. Scott Robertson, *op. cit.,* p. 303.) Soon thereafter, he was working on his biography of Florence Nightingale. Although Scott Robertson's statement that it took Cook only "five months" to write his two-volume *Life* of Ruskin (*op. cit.,* p. 294) seems incredible, Cook must always have been remarkably fluent in his use of such material as he had at hand.

[15] From a letter of Mr. F. J. Sharp, of Barrow-in-Furness, Lancashire (hereafter referred to as Mr. Sharp). Having in his possession books of John James Ruskin, Mr. Sharp informed me about this error in Cook's discussion of the watermark: see *Works,* I, p. xi: the last words on the page.

[16] These letters of 1894 and 1895 are now owned by Mr. Sharp, who most kindly has made them available for reproduction. See Figs. 15 and 16 after p. 56.

These two letters were sold in 1931 at Sotheby's and, having thus come from the Brantwood Collection, were all but indubitably known to Cook and Wedderburn.

Nevertheless, in Vol. XXXVI of their edition of the *Works,* Cook and

Wedderburn state unequivocally: "It was to [Miss Susan Beever], as she lay upon her death-bed [in October, 1893], that the last letter ever written in Ruskin's hand was sent." (P. cix.) In Vol. XXXVII they end by phrasing their footnote to this "Last" letter: "What is *believed* [my italics] to be the last letter. . . ." (P. 613, *n.*) The editors' definite statement in Vol. XXXVI is accompanied by the note: "See the *facsimile* in Vol. XXXVII."

However, Cook himself refers to Ruskin's letter of *1894,* to Lady Simon (addressed as "Dear Lady Simon*d*"), when he quotes the Simons' reply to Ruskin, in the second volume of his *Life* (1911), wherein he calls the October, 1893 letter to Miss Beever *"One* [my italics] of the last letters which [Ruskin] wrote in his own hand. . . ." (P. 531.)

This reference in Cook's *Life* should not be considered a correction, in 1911, of a mistake made in 1909, when Vols. XXXVI and XXXVII of the *Works* ("Letters") were published. The editor's "belief" and "The Last Letter" as a title for the facsimile facing p. 614 of Vol. XXXVII were not listed, in 1912, among the "Addenda et Corrigenda" in Vol. XXXVIII: see p. 384. (I never speak of editorial errors without due regard for the *errata* which are listed in Vol. XXXVIII. For example, see Note 9, p. 199.) Finally, in Vol. XXXIX this letter of October, 1893, is once more unequivocally identified as "R[uskin]'s last letter, written to [Miss Susan Beever]." (P. 45.)

This " 'Last' Letter" was originally presented in facsimile in the third edition (1902) of *Hortus Inclusus,* a selection of Ruskin's letters to Miss Mary and Miss Susan Beever ("Sister Ladies of the Thwaite, Coniston"), edited by Albert Fleming. In the "Preface to the Third Edition" Fleming states: "I have also added a reproduction of Mr. Ruskin's last letter to Miss Beever. It was written about the 20th October 1893. . . . I believe this to be the last complete letter that ever came from his pen." (*Works,* XXXVII, p. 622.) When Miss Susan Beever died (October 29, 1893), she bequeathed to Albert Fleming her Ruskin letters, of which about five hundred (now in the Henry E. Huntington Library and Art Gallery) had been addressed to her. The first of those published was written in November, 1873. By 1874 she had become to Ruskin "My dearest Susie."

Already "an old lady of sixty-eight when Ruskin first made her acquaintance" (*Works,* XXXVI, p. cviii), Miss Susan Beever shared Ruskin's interest in birds and flowers, and became one of the most intimate friends of his later years. As a near neighbor, she was also a close friend of Mrs. Arthur Severn. If sentimental values could alone determine which letter should be considered Ruskin's "Last," his letter of October, 1893, to Miss Susan Beever might appropriately be selected.

[17] On January 17, 1902, Norton wrote to Mrs. Severn (his "Dearest Joan"): "As to the new edition Allen seems to me grasping as usual. Between him & Wedderburn not much, I fear, will be left for you. You ought to have some entirely trustworthy & capable, confidential legal advisor who should be made to understand all the conditions, & who should maintain & protect your interests. A strong & efficient man is needed to deal with two such hard & gripe-all-characters, who have such advantage of position over you. You have been too yielding as regards Wedderburn, and have submitted to too much from him." (From a transcription kindly provided by Mr. Sharp from the original in his possession.)

[18] From unpublished letter of December 20, 1904; original in *The Charles Eliot Norton Correspondence.*

[19] A copy of this letter, addressed to the Editor of the London *Times* and dated July 31, 1852 (from Herne Hill), appears among *The Bowerswell Papers.* In an unpublished letter of August 2, 1852, John James Ruskin told George Gray, Sr. that the letter had appeared in "todays Times" (original in *The Bowerswell Papers;* henceforth, references to "George Gray" will signify *George Gray, Sr.*). Related correspondence shows that Ruskin had written this letter with reluctance and under pressure from his father. It was not included in Alexander Wedderburn's collection of Ruskin's "Public Letters," first published as *Arrows of the Chace* in 1880, or in the supplementary collection of Ruskin's "Letters" which Wedderburn published as *Ruskiniana* (1890). Chronologically arranged, the letters of Ruskin which Wedderburn thus published in 1880 and in 1890 comprise *Arrows of the Chace* in the Library Edition.

It seems inconceivable that this "Letter" to the Editor of the London *Times* (see col. 6, p. 7, of the August 2, 1852 issue) was unknown to Alexander Wedderburn and to others, although perhaps understandably (since Ruskin did not wish to write the letter in the first place) it has not been mentioned in any Ruskin bibliography. Working under Ruskin's auspices in 1880, Wedderburn would have omitted it from *Arrows of the Chace* if Ruskin did not wish to have it republished, and in deference to Ruskin, R. H. Shepherd would have deleted any reference to it in his *Bibliography of Ruskin* (1878). Later one finds Mrs. Arthur Severn, in an unpublished letter of April 27, 1894, remarking that Thomas J. Wise had already "done so much . . . [for Ruskin] in the Bibliography!" (1893) and concluding, with reference to a pending publication: "So I am much obliged by your assurance that I may have a voice in the matter." (Original letter, from Mrs. Severn to T. J. Wise, in the Symington Collection, Rutgers University Library.) Next, Mary E. Jameson states that Charles Eliot Norton had read in manuscript her *Bibliographical Contribution to the Study of Ruskin* (1901) and that although her bibliography represented "earnest research" it was not complete. Finally Wedderburn again ignored this letter when (so far as one can judge) he collected in the *Works* all other letters which had been already published. In Vol. XXXVIII, for example, the section of the *Addenda* devoted to "Additional Letters" concludes with a letter headed "A LETTER NOT INCLUDED IN 'ARROWS OF THE CHACE'": see *Works,* p. 349.

[20] For acid editorial comment upon Norton's edition of Ruskin's *Letters,* see *Works,* XXXVII, pp. 683–84. Unpublished letters in *The Charles Eliot Norton Correspondence* indicate the astonishment of Houghton Mifflin, as Norton's publishers, when Alexander Wedderburn stopped the sale, in England, of Norton's edition of these letters. According to English law, letters can be published and sold in England only with the consent of the literary executors of the man who wrote them — a permission Wedderburn refused to grant.

[21] For examples of fragmentary publication, see p. 7 and Note 30, p. 235. For an example of unindicated editorial omissions, see Note 33, p. 246. An illustration of how previous editors unobtrusively deleted parts of Ruskin's letters which were then republished by Cook and Wedderburn is provided

by Ruskin's letters to Alfred, Lord Tennyson, first edited by Hallam Tennyson and now in the Yale University Library.

[29] For example, frankly advertising his *John Ruskin* by a caricature of Ruskin on the cover-jacket, Peter Quennell concluded this "Portrait of a Prophet" with one of the most unpleasant stories about Ruskin I have ever read (see p. 288): without indicating why he believes that he is thus publicizing more than vicious gossip, Quennell recounts the tale as though it were a well-known fact; the story has, however, every earmark of the village talk which once was scandalously rife in Coniston. And although Derrick Leon's "Life" is of a very different order from Quennell's biography, Leon himself was undiscriminating in his use of sources other than those connected with *The La Touche Correspondence* (which he handled admirably, insofar as one can judge from his treatment of the Ruskin-La Touche-MacDonald letters, now in the Yale University Library). Leon, for instance, uncritically accepts such gossip as is represented by a story (which stems from Charles Augustus Howell) that Ruskin once gave the mineralogist, "Calvert," *a blank check* for some minerals he desired. Calvert, Leon states, had first vaguely quoted a price of about £300 and had "later filled in [the blank check] for £3,000." (*Op. cit.,* p. 338.) There is evidence that some chicanery was connected with Ruskin's purchase of these minerals. Nevertheless, every stroke of writing on the original check, made out to "John Calvert" for "Three Thousand Pounds/ £3000 · 0 · 0" and subsequently canceled, is beyond debate in Ruskin's script. (This "Calvert Check" is now in the possession of Mr. Sharp, who has most kindly provided me with a photographic copy, giving his permission for its use in reproduction. See Fig. 1 after p. 56.) The trouble is, of course, that to correct such individual misstatements — credulously and often inaccurately repeated — does little good until the very atmosphere in which they continue thus to flourish has been cleared.

CHAPTER 1

[1] Unpublished entry from *Diary,* 1885; in the Yale University Library. This *Diary* is in three "octavo" notebooks which contain the first version of that part of *Praeterita* written between January 1 and July 14, 1885. Through this period it was Ruskin's habit to begin each day with a brief dated comment on events of the preceding day, after which he picked up the story of his life from the point at which he had stopped the day before. These "Diary-Volumes" will be called the "First MS." of *Praeterita* when there is occasion to quote passages which were left unpublished, originally by Ruskin and later by Cook and Wedderburn. A revised and amplified version of *Praeterita,* in three "folio" volumes which contain autograph copy (not always in Ruskin's hand) and some pages of corrected proof, is also in the Yale University Library and will be referred to as the "Second MS." For further description of these two MSS., together with that of the MS. of *Praeterita* as printed, see *Works,* XXXV, p. lvii.

Before his work reached the point of publication, Ruskin was highly haphazard in his use of an apostrophe with the possessive — a convention habitually ignored by John James Ruskin in his letters; therefore an omitted apostrophe will not be indicated by *sic* in quotations from their writing, as it appears in manuscripts.

² *Works,* XXXV, p. 122.

³ Unpublished passage from "First MS." of *Praeterita:* originally, the concluding sentence of the paragraph which begins — "In looking back . . ." *Works,* XXXV, p. 127.

⁴ For example, Ruskin certainly knew that his mother's maiden name was *Cock:* see p. 75. He also knew that his Aunt Jessie was not Mrs. *Peter* but, rather, Mrs. *Patrick* Richardson: amongst the silver removed from Brantwood to be sold at auction was "A circular Salver . . . inscribed '*Mr. Patk. Richardson, of Perth, to J. J. Ruskin . . . June,* 1824'. . . ." (*Item 25,* in Sotheby & Co., *Catalogue of Old English Silver, etc.,* sold on April 29, 1931. For a copy of this *Catalogue* and for calling this detail to my attention, I am indebted to Mr. Sharp.)

More generally, *Praeterita* gives no evidence of Ruskin's having used information in those "grievous" and "humiliating" letters of his Croydon grandmother — lost, as yet, to Ruskin scholarship. Nor did he make use of information in letters of his Scottish grandmother (*The Catherine Tweddale Ruskin Correspondence*), which Mr. Sharp acquired after manuscripts at Brantwood had been dispersed at auction. The letters of his Croydon grandmother may have been destroyed long before the Brantwood manuscripts were thus scattered. I did not come across them when I was working with the material assembled in Ruskin's library, although at that time I found the letters of his Scottish grandmother. As noted in the "Introduction," Ruskin manuscripts were destroyed by Mrs. Severn, aided and abetted by Charles Eliot Norton and probably by Edward T. Cook and Alexander Wedderburn. Undoubtedly Mrs. Severn and others would have been much tempted to destroy the "humiliating" letters of his Croydon grandmother (see pp. 82–84) for what they would have considered the honor of John Ruskin.

⁵ See Alexander Carmichael, "The Ruskins," *Celtic Review* (April, 1906), Vol. II, pp. 343–51. Author of *Deirdire, Carmina Gadelica,* etc., Dr. Carmichael (*d.* 1912) had "made many archaeological discoveries in the Western Isles, and contributed many papers to transactions of various archaeological societies and to other publications, upon Celtic antiquities and literature; collected large masses of oral literature throughout the Highlands and Islands. . . ." (*Who Was Who, 1897–1916*). Dr. Carmichael gathered the material on "The Ruskins" in the district of Muckairn, in Argyllshire. Here, in Glenlonain, he learned from old inhabitants that a family of MacCalmans, who became known as the *Chlann Rusgain,* had owned a prosperous tanning house until the middle of the eighteenth century, and he talked with descendants of this family, thus assembling the most convincing evidence as yet produced about the possible backgrounds of the eighteenth-century Ruskins.

Summarizing the results of Dr. Carmichael's investigation, Cook and Wedderburn evidently depended on William Sinclair's version of the story (see "The Scottish Ancestors of Ruskin," *St. George,* Vol. IX) rather than on firsthand knowledge of Dr. Carmichael's report. Like Sinclair, for example, they state that the *great*-grandfather of Ruskin, rather than the *great-great*-grandfather (according to Carmichael), fought under the Earl of *Mar* (Carmichael having stated that this ancestor fought under the Earl of *Argyll* and having attempted to obtain specific evidence to this effect from the family papers of the Earl of Argyll). Citing Carmichael, they also place in direct quotation marks words used not by Carmichael but by Sinclair. They were highly skeptical about the Scottish ancestry ascribed by Carmichael, they themselves perhaps having been aware that the Ruskins came from Cheshunt, Hertfordshire: see p. 83. In any event, the reasons which they give for rejecting the erroneous conclusions which Dr. Carmichael had reached through singular but nonetheless conscientious investigation can seem patently absurd, if critically considered. Consequently, in 1946, on the basis of existing evidence (presented, to be sure, with sentimentality and without discrimination), Dr. George F. Black was justified in ignoring Cook and Wedderburn and in endorsing Dr. Carmichael when he listed "Ruskin" among *The Surnames of Scotland.*

Adding his mite, Dr. H. Cameron Gillies speaks of "Glen-lònian" as "the home of the 'Rusgain,' or Ruskins, of whom was the late prose-poet — John Ruskin. . . . 'A tradition still exists among the old people of the place that the Ruskins were "luchd ceaird," *artisans,* draoinich, sculptors,' " (*Place-Names of Argyll,* pp. 246–47.)

For a survey of etymological theories about the name *Ruskin,* see *Works,* XXXV, pp. lix–lxi. C. W. Bardsley does not include "Ruskin" in his *Dictionary of English and Welsh Surnames.* But as a further contribution, Ernest Weekley states, in his *Surnames* (1937), that "Ruskin" comes from the A. S. *Roscytel,* or *horse:* this word, he explains, "is fairly common in Middle English, and still survives as *Roskill* . . . while the derivative *Rosketin* . . . has given Ruskin. . . ." (Pp. 33–34.)

⁶ In 1950, J. B. Whitmore included "Ruskin" in Part III of *A Genealogical Guide,* citing [Messing Rudkin, "Some Ancient Rutland People,"] *The Rutland Magazine,* Vol. IV, No. 32 (October, 1910), p. 242. Rudkin maintains that during the eighteenth century, Ruskins live in Leicester: "There is, among the Leicester Wills at the Probate Register, Leicester, the will of Richard Ruskin of Rothley . . . of date 1792"; this statement is followed by a genealogical graph on which *Edward Ruskin,* a wheelwright, marries *Elizabeth,* by whom he has eight children. Therefore, in my behalf, Mr. Ernest Morris, of St. Margaret's Vicarage, Leicester, examined Leicester records and discovered that the name of this family was *Rushin,* not *Ruskin: Rushin* is thus spelled consistently and unmistakably in the will of *Richard Rushin* and in the entries of the baptism of every one of his eight children — he (not Edward) having been the wheelwright and the husband of Elizabeth. Whether Rudkin is more reliable in presenting evidence that Ruskins lived in Leicester from the fourteenth into the sixteenth centuries has not been determined. For those early Ruskins, see *Publications of the Harleian Society,* "Middlesex Pedigrees," Vol. 65, pp. 12–13; John Nichols, *The History and Antiquities of the County of Leicester,* Vol. II, p. 264.

⁷ *The Life and Works of John Ruskin,* Vol. I, pp. 6–7 (hereafter called *Life,* with all references applying to the two-volume edition of 1893 unless the revised one-volume edition of 1900 is designated). Collingwood removed this passage from the revised edition of the *Life,* in which he expressed his opinion that the Ruskins were English in origin, perhaps descending from "a tribe of Anglian settlers called Rusking," as is suggested by the place-name, *Ruskington,* in Lincolnshire." (*Life,* revised ed., p. 6.)

[8] Leon, Derrick, *Ruskin the Great Victorian,* p. 5.

[9] For general orientation, see "The Ruskin Family Tree," facing p. 40, on which italics indicate the names and dates which differentiate this "Tree" from the one presented by Cook and Wedderburn: see *Works,* XXXV, p. 603. The Cook and Wedderburn "Tree" was based upon the one prepared by Collingwood in 1893 and revised in his 1900 edition of the *Life.* Inasmuch as Cook and Wedderburn did not successfully correct one error made by Collingwood and introduced various errors while adding the barest modicum of accurate information (see Note 11), they created an entirely false impression when they called their *Family Tree* "revised and amplified" (*Works,* XXXV, p. 594, *n.*) beyond that of Collingwood, which remains the basis of my version. In 1912, under "Addenda et Corrigenda," Cook and Wedderburn noted only one error upon their "Tree," as follows: " 'Andrew' (Richardson) 'd. in Australia' should be 'd. on his way to Australia': see XXXV [p. 603]." (*Works,* XXXVIII, p. 382.)

[10] See Appendix A for information about the sources of all dates, places, and names used in the following discussion of the English Ruskins. Analogously, Appendix C serves to document all statements contingent upon Ruskin *Wills.*

[11] On their "Tree," Cook and Wedderburn erroneously state that this John Ruskin was "bapt. April 9, 1732, O. S.," Collingwood having erroneously entered "(1732–1780)" under *John Ruskin* on the "Tree" in his revised edition of the *Life.* Followed by Cook and Wedderburn, Collingwood obtained *1732,* as the birthdate, from a "Family Bible": see *Ruskin Relics,* p. 197 and *Works,* XXXIV, p. 702; moreover, on the manuscript version of his "Tree" (now in the possession of Mr. Sharp) Collingwood gave the baptismal date of this John Ruskin and the birthdates of his children, parenthetically noting "Family Bible" as his source. The date of death was all but certainly obtained from a mourning ring which remained at Brantwood until *c.* 1930 and which is now in my possession. Through what was evidently an error, complementary to the error in date of birth, made by some member of the family (probably Ruskin's great-grandmother), it is engraved upon this ring that John Ruskin died in 1780, aged *48* (see Note 17).

Reliable evidence now makes it possible to correct the birthdate error. In a Guildhall Library *Register of Burials* it is stated that this John Ruskin died in 1780, *"aged 45 years"* (my italics) — an entry which has been carefully re-examined. The correctness of this entry in the Guildhall *Register* would seem to be confirmed by complementary evidence: *"1734/5 Jan. 3"* appears as the date of baptism for John Ruskin in an original *Register* of Cheshunt, Herts. (now in the Hertfordshire County Record Office, Hertford). It follows that John Ruskin, born in late December, 1734, would have been 45 years old when he was buried on May 19, 1780. All facts considered, it seems as though henceforth the Cook and Wedderburn entry "bapt. April 9, 1732, O. S." should be disregarded.

As their only correct addition to the Collingwood "Tree," Cook and Wedderburn gave the names and dates of birth of five of the six siblings of John Thomas Ruskin — information which they may have obtained from the manuscript version of Collingwood's "Tree" (left with the "Early Records" of the family). It is symptomatic that, having decided to make this addition to the "Tree," Cook and Wedderburn should have failed to include Mary as a sister of John Thomas.

It is quite possible that the birthdates of both Margaret and Mary Ruskin are given incorrectly in the "Family Bible." According to Collingwood's transcription of these entries (kindly sent me in transcription by Mr. Sharp), Margaret was born on Saturday, July 3, 1756; Mary on December 6, 1757. According to epitaphs upon their tombstones in the Croydon Church-yard, Margaret would have been born in *1755*, Mary in *1756* (see Appendix A). No official record of the birthdates of these two children has as yet been found. It would not, however, be surprising eventually to discover that Margaret was born on Saturday, July *5, 1755;* Mary on December 6, 1756.

In all probability, the Bible which contains these birthdates has become an item in the Ruskin Collection of John Howard Whitehouse (a Collection which, beyond the *Diaries,* was evidently not made available even to Joan Evans as a biographer who with Mr. Whitehouse, according to announce-ment, is editing the *Diaries*). Collingwood describes it as a "Baskett Bible of 1749, nicely rebound in old red morocco, handsomely tooled, bear[ing] the family's earliest register. It is writte[n] in a big unscholarly hand in the blank space of the last page of Maccabees. . . ." (*Ruskin Relics,* p. 197.)

[12] For further details, see Appendix C. The daughter *Jane* mentioned in this *Will* may have been the "Infant" *Jane* who was buried in Cheshunt "1747/8 Mar. 7," without a surviving record of baptism: see Appendix A. (Note, too, that in 1753 a *Jane Ruskin* was buried in the Great Churchyard of the Parish of St. Bartholomew-the-Great.)

[13] See pp. 82–83.

[14] According to this *Will* (see Appendix C), upon the death of Ruskin's great-grandmother Mary (date unknown), property owned by his great-grandfather John would have passed into the possession of Ruskin's maternal grandmother Margaret, his paternal grandfather John Thomas, and their sister Mary. Such property could then have been inherited by Ruskin's mother from her mother or by Ruskin's father from his father, which might help to account for the curious coincidence that in Marylebone, after 1864, Ruskin made "efforts to reclaim part . . . of the lower-class dwellings of London. Half a dozen houses in Marylebone left by Mr. Ruskin's father, to which he added three more in Paradise Place, as it was euphemistically named, were subjects of [this] experiment." (W. G. Collingwood, *Life,* Vol. II, p. 415.) It has been impossible, to date, to trace the title-deeds of the house on Marylebone Road and of the five houses in Freshwater Place which Ruskin inherited: see *Works,* XXIX, p. 141 (from *Fors Clavigera,* June, 1877).

[15] Although this statement must be made with caveat, not to make it would seem to be close to splitting hairs in caution. In his *Will* John Ruskin refers to his wife *Mary.* Their first child was born in 1755 or 1756, John Ruskin having married Mary Carswell on June 26, 1754. Where they lived from 1754 to 1759 remains unknown. There is, however, no reason to suppose that the John Ruskin who married Mary Carswell in 1754 was not the John Ruskin who was baptized in Cheshunt on Jan. 3, 1735 and who died on May 16, 1780, aged 45 years old, as the husband of "Mary" and the great-grandfather of John Ruskin.

[16] See Fig. 2 after p. 56. This miniature, now in my possession, appears as *Item 282* in the *Catalogue* of the "Ruskin Exhibition Coniston July 21 to Sept. 15 1900," in which it is described as "Bracelet with miniature of his grandfather, John Ruskin, of Edinburgh, as a child."

[17] This mourning ring, now in my possession, appears as *Item 284* in the *Catalogue* of the "Ruskin Exhibition . . . 1900," in which it is erroneously described as "Ring with the hair of John Ruskin, of Edinburgh." The inscription on the mount shows that the hair must be that of Ruskin's great-grandfather, John Ruskin of London.

The engraving on the mount has become so worn that the date of death now reads: *"Ob   6th. of May,"* the *of* having been almost effaced; the *1* in the date *16* and the *it* of *Obit* have been completely worn away. The date of the death, *16 May, 1780,* is confirmed by the appearance of "May 19, 1780" as the date of burial for "John Ruskin in Great Churchyard aged 45 years" (see Appendix A). Upon the mourning ring the *8* in "aged 48" is clear but evidently is an error: see Note 11.

[18] From transcription of the *Deed of Indenture* (February 7, 1776) of John Thomas Ruskin; original in the possession of Mr. Sharp. Cook and Wedderburn misdated this document "February *16,* 1776": see *Works,* XXXV, p. lx.

[19] See Appendix C.

[20] From a letter of Mr. Lloyd Mead, Clerk, The Vintners' Company, London, who most kindly investigated the "Freedom Book" of the Vintners' Company. Completion of indentured service, Mr. Mead informs me, would not customarily have been recorded upon the *Deed of Indenture* but would have been regularly entered in the "Freedom Book." "As regards changing Masters during the period of the Indentures," Mr. Mead explains, "this would only be done if his original Master died, and I can only presume, although our records do not tell us, that Robert Walker died soon after the Indentures were sealed. . . . The normal procedure, of course, was that when the apprentice had completed his Indentures to the satisfaction of his Master, then he would take up his Freedom, and in due course his Livery. John Thomas Ruskin was not admitted to the Freedom, and I cannot say for what reason. It may have been due to the fact that he broke the Indentures, or that they were not completed satisfactorily, or to other causes such as that he did not wish to continue in the Wine Trade."

[21] *Life,* p. 7 (revised ed.); for example, Derrick Leon echoes that at the time of his marriage, John Thomas Ruskin was "a wine merchant in Edinburgh." (*Op. cit.,* p. 6.) For Cook's treatment of this matter (cited by Joan Evans) see p. 102 and Note 5, p. 226.

[22] From *Register of Births and Baptisms for the Parish of Edinburgh.* Born in 1783, Janet Ruskin (Mrs. Patrick Richardson of Perth) died on May 18, 1828: see Appendix B. Heretofore, her life has been erroneously dated: Collingwood listed it "1781–1821" (*Life,* Vol. I, p. 9), although he gave no dates for Janet Ruskin in the revised edition; Cook and Wedderburn gave the dates as "1781–1829" (*Works,* XXXV, p. 603), although they had at their disposal the entry for her birth, dated *1783,* as obtained from the *Register of Births* by the Rev. D. Butler ("John Ruskin's Grandfather,

A Merchant at the West of the Tron Kirk," *The Tron Kirk of Edinburgh,* p. 343), whose work Cook and Wedderburn cite.

Henceforth I shall not make it a practice to pause for specific correction of errors in detail or for controversy upon larger issues and interpretations. Differences which might give rise to special question will, however, be discussed, and documentary evidence in support of factual statements will always be provided.

[23] Sinclair, William, *op. cit.,* p. 247.

CHAPTER 2

[1] For example, to celebrate the New Year with a customary gift, Ruskin presented to his father in 1829, "A Battle" — an 89-line poem (unpublished) based on Scott's description in *Waverley* (Ch. LIX) of the skirmish at Clifton. (Original in "MS. XI," Bound volume: *Poems and Letters to his Father;* in the Yale University Library. Listing Ruskin's unpublished poems, Cook and Wedderburn mistakenly ascribed "A Battle" to 1828: see *Works,* II, p. 536.) Again, Chs. XLVI–XLVII of *Waverley* were transformed into Ruskin's "Battle of Preston Pans," 130 lines of verse composed in 1830. (Original in "MS. V," Notebook: *Poems, 1829–1832;* in the Yale University Library.)

[2] Boswell, James, *Journal of a Tour of the Hebrides,* pp. 11–12. A few days later, showing Johnson the sights of Edinburgh in 1778, Boswell and some friends "made him look up from the Cowgate to the highest building . . . thirteen floors or storeys from the ground upon the back elevation. . . ." (*Ibid.,* p. 25.)

[3] See Robert Chambers, *Traditions of Edinburgh,* Vol. I: this volume is devoted to a detailed description of the houses and living arrangements in Edinburgh from earlier days into the beginning of the nineteenth century. Though some districts understandably were more desirable than others, few if any neighborhoods were not "respectable" if one lived in upper stories, and very few indeed were socially acceptable if — as did John Thomas Ruskin — one occupied the ground floor. No biographer of Ruskin has recognized this fact, Collingwood having remarked: "For many years they lived in the Old Town, then a respectable neighbourhood, among a cultivated and well-bred society, in which they moved as equals. . . ." (*Life,* revised ed., p. 7.)

[4] Having noted industries recently established, W. L. Mathieson comments: "A few miscellaneous facts will illustrate the progress that was now being made. Between 1763 and 1790 the printing works of Edinburgh increased from six to sixteen, and the paper-mills in its vicinity from three to twelve — some of them the largest in Britain. The manufacture of paper rose from 6,400 reams to about 100,000; of printed cottons from 150,000 yards to 4,500,000; of candles from 1,400,000 lbs. to 3,000,000. In the twenty years from 1763–1783 the annual revenue of the Post Office expanded from about £12,000 to £40,000; and by 1786 the valued rent of the houses liable to the land-tax had more than doubled." (*The Awakening of Scotland, 1747–1797,* p. 253.) See also William Creech, *Edinburgh Fugitive Pieces,* pp. 62–83.

[5] Greig, James, *Sir Henry Raeburn,* pp. xviii–xix.

[6] Fyfe, W. T., *Edinburgh under Sir Walter Scott,* p. 2.

CHAPTER 3

[1] For the birth of Catherine Tweddale on August 14, 1763, see Appendix B. Ruskin having stated that Catherine was "sixteen" when she was married and that her first child was born within a year, Cook and Wedderburn became totally confused. Having first misdated Janet's birth *1781,* they dated Catherine's birth *1764,* though without evidence, they would nonetheless assert: "The actual date [of Catherine's marriage] is 1781." (*Works,* XXXV, pp. 603 and 62, *n.*) Yet the correct date of Catherine's birth was available in Hew Scott's *Fasti Ecclesiæ Scoticanæ,* to which they make references. For the date of Janet's birth, see Appendix B, *1783.* For the probable date of Catherine's marriage, see p. 50.

[2] For the Reverend Andrew Adair and his children (Catherine's nine cousins at Whithorn Abbey) see Hew Scott, *op. cit.,* Vol. II, p. 380. For the bequest left Catherine by her mother's brother John, see pp. 57 and 72. Her brother James was still more generously remembered, having been "left a considerable fortune by his uncle, Surgeon-General Adair." (P. H. M'Kerlie, *History of the Lands and Their Owners in Galloway,* Vol. I, p. 343; above, p. 112.) John Ruskin Tweddale, a son of Catherine's brother James, wrote his niece, Mrs. Arthur Severn, on October 24, 1886: " 'Dr. Adair, the physician, uncle of my father, was with General Wolff [*sic*] when he died at the battle he fought at Quebec. He was shot, and the ball entered near his heart. I have an engraving from a picture by B. West descriptive of the event. The doctor is holding a white handkerchief to the wound, and he seems to me to be a wonderfully good likeness of my late father.' " (Unpublished passage from a letter Ruskin had planned to include in *Dilecta;* taken from proof in the "Second MS." of *Praeterita.*)

[3] In 1746, Catherine's Aunt Mary (1723–1807) had married James Maitland, minister of Sorbie, and became mother of the Rev. John Garlies Maitland (1766–1835) of Fairgirth. Educated at the University of Glasgow, he, too, married the daughter of a minister and became father of the Rev. James Maitland (1797–1872). In 1837, Louisa, daughter of Charles Bellamy and "the Hon. Louisa Gordon, sister and heiress of Adam, last Viscount Kenmure," became the second wife of this James Maitland and the mother of "James Charles of Kenmure" (1850–1915). (See Hew Scott, *op. cit.,* Vol. II, pp. 372, 377, 413.) These backgrounds account for Cook and Wedderburn's entry (copied from Collingwood) on the "Family Tree" which identifies Mary Tweddale as "grandmother [*sic*] of J. E. [*sic*] Maitland of Kenmure Castle."

Catherine's connection with the Hannays, an old and reputable family of Galloway, is indicated by a letter which her brother, James Tweddale, wrote to John James Ruskin, from Wigtown, in February, 1838. Seventy years old by then, James Tweddale remarked: "I shall now proceed to give you a history of your family Tree — Cap'n Adair had 2 Sons & 3 daughters, viz. the Revd Adair & D'r John Adair. The Doctor never married. Rev Adair married a Sister of the present McDouall of Logans Grandfather; one of Cap^n Adairs daughters was my Mother, another of them Mr Maitland's Mother & a third Mr James Hannays Mother." (From original in the possession of Mr. F. J. Sharp, who kindly supplied this passage in transcription.) Although this letter remains, to my knowledge, the sole source of information about the Adair-Hannay marriage, I have preserved upon my version of the "Tree" Cook and Wedderburn's entry for *James Hannay,* without assuming, however, that *James* was necessarily the first name of the father of "Mr. James Hannay" or that these Hannays were necessarily "of Wigtown."

⁴ See p. 105. For the marriage of Captain Thomas Adair to Jean Ross of Balkail, Parish of Old Luce (rather than of Cook and Wedderburn's Balneil, Parish of New Luce), see P. H. M'Kerlie, *op. cit.,* Vol. I, pp. 600 and 607. For the Rev. Andrew Adair's inheritance of the Little Genoch (Cook and Wedderburn's "Gennoch") property from his father, Captain Thomas, who had been the heir of his father, John Adair, see *ibid.,* p. 586. For the marriage of this John Adair (Catherine's great-grandfather) to Mary Agnew (a cousin of the Sir Andrew Agnew who was the last hereditary Sheriff of Wigtownshire), and for his death in 1721, see *ibid.* For the prestige implicit in the family backgrounds of Catherine's great-grandmother, Mary Agnew Adair, see Sir Andrew Agnew, *The Hereditary Sheriffs of Galloway;* note, too, however, P. H. M'Kerlie's discussion of the extreme unreliability of this historical account of the Agnews: *op. cit.,* Vol. I, p. 428 ff.

⁵ What are today the counties of Wigtown (the extreme southwest tip of Scotland) and of Kirkcudbright (to the east of Wigtown) were known as "Galloway," whose men-of-old were famous for their bravery: hence the proverbial "wild Scots of Galloway." All of Ruskin's known Galloway ancestors were of Wigtownshire, having lived as ministers or landowners in the Parishes of Glenluce (or Old Luce), Sorbie, and Whithorn. Ruskin first received information about them through a letter of August 25, 1885, sent by his distant cousin, John Ruskin Tweddale, to Mrs. Arthur Severn. This letter, which Ruskin had set in type, was published in 1900, in Part III of *Dilecta:* see *Works,* XXXV, pp. 593–94; for his own comments on his "Galloway Ancestry," see *ibid.,* p. 607.

⁶ *Ibid.*

⁷ Vol. I, p. 8.

⁸ Learmonth, William, *Kirkcudbrightshire and Wigtownshire,* p. 101.

⁹ *Life* (revised ed.), p. 5.

¹⁰ *Works,* XXVIII, p. 148; from *Fors Clavigera,* September, 1874.

¹¹ *Ibid.,* XXXV, p. 63.

¹² *Ibid.,* p. 594; from letter of James Ruskin Tweddale to Mrs. Arthur Severn, August 25, 1885, published in *Dilecta* (see Note 5).

¹³ *Life* (revised ed.), p. 6. In 1908, repeating Collingwood's statement as though from personal knowledge, Cook and Wedderburn transformed into the " 'Solemn League and Covenant' " the document which John Ruskin Tweddale designated "the National Covenant of the Scottish Covenanters." (See *Works,* XXXV, pp. 602 and 594.) In kind response to an inquiry as to whether any Museum in Glasgow still owns a copy of the Covenant which might have come from the library of Ruskin's great-grandfather, Mr. C. W. Black, Depute City Librarian, The Mitchell Library, observed: "In spite of the fact that J. R. Tweddale states quite explicitly that the document handed over by the Baillie of Jarviswood was the *National* Covenant, the editors . . . make it the *Solemn League and Covenant,* being in obvious ignorance of the fact that these were two documents of different origins, dates and

formats. The National Covenant was a statement of faith drawn up by the presbyterian churchman of Scotland and applied to Scotland only. It was drawn up in 1638 on the basis of the Confession of King James VI in 1580 with additions by Archibald Johnston and Alexander Henderson and was circulated in all parts of Scotland by means of copies written on sheepskin. The Solemn League and Covenant was drawn up in 1643 and was a mutual bond between the Scottish presbyterians and the English Root and Branch reformers. It was circulated in printed copies with space for signatures, and went to all parts of the British Isles. There must have been many copies of the National Covenant as it was stated at the time of its signing that the leading Covenanters busied themselves in attesting duplicate copies, which were taken away by the considerable persons themselves or despatched into every shire, bailiary, stewartry, presbytery, parish, and Judicatory for signature. (J. King Hewison: 'The Covenanters,' 1908, Vol. 1, p. 270.) ¶There are many of these sheepskin documents still in existence. The above-mentioned Dr. Hewison made a census of existing copies for 'The Covenanters' and found that there were, in 1908, 39 copies known to be in public or private possession. Of these, four were in Glasgow. . . ."

[14] From description of the Kelvingrove Museum copy of the National Covenant, provided by Mr. C. W. Black, who also notes that this copy was "purchased about 1890 from David Pulsifer. . . . This copy might well be Tweddale's copy but the museum authorities are unable to give any information about its history." Of the four copies in Glasgow, only the one in the Kelvingrove Museum (signed in "various counties") could have come, however indirectly, from the library of the Reverend James Tweddale. A copy in the Glasgow University Library, Mr. Black continues, was "presented by Mr. James Wardrop, merchant in Glasgow in 1782. This copy was probably signed in Argyleshire." Two copies in The Mitchell Library were "purchased at the sale of the library of John Young, F.S.A., in 1875." One of these "is beautifully engrossed but bears no signatures"; the other "appears to have been signed in Biggar, Lanarkshire. . . ." One may add that of the 39 copies of the National Covenant known to have been extant in 1908, only the copy in the Kelvingrove Museum might reasonably be thought to have been owned by the Rev. James Tweddale, so far as one can judge from the descriptions and history of each copy given in *The Covenanters* by the Rev. J. King Hewison. Although this story may be but one more Ruskinian legend, Collingwood usually based his statements upon reliable first-hand knowledge, and in general the tale told by J. R. Tweddale would seem to warrant credence.

[15] In the *Deed of Indenture* it is stipulated: "He shall not commit Fornication, nor contract Matrimony within the said Term." (From transcription kindly made by Mr. Sharp from original in his possession.)

[16] Mr. E. A. Hogan, Registrar General for Scotland, most kindly conducted a search for the record of this marriage, without success. I am likewise indebted to Mr. Raymond Smith for information that registers in the Guildhall Library indicate that John Thomas Ruskin was not married in the Parish of St. Bartholomew-the-Great.

[17] Rusk, John McGill, *History of the Parish and Abbey of Glen Luce*, p. 85. Rusk provides two pictures which show the present church against its background of wooded hillsides and pasture land. This church was built in 1814 upon the site of the original structure, from which it does not differ

"very much . . . in outward appearance, as far as I have read and heard," its present minister, the Reverend David Galloway, informs me. "The old grave-yard is around the church and some of the dates on the tombstones are eighteenth century." For the Rev. James Tweddale, uncle of Catherine's father, see Hew Scott, *op. cit.,* Vol. II, p. 349.

[18] Rusk, John McGill, *op. cit.,* p. 95.

[19] Nicholson, John, *Historical and Traditional Tales in Prose and Verse, Connected with the South of Scotland,* p. 134.

[20] Rusk, John McGill, *op. cit.,* p. 121.

[21] *Ibid.,* p. 120.

[22] *Ibid.,* pp. 119–20.

[23] *Ibid.,* p. 120.

[24] *Ibid.;* from *Minutes* of a memorial service. The *Minute Book* from which Rusk drew his information is now in the custody of the Minister and Kirk Session of Old Luce. Having most kindly examined this MS., Mr. Galloway states that it contains no information about members of the Tweddale family: "The Minutes, written by the session clerk, deal chiefly with the business of the Kirk Session and the distribution of money to the poor of the parish. The Rev. Mr. Tweddale's opinion is not mentioned: he merely presided as Moderator of the Session."

[25] For Catherine's father and her grandfather, J. T. Tweddale, see Hew Scott, *op. cit.,* Vol. II, p. 349. Beyond the Agnews of Lochnaw, the Adairs of Little Genoch, and the Rosses of Balkail (see above, Note 4), Catherine would have been connected with the landed gentry through the marriage of her Uncle Andrew (of Whithorn Abbey) to Isabella M'Dowall (alternately, Isobel McDouall), daughter of John M'Dowall of Logan and Ann Johnstone of Kelton. (See P. H. M'Kerlie, op cit., Vol. II, pp. 299 and 307–308.)

[26] Learmonth, William, *op. cit.,* p. 123.

[27] Agnew, Sir Andrew, *op. cit.,* pp. 526–27. See also John Mactaggart, *The Scottish Gallovidian,* alphabetized entries under "Elf-Shot," "Smugglers," "Wraiths," etc.

[28] Scott, Hew, *op. cit.,* Vol. II, p. 349. Catherine's sister Janet, born February 15, 1765, married Alexander Brodie on August 26, 1784. Her parents had first had two daughters who died in infancy — Jean (named in honor of her grandmother), born February 6, 1761, and Frances, born February 8, 1762.

[29] For the death of Catherine's mother on May 23, 1775, see Appendix B. The entry therein cited lends support to the general reliability of J. R. Tweddale's account of the copy of the Scottish Covenant said to have been owned by Catherine's father. In the course of his story, J. R. Tweddale remarked that his father (Catherine's brother James) was "left an orphan at the age of ten [accurately, nine]. . . ." (See Note 14, p. 205.)

[30] The Rev. William Learmont (1742–1822) was presented with the living of the Parish of Old Luce on June 19, 1777 (Catherine's father having died on May 6). In 1782 he married Catherine's Cousin Sarah, daughter of the Rev. Andrew Adair. (See Hew Scott, *op. cit.,* Vol. II, p. 349.)

[31] See Fig. 3 after p. 56. This miniature, now in my possession, appears as *Item 285* in the *Catalogue* of the "Ruskin Exhibition . . . 1900," in which

it is described as "Miniature of John Ruskin, of Edinburgh, Mr. Ruskin's grandfather, as a young man."

[32] *Op. cit.,* Vol. I, p. 8.

[33] See Fig. 4 after p. 56. This miniature, now in my possession, appears as *Item 283* in the *Catalogue* of the "Ruskin Exhibition . . . 1900," in which it is described as "Miniature of his grandmother, Catherine Tweddale, wife of John Ruskin, of Edinburgh."

[34] For Ruskin's story of this marriage, see *Works,* XXXV, p. 62. The difficulty in finding a record of the ceremony supports belief that there was an elopement — a detail likely to have reached Ruskin through his parents.

[35] Trotter, Robert, *Galloway Gossip Sixty Years Ago,* p. 65. The general atmosphere in Catherine's time is suggested by a visitor who describes the custom of always identifying a man by naming his estate when he was introduced or otherwise referred to.

[36] Ruskin, *Works,* XXXV, p. 62.

[37] For a true copy of the whole entry, see Appendix B.

[38] From *The Oxford English Dictionary.*

[39] Chambers, Robert, "Edinburgh Merchants and Merchandise in Old Times," *Edinburgh Papers,* p. 3.

[40] *Ibid.*

[41] Speaking of the goods which a "Merchant" might handle, Robert Chambers writes that a man named Flockhart had left his wife "a good deal of money, together with his whole stock in trade, consisting of a multifarious variety of articles, such as ropes, tea, sugar, *whip-shafts,* porter, ale, beer, butter, sand, *caum-stane,* herrings, nails, cotton-wicks, papers, pens, ink, wafers, thread, needles, tapes, potatoes, rubbers, *gundy,* onions, *spunks,* coloured eggs in their seasons, &c., &c. — constituting what was then called a *merchant* and now a small *grocer.*" (*Traditions of Edinburgh,* Vol. II, pp. 290–91.)

[42] Thompson, H. W., *A Scottish Man of Feeling,* p. 35. Peter Williamson's distinction between a *Merchant* and a *Grocer* may be related to the fact that toward the beginning of the eighteenth century, as Thompson notes, gentlemen had sometimes been forced to enter trade, although this was "an occupation which by the opening of the nineteenth century was loftily avoided by Edinburgh gentles. In his *Edinburgh Papers,* Robert Chambers mentions several examples of [these early] merchant-gentlemen — and mentions them with a kind of snobbish astonishment." (*Ibid.,* p. 35, *n.*)

[43] From the beginning, Ruskin's parents hoped that their son would become a clergyman — his mother for religious reasons, to which his father readily subscribed, no one being more aware than he that the Church of England provided a career for "gentlemen." There were consequently plans for Oxford University, with the Dean of Christ Church College advising that if John James could afford to do so, he should enter his son as a Gentleman Commoner.

Thus John James obtained enormous satisfaction from Ruskin's being graciously accepted by the young noblemen who chanced to be his classmates. Ten years later he would write his friend George Gray: "He was invited to the Duke of Leinster's and many places he refused to go to — I have not named to any one, what Company he has kept since leaving

College — but I was gratified to find him admitted to Tables of Ministers, Ambassadors and Bishops. . . ." (Admiral Sir William James, *The Order of Release,* p. 131; from letter of August 31, 1848, which James misdates "1 August, 1848.") But even as he gloried in such triumphs of "my Son," he never forgot that he himself was *not* "a Gentleman."

After Ruskin's marriage, the brother of his wife (Euphemia Chalmers Gray, better known as "Effie") wished to come to London to work as a clerk in the office of some Colonial Broker, John James having done such work during his own early career in London; therefore he must now explain that as a clerk, the young George Gray would be no more socially acceptable than was he himself in the circles of Ladies and Gentlemen in which his Son could move: "It is not George alone, but Mrs. Ruskin and my self are equally excluded. John has brought Lords to our Table but we are very marked in regarding them as John's Visitors and when Sir Wm. and Lady James last breakfasted here John and Effie presided and neither Mrs. R nor I ever appeared. I have got them their House in Park St. to be among their own Set — when they like to put up with Wine Merchants or Colonial Brokers they may dine here now and then. . . ." (*Ibid.*) The trouble always came when Ruskin wished to lead his own life and not his father's.

⁴⁴ *Ibid.,* p. 130.

⁴⁵ Butler, The Rev. D., *op. cit.,* p. 341.

⁴⁶ *Ibid.*

⁴⁷ Collingwood, W. G., *Life* (revised ed.), pp. 10–11; from letter of March 15, 1808. (The date is supplied from the original letter, now in the possession of Mr. Sharp.)

⁴⁸ Ruskin, *Works,* XXXV, p. 602. Mr. Sharp has kindly told me that he likewise obtained this information through examining the *Will* of Dr. John Adair. One may therefore feel secure in accepting Cook and Wedderburn's statement.

⁴⁹ Through the kind help of Mr. C. S. Minto, City Librarian and Curator of the Central Public Library, Edinburgh, it has become evident that the Ruskins had moved to 15 St. James Square by 1796. The following information, obtained from a study of Edinburgh *Directories* from 1780–1810 (conducted by Mr. Minto), in part confirms and in part supplements (thereby, in effect, correcting) the results of a similar investigation made by the Rev. Dugald Butler and published in *The Tron Kirk of Edinburgh* (1906): see Notes 45 and 46.

The first entry of John (Thomas) Ruskin occurs in Williamson's *Directory* for 1786–88. (Williamson's *Directories* ran from 1773–96, although no *Directory* for 1779–80, 1785–86, 1792–93 is known to be extant.) His name does not appear in the *Directory* for 1788–90. For information about his residence and occupation between 1786 and 1796, as given by Williamson and presented by Butler, see pp. 56–57.

In Aitchison's *Directories,* which cover 1793–1803, with no copy known to be extant for 1798–99, John (Thomas) Ruskin appears in 1793–94 as "grocer, opposite Blackfriar's Wynd," and in 1796–97 as "merchant, No. 15 James's Square." Aitchison's *Directory* for 1795–96 does not include his name, which suggests that during this year he may have changed his residence from the Old to the New Town, even though he is identified as "grocer, opposite Blackfriar's Wynd" in Williamson's *Directory* for 1794–96. From 1796–1803 he regularly appears in Aitchison's *Directories* as a "merchant" who lived at 15 St. James Square, except that in the *Directory* of 1797–98 the *15* was apparently misprinted *25.*

In 1804–1805 his name does not appear in either Campbell's or Denovan's *Directory.* In Stark's *Directory* for 1805–1806 he appears as "Russken, John, Agent, 14 James's Square," and in 1806–1807 as "Rusken, John, 15 James' Square" — an entry which reappears in the *Post Office Directories* of 1807–1808, 1808–1809, 1809–10. "St. James' Square is variously spelt," Mr. Minto comments, "but in the opinion of this Library there is little doubt that all entries refer to the same place and that in spite of variations in numbering he [John Thomas Ruskin] occupied the same premises between 1796–1810. Alterations in numbering and inconsistencies in the Directories were both quite common at the time."

CHAPTER 4

[1] Nicolson, Alexander, *Memoirs of Adam Black,* Vol. I, pp. 3–4. As a publisher, in 1851 Adam Black purchased the Scott copyrights from Caldwell for £27,000; as a liberal politician, he gave such wise and generous leadership in burgh reform that he was twice elected Lord Provost; in 1848 he was offered, and declined, a knighthood. Today he is commemorated by a bronze statue, erected in 1877, three years after his death. (W. G. Blaikie, *DNB.*)

[2] Chalmers, George, *The Life of Thomas Ruddiman,* p. 17.

[3] The very frequency of such incursions into the ranks of "Gentlemen" must have played its part in developing the marked social hierarchy within the legal profession. Absolutely speaking, no one beneath the rank of *Advocate* could be considered a "Gentleman," as Sir Walter Scott would realize rather early in his career: see p. 66. On the other hand, one reason why Sir Walter Scott maintained that his birth could be considered not "sordid" but "genteel" was that his father had been a Writer to the Signet.

[4] In *Praeterita,* Ruskin's treatment of his father's education and of the "position" of his father's family in "Edinburgh circles" is suffused by fantasy. The atmosphere which colored his conception of his father as a "lad" of the Royal High School is, for instance, indicated by the comment: "He had learned Latin thoroughly, though with no large range of reading, under the noble traditions of Adam at the High School of Edinburgh: while, by the then living and universal influence of Sir Walter [*sic* — by 1800!] every scene of his native city was exalted in his imagination by the purest poetry, that ever hallowed or haunted the streets and rocks of a brightly inhabited capital." (*Works,* XXXV, pp. 123–24.) For the episode of Dr. Thomas Brown, which served as a chief pillar of his fantasy about family "position," see pp. 105–106, 120–22, and Note 15, p. 233.

[5] Lord Cockburn recalls: "I often think I see myself in my usual High School apparel, which was the common dress of other boys. It consisted of a round black hat; a shirt fastened at the neck by a black ribbon, and, except on dress days, unruffled; a cloth waistcoat, rather large, with two rows of buttons and of button-holes, so that it could be buttoned on either side, which, when one side got dirty, was convenient; a single-breasted

jacket, which in due time got a tail and became a coat; brown corduroy breeches, tied at the knees by a showy knot of brown cotton tape; worsted stockings in winter, blue cotton stockings in summer, and white cotton for dress; clumsy shoes made to be used on either foot, and each requiring to be used on alternate feet daily; brass or copper buckles. The coat and waistcoat were always of glaring colours, such as bright blue, grass green, and scarlet." (*Memorials of His Time,* p. 20.)

[6] *The Life of Sir Robert Christison, Bart.,* edited by his sons, Vol. I, p. 21. In 1809, about fifty students returned for a sixth year. (*Ibid.*)

[7] *Ibid.,* p. 23.

[8] Most kindly, Dr. D. S. M. Imrie, present Rector of the Royal High School, has informed me: "Examination of our records shows that in 1796 a certain John Ruskin was a member of Mr. Christison's class, since he paid a library fee of 1/- for the year. This seems to be the only evidence [available]. . . . There is no record of the books taken out from the school library."

[9] *Op. cit.,* p. 18.

[10] Lockhart, J. G., *Memoirs of the Life of Sir Walter Scott* (hereafter called *Life*), Vol. I, p. 27.

[11] Francis Horner studied under William Nicol from 1786–90 (Leonard Horner, ed., *Memoirs and Correspondence of Francis Horner, M. P.,* Vol. I, p. 3); therefore, the entering group of 1794 would have been the charge of William Nicol. Had John Thomas Ruskin been able to send his son to the Royal High School before Catherine received her legacy, John James, according to usual procedure, would have entered when he was eight years old, in October, 1793, and would have been in Luke Fraser's class, Luke Fraser having taught Lord Brougham from 1785–89; Francis, Lord Jeffrey from 1781–85; Sir Walter Scott from 1778–81, Scott having entered this class when it was in its second year.

[12] At the University, Froude comments, Carlyle said that he "learned little. . . . In the Latin class he was under Professor Christieson [*sic*], who 'never noticed him nor could distinguish him from another Mr. Irving Carlyle, an older, bigger boy, with red hair, wild buck teeth, and scorched complexion, and the worst Latinist of his acquaintance.' " (*Thomas Carlyle, A History of the First Forty Years of his Life,* Vol. I, p. 20.)

[13] *Op. cit.,* pp. 11–12.

[14] *Op. cit.,* Vol. I, p. 3.

[15] *Op. cit.,* pp. 5–6.

[16] These attacks, written by Gilbert Stuart, a cousin of Thomas Ruddiman, were published both in England and in Scotland. (See Henry, Lord Brougham, *The Life and Times of* . . . , Vol. I, pp. 50–51.)

[17] For a detailed story of the controversy, repeatedly referred to in memoirs of the time, see George Chalmers, *The Life of Thomas Ruddiman,* pp. 93–96 and *ibid.,* Appendix No. 5, pp. 390–404.

[18] Since the magistrates never changed their edict, Dr. Adam would introduce his *Grammar* by saying to the boys: " 'This is a prohibited book, and I do not wish, nor have I ever been under the necessity, to force it into use. There are a few questions which I wish to propose, and if you can answer them, I am content; but if you cannot, I must refer you to my

grammar, for the means of enabling you to give me a reply.' " (A. Henderson, *An Account of the Life and Character of Alexander Adam, LL.D.,* p. 109.)

[19] Division of opinion about the merit of Dr. Adam's *Grammar* was carried over into Ruskin's boyhood, as he recalls: "On the first day when I went to take my seat in Mr. Dale's schoolroom, I carried my old grammar to him, in a modest pride, expecting some encouragement and honour for the accuracy with which I could repeat, on demand, some hundred and sixty close-printed pages of it. ¶But Mr. Dale threw it back to me with a fierce bang upon his desk, saying (with accent and look of seven-times-heated scorn), 'That's a *Scotch* thing.' ¶Now, my father being Scotch, and an Edinburgh High School boy, and my mother having laboured in that book with me since I could read [*sic*], and all my happiest holiday time having been spent on the North Inch of Perth, these four words, with the action accompanying them, contained as much insult, pain, and loosening of my respect for my parents, love of my father's country, and honour for its worthies, as it was possible to compress into four syllables and an ill-mannered gesture. Which were therefore pure, double-edged and point-envenomed blasphemy." (Ruskin, *Works*, XXXIV, p. 365: from *Fiction, Fair and Foul;* the story recurs in *Praeterita*, in somewhat altered version.)

[20] *Waverley*, Appendix II, "Anecdotes of School Days."

[21] Nicolson, Alexander, *op. cit.,* Vol. I, p. 7.

[22] *Op. cit.,* p. 18.

[23] Lockhart, J. G., *Peter's Letters to His Kinsfolk*, Vol. II, pp. 3–4.

[24] Armstrong, Sir Walter, *Sir Henry Raeburn*, Vol. I, p. 43.

[25] Grierson, Sir Herbert J. C., *Sir Walter Scott, Bart.,* p. 18.

[26] Pottle, F. A., *Boswell's London Journal*, p. 331.

[27] As to Boswell's obvious insecurities, these would seem to have sprung from his personal relationship with his dominating father — filled with uncomprehending disapproval, and determined to have his eldest son an *Advocate*. Rebellious, and unable to lead his own adult life as he wished, Boswell apparently became obsessed by the need to demonstrate his "manhood" — which, by and large, he proceeded to do upon a level almost as adolescent (not least in its exhibitionism) as was the relationship which in actuality denied him his independence, or "dignity," as an adult. Hence, presumably, his theme-song: "Let me be *manly";* "I may be a *man* of *dignity*," etc. But the insecurity about his manhood which drove him so compulsively (often in conflict with the strong superego which causes him to lament his lapses in so many passages of high comedy) could not affect the absoluteness of the social security engendered by the regard and respect he would have received as eldest son of *his* family in the Edinburgh of his day. If there was one role that Boswell had no inner urge to play (sometimes freely and shrewdly putting even the revered Samuel Johnson, his *good* "father," on the wheel), it was that of sycophant, as Professor Tinker has maintained and as the *Journals* have attested. Conversely, the social *in*security that could be engendered in a proud and sensitive boy such as John James Ruskin, who happened to be born in the lower portion of the hierarchy, could be no less permanent and pervasive.

[28] Lockhart, J. G., *Life*, Vol. I, p. 25.

[29] *Ibid.,* p. 128.

[30] *Op. cit.,* p. 16. Heretofore, Sir Herbert further observes, he had "lived among those of the class to which his father's family belonged. . . ." Not incongruously, therefore, while in Kelso, he had had "an innocent love affair with a young girl [daughter of a small tradesman] whom later he would regard as socially undesirable. . . . The end of this youthful affair, . . . a termination which left in [the maiden's] mind 'a resentment that never subsided,' coincides probably with the crisis which marked his move up from the society of his father's apprentices to that of young budding Advocates, fully conscious of their social superiority to lawyers of the inferior branches, tradespeople, medical students . . . *et hoc genus omne.* . . . Scott, like most of his townsmen, was somewhat of a snob. . . ." (*Ibid.,* pp. 17–18.) To be sure, unless something of a rebel, or a reformer, one would have found it difficult *not* to have become somewhat of a snob.

[31] *Ibid.,* p. 3.

[32] Fergusson, Alexander, *The Honourable Henry Erskine,* p. 110.

[33] When Carlyle began his life in Edinburgh and found his few friends among the sons of peasants, it might have intensified his personal pride, but it would not have deepened his self-confidence in social relationships to have encountered the attitudes indicated by a passage in Scott's review of Burns (quoted by Sir Herbert Grierson in the essay "Scott and Burns") : " 'The dignity, the spirit, the indignation of Burns was that of a plebeian — of a high-souled plebeian indeed — of a citizen of Rome or Athens; but still of a plebeian untinged with the slightest shade of that spirit of chivalry which since feudal times has pervaded the higher ranks of society.' " Carlyle, Sir Herbert continues, was "like Burns a high-souled plebeian" who had come to Edinburgh in 1809, when he was fourteen, and who "during all the years that the novels were flowing from Scott's pen . . . was struggling to find a livelihood in or in the neighbourhood of Edinburgh. . . ." Scott, in contrast, was "a man of the world . . . if that means one who appreciated the world as he found it, who enjoyed those class differences which other men dislike or condemn. Scott accepted with joy the values of every class — distinction and refinement in the upper class, worth and enterprise in the middle class, honesty and good sense and kindliness in the lower. . . . He reconciled rich and poor, for Scott's aristocratic ideal, if a dream, was a generous dream. . . ." (*Essays and Addresses,* pp. 28–46, *passim.*) Through his father, as we shall see, it was this dream that John Ruskin inherited, retaining Scott's love of humanity while accepting the doctrines of Carlyle.

[34] Chambers, Robert, *Traditions of Edinburgh,* Vol. II, p. 248.

[35] Among the "sentiments" high and pure listed by Lord Cockburn, one finds: "May the hand of charity wipe the tear from the eye of sorrow"; "May the honest heart never feel distress"; "May the pleasure of the evening bear the reflection of the morning"; etc., etc. (*Op. cit.,* pp. 43–44.) Somewhat less genteel was the custom known as "Saving the Ladies": having escorted the ladies home, gentlemen would once more gather and, as a challenge, one would drink a toast to the lady whom he most admired; accepting the challenge, another gentleman would toast another lady, preferably with two drinks, to which the challenger would reply by drinking down four toasts, though the number of drinks was not always thus multi-

plied; and so it would continue "till one of the combatants fell unconscious to the floor." (Alexander Fergusson, *op. cit.,* p. 117; see also Robert Chambers, *Traditions of Edinburgh,* Vol. II, pp. 271–72.)

[36] Brougham, Henry, Lord, *op. cit.,* Vol. I, pp. 18–19. Lord Brougham assures us that the battered state of this coffin, eventually retrieved from the bottom of the river, attests the truth of the story.

[37] Cockburn, Henry, Lord, *op. cit.,* pp. 38–39.

[38] Speaking of the tradesmen of the West Bow as "in general humble but much more respectable" than any others of their rank throughout the town, Robert Chambers pauses to describe these admirable creatures: "Most of the shopkeepers are of long standing, and have reached, in the course of many years application to a small business, if not to wealth at least to easy circumstances. The greater part of them possess their own shops, and live in their own houses, and in such a community, *that* may be considered wealth. Whatever the fashionable merchants of Bridges or Prince's Street may think of them they are not to be despised for the darkness of their shops, or for the *un-business-like* antiquity and awkwardness of personal appearance . . . and while they keep a good balance on their own side at Sir William Forbe's and write themselves *lairds* of certain tenements in the labyrinthine purlieus of closes behind them, they can stand at their doors with their hands in their pockets and even with their hats on, conscious of being regarded by their neighbours with a high degree of respect and veneration." (*Traditions of Edinburgh,* Vol. I, p. 145.)

[39] Lockhart, J. G., *Life,* Vol. I, p. 34.

[40] In 1847, John James Ruskin wrote his son: "On the subject noticed in one of your letters on our different regard for public opinion, this is a malady or weakness with me, arising from want of self-respect. The latter causes much of my ill-temper, and when from misunderstanding or want of information I was losing some respect for you my temper got doubly bad." (*Works,* XXXVI, p. xix.)

[41] *Ibid.,* XXXIV, p. 699. The copy which was preserved at Brantwood was an edition of 1819 and therefore could scarcely have been, as Cook and Wedderburn assert, "his father's copy." (The date *1819* is given in a *Notebook* headed "Brantwood, 1873," in which Ruskin catalogued various items in his library; this *Notebook* is now in the Yale University Library.)

[42] Lockhart, J. G., *Life,* Vol. I, p. 26.

[43] McGilchrist, John, *Life of Lord Brougham,* pp. 17–18.

[44] Nicolson, Alexander, *op. cit.,* Vol. I, p. 6.

[45] *Op. cit.,* p. 4.

[46] *Op. cit.,* Vol. I, p. 41.

[47] "He remembered the fate of every boy at his school during the fifty years he had supervised it, and always traced their success or misfortunes entirely to their attention or negligence under his care." (J. G. Lockhart, *Life,* Vol. I, pp. 26–27.)

[48] Nicolson, Alexander, *op. cit.,* p. 6.

[49] *Life of Lord Jeffrey,* Vol. I, p. 11.

[50] *Memorials of His Time,* p. 13.

[51] *Op. cit.,* Vol. I, p. 21. When John James Ruskin was a clerk in London, his own attempts at "composition" significantly helped him to advance: see p. 115; as a merchant, he never lost his pride in writing business letters which his son called "monumental works of a master hand in its craft" (see p. 149); and as a father, he took far more than usual joy in the very earliest manifestations of talent in his son.

[52] *Ibid.,* p. 41.

[53] *Ibid.,* p. 21.

[54] Pinnington, Edward, *Sir Henry Raeburn,* p. 157. For Raeburn's portrait of Dr. Adam, see Fig. 5 after p. 56. Published with the permission of The National Galleries of Scotland.

[55] Lockhart, J. G., *Life,* Vol. I, p. 28.

[56] *Works,* XXXV, p. 461. By the time this story reaches us through Ruskin's memory of what Carlyle remembered from his youth, it bears a trace of the apocryphal. Yet the core of truth has not been lost, and in its telling I have made slight changes to conform with facts. For a contemporaneous description of Dr. Adam's funeral, see A. Henderson, *op. cit.,* pp. 158–61.

CHAPTER 5

[1] From unpublished letter of October 19, 1848; original in *The Bowerswell Papers.* In the original, *Pious* is not capitalized, but here I have substituted the capital letter as I shall elsewhere when it seems appropriate to do so. One peculiarity of John James Ruskin's handwriting is that he seldom capitalized the letter *p,* even when he wrote proper names such as *Perth, Portland Place,* or *Phemy* (pet name for his son's wife, Euphemia). This eccentricity can sometimes be so disruptive or misleading in effect, especially in his references to "phemy," that I have disregarded it in my transcriptions and have capitalized his *p's* when he would normally have used a capital letter, his use of capitals often being eloquent. Interestingly enough, the only other problem recurrently connected with his handwriting is created by his *s,* which, at the beginning of a word, he is inclined to make look like a capital letter; therefore when there is room for doubt, I have used a lower case *s* unless a capital *S* would seem particularly appropriate.

[2] Robert Chambers refers to the "first tenement in St. James Square [New Town, 1775]" (*op. cit.,* Vol. I, p. 173) and thus incidentally indicates that multiple dwelling houses characterized the neighborhood.

[3] No record for the death of the great-grandmother Mary Ruskin has been found, though registers of Edinburgh, Perth, Croydon, and the Parish of St. Bartholomew-the-Great have been searched.

[4] Collingwood, W. G., *Life* (revised ed.), p. 10.

[5] See Note 10, p. 230.

CHAPTER 6

[1] See Appendix B, which henceforth, for this section, will serve to document all otherwise unannotated references to the Patrick Richardsons and to Margaret Cock (or Cox), together with her parents and her Croydon relatives.

Heretofore, it has always been assumed that Jessie married a Mr. *Peter* Richardson (see *Works,* XXXV, p. 603, and XXXIX, p. 451), probably because in *Praeterita* Ruskin referred to his Perth uncle as "Peter — not Simon — the tanner" (*ibid.,* XXXV, p. 63) and incidentally called Patrick, the son, his Aunt Jessie's "Little Peter." (*Ibid.,* p. 65.) Yet Ruskin must have known his Uncle Patrick's name, if only because of his possession of the salver inscribed *"Mr. Patk. Richardson, of Perth, to J. J. Ruskin. . . ."* (see Note 4, p. 197.) His reference to "Peter . . . the tanner" occurs immediately after the remark that he was "not always entirely at ease in writing of [his] uncles the baker and the tanner," and the connotations of *Peter,* used with a Biblical reference (in contrast to the mundane actuality of *Patrick*), may have helped to relieve his own embarrassment as well as to confuse biographers.

² In 1848 the approaching marriage of their children led John James Ruskin and George Gray into correspondence about Mr. Gray's affairs, Mr. Gray having been placed under such pressure to meet "calls" on railroad stocks that he thought he would be forced into bankruptcy before the marriage ceremony. In this connection, John James Ruskin remarked: "Long since indeed I used to say jocularly that from the speculative propensities I believed to prevail in Perth I did not in a Business point of view value any Gentleman there as to property at 3 months purchase." (From unpublished letter of March 17, 1848; original in *The Bowerswell Papers.*) Mr. Gray having sent him more details, John James remarked in his response: "Excuse all this plain speaking or say writing — I had the same sort of thing with my Brother in Law whom I used to tell when he boasted of his property that I did not value any man in Perth at fifty shillings." (From unpublished letter of March 22, 1848; original in *The Bowerswell Papers.*)

³ See Fig. 6 after p. 56. This miniature, now in my possession, is a true and faithful copy of the one which appears as *Item 287* in the *Catalogue* of the "Ruskin Exhibition . . . 1900," described as "Miniature of Mrs. Richardson, of Perth, *née* Ruskin. . . ." The copy was made by Mrs. W. G. Collingwood for Mrs. Arthur Severn from the original, which I have been unable to locate. Mrs. Oscar Gnosspelius has written me: "The miniature you have is a replica of the original. I remember my mother's care to obtain an ivory of the exact size; and the extreme skill with which she reproduced the work in every detail so that when they were laid side by side they could scarcely have been told apart except by the frames." The likeness of Aunt Jessie which was made from this miniature and published in Ruskin's *Works* (XXXV, facing p. 62) is from a steel engraving; therefore (Mrs. Gnosspelius adds) because of the difference in medium, the engraving was "in no way so exact as the copy done in the same medium." Moreover, in the engraving, only the head and shoulders were reproduced, whereas in the original the gown, the background, the coloring were important to the effect of the whole, the result being that in the illustration published in *Praeterita,* much of the delicacy and femininity that characterized the young girl in the original has been lost.

⁴ *Works,* XXVIII, p. 602; from *Fors Clavigera,* May, 1876. Such use of double-entendre is a distinctive and highly functional characteristic of Ruskin's later style. (See also Note 15, p. 217; Note 67, p. 222; Note 3, p. 240.)

[5] Unpublished passage from "Second MS." of *Praeterita*. Originally it followed the paragraph which ends: ". . . their laborious youth": see *Works,* XXXV, p. 409.

[6] In addition to the material assembled in Appendix B (for these children, see also "Family Tree"), the *Burial Register of . . . Perth 1794–1823* records that there was "a still-born child with an almost undecipherable Christian name which looked like Baille (or Baillie) Richardson, on 13th February, 1823, father — P. Richardson (not necessarily Patrick Richardson)." (From letter of Miss E. L. Watson, hereafter referred to as Miss Watson.)

[7] Ruskin, *Works,* XXXV, p. 71. After the death of his sister, John James assumed the responsibility of helping his Perth nephews to get established, as *Praeterita* recounts (see *Works,* XXXV, pp. 409–12), and he remained loyal to all of them despite what he called, apparently with justice, the "palpable follies" of John and Andrew (occasionally discussed in unpublished letters from John James Ruskin to George Gray, in *The Bowerswell Papers*). Mary lived with the Ruskins for nineteen years and remained in close touch with them after her marriage, as did her brother William during his many years as a practicing physician in or near London. When Mary died in 1849, Ruskin said that to his parents her loss was "a severe trial" not least "as the breaking of the last *close* link with the memory of my fathers sister — for William and Andrew and John are of a different character, & besides, have been less with us. . . ." (From unpublished letter of June 28, 1849, to his wife; original in *The Bowerswell Papers*.) After Mary's marriage, Margaret Ruskin remained devoted to this niece, to the frequent irritation of Effie Gray, as a daughter-in-law.

[8] See Fig. 7 after p. 56. Published with the permission of Mr. E. A. Hogan, Registrar General for Scotland, who most kindly provided a photostatic copy of this entry. See, too, Appendix B, *February 2, 1818*.

[9] See Fig. 8 after p. 56. Published with the permission of The Croydon Corporation, from a photograph most kindly provided by Mr. T. E. Callander (hereafter referred to as Mr. Callander). See, too, Appendix C.

[10] For this *Certificate,* see Appendix B, *February 8, 1819.* In the Ruskin Museum, Coniston, this document is accompanied by a letter in which the Reverend James Boyd formally certifies that he had baptized "John Ruskin . . . on the 20th February 1819 at the house of his Father John James Ruskin Esq. 54 Hunter Street London" and then, addressing Ruskin's father, explains: "In answer to your letter . . . I beg to state that during the term of my ministry of the Caledonian Church, as the Congregation was in its infancy, there was no Register kept. The Parents of the Children whom I baptized, in general, rec^d. a note from me which they handed to D^r. Manuel who inserted the names of their children in the London Wall Register — From the result of your enquiries [it is? — torn edge] evident from some inattention on your p[art or? — torn edge] on my part, that this was not done in the case of your son. I have however a distinct recollection of his Baptism, and I trust the Certificate I send will suffice — " (From unpublished letter of November 14, 1837; original in the Ruskin Museum, Coniston.)

That Ruskin had never seen either the *Certificate* of his birth or the letter certifying his baptism is incredible, both documents having been preserved at Brantwood. For Cook and Wedderburn's knowledge of this "Birth Certificate" and, therefore, the correct names of Ruskin's mother and maternal grandfather, see *Works,* XXXV, lxi–lxii.

[11] Sending me photographs of the Cock and Richardson gravestones, for which he had instituted a search in the Churchyard of St. John the Baptist, Mr. Callander was the first to remark: "It seems almost unbelievable that Ruskin himself never saw them. It is hard to reconcile his affectionate references to his Croydon aunt with the thought that he never visited her grave, and he can hardly have done this without seeing his grandfather's name writ clear and X-less," — that is, on a tombstone which has no cross.

[12] Bardsley, Charles W., *Curiosities of Puritan Nomenclature,* p. 13.

[13] See *The Oxford English Dictionary.*

[14] Mencken, H. L., *The American Language,* p. 15. As the name of a woman, *cock* may also have been unpleasantly related to the feminine counterpart, *coquette* (from Fr. *coq*): "a woman who displays herself like a strutting cock." (J. T. Shipley, *Dictionary of Word Origins.*) For help in dealing with this problem, I am indebted to Dr. E. K. Sheldon, who had noted that *rooster* makes a late appearance in English dictionaries although in the *English Dialect Dictionary* Joseph Wright includes it as a word used in Scotland and in Surrey.

[15] *Works,* XIX, p. 128; from *The Cestus of Aglaia* (1865). The close association of the Wandel with his mother often led to double-entendre in Ruskin's references to this river and, on occasion, in his references to springs or wells: for example, see Note 19. What I have called this characteristic of Ruskin's later style first became significant in parts of *Modern Painters V* (1860) and was used repeatedly, and brilliantly, in some of his work that dates from the middle sixties (for example, in *Sesame and Lilies;* sometimes, meaningfully, in *The Ethics of the Dust*). Much less successfully, it manifests itself in those passages of *The Cestus of Aglaia* which flowed from his pen more or less freely ("to please myself"), as a stream of associations.

[16] *Ibid.,* XXII, p. 533; from *Readings in "Modern Painters."*

[17] *Ibid.,* XVIII, p. 385; from *The Crown of Wild Olive.*

[18] *Ibid.,* XXVIII, p. 177; from *Fors Clavigera,* October, 1874.

[19] *Ibid.,* XXII, p. xxiv.

[20] Steinman, G. S., *A History of Croydon,* p. 1.

[21] Bannerman, Ronald, *Forgotten Croydon,* p. 32.

[22] *Ibid.,* p. 25.

[23] From unpublished letter of August 16, 1856, from John James Ruskin to W. H. Harrison; original in *The Bowerswell Papers.*

[24] Anderson, John C., *A Short Chronicle concerning . . . Croydon . . . ,* p. 203.

[25] Ruskin, *Works,* XXXV, p. 122 and *n.* (from E. A. Martin, *Croydon,* p. 28). See, too, Fig. 9 after p. 56. Published with the permission of The Croydon Corporation, from a photograph taken *c.* 1890 of a site demolished shortly thereafter, and kindly provided by Mr. Callander; original copy in the Central Library, Croydon.

Making a tour of the old inns from section to section of the town, Bannerman comments: "Posting business with coaches, post chaises, vans and waggons was sufficient to keep at least three good houses busy in the centre of the town [*The Crown, Green Dragon, Greyhound*. The tour leads to] . . . King Street, now non-existent, which led to Middle and Market Streets. On the corner of King Street and behind the old Town Hall stood the King's Head, later known as the Old King's Head. Dated from the early eighteenth century, its chief interest was that the grandmother of John Ruskin was formerly landlady there. [Quotations are given from *Praeterita*, and then, the Ruskin interest having been exhausted, the author briefly notes later history, namely —] . . . In 1812 Margaret Cock was landlady, and in 1847 there was a Mark Griffin, who held the inn [*sic*] for a quarter of a century." (*Op. cit.,* pp. 31 and 49.)

²⁶ A nineteenth-century lease contains the ground-floor plan, kindly sent me in photostatic copy by Mr. Callander, together with the following information: "The old King's Head was quite definitely not an inn — this term is properly used only of houses where lodging can be obtained by travellers, and the old King's Head was not such a place. It could be correctly described as a tavern, but it did not include this word in its title. The property is described in a lease of 1847 as being 'Licensed as a public house or liquor shop.' . . . The old King's Head was conveyed by indenture of 24th March 1634 by John Rowse to John Webster and nine other parishioners and inhabitants of the Parish of St. Botolph, Old Aldgate, in trust for and on behalf of the poor of the Parish of St. Botolph. It was bought by the Croydon Corporation from the Aldgate Freedom Foundation in 1894. The Aldgate Freedom Foundation were administrators of a group of charities, into which the Rice charity had by 1894 become merged; but in 1847 the Churchwardens of the Parish of St. Botolph were letting the old King's Head to a tenant, and there is no doubt that this property was in the ownership of the Parish of St. Botolph during the whole of William Cock's lifetime. . . . William Cock describes himself in his will dated 14th June 1782 as '*Victualler.*' He may, at that time, have been landlord of The King's Head, but as tenant only. The owner of the tavern was the Parish of St. Botolph, Aldgate. . . . In general, I think that 'Merchant' was a very exaggerated description of William Cock. If he did in fact keep The King's Head, he was . . . the tenant of a small tavern in a humble part of Croydon. . . .''

²⁷ *Works,* XXXV, p. 122. The "narrow alley" must have been the "King Street" to which Bannerman refers.

²⁸ Unpublished passage from the "Second MS." of *Praeterita;* originally the conclusion of the paragraph which ends: ". . . to the lower town." (*Works,* XXXV, p. 122.) While writing this passage in the first draft of *Praeterita,* Ruskin recalled his Croydon grandmother as landlady "of the Bull, (*Black* Bull, I think). . . ." (From "First MS." of *Praeterita.*)

²⁹ For the death of Benjamin Cock, aged 66, in 1778, and of his widow Martha, aged 68, in 1780, see Appendix B. The name *Cock* "is not repeated in other Croydon records of the period," Mr. Callander states, and other attempts to confirm a relationship between William and Benjamin have been unsuccessful: their names, for example, do not appear in Yarmouth records. In the Registers of the Parish of St. Bartholomew-the-Great, of which William Cock was a resident in 1780 (see Fig. 10 after p. 56, and

Appendix B), there is a single entry that in 1764 a Margaret Cock was buried in the Great Churchyard: see Appendix B.

[30] See Fig. 10 after p. 56.

[31] The history of this property, from its acquisition by Ruskin's grandfather through its ownership by his mother and her sister has been thus summarized by Mr. Callander: "i) in 1782, by lease and release dated 19th and 20th May, William Cock of the parish of Croydon, Victualer, bought from Robert Blake of the same parish, Gardener, for the sum of £30 twenty rods of land in Pump Pail, Croydon. ii) By his will, dated 14th June 1782, William Cock left his whole estate to his wife Margaret. iii) By her will, proved 16th October, 1817, Mrs. Margaret Cock left nine freehold cottages in Pump Pail, Croydon (the total annual rental . . . being £44), to her daughters 'Margaret Cock of Perth . . . spinster, and Bridget Richardson wife of George Richardson of Croydon, baker' as tenants in common. iv) By indentures dated 14th October 1829, John James Ruskin of Herne Hill in the county of Surrey, Esquire, and Margaret his wife, late Margaret Cock, conveyed to George Richardson and Bridget his wife, and Richard Gray of Glasgow in North Britain, merchant, a trustee named by the several parties, in consideration of their natural affection and regard for Bridget, Margaret's half interest in the Pump Pail property. Bridget was to enjoy a life interest in the property with reversion to the heirs of her body. v) William Cock's will made no specific reference to this property. It is clear from the deeds of conveyance from Blake to Cock that Cock bought land only. The indentures cited in *iv* above, in reciting the title, rehearse that Margaret Cock, widow of William, was seized under the will of her late husband of the fee simple of nine messuages in Pump Pail. That is, the cottages on Pump Pail were built in the lifetime of William Cock, between 1782 and 1787. This suggests that William had some capital at the time of his marriage, which he invested in land and houses."

"The probate of Margaret Cock's will, which we have here [in the Central Library, Croydon]," Mr. Callander adds, "is not a holograph copy but is a lawyer's engrossment annexed to the probate, and it bears no original signatures."

[32] The gravestone of William Cock gives *31 March, 1787,* as the date of his death (see Note 11, p. 217).

[33] See Fig. 8 after p. 56, and Appendix C.

[34] From letter of Mr. Callander, who obtained the information from a Poor Rate Book of the Parish of Croydon.

[35] *Works,* XXXV, p. 18.

[36] *Ibid.*

[37] For example, in the course of thanking Ruskin for having promised her some horseback riding after they were married, Effie Gray remarked: ". . . Mrs. Ruskin will say I am sure the very first day after we have been out . . . that my neck is in danger and that she wonders how you can allow me to do such a madlike thing but perhaps when She sees how blooming & healthy we look after it she may gradually begin to think that there cannot be so much danger in the thing after all." (From unpublished letter of 9 February [1848]; original in *The Bowerswell Papers.*)

[38] *Works*, XXXV, pp. 96–97.

[39] Filling out the *Birth Certificate,* John James was called upon to give the name and *occupation* of Margaret's father. He resorted to interlinear script to provide, additionally, the first name of Margaret's mother and to state that both of these grandparents were "deceased." (See Appendix B, February 8, 1819.)

[40] Parish, The Rev. W. D., *A Dictionary of the Sussex Dialect and Collection of Provincialisms in Use in the County of Sussex,* p. 135. The Rev. Mr. Parish adds: "Their period of fishing was called cock-fare, and their nets cock-heaks." If this meaning of *cock* did not prevail in Margaret's contiguously northern County of Surrey, it was probably well known in Croydon, with the Sussex fish vans lumbering through that town. *Cox* is a plural of *cocks:* see, for example, Ernest Weekley, *Surnames,* p. 322; Nathaniel Bowditch, *Suffolk Surnames,* p. 201.

[41] See *Works,* XXXVI, p. 74, for a letter which records how he watched the unloading of herrings from a fishing fleet, in 1847; *ibid.,* XXVIII, pp. 32–33, for his publication of a lengthy letter from a correspondent (incorporated into his own text) in *Fors Clavigera,* February, 1874, in which the predicament of the individual herring fisherman is described, these remarks being followed, in the issue of October, 1874, by his discussion (unchanged when it was absorbed into *Praeterita*) of his grandfather as a sailor connected with the "herring business" in some way about which he was not entirely clear, his mother not having been "much communicative."

[42] See *Works,* XXXV, p. 38.

[43] *Ibid.,* p. 122.

[44] *Ibid.,* p. 18.

[45] *Ibid.,* p. 125.

[46] See Note 40, p. 247.

[47] Collingwood, W. G., *Life* (revised ed.), p. 7, *n.*; from letter of January 5, 1852, to Miss Mitford. (For Miss Mitford, see Note 8, p. 226.)

[48] Mr. Callander has kindly provided a photostatic copy of "Extracts from Particulars of Sale, dated 27th September 1809, giving details of George Richardson's premises in Middle Row, with a plan of the area showing the position of this property." The "Particulars of Sale" state that Bridget's "dwelling house" contained "a Baker's Shop, Four Rooms, and Cellaring." Ruskin refers to it as "the fashionablest [little house] in Market Street. . . ." (*Works,* XXXV, p. 19.)

[49] For this marriage, see Appendix B, *December 11, 1787.* The Croydon Rate Book of 1793 shows George Roberts "to have been living . . . in a property worth £20 a year, within fifty yards of the 'King's Head.' The Census of 1811 and the Poor Rate Book of 1812 show that George Roberts, husband of Mary Ruskin . . . was a victualler, and was landlord of 'The Bear' public house in Market Street, three doors away from George Richardson's bakery." (From letter of Mr. Callander.)

[50] See Appendix A, *1752,* for the marriage of a Robert Ruskin and Mary Pavitt, in Mayfair, St. George. It is not impossible that this Robert Ruskin, of Mayfair, was the brother of Ruskin's great-grandfather, John Ruskin, of St. Bartholomew-the-Great. But all things considered, it seems more

likely that the Robert Ruskin who remained in Cheshunt, marrying Hannah Adams in 1753, was the uncle of John Ruskin's daughter Margaret, wife of William Cock. Making his *Will* in 1747, the father of Robert Ruskin had appointed William Adams a "trustee" for his children, having married a Mary Adams in 1731. Robert Ruskin was their eldest son. For documentation of all statements about *Ruskins* made in the following pages, see Appendix A, except that data relevant to Margaret Cock, *née* Ruskin, will be found in Appendix B.

[51] See Appendix A, p. 180 (final sentence).

[52] See Fig. 10 after p. 56. Published with the permission of Mr. Raymond Smith, Librarian and Curator, Guildhall Library, London.

[53] From letter of Mr. Callander, commenting upon his discovery of Mrs. S. Rice's advertisement of her "Academy for Ladies," under the head "Traders, &c.," in the Croydon section of *The Universal British Directory of Trade, Commerce and Manufacture for 1791.*

The only other known reference to Mrs. Rice's "Academy" occurs in a reply sent by the Rev. East Apthorp, Vicar of Croydon, in January, 1788, to Archbishop Moore, who had sent the Vicar a questionnaire, known as an "archiepiscopal visitation." This document is now in the Central Library, Croydon. Mr. Callander remarks: "Amongst the other questions about the parish, the Archbishop enquired as to the schools, to which Mr. Apthorp replied: 'Schools kept by Mr. Hodgson, Green, Bisset, Dempster, Mrs. Rice.' Thus Apthorp merely mentions the fact that Mrs. Rice kept a school. . . . This school was certainly not in any way connected with the Parish Church, and although Ruskin in 'Praeterita' refers to his mother's having attended a fashionable school in Croydon, I cannot help feeling that this is another piece of characteristic embroidery."

[54] *Works,* XXXV, pp. 18 and 122.

[55] Urwick, William, *Nonconformity in Herts.,* p. 511.

[56] *Ibid.,* p. 512.

[57] *Ibid.,* p. 515.

[58] From unpublished letter of November 14, 1837, from the Rev. James Boyd to John James Ruskin; see Note 10, p. 216.

[59] Scott, Hew, ed., *op. cit.,* Vol. III, pp. 4 and 476. In his letter of November 14, 1837 to John James Ruskin (see Note 10), the Rev. James Boyd recalls having baptized Ruskin in his parents' home.

[60] For the course of study prescribed for children between the ages of eight and fourteen in a local school founded in 1714, see D. W. Garrow, "Croydon School Orders," *op. cit.,* p. 349 ff.

[61] See pp. 118–120.

[62] Lockhart, J. G., *Life,* Vol. I, p. 67.

[63] Chambers, Robert, *Traditions of Edinburgh,* Vol. II, p. 129, *n.*

[64] *Works,* XXVII, p. 609; from *Fors Clavigera,* September, 1873. On the preceding page he had noted Lockhart's description of Mrs. Scott. Emotionally identified with Sir Walter, Ruskin took increasing pleasure during later years in discovering parallels between his mother, his Scottish aunt, his experiences and those of Scott as he dwelt lovingly on Lockhart's *Life* (his annotated copy disappeared with the scattering of his library), collected Scott MSS., read aloud Scott novels, even as they had been read

aloud to him in childhood — thus (although not only thus) recapturing and reliving, in old age, his early years.

[65] From unpublished letter of July 23, 1845; original in the Yale University Library. For at least another decade Margaret (sixty-four years old in 1845) was able to travel with her son and husband, in their carriage, from morning until night.

[66] See Fig. 11 after p. 56. Published from *Works,* XXXV, facing p. 62, with the permission of George Allen and Unwin, Ltd. For the probable differences between this engraved reproduction and the original miniature, see Note 3, p. 215. After the Brantwood auction, the original (which I have never seen) was sold by Mrs. T. S. Telford, of Grasmere, to an unknown buyer (Mrs. Telford kindly relates) ; it has been, as yet, impossible to locate.

[67] *Works,* XXXV, p. 19. On this page, the endings of Sections 11 and 12 are framed to complement each other: at the end of § 11, Aunt Bridget takes in John James Ruskin whenever he is ill, with need "to be petted"; at the end of § 12, she takes in the starved and snappish vagrant, Towzer, transforming him into a brave and affectionate dog. There can be little doubt about what Ruskin is saying, characteristically through implication, although naturally he avoids making a specific application to his father as he concludes: "which was the kind of thing she did for every living creature that came in her way, all her life long."

[68] Mr. Callander states that no record for the marriage of Bridget Cock appears in Croydon Registers "from 1788 onwards . . . and it seems certain that she was not married in Croydon. Nor can I find any record of the birth of George Richardson in Croydon." A search of Edinburgh, Perth, and Kinnoull registers of marriages from 1799–1803 inclusive, kindly instituted by Mr. Hogan, proved similarly fruitless.

[69] Cook and Wedderburn follow Collingwood in identifying George Richardson as merely "Mr. Richardson, of Croydon." (See *Works,* XXXIX, p. 451.) Having called Mr. *Patrick* Richardson of Perth *"Peter . . . the tanner,"* Ruskin remarked: "By grotesque freak of Fors, both my aunts married a Mr. Richardson — and each left six children, four boys and two girls." (*Works,* XXXV, p. 409; here, wishing to make his point about the coincidental number of children, Ruskin was of course not strictly accurate.) He himself must have known perfectly well the name of his "Uncle George," although he chose not to mention it. In correspondence, he once inquired: "How is my uncle Richardson? I have nothing in your letters about Croydon." (From unpublished letter of April 30, 1852, from John Ruskin to his father; original in the Yale University Library.) Collingwood, one would assume, could readily have learned the first name of this uncle in the course of talk with Ruskin or with Mrs. Severn, whose knowledge was not unavailable to Cook. As to subsequent biographers, with Collingwood and Cook content to speak of "Mr. Richardson," of Croydon's "Market Street," why take the trouble to investigate a name?

[70] From unpublished letter of Catherine Tweddale Ruskin to "Miss Margaret Cox," July 15, 1809; original in the possession of Mr. Sharp, who provided this passage in transcription.

[71] Unpublished passage in "Second MS." of *Praeterita.* From a paragraph which begins: "There remained to me now of relatives whom I cared for outside of my own house-threshold, — this Croydon uncle — an altogether

gentle . . ." (as above) and which originally followed the account of the death of Charles Richardson: see *Works*, XXXV, p. 137.

[72] From unpublished note which Margaret penciled on a letter of February 27, 1836, from John Ruskin to his father; original in the Yale University Library.

[73] Ruskin having stated, in effect, that the death of his Aunt Bridget "sharply" marked the end of the first decade of his life (*Works*, XXXV, p. 87), Cook and Wedderburn evidently decided that "Mrs. Richardson of Croydon" must have died in *1829*, Ruskin having been born in 1819. Thus, through their typically rough-and-ready-guesswork (based on their naïve assumption that statements in *Praeterita* are accurate and literally truthful), Cook and Wedderburn could supply a date left *blank* on the *revised* version of the "Tree" prepared by Collingwood. They themselves nonetheless had published in Vol. II of the *Works* (p. 282, *n.*) Collingwood's statement that Ruskin's spaniel Dash was brought to Herne Hill in *1828, after* the death of Mrs. Richardson of Croydon, Collingwood having originally ascribed *1821* as the date of this death.

Sending rather unusual evidence in response to my request for information from local records about the death of Mrs. George Richardson of Croydon, Mr. Callander expressed surprise "that there should be any uncertainty about the date of her death. It is plain for all to see on her gravestone . . . [see Appendix B, *December 12, 1830*]. As you will see from the enclosed photographs [of the Cock-Richardson gravestones], she is buried with her mother and father in Croydon Churchyard."

[74] Unpublished passage from "First MS." of *Praeterita:* see p. 136. The distinction between a *Merchant* and a *Shopkeeper,* as it was impressed on Ruskin during his childhood, is suggested by the statement that his Father did not permit neighbors to cross the threshold of the Ruskins' Herne Hill home: "They [the neighbors] were for the most part well-to-do tradespeople, pure London shopkeepers of the better class. . . ." (This is the phrasing, in "Second MS.," of the last sentence of § 148 in the published version of *Praeterita:* see *Works*, XXXV, p. 130.) Specifically, thriving "grocers" were unacceptable; and when, in *Fors Clavigera*, Ruskin remarked that there was in London a "greengrocer" by the name of *Ruskin* (*ibid.*, XXVIII, p. 148), he doubtless was ironically amused.

[75] Unpublished passage from "Second MS." of *Praeterita*. From the paragraph which begins: "Bridget was a very different creature. . . ." (*Works*, XXXV, p. 88.) According to this paragraph, Cousin Bridget as a child had sometimes been a house guest at Herne Hill.

[76] From unpublished passage in the "Second MS." of *Praeterita*, as described in Note 75. In the "First MS." this sentence reads: "He was something a little above a tradesman, always an uncomfortable rank of life — " Ruskin notes that Bridget's "elder brother was already prospering" in Sydney, and adds that here "in a year or two [Bridget] died, I believe in childbirth." (Quoted from the "Second MS.") I am indebted to Dr. John Bradley of Clark University for having called my attention to a reference to Bridget's death, in an unpublished letter of February 24, 1852, from Ruskin to his father; original in the Yale University Library. (See Appendix B, *1852*.)

[77] See *Works*, XXXV, p. 20, for an account of the bitterness of the child's

disappointment, and of his unspoken but abiding resentment against the mother pilloried through this passage of tribute to the ill-advised behavior of his aunt.

[78] See Note 78, p. 253.

[79] *Works*, XXXV, p. 144.

[80] From unpublished letter of April 29, 1847, from Effie Gray to her mother, Mrs. George Gray; original in *The Bowerswell Papers*.

[81] From unpublished letter of August 16, 1856, to W. H. Harrison; original in *The Bowerswell Papers*. (It should be noted that *Chamounix* was consistently spelled *Chamouni* by Ruskin and members of his family.)

[82] *An Autobiography*, p. 75.

[83] See *Works*, XXXV, pp. 67–68. As Ruskin says, the dog which bit a piece out of the left corner of the lip "indeed had to go; but not Thomas. . . . The bitten side of the (then really pretty) mouth, was spoiled for evermore, but the wound, drawn close, healed quickly. . . ." The injury is doubtless related to the unpleasantly aggressive and obtrusive lower lip apparent in several photographs taken before Ruskin grew a beard. (One finds it stressed in caricature.)

[84] From unpublished note which Margaret penciled on a letter of March 25, 1836, from John Ruskin to his father; original in the Yale University Library.

[85] Collingwood, W. G., *Life*, Vol. II, p. 307.

[86] *Ibid.* (revised ed.), p. 10; from letter of March 15, 1808, the original (from which the date was taken) now in the possession of Mr. Sharp.

[87] From unpublished letter of April 23, 1811; original in the possession of Mr. Sharp.

[88] From unpublished page of thought and prayer, dated August 21, 1813; original in the possession of Mr. Sharp, who transcribed the quoted sentence, commenting upon its context.

[89] From unpublished letter of September 9, 1811; original in the possession of Mr. Sharp.

CHAPTER 7

[1] In 1801 it had a total population of 81,147. (Halévy, Élie, *A History of the English People in 1815*, Vol. II, p. 81.) The division into Old and New Town would have helped to create and to preserve homogeneity within the more fashionable section.

[2] Fyfe, W. T., *op. cit.*, p. 74; from a review of Mackenzie's *Life of Home*, in *Quarterly Review*, 1827.

[3] Pinnington, Edward, *op. cit.*, p. 36.

[4] In 1813 the circulation of the *Edinburgh Review* reached "what was then the enormous subscription of 12,000 . . . three years later the daily circulation of the London *Times* was only 8,000. . . ." (H. W. Thompson, *op. cit.*, pp. 342–43.)

[5] Schmitz, R. M., *Hugh Blair*, p. 2.

[6] *The Awakening of Scotland . . . 1747–1797*, p. 204.

[7] Meikle, H. W., *Scotland and the French Revolution*, p. 155.

[8] *Memorials of His Time*, p. 82. See *ibid.*, pp. 73–104 for a discussion of the terrible intolerance of the Tories, the need of reforms, and the impotence of a people without civic rights. Although the point of view in this discussion is that of a Whig reformer, as H. W. Meikle has said: "Cockburn's account of the intolerance pervading all ranks of society is amply confirmed from other sources." (*Op. cit.*, p. 155.)

[9] Meikle, H. W., *op. cit.*, p. 154.

[10] Cockburn, Henry, Lord, *Memorials of His Time*, pp. 162–63.

[11] The first issue of the *Edinburgh Review* having appeared, Francis Horner remarked: "You will not be surprised that we have given a good deal of disappointment by the temperate air of our politics; nothing short of blood and atheism and democracy were predicted . . . as the necessary production of our set." (*Op. cit.*, Vol. I, p. 210.)

[12] *Memorials of His Time*, pp. 162–63.

[13] In Black's *Memoirs*, Alexander Nicolson comments: "The effect of the Revolution in France in exciting the public mind at this time can hardly now be realised. It divided all society into two distinct factions, the friends of Order and the friends of Liberty. . . . Lord Cockburn . . . gives a very graphic and fair account of the political state of Edinburgh at this time. . . ."

CHAPTER 8

[1] The *Oxford English Dictionary* (from *Life*, III, p. 117, ed. 1839). In his *Autobiography*, De Quincey also gave reminder: "My father was a merchant; not in the sense of Scotland, where it means a retail dealer . . . but in the English sense." (*Ibid.*)

[2] *Memorials of His Time*, pp. 165–66. In England of that day the atmosphere was different. There, although the mercantile class would remain disenfranchised until 1832, social barriers were weakening as the *nouveau riche* bought country homes and thus joined the landed gentry. "Since 1688 financiers, bankers, merchants, and manufacturers had constantly exerted a decisive influence on the affairs of the nation. It was the acquisition of land which enabled these new men to insinuate themselves into the ranks of the old aristocracy. . . ." (Halévy, Élie, *op. cit.*, Vol. II, p. 35.) But through most of Scotland, and particularly in Edinburgh, the social barriers remained intact. As late as 1878, Matthew Arnold remarked: "In Scotland the landed aristocracy fills the scene, as is well known, still more than in England; the other classes are more squeezed back and effaced." ("Equality," *Mixed Essays*, p. 69.)

[3] See Note 49, p. 208. When he went to London, John James states, he lived with a "Mr. Moore for whom my Father was agent in Scotland": see Note 10, p. 230. It is not especially helpful to find nineteen *Moores* listed in the London *Post Office Directory* of 1800, with a "John Moore" described as "Wine & Brandy Mercht." Otherwise, there is no reason to believe that John Thomas Ruskin may now have been engaged in handling wine. One does find, however, that Stanger Moore, 17, Cheapside, was a wholesale Linen Draper and Warehouseman.

⁴ From unpublished letter of Catherine Tweddale Ruskin to John James Ruskin, November 2, 1807; original in the possession of Mr. Sharp.

⁵ *Life,* Vol. I, p. 14. Evidently Cook was not aware that John Thomas Ruskin was an agent of Mr. Moore, whom Cook believed to have been a resident of Edinburgh and the first employer of John James: see p. 114. In the *Life* he was content to call John Thomas Ruskin "a merchant of some sort in Edinburgh" (Vol. I, p. 5); later he identified John Thomas as a "calico-merchant" ("John Ruskin," *DNB*) — not necessarily on the basis of any evidence at his disposal.

⁶ I feel particularly indebted to Mr. Sharp for having examined *The Catherine Tweddale Ruskin Correspondence* in an attempt to discover whether any basis for Cook's identification of Mr. Moore is provided by these letters. "I can find in them nothing that could warrant Cook's statement," Mr. Sharp answered my inquiry. "Catherine mentions Mrs. Moore several times, Mr. Moore only twice, and nowhere is it stated where they live or what they do. Nor is it stated that John James Ruskin worked for them. Catherine in one letter asks Margaret to thank Mrs. Moore for her kindness to John James during one of his illnesses in London. John Thomas Ruskin was certainly in the employ of Mr. Moore, but the nature of his employment is not stated. It was in connection with his employment by Moore that John Thomas Ruskin found it necessary to travel about to Newcastle, Morpeth, etc. Knowing this, and knowing how Catherine in her letters to her husband complained about his long absences from home, makes one think that the business was not that of an Army Contractor. Had it been said that Mr. Moore was a 'Scotch Draper,' a trader in small wear, it would have seemed to fit in better with everything we know."

⁷ Nasmyth, James, *op. cit.,* pp. 55–56.

⁸ Collingwood, *Life* (revised ed.), p. 7, *n.*; from letter of January 5, 1852. Having met Ruskin in 1847, Miss Mitford (1787–1855) gained John James Ruskin's trust and friendship (marked by choice and generous contributions from his supply of sherry) at least partly through her unstinting admiration for the books of his son — her "dear John Ruskin," whom she considered "the most charming person" she had ever met; "the best letter-writer of his or any age"; an author whose writing was unequaled in its "richness and transparency"; and altogether a young man who was "just what if one had a son one should have dreamt of his turning out [to be]. . . ." (See *Works,* XXXVI, pp. xxix–xxx.) What happened to the letter of January 5, 1852, from John James Ruskin to Miss Mitford (to which evidently Collingwood alone had access) remains unknown.

For his part, Ruskin respected Miss Mitford as author of *Our Village,* and still valued her portrayal of "village children of the Lowlands" after she became "an authoress now forgotten." (See *Works,* XXXIII, p. 339; from *The Art of England,* lecture of 1883.) During her last years of life he expressed to her, with his usual thoughtfulness and bounty, his deep personal regard.

⁹ From unpublished letter of John James Ruskin to his son, July 5, 1845: original in the Yale University Library. For Catherine's reference to the temper of her husband, see p. 114.

¹⁰ *Works,* XXXV, p. 126.

¹¹ Fergusson, Alexander, *op. cit.,* p. 124.

[12] *Works,* XXXV, p. 28.

[13] *Ibid.,* p. 604; from letter of October 25, 1808; original in the possession of Mr. Sharp.

[14] Both the father and grandfather of Thomas Brown had been ministers of Kirkmabrech, a parish on the shore of Kirkcudbrightshire, just opposite Wigtown. (Malcolm M'L. Harper, *Rambles in Galloway,* p. 167.) Relatedly, John Smith — the father of Thomas Brown's mother — had been the Collector of Customs at Wigtown (Hew Scott, *op cit.,* Vol. II, p. 368), a position subsequently held by Catherine's brother, James Tweddale.

[15] *Works,* XXXV, p. 124; from letter of February 18, 1807. (The original is now in the possession of Mr. Sharp.)

[16] *Ibid.,* p. 125.

[17] Her presence and participation are described in an unpublished poem of December 26, 1830, "Going to Covent Garden Theatre / to see / The £100 Note & Harlequin Fat and Harlequin Thin"; original in "MS. V," Notebook: *Poems, 1829–1832,* in the Yale University Library.

[18] *Works,* XXXV, pp. 38–39.

[19] Nasmyth, James, *op. cit.,* p. 59.

[20] *Ibid.,* p. 60.

[21] Caw, Sir James L., "Alexander Nasmyth . . . ," *Scots Magazine,* N. S. Vol. 32 (February, 1940), p. 325.

[22] *Works,* XXXIV, p. 668; from a conversation, 1884, with M. H. Spielmann.

[23] For illustration, see *Works,* XXXV, facing p. xliv. In this photograph of Ruskin's bedroom, *Conway Castle* is the topmost picture on the left. Mr. Sharp has two other water colors, in the style of *Conway Castle,* signed by John James Ruskin.

[24] *Item 103,* Sotheby and Co., *Catalogue of the Collection of Pictures and Drawings Formerly the Property of . . . John Ruskin,* Sale of May 20, 1931.

[25] *Works,* XXIX, p. 539; posthumously published from MS. headed "Fors." The passage occurs in Ruskin's discussion of his ability to interpret Scott because, he explains, he could feel what Scott felt, with sympathetic understanding — as though they were akin, in a father-son relationship. "It has curiously happened to me also to have been educated in many particulars under the same conditions as Scott, and often in the same places. My father was a High School lad of Edinburgh; the first picture I ever saw with conscious eyes was of Edinburgh Castle. . . ." He was under the false impression that his father had studied drawing with Nasmyth while attending the Royal High School: see *ibid.,* XXXV, p. 38. Having been preserved at Brantwood, Nasmyth's *Edinburgh Castle* was sold at the Sotheby auction of May 20, 1931: see *Catalogue, Item 123.*

[26] Through poems, the prose narrative *Harry and Lucy,* Vol. II (complete with "plates"), and notes (prepared in cooperation with his father) on sights to see when traveling, Ruskin indicated in his childhood "Red Books" (in the Yale University Library) sights which he found memorable when John James Ruskin toured England and Scotland with his family. Somewhat later, in *The Iteriad,* we see them traveling through the Lake District:

With uplifted hands, and with praise never-ending,
The hill we were slowly, most slowly, descending;
And, feasting our eyes on the prospect before,
With lingering steps we were nearing the shore:
Until we were plunged, as we turned to the right,
In a wood that obscured the scene from our sight;
Save when some opening space for a moment revealed
The scene, scarce perceived when again 'twas concealed.

(Works, II, p. 288.)

The Rev. R. D. Rawnsley comments: "The more one reads the boy's poem the more one is struck with the way in which the little lad of eleven saw and noted what was really best worth seeing in the district." (*Ruskin and the English Lakes*, p. 4.) One should not forget, however, that it was the father who had planned the trip and who conducted his boy to the Romantic sights "best worth seeing."

[27] See Fig. 12 after p. 56. Published from *Works*, XXXV, facing p. 16, with the permission of George Allen and Unwin, Ltd. It was not Raeburn's habit to sign or date his pictures; "any lists of sitters and account books," Sir Walter Armstrong states, ". . . were destroyed or disappeared immediately after his death. . . ." (*Op. cit.*, Vol. II, pp. 87–88.) The maturity of John James' countenance in the Raeburn portrait suggests that he was closer to twenty than to sixteen when he was being painted. John Thomas Ruskin would also have been more likely to have commissioned a Raeburn portrait *c.* 1804 than during earlier years. (For John James' residence in Edinburgh during the later months of 1803 into late 1804 or early 1805, see pp. 113–114 and Note 19, p. 231.)

[28] Greig, James, *Sir Henry Raeburn*, p. lii. In 1802, H. W. Thompson states, "Raeburn made for one of the Mackenzie portraits his 'regular charge of fifteen guineas.'" (*Op. cit.*, p. 374, *n.*)

[29] This portrait now hangs in Brantwood. Mr. Sharp kindly gave me its dimensions.

[30] Armstrong, Sir Walter, *op. cit.*, Vol. II, p. 78. "His portraits of both men and women conform less to a type and are more fully individualised than those of any other painter of his time or school." (*Ibid.*, p. 91.)

[31] *Ibid.*, p. 67.

[32] "Ruskin's [hand] was all finger-grip," Collingwood informs us; "long, strong talons, curiously delicate-skinned and refined in form, though not academically beautiful. . . . But his palm, and especially the back of the hand, was tiny. When he rowed his boat he held the oars entirely in his fingers; when he shook hands you felt the pressure of the fingers, not of the palm. In writing, he held the pen as we are taught to hold a drawing-pencil, and the long fingers gave more play to the point than is usual in formed penmanship." (*Ruskin Relics*, pp. 136–37.) In George Richmond's portrait of the seated Ruskin, drawn in 1842, the left hand shows the characteristics Collingwood describes and suggests another version of the left hand in Raeburn's portrait of his father.

[33] *Works*, XXXIV, p. 668; from conversation, 1884, with M. H. Spielmann.

[34] ". . . I had always a hankering after Law not to have it dispensed to me but to dispense it to others —" (From unpublished letter, John James

Ruskin to George Gray, August 31, 1848; original in *The Bowerswell Papers*.)

CHAPTER 9

[1] From unpublished letter, John James Ruskin to George Gray, September 15, 1848; original in *The Bowerswell Papers*.

[2] The handicaps which John James Ruskin would have had to face had he tried to make his way in Edinburgh as his father's son are indicated by a letter in which a friend advised Lockhart to move to London. Speaking of Edinburgh as "the Mecca of social snobbishness," Sir Herbert Grierson notes: "At a much later date, in 1825, Lockhart's friend Wright, in urging him to come to London as editor of *The Representative,* tells him he had come to the conclusion that Edinburgh was not a sphere 'which your talents were calculated to adorn,' and goes on: 'For what Scotland affords in regard to preferment calculated to satisfy an ambitious and aspiring mind I thought the claimants with title and hopes far exceeded those in England, and that there preferment was not so independently bestowed, and that there was not with you that regard paid to powerful and useful talents which prevails here.'" (*Op. cit.,* p. 18, *n.*)

[3] See Note 11.

[4] Burne-Jones, Lady, *Memorials of Edward Burne-Jones,* Vol. I, p. 278.

[5] I am indebted to Mr. Sharp for the information that James Tweddale was left £8,000 by Dr. John Adair. (See Note 48, p. 208.) Having remarked that James Tweddale received "a considerable fortune" from his "Surgeon-General" uncle, P. H. M'Kerlie notes that "James Tweddell [*sic*]" then "became by purchase the owner of Glenlaggan, parish of Parton in Kirkcudbrightshire, and also had sasine of portions of the lands of the barony of Garthland . . . and as he is styled of Caldons in 1828, that farm must also have been purchased." (*Op. cit.,* Vol. I, p. 343. On the Cook and Wedderburn "Family Tree," *Caldons* appears as "Caldous." More meaningfully, Collingwood identified James Tweddale as "of Glenlaggan.")

[6] "He married Margaret, sister of John M'Taggart of Ardwell. . . ." (P. H. M'Kerlie, *op. cit.,* Vol. I, p. 343.) (On their "Family Tree," Cook and Wedderburn give *Cath[erine]* Mactaggart as the wife of James Tweddale, thus faithfully preserving an error originally made by Collingwood. *Ardwell* and *Ardwall* are variant spellings.)

M'Kerlie consistently uses the spelling *M'Taggart;* Cook and Wedderburn follow Collingwood in spelling the name *Mactaggart.* I have adopted the spelling used by John James Ruskin in all references to "Mr. McTaggart."

Margaret McTaggart's brother John has not heretofore been referred to in Ruskin scholarship, though Cook and Wedderburn follow Collingwood in noting that John James Ruskin's aunt by marriage was "aunt of Sir John Mactaggart, Bart. of Ardwell" (*d.* 1867) — possibly because this bit of information adds luster to Ruskin's "Family Tree."

[7] See Note 11.

[8] M'Kerlie, P. H., *op. cit.,* Vol. I, pp. 364–65.

[9] This firm may have been the "Fyfe & Stavley, Druggists, 25, Bartholomew-lane" listed in the London *Post Office Directory* of 1813.

[10] In the words of John James Ruskin: "I came to London at 16 years of Age with a Letter from my Uncle Tweddale to J^n McTaggart, one of the first Colonial Brokers in London & my aunts Brother — His House took no Connections but he promised to look out — meanwhile M^r. Moore for whom my Father was agent in Scotland, received me into his House . . . & my Father placed me with Fyfe Druggist to wait for Mr M^c.Taggarts Situation . . . I got nothing at the Druggists. . . ." (From unpublished letter of John James Ruskin to George Gray, September 1, 1848; original in *The Bowerswell Papers.* Henceforth in this section all direct quotations for which no source is given are taken from this letter, which is also the basis for some details left otherwise undocumented.)

[11] From unpublished letter of John James Ruskin to George Gray, September 9, 1848; original in *The Bowerswell Papers.*

[12] From unpublished letter of John James Ruskin to George Gray, August 24, 1848; original in *The Bowerswell Papers.* In letters of this period, John James Ruskin was trying to convince Mr. Gray that it would be unwise to start his son George on a mercantile career by establishing him in a London office of some Colonial Broker instead of keeping to a long-established plan of making George a Perth or Edinburgh lawyer. By now, Effie Gray had become Mrs. John Ruskin, both she and her father having hoped that if George could but get a foothold as a clerk, her marriage would help to launch him, socially and economically, upon a career in London.

In his attempts (at times excessively untactful) to make Mr. Gray see the problem realistically, John James Ruskin recalled his own experiences at the start of his career, resorting to forthright autobiography in his letter of September 1, 1848. Indirectly autobiographical in the unpublished letter of August 24, 1848, he also remarked: "Before taking the irretrievable step George should fully understand what he probably comes to here — To a Solitary Lodging or some family in the City to whom his Board is an object — " (Original in *The Bowerswell Papers.*) Although this statement does not apply to his life with the Moores, it characterizes the years he spent in lodgings after his return to London in 1804 or 1805. Telling this story of his early mercantile career, I interweave information scattered through several other letters.

[13] *Works*, XXXV, p. 123.

[14] *Life*, Vol. I, p. 14. It remained for Joan Evans to revive this story, and to dramatize it. Having told us that Cook's *Life* "will remain a classic" (*John Ruskin*, p. 11), she changes Cook's version by stating that the parents of John James (rather than the Moores) "forbade the marriage" (*ibid.*, p. 20) and comments, as part of her *finale:* "There are strange Aeschylean repetitions; Ruskin's father had in his youth been forbidden the girl he loved because she was a Catholic, yet saw, unprotestingly, his son's youth wrecked for the same reason." (*Ibid.*, p. 422.) Thus, continually — and unquestioningly, old tales are retold, with someone forever adding something else still more imaginatively new.

In an unpublished passage of the "First MS." of *Praeterita*, Ruskin states specifically that "to the match [with Adèle] . . . my Father never had any serious objection," and that his mother, he supposed, would have "consented to the match" if Adèle herself had been fond of him: originally, part of what appears as sentence 3, § 256: see *Works*, XXXV, p. 229. (For the improbability of Mr. Moore's having been an army contractor except in the imagination of Mr. Cook, see p. 102.)

[15] See Note 11. "Amyand, Amyand & Osborne, Merchts., 5 Lawrence-pountney-hill" are listed in *Kent's Directory for the Year 1781;* "Amyand & Osborne, Mer. [same address]" appear in *Lowndes's London Directory for the Year 1786;* "Amyand & Co. Merchts., 7 King's Arms-yard, Coleman-str." are listed in *The New Annual Directory for the Year 1800.* In 1813 the name *Amyand* does not appear in the *London Post Office Annual Directory.* (I have not had access to *Directories* for the years between 1800 and 1813.)

[16] From unpublished letter of Catherine Tweddale Ruskin to John James Ruskin, April 16, 1805; in the possession of Mr. Sharp, who most kindly provided a transcription of this passage.

[17] From unpublished letter of John James Ruskin to George Gray, August 24, 1848; in *The Bowerswell Papers.* In context the phrase reads: ". . . [I] lived very sparingly in a Roman Catholics House for 15 months & in a miserable Lodging House for four [sic] years till received into Gordon Co — " Thus, he did not bother to tell Mr. Gray that at the end of almost three years he had moved into still less desirable quarters (see Note 18). According to a letter of November 2, 1807, his address was "No. 1 Lawrence Pountney Hill," Mr. Sharp informs me; in the 1780's, the address of Amyand & Osborne was "5, Lawrence-pountney-hill" (see Note 15). It seems likely that John James took lodgings within a stone's throw of his work, even though the main address of the house of Amyand had been changed by 1805.

[18] From unpublished letter of John James Ruskin to Catherine Tweddale Ruskin and John Thomas Ruskin, February 29, 1808; in the possession of Mr. Sharp, who, kindly transcribing this passage, noted that in this letter John James Ruskin refers to having received, from his mother, the news of his father's business failure and indebtedness — an event usually dated 1809. (Writing to George Gray in 1848, John James Ruskin merely observed that when he was twenty-three years old, his "Father was by good living getting behind — ": see p. 115.) Some weeks later, Catherine asked: ". . . tell me particularly about your new Lodgings, and what your bedroom is like and if it be well aired and who the young men are and if you think you will be comfortable . . ." (Unpublished passage in letter of Catherine Tweddale Ruskin to John James Ruskin, March 15, 1808; in the possession of Mr. Sharp. For the main body of this letter, see Collingwood, *Life,* revised ed., pp. 10–11, and above, p. 124.)

[19] The following chronology emerges from the statements in this letter of September 1, 1848, from John James Ruskin to George Gray (see Note 10) — a chronology supported and supplemented by letters in *The Catherine Tweddale Ruskin Correspondence,* now in the possession of Mr. Sharp:

I. *First trip to London* for fifteen months of work at *Fyfe Druggist,* begun when he was still sixteen: early 1802 (sometime before May 10) into 1803 (lasting at least into early August).

II. *Return to Edinburgh* for "some months": late summer 1803 into late 1804 (or early 1805?).

III. *Return to London* for "four" years of work with Amyand Cornwall:

late 1804 (or early 1805?) to late 1808 (or early 1809?), with news of his father's business failure reaching him in February, 1808. These were the first "four" years through which he worked without a holiday. Leaving Amyand Cornwall "at the end of my Seventh year in London" (*viz.,* early 1802 into late 1808 or early 1809), he was earning an annual £100. It was in February, 1808, that he promised payment of his father's debts. He completed payment "nine" years later — that is, before the end of 1817 — so that he was free to marry in early 1818.

IV. *Five years with Gordon Murphy Co.,* to whom he went when he was still "23," now to work "5" years without a holiday: *viz.,* late 1808 (or early 1809?) to mid-August, 1813. (For "mid-August," see pp. 116 and 128.)

V. *Convalescence in Perth:* mid-August, 1813 into 1814.

VI. *Return to London* to join M. Domecq in sale of Haurie wine: (late?) 1814.

VII. *Founding of his firm,* Ruskin, Telford, and Domecq: 1815 (see Note 5, p. 238).

CHAPTER 10

[1] The fifteen months in 1802–1803 having proved so fruitless, the leave-taking of 1805 was in actuality the one which marked John James' "first" departure for veritable "business" in London. And since Margaret may not have been a member of her uncle's household when John James left for London in early 1802, it may have been for her, in reality, the "first" parting.

[2] See p. 124 (see also p. 115 for her uncle's " 'getting behind' ").

[3] *Works,* XXXV, p. 128.

[4] McKnight, George H., *Modern English in the Making,* p. 440.

[5] Pottle, F. A., *Boswell's London Journal,* pp. 8–9. "Professor of Oratory" (as Boswell called him), Thomas Sheridan had also given training in "correct" pronunciation to the young "Alexander Wedderburn, later Chief Justice and Lord Chancellor with the peerage titles of 1st Baron Loughborough and Earl of Rosslyn." (*Ibid.,* pp. 90, *n.* and 221, *n.*) While spending 1763 in London, Boswell wrote: ". . . I ought not to keep too much company with Scotch people, because I am kept from acquiring propriety of English speaking. . . ." (*Ibid.,* p. 177.)

[6] Francis Horner had three years at Edinburgh University and then was sent to England, for study under a private tutor, so that he could get "rid of the Scottish accent and pronunciation." (Leonard Horner, ed., *op. cit.,* Vol. I, p. 40.) Shortly after reaching England, he wrote his father: "With respect to one great object for which you were at the expense and trouble of placing me here, I think I am beginning to *pronounce* some *words* as Englishmen do, and just to *feel* the difference between the *rhythm* of their conversation and mine." (*Ibid.,* p. 7.)

More generally, speaking of Francis, Lord Jeffrey's prose, H. W. Thompson notes: ". . . for half a century Scottish writers had been meticulously careful with regard to style because they were writing a language not colloquial and their terrible pride made them unwilling to appear ridiculous for Scotticisms before English critics." (*Op. cit.,* p. 349.) Anxious to help his countrymen "attain purity of expression," Sir John Sinclair published a "collection of the most remarkable words and phrases by which the natives of North Britain excited the ridicule of their southern neighbours." (Catherine Sinclair, *Memoir of the Right Hon. Sir John Sinclair,* p. 4.)

On the other hand, a Londoner, William Kenrick, writing his *Introduction to A New Dictionary of the English Language* (1773), "points out as 'a phænomenon in the literary world, that, while our learned fellow subjects of Scotland and Ireland are making frequent attempts to ascertain and fix a standard to the pronunciation of the English tongue, the natives of England themselves seem to be little anxious for the honour or improvement of their own language.' 'There seems indeed,' he continues, 'a most ridiculous absurdity in the pretensions of a native of Aberdeen or Tipperary, to teach the natives of London to speak and to read.'" (George H. McKnight, *op. cit.,* p. 435.)

[7] George H. McKnight, *op. cit.,* pp. 500–501. (From *Sesame and Lilies: Works,* XVIII, p. 65.)

[8] John James Ruskin, who never lost his "rather broad" Scottish accent (Frederic Harrison, *Autobiographic Memoirs,* Vol. I, p. 205), had few associates in London who would have spoken with the accent of the well-educated Englishman. Most of the friends and neighbors of Herne Hill were prosperous tradesmen. When the Ruskins went to Perth, they were with the unpretentious family of Aunt Jessie; visiting Croydon, they were with relatives who lived above a bakery shop.

[9] *Works,* XXXV, p. 121.

[10] Unpublished passage from "First MS." of *Praeterita;* the original version of what appears as the first part of sentence 2, § 148: see *Works,* XXXV, p. 128.

[11] See Fig. 13 after p. 56. From Thomas Brown, *Lectures on the Philosophy of the Human Mind,* with *Memoir* by David Welsh.

Professor of Medicine at the University, Dr. James Gregory (1753–1821) attained widespread fame as "concocter of the dreadful Gregory's Mixture which still regulates Scottish health." (H. W. Thompson, *op. cit.,* p. 388.) Amusingly enough, in the 1860's, one finds John Everett Millais informing his daughter Mary that her sister "Miss Sophie is a wee bit out of sorts just now, and is subject to the power, and powder of Gregory." (From unpublished letter of November 8, 1874; original among *The Millais Papers,* in The Pierpont Morgan Library.) Dr. Gregory "had the leading consulting practice in Scotland until his death." (G. T. Bettany, *DNB.*)

[12] Brown, Thomas, *op. cit.,* p. xxii.

[13] *Ibid.*

[14] See p. 105 and Note 14, p. 227.

[15] *Works,* XXXV, p. 125. Giving further rein to fantasy, Ruskin adds that Sydney Smith had been trained "by the same Dr. Thomas Brown who had formed my father's mind and directed his subsequent reading." (*Ibid.,* p. 396.) Seven years older than Thomas Brown, Sydney Smith had helped to found the *Edinburgh Review* while Thomas was still a medical student.

[16] Although Cook stresses the mercantile rather than the aristocratic connections of Ruskin's family, he nonetheless remarks: "The fact that Dr. Thomas Brown, the Professor of Moral Philosophy, acted as [John James

Ruskin's] mentor in literary matters shows the position which the elder Ruskin held in the cultivated society of Edinburgh." (*Life,* Vol. I, p. 14.) Subsequent biographers have accepted this fallacious reasoning. It should also be remembered that neither before nor after he received his university professorship (delayed because of his sympathy with Whigs) was Dr. Brown an Edinburgh socialite. Instead, he lived with the mother to whom he was unusually devoted, "unwilling to go abroad" and enjoying the companionship of his sisters; "his youthful companions" came to him, spending "hour after hour" of discussion over his "favourite beverage . . . tea." (Thomas Brown, *op. cit.,* p. vii.)

[17] *Works,* XXXV, p. 124.

[18] See p. 148.

[19] *Works,* XXXV, p. 123.

[20] *Ibid.*

[21] *Ibid.* In view of the final secrecy of Margaret's marriage (see pp. 168–69), it is worth noting that this servant became Aunt Jessie's "Old Mause," who thus makes her first appearance in an incident associated with unpleasantness and disapproval.

[22] From unpublished letter of John James Ruskin to Catherine Tweddale Ruskin, February 29, 1808; original in the possession of Mr. Sharp, who kindly provided a transcription of this passage.

[23] From unpublished letter of Catherine Tweddale Ruskin to John James Ruskin, March 15, 1808; original in the possession of Mr. Sharp, who kindly provided a transcription of this passage.

[24] Collingwood, W. G., *Life* (revised ed.), pp. 10–11; from letter of March 15, 1808; original in the possession of Mr. Sharp, who kindly noted that Catherine wrote *"one* servant" rather than "our servant," as published by Collingwood.

[25] *Ibid.* The passages in double parentheses are taken from my transcription; queried words in brackets indicate differences from the version published by Collingwood. Original in the possession of Mr. Sharp.

[26] Recounted in an unpublished letter from Catherine Tweddale Ruskin to John Thomas Ruskin, July 11, 1809; original in the possession of Mr. Sharp.

[27] Republished in *Praeterita,* the story first appeared in *Fors Clavigera* of October, 1871. "My father began business as a wine-merchant, with no capital and a considerable amount of debts bequeathed to him by my grandfather. He accepted the bequest, and paid them all before he began to lay anything by for himself. . . ." (*Works,* XXVII, p. 15.) In *Praeterita* he adds: "My father came up to London; was a clerk in a merchant's house for nine years, without a holiday; then began business on his own account; paid his father's debts; and married his exemplary Croydon cousin." (*Ibid.,* XXXV, p. 19.) Finally: ". . . my father [showed his affection] in unremitting attention to the business on the success of which his marriage depended: and in a methodical regularity of conduct and correspondence which never left his mistress a moment of avoidable anxiety, or gave her motive for any serious displeasure. ¶On these terms the engagement lasted nine years; at the end of which time, my grandfather's debts having been all paid . . . the now not very young people were married. . . ." (*Ibid.,*

pp. 126–27.) The chief source of confusion in Ruskin's account of these events was his assumption that the "nine years" which marked (1) his father's work without a holiday, (2) his father's payment of the debts, (3) his father's engagement, covered the *same* time span, whereas in actuality only the last two were approximately concomitant. And how easily he could have drawn the wrong conclusion as he put together all the references to "nine years" that he must have heard his parents make!

[28] Mr. W. D. Collier, The Keeper, *Edinburgh Gazette,* Edinburgh, remarks, "I have to confirm that where a Scottish Court makes an Award of Sequestration (or bankruptcy) that fact is published in the Gazette . . . I regret, however, that there is no notice of such an award in the name of John Thomas Ruskin during the period of 1807–1813 inclusive." The indices for the *Gazette* of 1808, 1809, and 1810 were rechecked for possible variants in the spelling of the name *Ruskin.*

[29] From unpublished letter of Catherine Tweddale Ruskin to John James Ruskin, March 15, 1808; original in the possession of Mr. Sharp, who kindly provided this passage in transcription.

[30] From unpublished letter of Catherine Tweddale Ruskin to John James Ruskin, March 15, 1808; original in the possession of Mr. Sharp, who kindly provided this passage in transcription.

Having inadequately acknowledged the existence and significance of *The Catherine Tweddale Ruskin Correspondence* by noting that there were "at Brantwood a few letters written between 1805 and 1817 by Catherine Tweddale to her son . . . in London," Cook and Wedderburn selected two phrases (one at the beginning, the other at the end, of Catherine's long letter of March 15) and interwove them into a comment which biographers have used as a mainstay for their characterization of Ruskin's grandfather: ". . . John Thomas Ruskin's conduct, or misconduct of his affairs, as well as the condition of his health and mind, had long given anxiety to his family. His wife writes freely to her son on the subject, speaking of 'a father so unstable as yours' [see above, p. 123] who 'seldom knows his own mind for two hours together.'" (*Works,* XXXV, p. lx, *n.*) By thus linking these two widely separated phrases, quoted out of context and interpreted without regard for the circumstances which had impelled the letter as a whole, Cook and Wedderburn distort the spirit and to some degree the implications of Catherine's remarks about her husband, as she expressed, with gratitude, a mother's pride and love. In the long run, they could scarcely have been more destructive if they had exercised their editorial discretion with deliberate malice.

[31] From unpublished letter of Catherine Tweddale Ruskin to John James Ruskin, March 15, 1808; original in the possession of Mr. Sharp, who kindly provided this passage in transcription.

[32] From unpublished letter of John James Ruskin to Catherine Tweddale Ruskin, April, 1817; original in the possession of Mr. Sharp, who kindly provided this passage in transcription.

[33] From unpublished letter of Catherine Tweddale Ruskin to John James Ruskin, October 25, 1808; original in the possession of Mr. Sharp, who kindly provided this passage in transcription.

[34] From unpublished letter of Catherine Tweddale Ruskin to John Thomas Ruskin, July 11, 1809; original in the possession of Mr. Sharp, who kindly provided this passage in transcription, noting that the "good Hit or two"

refers to a disappointed Catherine's having said that she believed her husband had been away from home longer than was really necessary. In *The Catherine . . . Correspondence,* Mr. Sharp adds that, with one possible exception (see Note 41, below), this is the only time when Margaret's name appears as *Cock.* The "Mar*great Cock*" was at least an apt misspelling.

[85] From unpublished letter of Catherine Tweddale Ruskin to "Miss Cox, Mr. Ruskin, Dysart, Fife"; original in the possession of Mr. Sharp, who kindly provided this passage in transcription, noting that it was Catherine, rather than John Thomas, who decided to leave Edinburgh: "Catherine definitely states that 'going to Dysart was my idea, not his.' "

[86] *Works,* XXXV, p. 126.

[87] See pp. 145–46 and 150.

[88] From unpublished letter of Catherine Tweddale Ruskin to "Miss Margaret Cox," July 11, 1812; original in the possession of Mr. Sharp.

[89] Speaking of his father's death, Ruskin remarks that his "own principal feeling was certainly anxiety for her, who had been for so many years dependent on my father's wishes . . ." (*Works,* XXXV, p. 535.) All evidence in letters and other material related to Margaret's married life indicates that she spent herself in caring for and pleasing John James Ruskin, who phenomenally dominated both her life and their son's. From the beginning, she had taught Ruskin to love, respect, and obey his father as the household god.

[40] See p. 147.

[41] It is barely possible that before she was engaged, Margaret had tried to caution her cousin against assuming the payment of his father's debts as a personal obligation. In the letter of March 15, 1808, in which Catherine thanked John James for having promised to make good whatever sum John Thomas owed, one finds the statement: "Miss [*Cook?* or *Cock?*] desires me to say that it is moraly [*sic*] wrong to promise and not to perform and *might be avoided.* . . ." (From transcription kindly provided by Mr. Sharp, from the original in his possession; my italics.) Because the queried name appears in cross-script on a page that is otherwise most crowded, strokes overlap so that we will never know whether Catherine wrote Miss *Cock* or Miss *Cook.* Elsewhere, however, Catherine addresses letters to her niece as Miss *Cox* and speaks of her, informally, as *Margaret, Margt, Meggy,* etc.; under the immediate circumstances, for Catherine to have referred to *Margaret* as "Miss Cock" would have been especially incongruous. Hence there is good reason to believe that Catherine wrote the name *Miss Cook* — a probability allied to one detail in Ruskin's version of this story: ". . . [my father's] friends, as a body . . . dissuaded him from the chivalry of such sacrifice to honour." (See p. 147.) Yet surely Margaret, too, would have believed that it is "moraly" wrong to promise and not to perform.

At first, apparently, John James Ruskin put aside his extra money, to be invested, in 1815, in his own business: see p. 132. The debts, one would infer, were paid after 1815 and before 1818 through his work as the head partner in Ruskin, Telford, and Domecq.

[42] *Works,* XXXV, p. lx, *n.*

[43] From unpublished letter of Catherine Tweddale Ruskin to "Mr. [John James] Ruskin, Red Lion Inn, Ferry Bridge, Yorkshire," postmarked

August 15, 1813; original in the possession of Mr. Sharp, who kindly
provided the passage in transcription, noting that in the next letter, "Perth,
August 21, 1813, to 'My dearest John and Margt.' John James is
better. . . ."

[44] These words mark the beginning of "a separate sheet, starting August
21st, 1813 — a sheet of Catherine's own, giving her thoughts and prayers
in regard to John James Ruskin's improvement and safety." Original in the
possession of Mr. Sharp, who kindly provided the transcription, describing
this page of the manuscript.

[45] From unpublished letter, postmarked Perth, August 21, 1813, of Catherine
Tweddale Ruskin to John James Ruskin and Margaret Cox, who were
still in Ferry Bridge; original in the possession of Mr. Sharp, who kindly
provided the transcription.

[46] On April 13, 1815, John James Ruskin posted from Stirling a letter
addressed to "Mrs. Ruskin, Bowerswell, Perth." Mr. Sharp states that
among the letters in *The Catherine Tweddale Ruskin Correspondence*,
this is the first which provides definite evidence that the Ruskins had
become residents of Bowerswell. (The extremely kind effort of Mr.
Tait and Miss Watson to discover when the Ruskins lived at Bowerswell
proved unsuccessful, no Perth tenancy lists for this period having survived,
so far as can be learned.)

[47] See Admiral Sir William James, *op. cit.*, p. 6. See also above, p. 167.

[48] Mrs. George Gray (*née* Sophia Margaret Jameson) had a niece, Eliza
Jameson (daughter of her brother Melville), who "wrote down some reminiscences of her own recollections, and of what her family had told her."
When Effie's daughter Carrie, mother of the Hon. Clare Stuart Wortley,
planned to write the story of Effie's marriage to Ruskin, she copied passages from Eliza Jameson's reminiscences, including the following passage:
"Aunt [Sophia] Gray told me the first time she saw J[ohn] R[uskin] was
when his mother brought him with her to call on Aunt G[ray] at Bowerswell when he was 8 years old. ¶ . . . Mrs Ruskin had evidently a dislike
to enter the house and asked that her visit to Aunt G[ray] might be in
the garden — " (From unpublished MS. in *The Bowerswell Papers.*) In
letters to George Gray, John James Ruskin refers to his wife's "superstitious" dread of Perth; in letters to his father, Ruskin also speaks of the
intensity of emotion this place aroused in his mother. After Jessie's death
in 1828, neither Margaret nor John James Ruskin would return to Perth —
not even to attend their son's wedding: see p. 164.

[49] *Works, XXXV*, p. 123.

[50] From unpublished letter of John James Ruskin to Catherine Tweddale
Ruskin, April 13, 1815; original in the possession of Mr. Sharp, who most
kindly provided a copy of the original so that I could check the transcription I had made at Brantwood.

CHAPTER 11

[1] From unpublished letter of September 1, 1848, to George Gray; original
in *The Bowerswell Papers.*

[2] *Ibid.*

[3] *Ibid.*

⁴ *Ibid.* For changes in the firm of John McTaggart, see P. H. M'Kerlie, *op. cit.,* Vol. I, pp. 364–65.

⁵ From unpublished letter to W. H. Harrison, July 12, 1859; original in *The Bowerswell Papers.* The reference to "44 years" of partnership provides evidence that John James Ruskin's firm was founded in 1815.

⁶ *Works,* XXXV, pp. 27–28.

⁷ "John Ruskin, Wine Propagandist," *Ridley's Wine and Spirit Trade Circular,* August 14, 1933, p. 616. Some statements in this article are evidently based upon the *Praeterita* account of the founding of Ruskin, Telford, and Domecq, and are in consequence mistaken.

⁸ Yeats, John, *A Manual of Recent and Existing Commerce — 1789–1872,* p. 11. "This idea is not well founded," Yeats continues, "for the merchants of Xeres 'must' purchase from the adjoining, and even the distant vineyards, and high-class wines are also made at Port St. Mary."

⁹ *Works,* XXXV, pp. 26–27. Apparently, however, the problem was less simple than Ruskin thought. In later years, M. Domecq wrote John James Ruskin: "The old shipments of some wines I saw in London [were] right in *colour,* but not in quality; they were all thin wines, but I think the same colour can be sent with more quality in them. I saw some wines of Dastis at Morris, just the same, pale and thin, and could not sell them; sour taste. I have told my brother to destine the fullest wines for the pale. I think he will exert himself as much as it is possible in colour and quality. Our adversaries have done much in pale and succeeded often, but have had great losses for thin wines; it is not easy in low pale wines to say how they will turn; they very often get thinner after shipping. Low wines have still to ferment, and fermentation makes wines thinner, unless they are overloaded with brandy, which checks fermentation. Older wines ferment less, and get less thin, and you can better tell how they will turn; at all times it is an obscure matter. So many things [have] influence on wines in the course of time which you cannot forsee, and do not show at first — long pruning, bad cultivation, young vines, manure, and God knows what." (From unpublished letter of June 20, 1836, in proof sheets intended for *Dilecta;* in "Second MS." of *Praeterita;* in the Yale University Library. Original letter in the possession of Mr. Sharp, who notes that the version in proof has been edited for punctuation and capitalization.)

¹⁰ See Note 1, p. 237.

¹¹ *Ibid.*

¹² *Works,* XXXV, p. 27.

¹³ From unpublished letter of June 20, 1836, in proof sheets intended for *Dilecta;* in "Second MS." of *Praeterita;* in the Yale University Library.

¹⁴ *Works,* XXXV, p. 26. Elsewhere, Ruskin states: "Some considerable time during my father's clerkdom had been passed by him in Spain, in learning to know sherry, and seeing the ways of making and storing it at Xerez, Cadiz, and Lisbon." (*Ibid.,* p. 100.) His own uncertainty about the facts is suggested by the first version of this sentence: "Some considerable time during the nine years of my fathers engagement had been passed. . . ." (From "First MS." of *Praeterita.*) John James Ruskin's own story of his life as a London clerk makes it clear that he had not spent any time

in Spain before he left Gordon Murphy; with the continent shut off by war, it seems highly improbable that he could have gone abroad before 1815. Apparently, however, he visited Spain between 1815 and 1817, and he may have made a special effort to see the Domecq vineyards before the founding of his firm. Ruskin states that his father met his friend Richard Gray, of Camberwell, when he was in Lisbon. (*Ibid.*, p. 100.) Then too, during boyhood Ruskin wrote a poem (see below) which in all probability is based upon his father's account of what he had observed in Spain as an aftermath of the Napoleonic Wars. On the other hand, it is not likely that John James Ruskin would have spent "considerable time" in Spain while he was the head of a firm not yet securely established.

[15] Four of M. Domecq's five daughters would make distinguished marrigaes, and that of Clotilde (the Adèle of *Praeterita*) to the Baron Duquesne becomes intimately interwoven with Ruskin's story. In his letter of June 20, 1836, to John James Ruskin, M. Domecq describes the wealth and position of the family into which one of his daughters was being married and the general fanfare which accompanied the signing of the marriage contract — for example, "the politeness and kindness shown me by the royal family," including a conversation with the King; the "immense concourse of people" assembled for the actual signing of the contract, "consisting of Marshals, Generals, Ministers, Ambassadors, and other notabilities, Dukes, etc., etc., and their ladies." (From proof sheets intended for *Dilecta;* in "Second MS." of *Praeterita*. Original in the possession of Mr. Sharp.)

[16] From unpublished poem dated May 10, 1835, in "MS. XI," Bound volume: *Poems and Letters to his Father;* in the Yale University Library. The poem has as subtitle: "A Dream and no dream." Although the dream does not carry the poet specifically to Spain before the fifth stanza, it is interesting that in *Praeterita* Ruskin should specifically have mentioned his father's observation of ways of "storing" wine, and that the second stanza of the poem describes the appearance of the vaults after long neglect:

> Methought that my way I was wending
> Where casks had been heaped up with toil
> And guided through vaults never ending
> By feeble lamps, dripping with oil[.]
> In disorder, in damp, and in dust
> The casks were laid low on the ground
> And the spider in mould and in must
> Was weaving his cobwebs around.

The third stanza likewise refers to conditions that might well have prevailed after the Napoleonic Wars:

> No wine had attained to old age here,
> It was new, it was sour, it was dead
> Oh, here was no voice of the gauger;
> Nor sound of the cellarmans tread. [etc.]

With exports from Spain shut off, English sherry drinkers might also have known, to some degree, the suffering described in stanza four:

> But though there was feasting enough,
> When I looked for the soul of the cheer,
> They had but some pitiful stuff

> Some wine had been vintaged that year.
> There came not, to make them all merry
> The spirited juice from Champagne,
> There came what was said to be sherry,
> But had never been ripened in Spain.

Altogether, the poem reads as though the boy was versifying John James' talk about his early days as head of the firm, with emphasis on what M. Domecq almost certainly would have found on his return to Macharnudo. Did John James accompany him to Spain or follow shortly after? Or perhaps did M. Domecq describe by letter the conditions he must overcome?

CHAPTER 12

[1] Trevelyan, G. M., *A Shortened History of England,* pp. 408–409.

[2] See Note 1, p. 237.

[3] *Works,* XXXV, p. 26: another example of Ruskin's use of double-entendre.

[4] Halévy, Élie, *op. cit.,* Vol. II, p. 45. "From 1809 onwards there were over 100 enclosures a year." (*Ibid.,* p. 32, *n.*)

[5] *Works,* XXVII, p. 89; from *Fors Clavigera,* May, 1871.

[6] Halévy, Élie, *op. cit.,* Vol. II, p. 108.

[7] For the enslavement of tailors in sweat shops, see *Alton Locke.* For what was in reality the slave labor of women and especially children in the coal mines, see Disraeli's *Sybil.* The reports to Parliament of various Commissions during these and later years make genuinely horrendous reading, as, before Marx and Engels, Carlyle had discovered.

[8] See *Works,* XXXVI, p. 436; letter to Charles Eliot Norton, March 10, 1863. Ruskin was then spending the winter in Mornex: ". . . the loneliness is very great, in the peace in which I am at present, and the peace is only as if I had buried myself in a tuft of grass on a battlefield wet with blood, for the cry of the earth about me is in my ears continually if I do not lay my head to the very ground."

[9] Unpublished passage from "MS. IVB," Red Book: Travel notes, miscellaneous diagrams, mineralogical material, etc.; in the Yale University Library.

CHAPTER 13

[1] See Note 40, p. 213.

[2] Unpublished passage in letter of August 10, 1862; original in the Yale University Library. Cook and Wedderburn published this letter in large part, without indicating omissions: see *Works,* XXXVI, p. 419; see also below, Note 33, p. 246.

[3] See p. 137.

[4] In "The Wine Merchant," an essay written in the 1860's, Anthony Trollope remarks that "the good old time when men laid down great cellars" was of the past. Reminiscing, he said that the good merchant, that is, the man whose wares could be trusted, was called a "Prettyman"; that although his prices were high, no one would ever think of asking

him for a discount; that he sent his bill once a year, waited a year for payment without remark, and then sent a reminder. (*London Tradesmen,* p. 76.) In 1815, after the long years of isolation from the continent, the wine cellars of England were doubtless in a state conducive to unusually large orders.

⁵ Yeats, John, *op. cit.,* p. 71.

⁶ See p. 132 and Note 1, p. 237.

⁷ From unpublished letter of John James Ruskin to W. H. Harrison, November 17, 1849; original in *The Bowerswell Papers.*

⁸ See pp. 69–70, *passim.*

⁹ From unpublished letter of John James Ruskin to George Gray, August 24, 1848; original in *The Bowerswell Papers.*

¹⁰ From unpublished letter of John James Ruskin to George Gray, August 24, 1848; original in *The Bowerswell Papers.*

¹¹ *Works,* XXXIV, p. 601; from letter to Editor of the *Pall Mall Gazette,* January 7, 1887.

¹² In penciled notes added to unpublished letters of 1835 from John Ruskin to his father, Margaret Ruskin twice speaks of Mr. Telford's having called: original letters (of February 18 and March 11, 1835) in the Yale University Library.

¹³ *Works,* XXXV, p. 171.

¹⁴ From unpublished letter of John James Ruskin to George Gray, October 4, 1848; original in *The Bowerswell Papers.*

¹⁵ *Works,* XVII, p. lxxvii.

¹⁶ From "Second MS." of *Praeterita.* In the "First MS.," the conclusion of this passage reads: "This was frankly represented to him at the time by his best friends, and as I see things now, his friends were right. The feeling in which my grandfathers debts were paid, was exactly the same in which my mothers relations were kept at a distance, and in which the threshold of our house Herne Hill became impassable to our neighbours." Originally, this passage appeared between what are now sentences 2 and 3 of the third paragraph of § 147: see *Works,* XXXV, p. 127. (Ruskin may have had in mind the first version of this passage when he wrote, in the second version, *"As before noticed* [my italics], his friends . . . dissuaded him. . . ."; see also Note 41, p. 236.)

¹⁷ Norton, C. E., ed., *op. cit.,* Vol. I, p. 20. Norton indicates that John James Ruskin had attended the whole series of lectures on Shakespeare and Milton but relies, in his comments, exclusively on the memories of W. H. Harrison.

¹⁸ Having discussed his parents' long engagement in the passage eventually left unpublished (see p. 147), Ruskin continued: "Of the heroism and patience with which the sacrifice was made, on both sides, I cannot judge; — but that it was greater than I should myself have been capable of, I know, and I believe that it was unwise. For during these years of waiting, my father fell gradually into a state of ill-health, from which he never entirely recovered. . . ." (*Works,* XXXV, pp. 127–28.) The *yes-and-no* of the whole problem is well indicated by Ruskin's having written on the next page: "My father's failure of health, following necessarily on the long

years of responsibility and exertion, needed only this repose [gained through marriage] to effect its cure." See also Note 24.

[19] See pp. 116 and 153.

[20] By October, 1859, difficulties had developed which thereafter, despite periods of improvement, caused him very real inconvenience and finally affected his general strength and health. (He refers to "October last year" as the beginning of this trouble in an unpublished letter of October 6, 1860, to W. H. Harrison; original in the possession of Mr. Sharp.) By 1862, having gone to Norwood for a rest, he described the malady: "My own case is the worst, a very material Organ having declined any longer to perform its function without frequent aid which if not given the said Organ vents its displeasure in severe spasms —. . . . [sic] pains night & day have taken flesh entirely away & the object now seems to be to get back some strength . . . [sic] I hope I may be in better plight before my Foreign friends come. . . ." (From unpublished letter to W. H. Harrison, June 12, 1862; quoted from typed transcript in *The Bowerswell Papers*; original in the possession of Mr. Sharp.) Nevertheless, six months before his father's death, Ruskin wrote: "I'm so glad you have set yourself in your business chair, and mean to stay there." (From unpublished letter of John Ruskin to his father, October 22, 1863; original in the Yale University Library.)

[21] Mentioned in unpublished passage of the "First MS." of *Praeterita*, in conjunction with his father's relationship with Dr. Grant: see *Works*, XXXV, p. 98.

[22] In unpublished letter from John Ruskin to his father, September 20, 1863; original in the Yale University Library.

[23] In late 1849 he was troubled by jaundice under circumstances which suggest that this ailment may have appropriately expressed a certain bile of spirit. At the time, Ruskin and his wife were en route to Venice — to John James a far from desirable development; and he had just received from Ruskin two "very satisfactory" letters, "but again I see you change your plans . . . I have quite a disease about changing plans — and am sure my Illness was increased by constantly changing my plans in the last month of our [summer] Tour — missing Bourges &c I got quite a contempt for myself & this increases Jaundice — Do not tell me of any plan you have because I dislike to see it changed." (From unpublished letter from John James Ruskin to his son, October 23, 1849; original in the Yale University Library.)

Three months later he told George Gray: "I have drank [sic] nothing but Toast & Water since 1 Jany with Sherry on my Table worth £200 a Butt & not a drop of Tea, although I would have sooner wanted my Dinner than my usual 3 Cups & have very fine Tea from China direct[.] It really required resolution to cut off Puddings Pies Chees[e] & a good pint of fine Sherry & 3 cups Tea — but I get my rest & am able for Business. The Doctors all say I am very wrong in giving up Wine — & I hope I am for the Sake of my Trade. I shall take the earliest opportunity of renewing my acquaintance with my own good Sherry at least — " (From unpublished letter of February 11, 1850; original in *The Bowerswell Papers*.)

Two years later we find Ruskin writing: "I have regretted sending that note about Veronese [expressing his wish to buy the picture] hundreds of times, and I was sadly afraid it would make you ill, when you told me your liver was wrong again; so that I am a good deal relieved when I find you are not vexing yourself — I hope you will think no more about it." (From unpublished letter of John Ruskin to his father, February 27, 1852; original in the Yale University Library.)

[24] *Works*, XXXV, p. 71. In *Praeterita*, as probably in life, the general condition of John James' health was subject to helpful variations. Speaking of his father's weekday occupation, Ruskin states that "he gave his full energy to counting-house work in the morning, and his afternoons to domestic rest. With instant perception and decision in all business questions, with principles of dealing which admitted no infraction, and involved neither anxiety nor concealment, the counting-house work was more of an interest, or even an amusement, to him, than a care." His marriage having brought him a home of perfect peace, his "failure of health, following necessarily on the long years of responsibility and exertion [the nine years without a holiday], needed only this repose to effect its cure." (*Ibid.,* p. 129.) On Sundays, however, "My father, who was still [*c.* 1828] much broken in health, could not go to the long Church of England service. . . ." (*Ibid.,* p. 71.)

[25] *Ibid.,* XXXVI, p. 469; from letter to Henry Acland, March 7, 1864.

[26] *Ibid.*

[27] Expressions of solicitude about John James' health are to be found in notes which Margaret penciled on her son's letters to his father during the 1830's (original letters in the Yale University Library); in general, overanxiety about the health of those she loved seems to have been part of Margaret's pattern of behavior. More complete discussion of this problem and of others closely related to it will become possible after 130 post-marital letters written by Margaret to her husband and bought by J. H. Whitehouse at the Sotheby sale of May 18, 1931, have been either published as a whole or otherwise made available for study. To date I can only regret having been denied permission to acquaint myself with this supplementary group of letters, which I did not read at Brantwood when I studied Ruskin's *Diaries,* his letters to his father, *The Catherine Tweddale Ruskin Correspondence,* and other such material (as noted in the "Introduction").

[28] In an unpublished letter of February 23, 1848, John James Ruskin wrote George Gray: "It is just 30 years this 1848 [he was married on February 2, 1818] since I Slept in a friends house." When he traveled, he explained, he always stayed at Inns. (Original in *The Bowerswell Papers.*)

[29] See p. 78.

[30] For fifteen years or more (to recapitulate), Margaret had been trained by John James' mother in the details of household management, and with anxious sympathy and loving protectivity (not unmaternal in emotional overtones), she had known John James' individual ambitions, tastes, needs, and habits from his very adolescence. Through illnesses she had been his nurse; when she first became a member of their family, the almost five years' difference in their ages would have made her seem, to her young cousin, much "older" than she really was. In her respect for "learning," in her love for gardening, in her relationships with servants, in the quality of her religious faith, there is also every reason to believe that Margaret

resembled Catherine. Hence it does not signify mere repetition of, or empty application of, a Freudian cliché to state that John James Ruskin found in Margaret what modern psychologists would doubtless call a "mother substitute" or "mother image" — this interpretation being supported by a good deal that is known about their relationship as man and wife.

CHAPTER 14

[1] Digest of an unpublished letter from John James Ruskin to his mother, June 30, 1815; original in the possession of Mr. Sharp.

[2] From unpublished letter of Catherine Tweddale Ruskin to Mrs. Lithgow, September [1817]; original in the possession of Mr. Sharp.

[3] See Fig. 14 after p. 56. This miniature, now in my possession, appears as *Item 286* in the *Catalogue* of the "Ruskin Exhibition . . . 1900," in which it is described as "Miniature of the same [John Ruskin, of Edinburgh . . .] in middle life."

[4] From unpublished letter of August 31, 1848, from John James Ruskin to George Gray; original in *The Bowerswell Papers*.

[5] See p. 127, for the note of 1809 in which John Thomas Ruskin remarked: "Miss Margreat Cock must bring this carefully down with her to Scotland. . . ." (See also Note 41, p. 236.)

[6] See p. 129.

[7] "Margaret Cock, widow of William Cock, appears in the Poor Rate Book of the Parish of Croydon dated 3 May 1815 as former occupier of The King's Head, with the endorsement 'now Smith's.' In the Rate Book of the following year, the property is shown as in the occupation of Nicholas Smith. It appears that Margaret Cock gave up the tenancy of The King's Head shortly before May 1815." (From a letter of Mr. Callander.)

That Margaret's mother (by then, fifty-nine or sixty) should have withdrawn from her work as landlady of this tavern at approximately the time when the firm of Ruskin, Telford, and Domecq was being founded must have gratified John James: more than a happy coincidence may have been involved in the timing of these two events.

[8] See pp. 167–68.

[9] See Note 40, p. 237.

[10] Admiral Sir William James erroneously states: "He [George Gray] bought Bowerswell from John James Ruskin. . . ." (*Op. cit.,* p. 12.) The title deeds of Bowerswell (sometimes known as Bower's Well) are now held by the Perth Corporation City Clerk's Department and were searched through the kindness of Mr. Tait and Miss Watson, of the Sandeman Public Library. Miss Watson writes: "Bowerswell was *never* owned by *any* of the Ruskin family. This house was first built by a Bailie John McEwan about 1800. It was sold and re-sold until 1827, when it was bought by George Gray, with the adjoining grounds. No Ruskin name appears on the title-deeds." The builder, Miss Watson notes, owned Bowerswell until 1815, when he sold it to James Henderson. In 1816, Mr. Henderson sold it to Patrick Taylor, who owned it until 1820. After 1817, one might add, it would have been the last house in the world which John James Ruskin would have wished to buy: see pp. 163 and 167.

[11] The second Bowerswell had been built by 1848, when George Gray was struggling to avoid bankruptcy and John James Ruskin answered one of his letters by remarking: "Do not let your slumbers be disturbed about your new House or about what people will say — you perhaps have been envied & sometimes evil spoken of in your present mansion — you will be more loved in a smaller & I utterly abhor Gas & Bowling Greens — " (From unpublished letter of August 24, 1848; original in *The Bowerswell Papers.*)

On the night of January 10, 1892, this so-called "mansion" was reduced to "a smoking ruin" by a fire. "The fire engines from Perth came but too late to save but a small fragment of the building." (From unpublished letter of January 11, 1892, from John Everett Millais to his daughter Mary; original in The Pierpont Morgan Library.) In 1946 the reconstructed Bowerswell became the Perth Corporation's Even-Tide Home.

[12] In one of his early poems, the child Ruskin would commemorate the view:

.   .   .   .

walk on the top of that rock and look down
from thence upon the tay the precipice
tween thee and it doth make thee giddy
it is so high that from it seen the tay
appears like a little rivulet among the hills
dwindling into nothing mong the distant mountains.

(From unpublished poem, "The hill [*sic*] of Kinnoull" [1827?]; in "MS. No. III," Red Book: *Harry and Lucy, Vol. II, and Poems;* in the Yale University Library.

[13] From unpublished letter of March 21, 1855, from Euphemia Chalmers Gray to Rawdon Brown; original in *The Bowerswell Papers.*

[14] *Works,* XXXV, p. 15.

[15] *Ibid.,* p. 65.

[16] See Appendix B, *1818.*

[17] As Ruskin recalled Margaret's description: ". . . white swelling came in the knee; he suffered much, and grew weaker gradually, dutiful always, and loving, and wholly patient. She [Jessie] wanted him one day to take half a glass of port wine, and took him on her knee, and put it to his lips. 'Not now, mamma; in a minute,' said he; and put his head on her shoulder, and gave one long, low sigh, and died." (*Works,* XXXV, p. 65.)

[18] *Ibid.*

[19] *Ibid.*

[20] See Appendix B, *1817.*

[21] See Appendix B, *1817.* Were it not for Margaret's memory of Jessie's dream and of the quickly successive loss of the two children, one might assume that Sievwright's record of the death of little Margaret (see Appendix B, *1774*) is mistaken, since, inexplicably, this death does not appear in the *Burial Register of the Town of Perth 1794–1823.* Nevertheless, what Ruskin would have called a strange "freak of Fors" seems to have provided these two dates to support his memory of his mother's story.

[22] Burne-Jones, Lady, *op. cit.,* Vol. I, p. 300.

[23] Anne Strachan died in 1871, aged seventy-two. John James' statement that in 1814 he was ill in Perth sufficiently indicates how Anne, eighteen years younger than Margaret, could have been, first, the "nurse" of John James Ruskin, a student at the Royal High School during the year of Anne's birth. Entering the Ruskin's service in 1814, she would have been fifteen, as Ruskin states. (See *Works*, XXVII, p. 518.)

[24] *Ibid.*, XXXV, p. 30.

[25] *Ibid.*, pp. 30–31.

[26] *Op. cit.*, Vol. I, pp. 300–301.

[27] *Works*, XXXV, p. 31. When this passage was republished in *Praeterita*, having first appeared in *Fors Clavigera*, *verily* appeared as *very*. I have retained the original reading: see *ibid.*, XXVII, p. 518.

[28] *Ibid.*, XXXV, p. 31, *n.*; from diary entry of March 31, 1871.

[29] *Ibid.*, p. 30.

[30] *Ibid.*, p. 66.

[31] From letter of March 6, 1830; original in the Yale University Library. See *Works*, II, p. xxxv, for Cook and Wedderburn's publication of this sentence without indicating their omission of the words enclosed in double parentheses. The "farthing bargain" refers to the stipend John James had agreed to pay for the composition of *The Iteriad*. In this letter the boy proceeds to ask: "May I not myself amuse / In writing nonsense if I choose / May I not employ my brain / in calling past delights again[?]"

[32] From unpublished letter of May 10, 1829; original in the Yale University Library.

[33] In 1862 (to give but one example), when Ruskin was being driven — for once, beyond endurance — first by John James' opposition to further essays on political economy and, second, by John James' immediate insistence that he keep a promise to visit various wealthy and aristocratic members of the Domecq family, Ruskin finally wrote: "My promise was of course made, and to be understood — on terms of health and life. ((Had I broken both my legs, I should yet have gone to Ville Tertre [home of Elise Domecq, now Comtesse des Roys]. But I will not go with disease in my brain.))" (*Works*, XXXVI, p. 419; from letter of August 10, 1862; original in the Yale University Library. Publishing parts of this letter, Cook and Wedderburn omitted the two sentences in double parentheses without indicating that material had been omitted.) In another omitted passage, Ruskin remarked: "Permit me — respecting this breaking of my word, only to remind you — that you have not the least objection to my breaking it to poor and vulgar persons; you only dislike me to break it to rich ones and well bred ones."

As to the later years, there is extremely moving evidence (especially in letters and diaries postdating 1878, much of it as yet unpublished) of Ruskin's often keen and almost objective awareness of mental illness, as well as of his efforts to lead his life so that the "disease" might be controlled, above all because he wished to carry on his work. See, for example, *Memories and Friends* (pp. 22–31) for Arthur C. Benson's account of the glimpse he caught (at Eton, in 1880) of this long and losing, though scarcely fruitless, struggle — *Praeterita* being but one result.

[34] *Works,* XXXVI, p. 5, *n.*; from the postscript addressed to Mr. [George?] Gray and written on a letter of January 15, 1833, from John Ruskin to his father; original in the Yale University Library. Publishing an excerpt from this postscript, Cook and Wedderburn did not include the words enclosed in double parentheses and mistakenly remarked that John James was forwarding his son's letter to "Mrs. Richard Gray." The postscript begins: "My dear Gray," and it seems much more likely that Ruskin's father was addressing his friend George Gray of Perth than Mr. Richard Gray of Camberwell. John James' postscript is dated "Lynn, 17 Jany 1833."

[35] *Ibid.,* p. 319; from *Fors Clavigera,* May, 1875. He wrote this issue of *Fors* knowing that Rose La Touche was very ill (she died on May 26, 1875). Helped by Effie (now Mrs. John Everett Millais), Mr. and Mrs. La Touche had kept Rose from marrying Ruskin; Rose, in the course of her suffering, had become insane.

[36] *Works,* XXVIII, p. 719; from *Fors Clavigera,* October, 1876.

[37] From unpublished letter, *n.d.* [17? October 1851]; quoted from a typed copy in *The Bowerswell Papers;* original in the possession of Mr. Sharp.

[38] For this letter of April, 1815, see p. 130.

[39] See *The Letters of Elizabeth Barrett Browning* (ed. F. G. Kenyon), Vol. I, pp. 196–97. Mrs. Browning was fairly overcome by her astonishment: "For she [Miss Martineau] is better and likely still to be better; she has recovered appetite and sleep, and lost the most threatening symptoms of disease; she has been out for the first time for four years and a half, lying on the grass flat, she says, with my books open beside her day after day. . . . And the means — the means! . . . It is *mesmerism.* She is thrown into the magnetic trance twice a day; and the progress is manifest; and the hope for the future clear. . . . She suggests that I should try the means — but I understand that in cases like mine the remedy has done harm instead of good. . . . But her experience will settle the question of the reality of magnetism for a whole generation of infidels." (From letter of "[about September 1844].")

[40] From unpublished letter of June 28, 1849; original in *The Bowerswell Papers.* It is highly probable that Margaret herself was the immediate source of this information; other unpublished letters of this period show that both she and John James Ruskin were much concerned about the cause and cure of Effie's illness and discussed the problem with Ruskin while they were on the continent with him. One can almost hear Margaret saying, "When I was Effie's age . . ." although in actuality Effie was only twenty-one in 1849, whereas Margaret's similar illness, as contemporaneously described, caused alarm in 1815 when she was thirty-six. It is therefore possible that Margaret had been in a similar state in 1802 (when she was twenty-one) and that her illness of 1815 was a recurrence of earlier difficulties which may have helped to motivate her joining the family of her Edinburgh aunt and uncle.

Although at this point it would be inappropriate to discuss analytically Admiral Sir William James' handling of the more than 1,200 documents, predominantly long letters, now assembled in *The Bowerswell Papers,* it seems desirable to repeat that in *The Order of Release* Admiral James' use of the material at his disposal was highly selective and that through his publication of letters from the correspondence of 1849 the reader gets at best an incomplete if not (as I believe) a seriously misleading impression of Ruskin's response to Effie's illness.

Although no longer in love with Effie, Ruskin himself was genuinely bewildered and distressed both by his wife's unhappiness and by her failing health. Returning from the continent, he put aside his work for *Modern Painters III* (not published until 1856) because of his desire to do work that would be more compatible with Effie's happiness: hence their trip to Venice in November of this year, leading to *The Stones of Venice.* The whole story of his marriage, as of his life and work, would be more simple had he been guilty of deliberate wrong-doing, together with hypocrisy and deliberate cruelty, as members of Effie's family, and their descendants, were much too ready to believe. Ruskin could no more understand his wife's illness as an outcome of emotional stress in an extremely headstrong and self-centered personality (as unpublished letters, now in The Pierpont Morgan Library, of John Everett Millais also clearly show) than he could understand why his own health suffered, both before and after marriage, with the intensification of *his* resentments, although before his father's death he realized that if he was to preserve a modicum of health, he could not go on living with John James at Denmark Hill (hence his life abroad, for the most part, between 1862 and 1864). His whole story, inclusive of his relationships with Effie and with his parents, unfortunately demonstrates that good intentions do not necessarily result in happiness and health.

[41] The question of how it was possible for Ruskin to retain his Evangelical beliefs through the so-called "forty years" and of how it then became possible for him to break with them is explored in the "Introduction" to my forthcoming edition of his *Sermons on the Pentateuch* (written during boyhood).

[42] *Works,* XXXII, p. 166; from *Roadside Songs of Tuscany* (1884). Analogously: "For — and I must again and again point out this to the modern reader, who, living in a world of affectation, suspects 'hypocrisy' in every creature he sees — the very plague of this lower evangelical piety is that it is *not* hypocrisy. . . ." (*Ibid.,* XXXIV, p. 392; from "Fiction, Fair and Foul — V," *On the Old Road,* 1881.) There are many other passages in which Ruskin stresses, if only through implication, the profound effect on his own life of the vital force in Margaret's religious faith. He himself had already suffered from his former wife's charges that he had been only hypocritically religious while he was still an Evangelical.

[43] *Ibid.,* XXXV, p. 40.

[44] *Ibid.,* p. 128.

[45] *Ibid.,* p. 42.

[46] *Ibid.*

[47] *Ibid.*; see also XXXVI, p. 153.

[48] In *Matthew 5, 6, 7,* we have the Sermon on the Mount; in *I Corinthians 13,* Paul's exposition of the meaning and power of charity: "Though I speak with the tongues of men and of angels, and have not charity, I am become as sounding brass . . ."; in *I Corinthians 15,* Paul's summary of the Gospel: "And if Christ be not raised, your faith is vain; . . . / For as in Adam all die, even so in Christ shall all be made alive. / . . . / So

. . . Death is swallowed up in victory." *Acts 26,* Paul's apologia *pro vita sua,* includes his description of what Ruskin calls the "most conspicuous and violent conversion on record" (*Works,* XII, p. 581; from *Essay on Baptism,* 1850–51), the experience of conversion being of great moment to Evangelicals. Through incandescent imagery and all the marvels leading up to a tremendous climax, *Revelation 5* and *6,* the opening by the Lamb of the first six seals of the Seven-Sealed Book, might reasonably be expected forever to impress on a child's mind the coming of the Day of Judgment. In *Isaiah 58,* on the proper observation of fasts and of the Sabbath, one finds a chapter important to the evangelical regard for Sunday. Then, in *Proverbs 2* and *3,* "my son" directly, and how tenderly, is exhorted to search for wisdom, whose source is God, whose paths are those of righteousness and justice and of life, whose reward is length of years in plenty and honor. In *Proverbs 8,* wisdom herself calls on men for prudence, knowledge, and discretion, for hatred of all arrogance, proclaiming herself eternal: "Now therefore hearken unto me, O ye children: for blessed are they that keep my ways." Finally, through sundry precepts, *Proverbs 12* contrasts the behavior of the foolish and the prudent, the righteous and the wicked, this theme being complemented by *James 4,* with its warnings against self-indulgence, self-righteousness, and procrastination: "Submit yourselves therefore to God. . . . For what is your life? It is even a vapour, that appeareth for a little time, and then vanisheth away."

⁴⁹ Read as chapters that might have become particularly meaningful to Margaret because associated with personal experience, her selections fall into five groups:

I. *Exodus 20,* for Margaret the Ten Commandments being ever imminent, from her first days to her last, by her conceived to have been in actuality delivered midst "the thunderings, and the lightnings, and the noise of the trumpet, and the mountain smoking," whereafter "the LORD said unto Moses, . . . Ye have seen that I have talked with you from heaven."

II. Chapters especially endeared to her during the years of affliction:

Psalm 32 — God's punishment of her for her transgressions, and the blessedness of His forgiveness: "Blessed is he whose transgression is forgiven, whose sin is covered. / . . . / For day and night thy hand was heavy upon me: my moisture is turned into the drought of summer. / . . . / Thou art my hiding place; thou shalt preserve me from trouble; thou shalt compass me about with songs of deliverance."

Psalm 90 — The eternity of God and the ephemeralness of man, whose life is but three-score years and ten: "Return, O LORD, how long? and let it repent thee concerning thy servants. / . . . / Make us glad according to the days wherein thou hast afflicted us, and the years wherein we have seen evil."

Psalm 91 — God as her refuge and protection in time of terror: "I will say of the LORD, He is my refuge and my fortress: my God; in him will I trust. / Surely he shall deliver thee from the snare of the fowler . . . / . . . / Thou shalt not be afraid for the terror by night; nor for the arrow that flieth by day; / . . . / Because thou hast made the LORD, which is my refuge, even the Most High, thy habitation; / . . . / For he shall give his angels charge over thee, to keep thee in all thy ways."

Psalm 119 — See p. 160.

Psalm 139 — The wonder and the inescapability of God's knowledge of her most secret thoughts: "O LORD, thou hast searched me, and known me. / . . . / Thou hast beset me behind and before, and laid thine hand upon me. / . . . / Surely thou wilt slay the wicked, O God: depart from me therefore, ye bloody men. / . . . / Do not I hate them, O LORD, that hate thee? / . . . / Search me, O God, and know my heart: try me, and know my thoughts: / And see if there be any wicked way in me, and lead me in the way everlasting."

III. Chapters of thanksgiving for delivery:

Psalm 23 — "The LORD is my shepherd . . . / . . . / He restoreth my soul . . . Thou preparest a table before me in the presence of mine enemies . . . / Surely goodness and mercy shall follow me all the days of my life . . ."

Psalm 103 — The mercy of God to all who keep His commandments: "Bless the LORD, O my soul: and all that is within me, bless his holy name. / . . . / Who forgiveth all thine iniquities; who healeth all thy diseases; / Who redeemeth thy life from destruction; who crowneth thee with lovingkindness and tender mercies; / Who satisfieth thy mouth with good things; so that thy youth is renewed like the eagle's. / The LORD executeth righteousness and judgment for all that are oppressed. / . . . / He hath not dealt with us after our sins; nor rewarded us according to our iniquities."

IV. Chapters of triumph:

Exodus 15 — The song of Moses and the Israelites after Pharaoh's host has been destroyed in the Red Sea; "And Miriam the prophetess . . . took a timbrel in her hand; and all the women went out after her with timbrels and with dances. / And Miriam answered them, Sing ye to the LORD, for he hath triumphed gloriously; the horse and his rider hath he thrown into the sea."

Deuteronomy 32 — The last song of Moses, in praise of a just God most terrible in vengeance against those who are perverse and corrupt: "For their vine is of the vine of Sodom, and of the fields of Gomorrah: their grapes are grapes of gall, their clusters are bitter: / Their wine is the poison of dragons, and the cruel venom of asps. / . . . / Rejoice, O ye nations, with his people: for he will avenge the blood of his servants, and will render vengeance to his adversaries, and will be merciful unto his land, and to his people."

II Samuel 1, verse *17* to end — David's lament for the deaths of Saul and his son Jonathan: ". . . how are the mighty fallen! / Tell it not in Gath. . . ."

V. The dedication of her own home:

I Kings 8 — Solomon's dedication of the temple, with prayer that God hear all those who dwell therein and heed His ways, forgiving them their sins. See also p. 174.

[50] James, Admiral Sir William, *op. cit.,* p. 22; from letter of April 28, 1847.

[51] From unpublished letter of February 23, 1848; original in *The Bowerswell Papers.*

[52] *Works,* XXXIV, p. 393; from "Fiction, Fair and Foul, V," *On the Old Road,* 1881.

[53] *Ibid.,* V, p. 366; from *Modern Painters III.*

[54] *Ibid.,* XXXII, p. 165; from *Roadside Songs of Tuscany,* 1885.

[65] *Ibid.*, XXIX, p. 457; from *Fors Clavigera*, November, 1883.

[66] "Glen Luce seems to have had an uncanny reputation in the matter of ghosts. Many traditional tales have been told of the appearance of the wraiths of former inhabitants of the Castle Park, and of the efforts of the local minister to get them 'laid.' . . . a ghostly character which was personified as 'The Deil o' Glen Luce' seems to have acquired a national reputation about the year 1638. . . ." (Robert M. Rusk, *op. cit.*, p. 112.)

[67] *Works*, XXVIII, p. 546; from *Fors Clavigera*, March, 1876. Mrs. Arthur Severn (granddaughter of Catherine's brother, James Tweddale) had seen "the shade — or rather light — of her sister, at the time of that sister's death on the other side of the world. . . ."

[58] *Ibid.*, XXIX, p. 455; from *Fors Clavigera*, November, 1883. He made the comment to explain the "absolute frankness and simplicity" with which Scott employed the supernatural in *Waverley: e.g.*, ". . . I see his winding sheet high upon his breast" (Ch. XLVI); "The spectre seemed to beckon and to smile as he faded from my sight" (Ch. LXIX). As a child, Ruskin would all but certainly have discussed such passages with his mother; during later years the memories, feelings, of his childhood returned to him with increasing power and vividness, until finally he was ready to relive those years through *Praeterita*, written with the effortless spontaneity revealed by the first version (in the diary volumes of the manuscript). Hence, by 1883, he could refer to such a "supernatural phenomenon" as "second-sight" as though there were no doubt about its "reality." In contrast, during the middle years he often sought proof which would remove all doubt from his belief in such "realities" — as when, in 1849 he paid for excavations, in Chamouni, at a spot where children reported having seen a ghost; or in the 1860's, when he hoped at last to find evidence of the return of spirits through seances conducted by D. D. Home and became almost convinced, but not quite. One can scarcely doubt that his mother, aided by Nurse Anne, initially instilled conviction, at least through her own belief in "second-sight."

[59] *Works*, XXXV, p. 128.

[60] From unpublished letter, n.d. [17? October 1851]; quoted from a typed copy in *The Bowerswell Papers;* original in the possession of Mr. Sharp.

[61] From unpublished letter to George Gray, July 4, 1849; original in *The Bowerswell Papers*.

[62] From unpublished letter to W. H. Harrison, October 6, 1860; quoted from a typed copy in *The Bowerswell Papers;* original in the possession of Mr. Sharp.

[63] Viewing an event forty-four years remote, through lenses Ruskin had provided in *Praeterita*, Lady Burne-Jones recorded and interpreted her memory: "The little old lady who ruled the house from her low seat by the fireside was less easy to understand. She had had an accident not long before we saw her — a fall, in which what she always called her 'limb' was broken — and though it had been properly set it had stiffened in some way, so that she could not walk without help. It was her nature, I suppose, which made her choose for support the back of a chair rather than the arm of either husband or son: at all events, bidding us all precede her, she walked from the drawing-room to the dining-room, leaning upon a chair which

moved easily on castors as she pushed it before her, and evidently carrying out an established custom." (*Op. cit.,* Vol. I, p. 252.)

[64] *Works,* XXXV, p. 535. Should it be objected that she left her husband when Ruskin was at Oxford, one need merely remark that she would never have gone to Oxford had not her husband so desired and that during those years, as always, his son seemed to John James Ruskin more important than his wife.

[65] From unpublished letter of October 12, 1849, from John James Ruskin to his son; original in the Yale University Library.

[66] Collingwood, W. G., *Life* (revised ed.), p. 283.

[67] From "Second MS." of *Praeterita;* on publication, *much* was significantly changed to read *perhaps:* see *Works,* XXXV, p. 126.

[68] Collingwood, W. G., *Life,* Vol. I, p. 13. Collingwood adds, "in the Scotch fashion," which is erroneous if the phrase signifies "by a justice of the peace." The statement that Margaret's minister helped John James to persuade her into a "prompt" marriage was probably part of the story which Margaret told Ruskin, whom Collingwood could sometimes consult while he was writing the biography. Margaret's marriage was, however, "regularly proclaimed" (see Appendix B, *February 2, 1818*), which indicates that although she was married on a Monday, her intention to marry John James Ruskin (and *v.v.*) had been "regularly proclaimed" in her church on three successive Sundays, as is the habit of Scots Presbyterians who are "regularly" married by first having had their "banns" proclaimed.

[69] *Works,* XXXV, p. 127.

[70] See Appendix B, *September 30, 1817.*

[71] See Appendix B, *October 13, 1817.*

[72] Unpublished letters in which Derrick Leon arranged, and then discussed, an interview held in 1944 with the Hon. Clare Stuart Wortley are in *The Bowerswell Papers:* in *Ruskin the Great Victorian,* Leon thanks Lady Clare "for information" (p. xviii).

[73] Leon, Derrick, *op. cit.,* p. 8. It is possible, though undemonstrable, that the Helen who died "aged 3 weeks" (see Appendix B, *October? 1817?*) was born in the autumn of 1817 and that Catherine Tweddale Ruskin died at the christening of this child, according to the story preserved by oral tradition and finally reported by Leon. There seems to be no Perth *Register of Baptisms* for this period, and the *Register of Burials . . . 1794–1823* contains no entry for Helen's death (or for the death of Margaret, in January, 1817; see Appendix B). Discussing these matters, Leon was confused about dates, but evidence connected with the death of John Thomas Ruskin now supports the gist of the story he recounted. The absence in the *Burial Register* of any entry of Helen's death suggests that under the stress of events in their family at this time, the Richardsons may have failed to report, officially, their loss of this child.

[74] See Appendix B, *October 13* and *October 30, 1817.* The unusual delay in Catherine's burial may have been related to the mental condition of her husband during the aftermath of shock, and/or to the absence of members of the family. Margaret probably was in Croydon; John may even have been in Spain. In Perth, the Richardsons probably had the infant Helen as well as John Thomas Ruskin to care for.

Through the kindness of Mr. Tait and Miss Watson, issues of *The Perthshire Courier* (a bi-weekly newspaper) for "the years 1817 and 1818 were thoroughly checked and rechecked for suicides, sequestrations, and deaths — in vain." (From letter of Miss Watson.)

[75] From unpublished typed material in *The Bowerswell Papers;* it is presumably manuscript prepared by Effie's daughter, Caroline, Lady Charles Stuart Wortley, in an attempt to write her mother's life. (This MS. seems to have been a basis for Admiral James' Chapter II in *The Order of Release.*) Explaining that Mrs. George Gray's niece, Eliza Jameson, wrote down her own reminiscences and what her family had told her about the Ruskins and the Grays, Lady Alice Caroline quotes from Eliza Jameson's manuscript. After copying *"The reason old Mr John Ruskin took his life was . . . because his only son . . . had married his first cousin,"* Lady Alice Caroline added in parentheses: "(N. B. This is incorrect, as they were not married till afterwards.)" She therefore must have known the story which her daughter, the Hon. Clare Stuart Wortley, apparently told Derrick Leon in 1944. The incorrect account is significant, however, as preserving what was said in early days.

[76] Miss Watson writes: "I am told to presume that [the *Burial Register . . . 1794–1823*] was the Register for Greyfriar's Burying Ground, since no other burying-ground existed at that time, and no cemetery is named in the Register. There are no lair numbers to show where these Ruskins lie. Until recent years this record was in the City Chambers custody, but at some time in the past there was a fire, destroying, so the Cemeteries Dept. believe, the key volume containing the lair numbers. Nevertheless, Sievwright does not mention these Ruskins in his volumes on Greyfriar's Burying-ground, so they have apparently always remained therein anonymous."

[77] See Appendix B, *February 2, 1818.* Cook and Wedderburn (unfailingly) have misdated this marriage February 27: see *Works,* XXXV, p. 127, *n.*

[78] That John James, as described in the *Register of Marriages,* should have been "presently residing in the East Church Parish" suggests that he had been living in Perth for at least some weeks, if not continuously since his father's death. Both he and Margaret were doubtless living with the Richardsons, their home as well as Bowerswell having probably been within the East Church Parish. (Having kindly examined old guide books, Miss Watson states that the boundaries of the East Church Parish cannot clearly be determined but that "Bowerswell is on the same side of the river as Bridgend, with only a quarter-of-an-hour's walk between them. . . .")

[79] *Works,* XXXV, p. 64.

[80] *Ibid.,* p. 465.

[81] *Ibid.,* pp. 64–65.

[82] From unpublished letter of February 23, 1848, from John James Ruskin to George Gray; original in *The Bowerswell Papers.*

CHAPTER 15

[1] *Works,* XXVII, p. 584; from *Fors Clavigera,* August, 1873.

[2] *Life,* Vol. I, pp. 3–4. Collingwood, however, is inclined to consider innate characteristics the chief reason for Ruskin's being so distinctly "a

Scotsman." For example: "At five he was a bookworm, and the books he read at once fixed him in certain grooves of thought; or rather, say they were chosen as favorites from an especial interest in their subjects, an interest which arose from his character of mind, and displayed it." (*Ibid.*, pp. 25–26.) Yet realistically, one should not ignore the highly pertinent fact that until Ruskin was much older than five, he read the books his parents chose for him and followed out the interests they instilled, these books and interests being predominantly and directly reflective of their Edinburgh backgrounds.

[3] See, for example, Note 33, p. 246, for one indication of a prolonged development that reached a crisis in 1862 and that was outwardly resolved only when his father died in 1864.

[4] *Works*, XXXVI, p. 471; from letter of March 9, 1864, to Henry Acland.

[5] *Ibid.*, XXXV, p. 535.

[6] See p. 159.

[7] Most of Margaret's letters to her husband are now in the possession of J. H. Whitehouse: see Note 27, p. 243.

[8] Margaret was sixty-six years old in 1847, the first year in which the letters of Euphemia Chalmers Gray contain references to her. After her marriage to Ruskin, Effie was by no means objective in her observations of his parents, nor were the selections from her letters as published in Admiral James' *The Order of Release* chosen with objectivity.

The first outsider to record impressions was James Smetham, a student at the Working Men's College, who saw Margaret when she was seventy-four. Five years later (1860) Frederic Harrison dined at Denmark Hill one Sunday afternoon, to find dark shades, which Ruskin thought essential, protecting water colors against the light. Therefore, to the Margaret-legend Harrison contributed the story (subsequently embellished) that Margaret insisted that Ruskin keep his pictures covered on the Sabbath. Charles Eliot Norton gives us an interesting glimpse of her when she was seventy-six and finally, influenced by *Praeterita,* added general remarks. Lady Burne-Jones knew her after she reached eighty, and wrote the *Memorials* after having read *Praeterita,* delighted by what she called its "genius for truth." (Vol. I, p. 261.) Biographically, however, "truth" does not result from mistaking for *literal* truth, essential truths within *Praeterita* and from insufficient recognition of the fact that changes are always likely to occur between a woman's youth, her prime, and her old age.

[9] Speaking of Ruskin's funeral, his friend and neighbor of later years, the Rev. R. D. Rawnsley, states: "He had had his own mother's coffin painted sky-blue. . . ." (*Op. cit.,* p. 191.) To me this statement seems not incredible, though I have found no other reference to a detail which may represent a wish that Ruskin did not actually translate into fact. As either wish or fact, it would naturally have been well known to Mrs. Arthur Severn but no less naturally withheld by any biographer whose work was conducted under her auspices, not that Sir Edward T. Cook, personally, would have desired to publicize anything connected with sky-blue coffins.

[10] *Works*, XXII, p. xxiv.

[11] From unpublished material included in typed copy of *Letters from John Ruskin to Dr. John Brown;* in the Yale University Library.

[12] *I Kings 8: 13–26, passim.* See p. 160. The whole chapter articulates with intensity a prayer which any religious woman might have offered about her own home as also a house of God. Ruskin says that the pages of the Bible from which he learned this long chapter, surely closely related to Margaret's feelings about her home, "are worn somewhat thin and dark." (*Works,* XXXV, p. 42.)

Bibliography

Unpublished Sources

I. DOCUMENTS

1. *Photographs and Photostats:*

Check of February 8, 1868, from John Ruskin to John Calvert, for £3000; "Orders from the Drawer / Not to Pay" entered at upper left, and "Cancelled" written over Ruskin's signature in Ruskin's script. (Original in the possession of Mr. F. J. Sharp of Barrow-in-Furness, Lancashire.)

Entry in Perth Parish Register of marriage of John Rusken (sic) and Margaret Cock, February 2, 1818. (From Register kept at the General Registry Office, Edinburgh.)

Entry in Register of Marriages 1773–1786 of marriage of William Cock and Margaret Ruskin, June 19, 1780, with original signatures of William and Margaret, and of Mary Ruskin as a witness. (From Register of the Parish of St. Bartholomew-the-Great, GLMR. Ms. 6779/3, in the Guildhall Library, London.)

Extracts from Particulars of Sale, September 27, 1809, with description of George Richardson's premises in Middle Row, Croydon. (Original in the Central Library, Croydon; property of The Croydon Corporation.)

Ground floor plan of The King's Head Public House, from nineteenth-century lease. (Original in the Central Library, Croydon; property of The Croydon Corporation.)

The "Last" Letters of John Ruskin, one addressed to Lady Simon (spelled "Simond") and dated March 3, 1894; the other written to Sir John Simon (addressed as "Brother John") and dated October 12, 1895. (Originals in the possession of Mr. F. J. Sharp.)

Plan of area, showing position of George Richardson's premises in Middle Row, Croydon. The site of *The King's Head Public House* has been marked on my copy of the plan. (Original in the Central Library, Croydon; property of The Croydon Corporation.)

Will of William Cock, of Croydon, Surrey, dated June 14, 1782, with original signature of William Cock. (In the Central Library, Croydon; property of The Croydon Corporation.)

Will of Frances Ruskin, of Saint Mary Stoke Newington, Middlesex; proved at London, February 18, 1741. (True copy of the original; in Somerset House, London. *Reference:* Tremley / 1742: . . . folio 65.)

Will of John Rusken (sic), of Writtle, Essex; given by word of mouth to Goodman Green and proved at London (December?) 13, 1686. (True copy of the original; in Somerset House, London. *Reference:* Peculiar of Writtle, Essex / Calendar / 1618–1851.)

Will of John Ruskin, of Cheshunt, Hertfordshire (the great-great-grandfather); proved at London, February 23, 1753. (True copy of original; in Somerset House, London. *Reference:* Searle / 1753 . . . folio 60.)

Will of John Ruskin, of the Parish of St. Bartholomew-the-Great, London (the great-grandfather), with original signature of John Ruskin; proved at London, July 1, 1780. (In Consistory Court of London. *Reference:* Register 1777–1781, folio 304.)

Will of Robert Ruskin, late of Edmonton, Middlesex, but now of Stansted Abbot, Hertfordshire; signed by his "marke" and proved (place not specified) January 18, 1741. (True copy of original; in Somerset House, London. *Reference:* Arch. of Middlesex (Essex & Herts.) / Pae flie / 1732–50 / folio 196.)

2. *Certified Extracts of Entries in Registers* kept at the General Registry Office, Edinburgh:

Baptism of Catherine Tweddell (sic), Ruskin's grandmother; August 15, 1763.

Birth of Janet Ruskin, Ruskin's "Aunt Jessie"; November 20, 1783.

Death of Janet Adair Tweedale (sic), Ruskin's great-grandmother; May 23, 1775.

Death of The Rev. Mr. [James] Tweedale (sic), Ruskin's great-grandfather; May 6, 1777.

Marriage of Janet Ruskin and Patrick Richardson, Ruskin's Aunt Jessie and the so-called "Peter" Richardson of Perth; November 1, 1804.

3. *Transcriptions:*

Baptismal Certificate of John Ruskin, followed by *letter of November 14, 1837, from the Rev. James Boyd to John James Ruskin.* (Provided by Mrs. Oscar Gnosspelius, Curator, from original in the Ruskin Museum, Coniston.)

Birth Certificate of John Ruskin, dated November 30, 1837. (Provided by Mrs. Oscar Gnosspelius, from original in the Ruskin Museum, Coniston.)

Deed of Indenture of John Thomas Ruskin, dated February 7, 1776. (Provided by Mr. F. J. Sharp, from original in his possession.)

Entries from Original Registers of Cheshunt County, Hertfordshire, 1688– 1760. (Provided by Lambert & Raggett, Watford, Hertfordshire, from Registers in the Hertfordshire County Record Office, Hertford.)

Letter of January 17, 1902, from Charles Eliot Norton to Mrs. Arthur Severn. (Provided by Mr. F. J. Sharp, from original in his possession.)

Passage from letter of February, 1838, from James Tweddale to John James Ruskin. (Provided by Mr. F. J. Sharp, from original in his possession.)

Passages from The Catherine Tweddale Ruskin Correspondence, 1805–17. (Provided by Mr. F. J. Sharp, from MSS. in his possession, to supplement transcriptions I made from these MSS. shortly before they were sold at Brantwood auction.)

4. *Evidence from Documents, Recorded in Letters* that give results of research most kindly conducted in my behalf by —

Callander, T. E., Chief Librarian, Central Library, Croydon.
Collier, W. D., The Keeper, *Edinburgh Gazette,* Edinburgh.
Galloway, The Rev. David, Glenluce, Wigtownshire.
Gnosspelius, Mrs. Oscar, Curator, Ruskin Museum, Coniston.
Hogan, E. A., Registrar General for Scotland, Edinburgh.
Imrie, Dr. D. S. M., Rector, The Royal High School, Edinburgh.
Lambert & Raggett, Genealogists and Record Searchers, Watford, Hertfordshire.
Ledger, Miss Vera J., Research Assistant, London.
Mead, Lloyd, Clerk, The Vintners' Company, London.
Minto, C. S., City Librarian and Curator, Central Public Library, Edinburgh.
Morris, Ernest, F. R. Hist. S., Clerk (and author of *Bells of All Nations*), St. Margaret's Vicarage, Leicester.
Paterson, A. B., City Librarian, and G. W. Black, Depute City Librarian, The Mitchell Library, Glasgow.
Smith, Raymond, Librarian and Curator, Guildhall Library, London.
Tait, A. J., City Librarian, and Miss E. L. Watson, Principal Assistant, Sandeman Public Library, Perth.
Wallbank, The Rev. Dr. N. E., Rector, St. Bartholomew-the-Great, London.

II. RUSKIN MSS.:

The Bowerswell Papers. (These *Papers* comprise *c.* 1250 Ruskin-Millais documents, chiefly letters, inclusive of *c.* 100 letters from John James and Margaret Ruskin to several correspondents, some of these letters of Ruskin's parents being typed copies of originals now owned by Mr. F. J. Sharp.) In the Pierpont Morgan Library.
The Catherine Tweddale Ruskin Correspondence, 1805-17. In the possession of Mr. F. J. Sharp.
The Charles Eliot Norton Correspondence (inclusive of letters discussing plans for, and the progress of, the Library Edition of Ruskin's *Works*). In The Houghton Library, Harvard University.
The Millais Papers. (These *Papers* include hundreds of letters from the correspondence of Sir John Everett Millais — these covering a wide range in date.) In the Pierpont Morgan Library.
Ruskin, John, JUVENILIA:
  "MS. III," Red Book: *Harry and Lucy, Vol. II and Poems.* In the Yale University Library.
  "MS. IVB," Red Book: *Travel Notes, etc.* In the Yale University Library.
  "MS. V," Notebook: *Poems, 1829–1832.* In the Yale University Library.
  "MS. XI," Bound volume: *Poems and Letters to his Father.* (In these letters Margaret Ruskin often penciled messages to her husband.) In the Yale University Library.
Ruskin, John, *Letter to George Allen,* of April 2 [1882], accompanied by a *Letter to Henry Champ, Esq.,* of December 11, 1913, from The Encyclopædia Britannica Company, Ltd. These letters are in one of the red

morocco folders, dated 1912, which were designed to contain an original autograph Ruskin letter, to be presented to individuals who bought the Library Edition of Ruskin's *Works,* as distributed by The Encyclopædia Britannica Company. In The Pierpont Morgan Library.

Ruskin, John, *Letters to Alfred, Lord Tennyson.* In the Yale University Library.

Ruskin, John, *Letters to Dr. John Brown* (in typed transcript). In the Yale University Library.

Ruskin, John, *Letters to His Father, John James Ruskin* (published in part). In the Yale University Library.

Ruskin, John, *Notebook,* 1873. In the Yale University Library.

Ruskin, John, *Praeterita* and *Dilecta,* in manuscript version and/or in proof, but not complete: three "octavo" diary volumes and three "folio" volumes. In the Yale University Library.

The Ruskin–La Touche–MacDonald Correspondence. (The letters used by Derrick Leon in *Ruskin the Great Victorian,* except for those from Ruskin to Mr. and Mrs. William Cowper, later Lord and Lady Cowper-Temple.) In the Yale University Library.

Severn, Mrs. Arthur, *Letter of April 27, 1894 to Thomas J. Wise.* In the Symington Collection, Rutgers University Library.

Wedderburn, Alexander, two *Letters to W. G. Collingwood,* of December, 1902 (in regard to using Collingwood's edition of Ruskin's *Poems, The Poetry of Architecture,* etc., in the Library Edition), and a copy of W. G. Collingwood's reply. In my possession.

Published Sources

Agnew, Sir Andrew, *The Hereditary Sheriffs of Galloway, Their "Fore-bears" and Friends, Their Courts and Customs of Their Times. With notes of the early history, ecclesiastical legends, the baronage and place-names of the province.* 2 vols., Edinburgh, David Douglas, 1893.

Anderson, John Corbet, *A Short Chronicle Concerning the Parish of Croydon in the County of Surrey,* Edinburgh, Ballantyne, Hanson and Co., 1882.

Armstrong, Sir Walter, *Sir Henry Raeburn,* London, William Heinemann, 1911.

Arnold, Matthew, *Mixed Essays, Irish Essays, and Others,* New York, The Macmillan Co., 1904.

Bannerman, Ronald, *Forgotten Croydon,* Croydon, Croydon Times, Ltd., 1933.

Bardsley, Charles Wareing, *Curiosities of Puritan Nomenclature,* London, Chatto and Windus, 1888.

Bardsley, Charles Wareing, *A Dictionary of English and Welsh Surnames,* London, H. Frowde, 1901.

Benson, Arthur Christopher, *Memories and Friends,* New York, G. P. Putnam's Sons, 1924.

Benson, Arthur Christopher, *Ruskin; A Study in Personality,* New York, G. P. Putnam's Sons, 1911.

Bettany, George Thomas, "Gregory, James," *DNB.*

Black, George F., *The Surnames of Scotland, Their Origin, Meaning, and History,* New York, The New York Public Library, 1946.

Blaikie, W. G., "Black, Adam," *DNB.*

Boswell, James, *Journal of a Tour to the Hebrides with Samuel Johnson, LL.D.* (ed. Frederick A. Pottle and Charles H. Bennett), New York, The Viking Press, 1936.

Bowditch, Nathaniel Ingersoll, *Suffolk Surnames,* London, Trübner and Co., 1861.

Brougham, Henry Peter, Lord, *The Life and Times of Henry Lord Brougham, Written by Himself,* 3 vols., Edinburgh, William Blackwood and Sons, 1871.

Brown, Thomas, *Lectures on the Philosophy of the Human Mind,* with a *Memoir* of the author by David Welsh, London, William Tegg and Co., 1858.

Burne-Jones, Georgiana, Lady, *Memorials of Edward Burne-Jones,* 2 vols., The Macmillan Co., 1906.

Butler, The Rev. Dugald, *The Tron Kirk of Edinburgh; or Christ's Kirk at the Tron; A History* (Ch. XIII, "John Ruskin's Grandfather, A Merchant at the West of the Tron Kirk"), Edinburgh, Oliphant, Anderson and Ferrier, 1906.

Carmichael, Sir Alexander G., "The Ruskins," *Celtic Review,* No. 8, Vol. II (April 16, 1906), pp. 343–51.

"Carmichael, Alexander," *Who Was Who, 1897–1916,* London, A. and C. Black, Ltd., 1920.

Catalogue: Ruskin Exhibition at Coniston, July 21 to September 15, 1900, Fourth Edition, Revised.

Caw, Sir James L., "Alexander Nasmyth, 'The Father of Scottish Landscape Painting,' 1758–1840," *Scots Magazine,* N. S. Vol. 32 (February, 1940), pp. 325–35.

Chalmers, George, *The Life of Thomas Ruddiman,* London, John Stockdale, 1794.

Chambers, Robert, "Edinburgh Merchants and Merchandise in Old Times," *Edinburgh Papers,* London, William and Robert Chambers, 1859.

Chambers, Robert, *The Life of Sir Walter Scott,* New York, William Stodart, 1832.

Chambers, Robert, *Traditions of Edinburgh,* 2 vols., Edinburgh, W. and C. Tait, 1825.

Christison, The Life of Sir Robert . . . Bart., ed. by his sons, 2 vols., Edinburgh, William Blackwood and Sons, 1885–86.

Cockburn, Henry Thomas, Lord, *Life of Lord Jeffrey. With a Selection from his Correspondence,* 2 vols., Philadelphia, Lippincott, Grambo and Co., 1852.

Cockburn, Henry Thomas, Lord, *Memorials of His Time,* New York, D. Appleton and Co., 1856.

Collingwood, W. G., *The Life and Work of John Ruskin,* 2 vols., Cambridge, The Riverside Press, 1893.

Collingwood, W. G., *The Life of Ruskin* (revised ed.), London, Methuen and Co., 1905.

Collingwood, W. G., *The Poems of John Ruskin,* 2 vols., Orpington, George Allen, 1891.

Collingwood, W. G., *Ruskin Relics,* London, Isbister and Co., Limited, 1903.

Cook, E. T., *The Life of John Ruskin,* 2 vols., New York, The Macmillan Co., 1911.

Cook, E. T., "Ruskin, John," *DNB.*

Cook, E. T., *Studies in Ruskin: Some Aspects of the Work and Teaching of John Ruskin,* Orpington, George Allen, 1890.

Creech, William, *Edinburgh Fugitive Pieces,* Edinburgh, William Creech, 1791.

Dick, Rev. C. H., *Highways and Byways in Galloway and Carrick,* London, Macmillan and Co., Ltd., 1916.

Evans, Joan, *John Ruskin,* New York, Oxford University Press, 1954.

Fergusson, Alexander, *The Honourable Henry Erskine, Lord Advocate for Scotland; with Notices of Certain of His Kinsfolk and of His Time. Compiled from Family Papers and Other Sources* . . . Edinburgh, W. Blackwood and Sons, 1882.

Froude, James Anthony, *Thomas Carlyle, A History of the First Forty Years of His Life, 1795–1835,* 2 vols., New York, Charles Scribner's Sons, 1897.

Fyfe, W. T., *Edinburgh under Sir Walter Scott,* New York, E. P. Dutton and Co., 1907.

Garratt, G. T., *Lord Brougham,* London, Macmillan and Co., 1935.

Garrow, David William, *The History and Antiquities of Croydon, with a Variety of Other Interesting Matter,* Croydon, W. Annan, 1818.

Gillies, H. Cameron, *The Place-Names of Argyll,* London, David Nutt, 1906.

Goodwin, Gordon, "Gregory, James," *DNB.*

Grant, James, *Cassell's Old and New Edinburgh: Its History, Its People and Its Places,* 3 vols., London, Cassell, Petter, Galpin, and Co., 1882.

Greig, James, *Sir Henry Raeburn, R. A., His Life and Works,* London, "The Connoisseur," 1911.

Grierson, Sir Herbert J. C., "Scott and Carlyle," *Essays and Addresses,* London, Chatto and Windus, 1940.

Grierson, Sir Herbert J. C., *Sir Walter Scott, Bart.,* New York, Columbia University Press, 1938.

Halévy, Élie, *A History of the English People in 1815,* 3 vols., Harmondsworth, Penguin Books Ltd., 1937.

Hallen, A. W. Cornelius, ed., *London. St. Botolph Parish, Bishopgate Registers,* 3 vols., Edinburgh, T. and A. Constable, 1889–95.

Harper, Malcolm McLachlan, *Rambles in Galloway,* Dalbeattie, Thomas Fraser, 1896.

Harrison, Frederic, *Autobiographic Memoirs,* 2 vols., London, Macmillan and Co., 1911.

Henderson, Alexander, *An Account of the Life and Character of Alexander Adam, LL.D.,* Edinburgh, D. Schaw and Son, 1810.

Hertford County Records, Notes and Extracts from the Sessions Rolls 1581 to 1833, 9 vols., Hertford, Charles E. Longmore, 1905–39.

Hewison, The Rev. James King, *The Covenanters; a History of the Church in Scotland from the Reformation to the Revolution,* 2 vols., Glasgow, J. Smith and Son, 1908.

Horner, Leonard, ed., *Memoirs and Correspondence of Francis Horner, M. P.,* 2 vols., Boston, Little Brown and Co., 1853.

James, Admiral Sir William, ed., *The Order of Release: The Story of John Ruskin, Effie Gray and John Everett Millais Told for the First Time in Their Unpublished Letters,* London, John Murray, 1948. (Originally published as *John Ruskin and Effie Gray,* with same pagination but without illustrations; New York, Charles Scribner's Sons, 1947.)

Jameson, Mary Ethel, *A Bibliographical Contribution to the Study of John Ruskin,* Cambridge, The Riverside Press, 1901.

Jamieson, John, *An Etymological Dictionary of the Scottish Language,* 4 vols., Paisley, Alexander Gardner, 1879–82.

"John Ruskin — Wine Propagandist," *Ridley's Wine & Spirit Trade Circular,* No. 1,030, August 14, 1933, pp. 615–19 and No. 1,031, September 14, 1933, pp. 693–97.

Kent's [London] Directory for the Year 1781, London, Richard and Henry Causton, 1781.

Learmonth, William, *Kirkcudbrightshire and Wigtownshire,* Cambridge University Press, 1920.

Leon, Derrick, *Ruskin the Great Victorian,* London, Routledge and Kegan Paul Ltd., 1949.

Lockhart, John Gibson, *Memoirs of the Life of Sir Walter Scott,* 5 vols., Boston, Houghton Mifflin Co., 1901.

Lockhart, John Gibson, *Peter's Letters to His Kinsfolk,* 3 vols., Edinburgh, William Blackwood, 1819.

[London] *The New Annual Directory* (for the year *1800;* and for *1813*), London, T. Maiden, 1800 and 1813.

London *Times,* August 2, 1852.

Lowndes's London Directory for the Year 1786, London, W. Lowndes, 1786.

Mactaggart, John, *The Scottish Gallovidian Encyclopedia,* London, Hamilton, Adams and Co., 1876.

Mathieson, Willam Law, *The Awakening of Scotland; a History from 1747 to 1797,* Glasgow, James Maclehose and Sons, 1910.

McGilchrist, John, *The Life of Lord Brougham,* London, Charles Griffin and Co., 1868.

McKnight, George H., *Modern English in the Making,* New York, D. Appleton and Co., 1928.

Meikle, Henry William, *Scotland and the French Revolution.* Glasgow, James Maclehose and Sons, 1912.

Mencken, H. L., *The American Language,* New York, Alfred A. Knopf, 1921.

M'Kerlie, Peter Handyside, *History of the Lands and Their Owners in Galloway, with Historical Sketches of the District,* 2 vols., Paisley, Alexander Gardner, 1906.

Mills, John Saxon, *Sir Edward Cook, K. B. E., A Biography,* New York, E. P. Dutton and Co., 1921.

Murray, Sir James Augustus Henry, ed., *The Oxford English Dictionary,* 13 vols., Oxford, Clarendon Press, 1933.

Nasmyth, James, *James Nasmyth, Engineer. An Autobiography* (ed. by Samuel Smiles), New York, Harper and Bros., 1883.

Nichols, John, *The History and Antiquities of the County of Leicester,* 4 vols. in 8, London, John Nichols, 1795–1815.

Nicholson, John, *Historical and Traditional Tales in Prose and Verse, Connected with the South of Scotland,* Kirkcudbright, John Nicholson, 1843.

Nicolson, Alexander, ed., *Memoirs of Adam Black,* Edinburgh, Adam and Charles Black, 1885.

Norton, Charles Eliot, Letters of (ed. by Sara Norton and M. A. DeWolfe Howe), 2 vols., Boston, Houghton Mifflin Co., 1913.

Parish, The Rev. William Douglas, *A Dictionary of the Sussex Dialect and*

Collection of Provincialisms in Use in the County of Sussex, Lewes, Farncombe and Co., 1875.

Paul, James B., "Adam, Alexander," *DNB.*

Phillimore, W. P. W., ed., *Hertfordshire Parish Registers, Marriages,* 3 vols., London, Phillimore and Co., 1907–14.

Phillimore, W. P. W. and G. E. Cokayne, *London Parish Registers,* 4 vols., Hertford, Stephen Austin and Sons, 1900.

Phillimore, W. P. W., ed., *Middlesex Parish Registers, Marriages,* 9 vols., London, Phillimore and Co., 1909–38.

Pinnington, Edward, *Sir Henry Raeburn,* London, The W. Scott Publishing Co., 1904.

Pottle, Frederick A., ed., *Boswell's London Journal, 1762–1763,* New York, McGraw-Hill Book Co., 1950.

Publications of the Harleian Society. Middlesex Pedigrees as Collected by Richard Munday in Harleian MS. No. 1551 (ed. by Sir George John Armytage), Vol. 65, London, Harleian Society, 1914.

Publications of the Harleian Society. The Register Book of Marriages Belonging to the Parish of St. George, Hanover Square, in the County of Middlesex (ed. by George J. Armytage), Vol. 24, London, Harleian Society, 1897.

Publications of the Harleian Society. The Registers of Baptisms and Marriages at St. George's Chapel, Mayfair, 1740–1754 (ed. by George J. Armytage), Vol. 15, London, Harleian Society, 1889.

Publications of the Harleian Society. The Registers of Christ Church, Newgate, 1538–1754 (ed. by Willoughby A. Littledale), Vol. 21, London, Harleian Society, 1895.

Publications of the Harleian Society. The Registers of Marriages of St. Mary le Bone [Parish], Middlesex (ed. by W. Bruce Bannerman and Capt. R. R. Bannerman), Vols. 48, 51, 54, London, Harleian Society, 1918–25.

Publications of the Harleian Society. The Registers of St. Bene't and St. Peter's, Paul's Wharf, London, "Marriages" (ed. by Willoughby A. Littledale), Vols. 39 and 40, London, Harleian Society, 1910–11.

Quennell, Peter, *John Ruskin, The Portrait of a Prophet,* New York, The Viking Press, 1949.

Rawnsley, The Rev. R. D., *Ruskin and the English Lakes,* Glasgow, James Maclehose and Sons, 1902.

Robertson Scott, J. W., *The Life and Death of a Newspaper. An Account of the Temperament, Perturbations, and Achievement of John Morley, W. T. Stead, E. T. Cook, Harry Cust, J. R. Garvin and Three Other Editors of the Pall Mall Gazette,* London, Methuen and Co., 1952.

Ross, William C. A., *The Royal High School,* Edinburgh, Oliver and Boyd, 1934.

Rudkin, Messing, "Some Ancient Rutland People," *The Rutland Magazine,* Vol. IV, No. 32 (October, 1910), pp. 235–43.

Rusk, John McGill, *History of the Parish and Abbey of Glen Luce,* Edinburgh, William Blackwood and Sons, Ltd., 1930.

Ruskin, John, *The Complete Works of John Ruskin* (ed. by E. T. Cook and Alexander Wedderburn), 39 vols., London, George Allen, 1903–12.

Ruskin, John, *Letters to Charles Eliot Norton* (ed. by C. E. Norton), 2 vols., Boston, Houghton Mifflin Co., 1904.

Schmitz, Robert M., *Hugh Blair,* New York, King's Crown Press, 1948.

Scott, Hew, ed., *Fasti Ecclesiæ Scoticanæ. The Succession of Ministers of the Church of Scotland from the Reformation,* 7 vols., Edinburgh, Oliver and Boyd, 1915–28.

Scott, Sir Walter, *Waverley or 'Tis Sixty Years Since,* Edinburgh, Adam and Charles Black, 1892.

Shepherd, R. H., *The Bibliography of Ruskin. A Bibliographical List Arranged in Chronological Order . . . (from 1834 to 1881),* Fifth Edition, revised and enlarged, Elliot Stock, *n.d.* (first published 1878).

Shipley, Joseph T., *Dictionary of Word Origins,* New York, The Philosophical Library, 1945.

Sievwright, William, *Supplement to Greyfriar's Burying-Ground, Perth: Its Epitaphs and Inscriptions,* Perth, Alexander Wright, 1895.

Sinclair, Catherine, *Memoir of the Right Hon. Sir John Sinclair, Bart.,* Edinburgh, William and Robert Chambers, 1853.

Sinclair, William, "The Scottish Ancestors of Ruskin," *St. George,* Vol. IX (October, 1906), pp. 238–47.

Sotheby and Co., *Catalogue of Old English Silver . . . The Property of the Late Professor John Ruskin, Removed from Brantwood, Coniston, and The Property of the Late Joseph Arthur Severn;* Sale: April 29, 1931.

Sotheby and Co., *Catalogue of the Collection of Pictures and Drawings Formerly the Property of . . . John Ruskin . . . ;* Sale: May 20, 1931.

Spender, John Alfred, "Cook, Sir Edward Tyas," *DNB.*

Steinman, George S., *A History of Croydon,* London, Longman, Rees, Orme, Brown, Green, and Longman, 1834.

Stephen, Leslie, "Brown, Thomas," *DNB.*

Stewart, Dugald, *Biographical Memoirs of Adam Smith, of William Robertson, and of Thomas Reid,* Edinburgh, George Ramsay and Co., 1811.

Thompson, Harold W., *A Scottish Man of Feeling. Some Account of Henry Mackenzie, Esq., of Edinburgh and of the Golden Age of Burns and Scott,* London, Oxford University Press, 1931.

Trevelyan, George M., *A Shortened History of England,* London, Longmans, Green and Co., 1942.

Trollope, Anthony, "The Wine Merchant," *London Tradesmen,* London, Elkin Mathews and Marrot, Ltd., 1927.

Trotter, Robert de Bruce, *Galloway Gossip Sixty Years Ago; being a Series of Articles Illustrative of the Manners, Customs, and Peculiarities of the Aboriginal Picts of Galloway,* Choppington, Northumberland, Robert Trotter, 1877.

Unwin, Rayner, ed., *The Gulf of Years. Letters from John Ruskin to Kathleen Olander,* London, George Allen and Unwin Ltd., 1953.

Urwick, William, *Nonconformity in Herts. Being Memorials of Puritanism and Nonconformity in All the Parishes of the County of Hertford,* London, Hazell, Watson, and Viney, Ltd., 1884.

Wedderburn, Alexander, ed., *Arrows of the Chace. Being A Collection of Scattered Letters Published Chiefly in the Daily Newspapers, — 1840–1880 . . . and Now Edited by An Oxford Pupil [Alexander Wedderburn] with a Preface by the Author,* 2 vols., Orpington, George Allen, 1880.

Weekley, Ernest, *Surnames,* New York, E. P. Dutton and Co., 1937.

Whitmore, John B., *A Genealogical Guide,* Part III, London, John Whitehead and Son, 1950.

Wilenski, R. H., *John Ruskin. An Introduction to Further Study of His Life and Work,* London, Faber and Faber, 1933.

Wise, Thomas J., ed., and James P. Smart, *A Complete Bibliography of the Writings in Prose and Verse of John Ruskin, LL. D., with a List of the More Important Ruskiniana,* 2 vols., London, R. Clay and Sons, Ltd., 1893.

Wright, Joseph, *The English Dialect Dictionary,* 6 vols., London, Henry Frowde, 1898–1905.

Yeats, John, *A Manual of Recent and Existing Commerce — 1789–1872,* New York, Scribner, Welford, and Armstrong, 1878.

Index

A superior numeral after a page number indicates the relevant note in the Note section, beginning on p. 191. Italicized page numbers indicate that on such pages, some or all of the cited material is derived from MSS. which have remained unpublished in part or whole.